MISMATCH

MISMATCH

HOW AFFIRMATIVE ACTION HURTS STUDENTS IT'S INTENDED TO HELP, AND WHY UNIVERSITIES WON'T ADMIT IT

Richard Sander
Stuart Taylor, Jr.

BASIC BOOKS

A Member of the Perseus Books Group

Books published by Basic Books are available at special discounts for bulk purchases in the United States by corporations, institutions, and other organizations. For more information, please contact the Special Markets Department at the Perseus Books Group, 2300 Chestnut Street, Suite 200, Philadelphia, PA 19103, or call (800) 810-4145, ext. 5000, or e-mail special.markets@perseusbooks.com.

Editorial production by Lori Hobkirk at the Book Factory
Design by Cynthia Young at Sagecraft

GRAPHICS

Artwork by Peter Bell and Ryan Morris

"Institution" symbol used on pages 21–24, and 138 is by Thibault Geffroy from thenounproject.com collection.

"Man" symbol on pages 22–23, 53, and 80 is by The Noun Project from thenounproject.com collection.

A CIP catalog record for this book is available from the Library of Congress.

978-0-465-02996-9

10 9 8 7 6 5 4 3 2 1

From Richard Sander:

To Fiona, with all my love

From Stuart Taylor Jr.:

To Gwennie, Rodger, Clare, and Jack,
with much love

CONTENTS

IV. LAW AND IDEOLOGY

V. THE WAY FORWARD

LIST OF FIGURES

I know that most men, including those at ease with problems of the greatest complexity, can seldom accept even the simplest and most obvious truth if it be such as would oblige them to admit the falsity of conclusions which they have delighted in explaining to colleagues, which they have proudly taught to others, and which they have woven, thread by thread, into the fabric of their lives.

—LEO TOLSTOY

PREFACE

AFFIRMATIVE ACTION IN HIGHER EDUCATION is one of those issues that, like abortion and prayer in schools, divides people so deeply that dialogue across the chasm often seems impossible.

This book attempts to bridge the chasm.

We see merits on both sides of the moral issues raised by affirmative action. But moral arguments have dominated our national dialogue on the issue for decades, and they have neglected a more fundamental question: Does it work?

When the focus shifts from "Is it right?" to "Does it work?" a whole series of important real-world questions open up. And ideology becomes less important. Although people profoundly disagree on whether racial preferences are a legitimate way of expanding opportunity, almost everyone agrees on the underlying goal—expanding opportunity. And we hope that almost everyone would agree that if current programs are actually leading many or most preferred-minority students into academic distress and self-doubt as well as damaging their long-term success, something has to change.

This book demonstrates in detail how racial admissions preferences often undermine the success of the people they are intended to help. As if that were not bad enough, the pervasive secrecy that veils the operation and effects of racial preferences even from most academics has led to deception, ostracism of truth-tellers, lack of accountability, and an unwillingness to face awkward facts and undertake needed reforms. This book takes you on a tour of this largely hidden world.

We reveal much that is shocking, but we also see reason for hope. We find that neither tinkering by the Supreme Court nor the outright bans adopted by six states have effectively addressed the core problems. We think some moderate but dramatic reforms—limiting some particular abuses, improving the focus of preferences on the nonaffluent of all races, and making higher education admissions and outcome highly transparent—can go a long way toward correcting the worst abuses and could set in motion a cycle of virtuous self-reform that could turn a dysfunctional system into a highly effective, genuinely helpful one.

Given the emotional nature of this issue, we thought it would make sense to introduce ourselves and explain why we decided to write this book.

RICK SANDER

I am white, and I grew up in a conservative rural town in the Midwest. But by the time I finished college I knew that what I most wanted to do was work on issues of racial justice, especially those played out in our largest cities, which at the time (the end of the 1970s) were reeling. I became a community organizer in a nearly all-black neighborhood on Chicago's South Side and then worked for other groups that dealt with issues of race and urban revitalization. I was part of a network of young progressives who were tremendously energized by the 1983 campaign of Harold Washington to become Chicago's first black mayor, and when he shocked everyone by actually winning, I worked on his transition team to formulate housing and tenant law reforms. Some reforms passed, but most got mired in gridlock.

Around this time I developed the mantra that has guided my professional life ever since: Opportunities for real reform are rare and should be seized. When they come, it is incredibly important for reformers to *get it right*. Political capital should not be spent on programs that do not work or that produce harmful, unintended side effects. This, in turn, implies that those who really believe in reforms must also be their most demanding critics; they must seek out data to evaluate what works and what does not, and above all they must follow the facts where they lead.

I returned to school to study economics and law, and I became very interested in the problem of housing segregation. Despite the passage of fair housing laws, black-white segregation remained very high in the cities, and many liberals concluded that the laws were simply ignored. But there was some impressive, overlooked evidence that actual discrimination rates had fallen sharply since the 1960s. I developed and tested explanations of segregation that could reconcile these facts and that pointed toward different and more effective ways of tackling segregation directly. As I became closely involved in civil rights work, I was struck again and again by the way strongly held beliefs about public policy could blind people on all sides of important issues to the actual state of affairs. Otherwise smart and honest people often screened out inconvenient facts or felt that acknowledging weaknesses in their position only gave aid and comfort to their opponents. I saw this while serving as board president of a large fair housing organization, when some of my colleagues were reluctant to confront and address obvious cases of corruption or incompetence because to do so would embarrass "the movement."

As I recount in Chapter Four, I started to examine the operation and effects of affirmative action when, as a young law professor at UCLA in the mid-1990s, I became involved in efforts to improve the quality of academic support for struggling law students, many of whom had been admitted with large racial preferences. It soon became clear that these preferences were undermining rather than helping the students they were intended to aid. When California voters passed a ban on the use of racial preferences in 1996 (known as Proposition 209), I worked with colleagues at the law school to develop a race-neutral system of smaller, socioeconomic preferences that would expand opportunity while also improving academic performance. The class that we admitted in 1997 was not only (by economic measures) the most diverse we had ever seen; it also went on to have the highest bar-passage rate in the school's history.

Within a few years, however, efforts to evade Proposition 209 and bring race back into admissions decisions got under way in various parts of the University of California, including some of its law schools. At around the same time I found better data that would let me test my hypotheses about the effects of large racial preferences. In January 2005 I published an article that laid out for the first time the detailed operation of preferences in a sector of higher education and presented an array of evidence suggesting that the current system generally made black students worse off, both individually and collectively. This article generated enormous interest and debate; there was clearly a hunger in the legal academic community in general—and in particular from black students—for information on the largely hidden system of racial preferences.

That was the good news, but on the bad side were all the unhappy problems I had encountered in other areas of social policy, especially those touching on race. Those who believed in affirmative action—including some close and wise friends—were upset to see its inner workings revealed and critically examined; they saw this as simply providing aid and comfort to opponents who wished to abolish all racial preferences. Other prominent friends privately cheered my article as a necessary step toward reform but felt they must remain silent about their views for fear of stepping into the withering ideological crossfire between partisans on either side. And the leading institutions of legal education not only refused to take up the issue of reform but also took steps to make it more difficult for anyone to continue any evaluation of law school preference programs.

I took three lessons from the reception to my article. First, I needed to figure out a way to talk about racial preferences that didn't cause people to shut down. I sought out and interviewed dozens of people who, as students, had received racial preferences, and I developed a deeper sense of how it was experienced, how its benefits and harms were perceived, and more nuanced ways of discussing these. Second, I realized that a phenomenon as interesting and difficult as affirmative action itself is the culture of secrecy and doubletalk that surrounds it. That needed to be excavated. Third, it seemed important to bring more careful, dispassionate empiricists into the discussion about racial preferences; I worked with other scholars and foundations to find and make available databases and funding mechanisms that fostered neutral, careful empirical research on the operation and effects of racial preferences in higher education. Coincidentally, other scholars were getting interested in this subject as well, and over the past few years a rich mosaic of important research—still largely unknown to the public—has materialized. It is now fair to talk about an emerging consensus on many issues.

I had been deeply impressed by the work of my friend Stuart Taylor in exposing doubletalk and malfeasance in a variety of American institutions, and in November 2010 I suggested to him that there was a real need for an analytic but accessible book on racial preferences that would call universities to account while also reporting on the new wave of research and suggesting paths toward sensible reforms that cut across hardened ideological lines. Events since we started work on the project have propelled the issue of racial preferences into public discussion, and there are some signs of a healthier debate. Colleagues have told me for years that someday—but not quite yet—a time would arrive when there could be honest public discussion about the problems of affirmative action and some degree of consensus among liberals and conservatives about a constructive path forward. Stuart and I hope that this day has come.

STUART TAYLOR

As a journalist, I have been consistently drawn to investigate and write about situations in which influential people and institutions dodge the truth and engage in cover-ups. I am even more motivated to jump in when I sense that groupthink and moral cowardice have made the truth taboo—and as this book shows, these have been endemic features of much public discussion on racial preferences.

In the political world I have made it something of a specialty to expose abuses by powerful politicians of both parties while taking on and proving wrong the journalistic conventional wisdom. I have done this in major controversies including the phony "House Bank" scandal of 1992, when I roasted the first Bush administration and sensationalistic journalists for politically driven smears of House Democrats; the much bigger and even more phony "Iraqgate" scandal, also of 1992, when House Democrats and major news organizations polluted a presidential campaign with bogus allegations of high-level criminality by the same Bush administration; the widely ridiculed sexual harassment claim of Paula Jones against President Clinton, which led to a 1997 Supreme Court ruling against him; the related Monica Lewinsky affair, which led to his 1998 impeachment; and the Duke lacrosse rape fraud of 2006–2007, which led to the disbarment of rogue prosecutor Mike Nifong. My book on that fraud, *Until Proven Innocent: Political Correctness and the Shameful Injustices of the Duke Lacrosse Rape Case*, coauthored by K. C. Johnson, also showed how scores of Duke professors, leaders, and the news media en masse joined in a disgraceful mob rush to judgment against white Duke students falsely accused by a black stripper. The race-driven campus and media pathologies explored in that book closely relate to those explored in this one.

I have also written scores of news stories and commentaries about racial preferences as a reporter and Supreme Court correspondent for the *New York Times* and writer for the *American Lawyer, Legal Times*, and *National Journal*. Over those same years I have evolved from an affirmative action supporter to an increasingly skeptical critic of the enormous, pervasive, and carefully concealed system of racial preferences into which it has morphed. My concerns have been fueled by in-depth reporting of facts, evidence, and impact on real people of all races, ranging from firefighters in Alabama, Ohio, and Connecticut, to students and teachers around the country. My major essay on racial preferences in 2004—"The Affirmative Action Cases," a chapter in a book entitled *A Year at the Supreme Court*—detailed how large racial preferences harm black students, including academic mismatch, fueling stereotypes of black inferiority, stigma, disincentives to study, papering over the ruinously bad educations of many blacks from birth to age eighteen, and the need for radical reform of our K-12 schools.

I have been privileged to discuss affirmative action privately with the only two African Americans ever to sit on the Supreme Court, the late, great liberal Thurgood Marshall, a passionate devotee, and the arch-conservative Clarence Thomas, a passionate critic. I used to visit Marshall's chambers occasionally, savoring every minute I could spend with this singularly unpretentious living legend. He loved to tell stories about his years of dangerous duty representing black murder defendants in racist southern towns, tangling with General

Douglas MacArthur over mistreatment of black soldiers in Korea, and much more. The stories usually had a humorous twist. But once, when I wondered aloud whether the time was coming to wind down racial preference, Marshall turned grave. "I think we need it," he said, fixing me with a steady gaze. "Can you tell me you never got any advantage from being white?" I said no. "Well," Marshall continued, "you owe something."

I wonder what Justice Marshall would think now of large racial preferences were he alive and aware of the evidence in this book, which is quite consistent with Justice Thomas's forceful depictions of mismatch and other grievous harms to his fellow blacks. I loved Marshall. I like Thomas very much. I have learned from both.

I became acquainted with Rick Sander after writing admiring commentaries about his work. Rick asked me in late 2010 to coauthor a book that would seek a broader audience and would at the same time show how mismatch harms intended beneficiaries at undergraduate colleges as well as at law schools. I was aware that university leaders and the California State Bar had blocked Rick and other scholars from accessing databases that could go a long way toward proving—or disproving—his mismatch thesis. It struck me as a classic example of entrenched interests attacking a truth-teller.

I agreed to be coauthor subject to studying more closely the many critiques of Rick's statistical analyses by prominent scholars. My nonexpert conclusion was that Rick had much the better of the arguments with each of his critics. This reinforced my sense that his interpretations of the data were far more plausible. In addition, some critics had stooped not only to the usual dodging and distorting of data but also to ugly personal vilification. There they go again. I was in.

* * *

To hold this book to a reasonable length and to keep it accessible to a wide audience, we have kept out technical or elaborating material that many readers might value. Those readers should visit the book's website, http://www.mismatchthebook.com, which has an array of supplemental materials.

A NOTE ON TERMINOLOGY

Much of this book is about the consequences of racial admissions preferences on student learning in American higher education. Most public discussions of this issue (and related issues) use terms that have multiple or ambiguous meanings, so this note explains and defines a few key ideas and introduces usages we use henceforth.

Affirmative action is a particularly confusing (and often political) term. In this book we generally distinguish between affirmative action and *racial preferences*. We use affirmative action to refer to proactive efforts to prevent discrimination against minorities and promote genuinely equal opportunity by ensuring that selection procedures are fair and by using outreach and recruiting to correct past patterns of exclusion. Racial preferences, in contrast, describe programs that allocate college admissions or other opportunities based partly on the race of a candidate.

In common parlance "affirmative action" usually refers both to the pool-expanding efforts we note above as well as racial preferences. Advocates of racial preferences often use this broad sense of affirmative action because there is—as hundreds of polls confirm—much more public support for affirmative action in some form than there is for racial preferences. We sometimes use "affirmative action" in this broad sense when we refer to general usage, as in "the affirmative action debate."

By *higher education* we mean all postsecondary schooling in the United States. We often refer to "colleges and universities" similarly to refer to higher education, and sometimes we use *college* alone to refer to undergraduate education and *universities* to refer to institutions that confer both undergraduate and graduate degrees.

We use an *academic index* to roughly quantify and compare the academic preparation of people applying for admission to a college or graduate program and to make discussions of things like racial preferences more concrete. When expressed as a number, the academic index runs from 0 to 1,000; applicants may receive up to 600 points based on their score on a standardized admissions test taken for a particular program (e.g., the SAT I for college applicants, the GRE for applicants to doctoral programs, the LSAT for law school applicants, etc.), and up to 400 points based on their GPA in whatever academic program they have most recently completed (e.g., high school for college applicants, college for graduate school applicants). Thus, for example, a high school senior who received an 1800 on the SAT I and had a 3.5 high school GPA would have an academic index of 750 (400 points for the SAT I score, because the student got two-thirds of the possible points on it, and 350 points for the HSGPA, because the student got seven-eighths of the possible points for that). Many higher education programs use some variation on this academic index, though they have many different methods of giving weight to test scores and grades. But however an academic index is defined, it is generally a strong predictor of whether a student will be admitted. At most law schools, for example, one can predict over 80 percent of the applicants who will be offered admission simply by knowing each applicant's academic index.

Sometimes, with academic indices and other measures of academic preparation, we will use *percentiles* to compare students or applicants. If Student Jones has an academic index at the 90th percentile of applicants to a particular school, that means that 90 percent of the other applicants have lower academic indices than Jones does. If Student Lee is at the 20th percentile, that means that 20 percent of the other applicants have lower academic indices than Lee does. Similarly, a decile refers to tenths of a distribution. A student in the top decile of her class is in the top tenth and is at the 90th percentile or above.

The concept of the academic index can help us distinguish between *large* and *small* admissions preferences. These are obviously subjective terms, but when we refer to a *large admissions preference*—whether it be based on race, alumni connections, or athletic ability—we generally mean a preference that is equivalent to adding 80 or more points to the academic index of a an applicant. This would be equivalent to a 240-point upward adjustment to an applicant's modern SAT I score. We discuss these ideas in more depth in Chapter Two.

We use *black* as a shorthand reference for African American, *white* as shorthand for Caucasian Americans, Hispanic as shorthand for *Hispanic Americans* (which subsumes the terms Latino, Chicano, Cuban American, Mexican American, etc.); we use *Asian* as shorthand for *Asian Americans*, including all American residents whose ethnic origins are in Asia; we use *American Indian* as shorthand for anyone who traces ancestry to one or more of the native tribes indigenous to the territory of the United States. We generally eschew the term minority, but when we do use it we are referring to all nonwhite groups. Racial preference programs often focus on *underrepresented minorities*, a term that includes any ethnic group that would be accepted at a lower-than-average rate under a race-neutral admissions program. Depending on the program and the context, Filipino Americans, Cambodian Americans, Cuban Americans, and many other ethnic groups might or might not be included. Because this can be a confusing term and is not widely used in common discourse, we generally avoid it. Moreover, in much of the book we do not specifically mention American Indians as the beneficiaries of admissions preferences, partly to simplify the discussion but more often because the relevant numbers are so small that we cannot make confident generalizations.

I.

INTRODUCTION

CHAPTER ONE

THE IDEA OF MISMATCH, AND WHY IT MATTERS

A FFIRMATIVE ACTION in university admissions started in the late 1960s as a noble effort to jump-start racial integration and foster equal opportunity. But somewhere along the decades since, it has lost its way.

Over time it has become a political lightning rod and one of our most divisive social policies. It has evolved into a regime of racial preferences at almost all selective schools, preferences so strikingly large and politically unpopular that administrators work hard to conceal them. The largest, most aggressive preferences are usually conferred on upper-middle-class minorities on whom they often inflict significant academic harm, whereas more modest policies that could help working-class and poor people of all races are given short shrift. Academic leaders often find themselves flouting the law and acting in ways that aggravate the worst consequences of large preferences. They have become prisoners of a system that many privately deplore for its often perverse unintended effects but feel they cannot escape.

We document these claims in detail and show how to reform affirmative action in ways that would be good for students of all races. We explain the outpouring of scholarly research in recent years showing how large racial preferences backfire against many and, perhaps, most recipients, to the point that they learn less and are likely to be less self-confident than had they gone to less competitive but still quite good schools.

This is what we mean by "mismatch." Mismatch largely explains why, even though blacks are more likely to enter college than are whites with similar backgrounds, they will usually get much lower grades, rank toward the bottom of the class, and far more often drop out; why there are so few blacks and Hispanics with science and engineering degrees or with doctorates in any field; and why black law graduates fail bar exams at four times the white rate.

It is not lack of talent or innate ability that drives these students to drop out of school, flee rigorous courses, or abandon aspirations to be scientists or scholars; it is, rather, an unintended side effect of large racial preferences, which systematically put minority students in academic environments where they feel overwhelmed. Because of the mismatch effect as well as the related role of racial preferences in fueling pernicious stereotypes of black intellectual inferiority, we will argue that the biggest problem for minorities in higher education is no longer race but rather racial preferences.

The mismatch effect happens when a school extends to a student such a large admissions preference—usually, but not always, because of the student's race—that the student finds herself in a class where she has weaker academic preparation than nearly all of her classmates. The student who would flourish at, say, Wake Forest or the University of Richmond, instead finds herself at Duke, where the professors are not teaching at a pace designed for her—they are teaching to the "middle" of the class, introducing terms and concepts at a speed that is challenging even to the best-prepared student. The student who is underprepared relative to others in that class falls behind from the start and becomes increasingly lost as the professor and her classmates race ahead. Her grades on her first exams or papers put her at the bottom of the class. Worse, the experience may well induce panic and self-doubt, making learning even harder.

When explaining to friends how academic mismatch works, we sometimes say: Think back to high school and recall a subject at which you did fine but did not excel. Suppose you had suddenly been transferred into an advanced class in that subject with a friend who was about at your level and eighteen other students who excelled in the subject *and* had already taken the intermediate course you just skipped. You would, in all likelihood, soon be struggling to keep up. The teacher might give you some extra attention but, in class, would be focusing on the median student, not you and your friend, and would probably be covering the material at what, to you, was a bewildering pace.

Wouldn't you have quickly fallen behind and then continued to fall farther and farther behind as the school year progressed? Now assume that you and the friend who joined you at the bottom of that class were both black and everyone else was Asian or white. How would that have felt? Might you have imagined that this could reinforce in the minds of your classmates the stereotype that blacks are weak students?

So we have a terrible confluence of forces putting students in classes for which they aren't prepared, causing them to lose confidence and underperform even more while at the same time consolidating the stereotype that they are inherently poor students. And it's easy to see how at each level there are feedback effects that reinforce the self-doubts of all the students who are struggling.

Mismatch problems are particularly easy to see in technical subjects like science and math, where every new concept builds on the ones that come before. If you fall behind at the start, you become less and less prepared as the material gets more and more complicated. Mismatch problems have been especially well documented in law schools, where an unusual amount of good data is available and where all graduates take a standardized exam that assesses their learning. But mismatch can and does occur throughout higher education, wherever very large preferences are used. In a recent article—not about affirmative action but about why online education often doesn't work—a professor captured very well this idea behind mismatch:

> With every class we teach, we need to learn [where] the people in front of us . . . are intellectually. . . . In the summer Shakespeare course I'm teaching now, I'm constantly working to figure out what my students are able to do and how they can develop. . . . Is the language hard for them, line to line? Then we have to spend more time going over individual speeches word by word. Are they adept at understanding the plot and the language? Time to introduce them to the complexities of Shakespeare's rendering of character. . . . The best . . . lecturers are highly adept at reading their audiences . . . they have a sort of pedagogical sixth sense.

In making these constant small adjustments and decisions about content, pace, and complexity, professors will generally focus on the broad middle of the class. Outliers at the top will be bored; outliers at the bottom—our focus here—will tend to struggle and fall behind.

In the chapters that follow we will explore and document several examples of the mismatch effect in operation, situations in which students receiving preferences end up having high academic attrition or failure, thereby earning fewer degrees, obtaining fewer professional licenses, giving up on aspirations, and emerging from higher education with a deep-seated sense that they didn't have what it takes to succeed.

But nearly all of these students **do** *have what it takes to succeed.* If they were at good but less-selective schools, their chances of achieving long-term success in school and in life would likely be higher. Their rate of learning and sense of mastery over their subjects would almost certainly be higher. But they aren't told of their significant disadvantage when they enter, and so they're effectively being set up to fail.

Much of the evidence in this book comes from studies that track students from high school through college and sometimes beyond. Most have been done by scholars analyzing databases to compare how similar students fare in different educational environments.

An especially compelling case for mismatch comes in Part III, where we chronicle and analyze a "natural experiment" that occurred when California voters passed the highly controversial Proposition 209, banning the state government's use of racial preferences, which forced the massive University of California system to abruptly shift from the widespread use of preferences to their virtual elimination. For all of the discord it caused, Prop 209 ultimately made it possible to observe how minority behavior and outcomes change when preferences disappear. Because it affected thousands of students, we can also better measure the aggregate effects of mismatch. Using data we obtained through extensive negotiations with the university, this book presents for the first time a detailed assessment of what the preference ban actually did and how it affected—and in several important ways benefited—black and Hispanic students.

We and several colleagues have also conducted well over one hundred interviews with people from all walks of life who shared the experience of receiving racial preferences in college, and who have endured or seen classmates endure traumatic university experiences, in many cases ending in frustration and failure. We also interviewed more than thirty college counselors, administrators, and faculty who have witnessed mismatch issues firsthand. In some cases mismatched students emerge only with bruised self-confidence; in others they end up without a profession and deeply in debt. Although our arguments rely first and foremost on data and empirical tests, we will include many of these voices and the vivid stories that they told us about struggling students to illustrate the lived experience of mismatch.

We are also convinced that the main victims of large racial preferences, at least in terms of the ultimate effect on their lives, are not the many whites and Asians who get passed over but rather the many blacks and Hispanics who receive preferences and do badly. This is not to minimize the harms to passed-over whites and Asians whose dreams of going to college X or Y are dashed, or to dismiss concerns about basic fairness. But almost all of these students will have other excellent choices of schools. Compare the impact on mismatched black and Hispanic students. Their intellectual self-confidence has been undermined, their career aspirations have in many cases been derailed, and they must deal with the stigma of being "affirmative-action admits." In the words of liberal scholar Christopher Jencks, "A policy that encourages the nation's future leaders to believe that blacks are slow learners will . . . do incalculable harm over the long run, because blacks cannot shed their skin after graduation."

For many black and Hispanic students, in short, the preference has proved to be a curse.

This brings us to an obvious question and to the second major theme of this book: Why, if admissions preferences have produced such harms to their intended beneficiaries and other large costs, have our universities not faced and solved the problem? Why do they instead pretend that there *is* no problem, a pretense that at best avoids some short-term pain and embarrassment but does so only by making the long-term problems both worse and far more lasting?

At least part of the answer lies in the tortured nature of public dialogue about race in this country, in which it is often taboo even to mention awkward statistical facts that are undisputed among scholars familiar with the data. This avoidance of candid discussion—which is indispensable to wise policymaking—is particularly pervasive on university campuses and in the news media. We will explore several examples of this phenomenon in detail, and Chapters Eleven and Twelve will grapple with why it occurs.

Defenders of affirmative action often suggest that they fear that openness and dialogue on the nature and operation of racial preferences will lead to demagoguery on the right. Certainly there are historical grounds for that concern, though in recent years many of the "conservative" critics of racial preferences have done nothing more than point out unpleasant facts. We agree that sensitivity is important. But too much sensitivity in the face of overwhelming evidence that the status quo is not working only perpetuates a system that hurts the people it is supposed to help. In our view this is both morally and logically indefensible.

Recent years have seen the US Commission on Civil Rights—an independent, bipartisan federal fact-finding agency created by the Civil Rights Act of 1957 to inform national civil rights policy—issue two thoughtful, concerned reports about academic mismatch. The higher education community has utterly ignored both reports. Scholars doing serious, important work on mismatch issues are, not infrequently, summarily dismissed as racists. This is a profoundly unhealthy state of affairs.

A powerful example that captures these problems comes from UCLA, an elite school that used large racial preferences until the Proposition 209 ban took effect in 1998. The fear that a ban on preferences would have devastating effects on minorities at UCLA and Berkeley were among the chief exhibits of those who attacked Prop 209 as a racist measure. Many predicted that over time blacks and Hispanics would virtually disappear from the UCLA campus. And there was indeed a post-209 drop in minority enrollment as preferences were phased out. Although it was smaller and more short lived than anticipated, it was still quite substantial: a 50 percent drop in black freshman enrollment and a 25 percent drop for Hispanics. These drops precipitated ongoing protests by students and continual handwringing by administrators, and when, in 2006, there was a particularly low yield of black freshmen, the campus was roiled with agitation, so much so that (as we document in Chapter Ten) the university reinstituted covert, illegal racial preferences.

Throughout these crises university administrators fed agitation against the preference ban by emphasizing the drop in undergraduate minority admissions. Never did the university point out one overwhelming fact: *The total number of black and Hispanic students receiving bachelor's degrees was the same for the five classes after Prop 209 as for the five classes before.*

How was this possible? First, the ban on preferences produced better-matched students at UCLA, students who were more likely to graduate. The black four-year graduation rate at UCLA doubled from the early 1990s to the years after Prop 209. Second, strong black and Hispanic students accepted UCLA offers of admission at much higher rates after the preferences ban went into effect; their choices seem to suggest that they were eager to attend a school where the stigma of a preference could not be attached to them. This mitigated the drop in enrollment. Third, many minority students who would have been admitted to UCLA with weak qualifications before Prop 209 were admitted to less elite schools instead; those who proved their academic mettle were able to transfer up to UCLA and graduate there.

Thus, Prop 209 changed the minority experience at UCLA from one of frequent failure to much more consistent success. The school granted as many bachelor degrees to minority students as it did before Prop 209 while admitting many fewer and thus dramatically reducing failure and drop-out rates. It was able, in other words, to greatly reduce mismatch. But university officials were unwilling to advertise this fact. They pretended that Prop 209's consequences had caused unalloyed harm to minorities and suppressed data on actual student performance. The university never confronted the mismatch problem, and rather than engage in a candid discussion of the true costs and benefits of a ban on preferences, it engineered secret policies to violate Prop 209's requirement that admissions be color-blind.

The odd dynamics behind UCLA's official behavior exist throughout the contemporary academic world. The quest for racial sensitivity has created environments in which it is not only difficult but downright risky for students and professors alike, not to mention administrators, to talk about what affirmative action has become and about the nature and effects of large admissions preferences. Simply acknowledging the fact that large preferences exist can trigger accusations that one is insulting or stigmatizing minority groups; suggesting that these preferences have counterproductive effects can lead to the immediate inference that one wants to eliminate or cut back efforts to help minority students. The desire to be sensitive has sealed off failing programs from the scrutiny and dialogue necessary for healthy progress.

The ideology of racial inclusion has another unhealthy side effect that forms a third major theme of this book: Most universities' pervasive neglect of poor, working- and even middle-class students and its relationship to their single-minded focus on racial identity. We will shed light on the socioeconomic backgrounds of most students who receive racial preferences and how many of them have been advantaged over less well-off, better-prepared students of all races. Some of the most important facts in our book are these: Black students are, today, about a third more likely than are white students with otherwise similar characteristics to start college (although blacks are less likely than similar whites to finish college—in large part, we believe, because of mismatch). Meanwhile, low-income students of all races are 70 percent less likely than their affluent counterparts to enter college. In other words, the problem of access (which financial aid and moderate, targeted preferences can address) is social and economic. The problem of persistence—of ending up with the degrees that students start college to achieve—has become a racial problem largely because of the pervasive use of very large racial preferences.

Because this is mostly an empirical book, our facts are more important than our policy recommendations. But we do think some fairly simple, nonideological solutions could dramatically ameliorate the problems we examine. We do not think that the total bans on racial preferences that some states have adopted have proved to be workable, because experience has shown that such bans are usually evaded in ways that can make the mismatch effect even worse. But we do think that race-based financial aid can and should be banned because it leads to practices hard to justify on any public policy grounds. Law schools, for example, currently provide four times as much scholarship aid (on a per capita basis) to high-income blacks as to low-income whites and Asians, a practice that insiders concede exists only because of the zero-sum competition among law schools for scarce black candidates. Prohibiting the use of race in scholarships would help schools refocus aid on actual need.

More important, we argue that the racial preferences used by any university should not be permitted to exceed in size the preferences (if any) that the same school uses for socioeconomically disadvantaged students of all races. This would not cut racial preferences off altogether; it would push schools to focus on individual hardship and barriers to opportunity rather than group entitlements and racial balancing. Our proposals would do far more than the current regime to counter the disturbing trend toward increasing income inequality in America. And, as we will explain, broadening the range of relatively well-qualified students who qualify for preferences tends to make the size of preferences smaller, which helps to contain mismatch effects.

Perhaps most important, we propose that universities make their preference systems transparent, not just as to racial preferences but also as to legacies and athletes. Students and outsiders should also have ready access to information not only on how they were admitted but on how similarly qualified students fared at the school. At what rate did they persist in science majors? At what rate and how quickly did they graduate? Did they get jobs after graduation? Transparency empowers students to evaluate the dangers of mismatch against the already well-known benefits of attending a more elite school. And by giving colleges and universities powerful incentives to improve the outcomes of their students, transparency creates a powerful engine for reform.

Although our book does not examine in any detail the moral and philosophical issues that have tended to dominate debates over affirmative action, we discuss in some detail the politics surrounding the issue. That is the focus of our chapter on the tumultuous Proposition 209 campaign, in which the tactics used by many leading opponents relied on even greater distortions of fact in the political arena than those we examine in the academic arena. We also discuss both the media coverage of and the major Supreme Court decisions on racial preferences in higher education. Juxtaposing these discussions with our empirical findings on the operation and effects of preferences helps, we think, to bring a fresh and revealing perspective to the old debates.

* * *

Our story proceeds through five parts. Part I introduces the themes of the book and, in Chapter Two, lays out the surprising but largely undisputed basic facts on how racial preferences operate. Part II explores how the mismatch effect was first documented empirically, examines the effects of racial preferences in specific contexts, and weighs the evidence for and against mis-match. Part III takes up America's largest experiment in banning racial pref-erences—California's Proposition 209—and its little-heralded beneficial effects at UC.

In Part IV we turn from the experience of students to the behavior of institutions. Racial preferences have been widely supported by American elites and widely opposed by the American public. This tension as well as the growing evidence of dysfunctional preference policies have produced often scandalous but always fascinating behavior from institutions ranging from the California Bar to Duke University, from the American Bar Association to the Supreme Court.

In Part V we turn to the elements of reform. Chapter Sixteen documents the poor socioeconomic targeting of preferences mentioned earlier. Chapter Seventeen examines in detail the underlying reason why racial preferences exist in the first place—that is, the huge racial gap in average academic achievement that exists before kindergarten and steadily expands through ele-mentary and secondary school. Although this problem, often called the "test-score gap" for short, has defied the best efforts of countless reformers more expert than us, we think that much has been learned over the past fifteen years about the causes of the gap and the most promising reforms for reduc-ing it. And in Chapter Eighteen we detail our proposals for reforming racial preferences and explain how the pending Texas case, to be argued before the Supreme Court in October 2012, presents an opportunity to move the law in a healthier direction.

* * *

We write this book in 2012 because affirmative action is clearly at a turn-ing point. The spurs for change come from five directions:

- The undeniable and extremely disturbing accumulation of evidence of mismatch, primarily through the steadily growing flow of research that this book describes.

- The deep dissatisfaction with the fictions and frauds of the current racial-preference regime privately expressed (to us and others) by more and more academics and administrators, who want reform but are afraid to speak out.

- The Supreme Court, which in 2012 agreed to hear its first major case in nine years on higher education racial preferences.

- The transformation of America into an increasingly multiracial society that is rapidly erasing the old lines pitting white beneficiaries of past discrimination against black victims and their children. Indeed, increasingly, racial admissions preferences are used to advantage Hispanics, biracial Americans, and black foreign nationals and to disadvantaage Asian Americans.

- The changing views of black and Hispanic people, now expressing a rising sense that the racial preference system may have outlived its usefulness and that the time is ripe for reappraisal and reform.

On this last point consider the views of three prominent black thinkers with impeccable liberal credentials. William Coleman was an academic star at Harvard Law School, a cocounsel with Thurgood Marshall in *Brown v. Board of Education*, a longtime chair of the NAACP Legal Defense and Education Fund, and a US cabinet member. In his 2010 memoir Coleman wrote,

> Today, race in and of itself usually is not an impediment to success at the highest levels of our society or at any level for that matter. We need therefore to modify our diversification policies to focus more on creating opportunities for people entrapped in a cycle of poverty and those with special needs and challenges or who have not had the benefit of strong family and community support systems. . . . We must also take into account generations of poor whites in rural and urban areas, some of whom have been disadvantaged by government policies that focus only on providing racial preferences, regardless of circumstances. . . . [We should consider] abolishing all distinctions based on race and ethnicity except targeted programs to assist African-Americans still in need in order to remedy the vestiges of slavery and [government-sanctioned] . . . racial discrimination.

Coleman's point that the racial scene has fundamentally changed was made almost at the same time by Ellis Cose, who as recently as 1994 wrote about the tendency of subtle but pervasive discrimination to erode blacks' sense of citizenship. In late 2010 Cose wrote, "Few people of any race would claim that full racial equality has arrived in America. . . . Still, so much has changed. . . . It's not that discrimination has stopped or that racist assumptions have vanished. But they are not nearly as powerful as they once were. Color is becoming less and less a burden; race is less and less an immovable barrier." Although race still seriously affects opportunities for blacks, Cose concludes, it can no longer "prevent them from getting where they want to go."

And *Washington Post* columnist and Pulitzer Prize–winner Eugene Robinson points out in his 2011 book, *Disintegration*, that the black upper-middle class has truly entered the mainstream and henceforth should "be on its own." Policies like affirmative action need to shift from a racial focus to one that focuses on effective help for those truly in need. This would take "considerable courage" from America's black leaders, Robinson notes, but only then can blacks begin to "un-hyphenate ourselves" and move beyond the invisible shackles created in part by race-based categories of treatment.

In the spirit of Coleman, Cose, and Robinson, we embark on this inquiry.

CHAPTER TWO

A PRIMER ON
AFFIRMATIVE ACTION

ONE OF THE CURIOUS THINGS about the way affirmative action works in higher education is that although it is widely misunderstood by the public and even many seeming "insiders," scholars of all political stripes agree on many of its basic characteristics and effects. If you haven't been following the literature, some of what we will describe in this chapter may shock you, but virtually none of it is controversial among scholars who have studied the relevant data (we will make note where particular features of the system are still uncertain or debated). What follows is a guide to its general operations and vocabulary; this will make the stories in later chapters easier to follow.

1. Contemporary affirmative action in higher education is primarily about racial preferences.

When the term "affirmative action" first came into general usage in the 1960s, it was understood to refer to organized efforts by government and other institutions to make sure that opportunities (e.g., benefits from federal programs or hiring by federal contractors) were truly open to all and did not simply pass through "old boy networks." Affirmative action was a way of pushing these institutions to break their habit of bypassing (if not deliberately excluding) traditionally disadvantaged groups; in these early years the predominant focus was on opening access to African Americans. At universities in the mid-1960s it meant reaching out to counselors at black high schools in places such as Harlem or Boston's Roxbury district or the South Side of Chicago, who had always assumed, with reason, that elite private colleges would never take their students seriously. It also meant sponsoring summer programs in which minority students were brought to campuses to meet with professors, explore the facilities, and hear talks about why they should seriously consider college in general and the host school in particular.

But starting in 1967 and 1968, first elite colleges and then professional schools shifted their focus from institutional reform to racial preferences. College and university leaders realized that outreach alone would bring no more than a small number of blacks to their campuses. Colleges—especially private colleges—that were accustomed to giving an admissions "plus" to all sorts of applicant characteristics, began to do so for blacks. Within a year or two they realized that even a conventional "plus," like the points that might be given to a farm boy from Iowa, were not going to produce significant minority enrollment either. As a result, the racial preferences grew in size and soon became very large (as detailed below); they were extended from blacks to other racial groups, such as Native Americans, Hispanics, and sometimes southeast Asians, and they became more automatic. Soon large racial preferences overshadowed the old outreach efforts.

By 1980, more than three-quarters of the black students, and a majority of the Hispanic students at selective colleges and professional schools were there not because of some traditional form of outreach, but because they had received a preference (and often a race-based financial award as well).

2. Racial preferences are far more than mere "tie-breakers."

As we explained in A Note on Terminology, we use the term "academic index" throughout this book to describe in a consistent way the test scores and grades that admissions officers heavily rely upon in making admissions decisions. For undergraduates, the index summarizes the SAT I scores and high school grades of students, with "0" meaning that a student received a 200 on each SAT I component and had a 0.0 high school GPA, and a "1000" meaning that a student received perfect scores on each SAT I component and had a 4.0 high school GPA. Many colleges and universities use some index of this kind; those that do not have some more informal way of comparing these key measures of prior academic success across their applicants.

Suppose that a college admissions officer reviews an applicant pool and sees that black applicants have academic index scores that are, on average, about 130 points below those of white applicants. The officer has been instructed to put together a student body that roughly mirrors the racial makeup of the applicants, of whom 9 percent are black. (These targets typically emerge from a consensus among the college president, a faculty admissions committee, and the dean of admissions.) To meet this target, the officer must somehow insulate the black applicants from direct competition with the generally higher-scoring Asian and white applicants. The simplest way to do this is to "race-norm" the academic index—that is, add 130 points to each black applicant's index.

Now, college admissions officers and presidents and even some affirmative action scholars will not readily concede that colleges "race-norm" applications. That's because explicit race-norming is pretty clearly unconstitutional under the Supreme Court's 2003 decision in *Gratz v. Bollinger*, discussed in Chapter Thirteen. It is also illegal for schools to compare the academic index of scores of blacks and Hispanics only with those of other blacks and Hispanics and not with whites and Asians—a practice that, according to a recent survey described in *Inside Higher Ed*, is quite common at elite schools.

We have examined dozens of admissions datasets from many elite colleges and professional schools, and we almost invariably find that the racial gap in academic indices among applicants is very similar to the racial gap in academic indices among admitted students.

This implies that racial preferences will vary across racial groups, with blacks preferred over Hispanics, both groups preferred over whites, and whites preferred over Asians. Nationwide, the academic index of whites taking the SAT is about 140 points higher than the academic index for blacks (corresponding to a 300-point black-white gap on the current SAT I test, and a 0.4 GPA gap in high school grades), and it has hovered in that range for the past twenty years. Hispanics, in contrast, have an average academic index that is about 70 points lower than that of whites. The gap for American Indians is very similar to the black-white gap, and the academic index of Asians is about thirty points higher than that of whites. Something close to these differences will show up in most college applicant pools, and with racial preferences, similar gaps will carry over to the college's enrolled student body.

These average differences across races in academic preparation carry over to virtually all of the academic measures that admissions officers rely on. There are, for example, substantial racial differences in the proportion of students who have taken AP classes, how many they have taken, and what scores they have obtained. Through the use of racial preferences, all of these differences become replicated in the student bodies of colleges and universities.

A number of scholars have carefully documented these gaps. For example, Thomas Espenshade, a leading expert on (and supporter of) affirmative action, and his coauthor Alexandria Walton Radford obtained academic data on a large number of students at a sample of selective, mostly private colleges. In their 2009 book on race in higher education, *No Longer Separate, Not Yet Equal,* they reported that black applicants received "an admissions bonus . . . equivalent to 310 SAT points" relative to whites and more relative to Asians. This translates to 155 points on our academic index. Other studies focus on the vastly greater chance that a black applicant has of being admitted compared with a white applicant with the same academic index score.

There are two important points here. First, racial preferences are not remotely close to being the "tie-breakers" they are sometimes claimed to be. They require admissions offices to give priority to minority applicants over hundreds or thousands of white and Asian applicants with substantially higher academic indices. And second, because of the large differences in average academic indices across racial lines, large racial preferences follow ineluctably if elite schools want student bodies whose racial mix reflects their applicant pool. (We explore the sources of and possible cures for racial difference in pre-college learning in Chapter Seventeen.)

3. Virtually all colleges and universities that use racial preferences have either an explicit or an implicit weight assigned to race.

Every analyst who has studied actual data on admissions at selective colleges or professional schools understands that these schools not only use large racial preferences; they also use them consistently. That is to say, the effect of the preference at these schools is essentially equivalent to adding a certain number of points to each black student's test scores or GPA. Or, to put it differently, there is some range of academic credentials in which white and Asian applicants are almost certain to be denied, whereas blacks and American Indians are almost certain to be admitted and Hispanics are a coin toss.

These schools often refer to their admissions processes as "holistic," as though each file is deeply meditated upon and each admissions decision is more intuitive than mechanical. (As we shall see, current Supreme Court doctrine nearly requires schools to at least pretend this is the case.) At most large schools such descriptions are completely fanciful; admissions are driven by fairly mechanical decision rules. But even at schools that truly do make decisions on a case-by-case basis, there is some kind of systematic heuristic—

a detailed mental sorting system—that guides choices. If we could sit down with the admissions staff and give them a series of hypothetical candidates who differed only on one or two characteristics, we could reconstruct the implicit weight given to a well-written essay, an enthusiastic letter of recommendation—or the applicant's race. Given the observed results of admissions decisions, we know that such an implicit weight exists and that, for race, it is generally very large indeed.

4. Racial preferences produce a "cascade effect."

One striking feature of our system of preferences is its tendency to cascade like a row of dominoes. The elite schools get their pick of the most academically qualified minorities, most of whom might have been better matched at a lower-tier school. The second tier of schools, deprived of students who would have been good academic matches, must then in turn use preferences to produce a representative student body, and so on down the line.

Figure 2.1 illustrates the cascade effect for black students by showing the relative supply of blacks to whites at various levels of the academic index in the national pool of college applicants in 2008. In this very simplified example the most elite colleges set racial diversity goals, admit the blacks with the highest academic indices, and then continue using preferences as large as necessary to reach down into the black pool until they achieve their admissions goals, a process that absorbs the top five cohorts of blacks. The second tier of colleges start where their more elite competitors leave off, but even their strongest black admits will have academic indices well below the white average. To avoid too large an academic index gap between whites and blacks, the second-tier schools end up admitting a smaller proportion of blacks than the top-tier schools, but those blacks nonetheless have a larger academic index gap (and thus more vulnerability to mismatch) than do their counterparts at the most elite schools. And so on down the line. Only when one drops below the midpoint of academic index distribution does the supply of black candidates become large enough to start dampening the cascade effect.

We can draw two important lessons from Figure 2.1. First, the cascade effect multiplies with the number of institutions using—and the number of students receiving—racial preferences. In Tier 2 on down, it's the case that if higher-ranked schools practiced strict race neutrality, then schools in every lower tier would be able to use much smaller preferences, or none at all, to achieve their racial diversity goals. Second, the cascade effect amplifies the academic index gap as it sweeps across the tiers. Because the most elite schools "go first," they are in the unique position of being able to admit both the minority students who qualify for their schools without preferences and the best students who can qualify with relatively small preferences. Tier 2 schools must reach much further down into the pool of students and thus end up with a larger black-white academic index gap. And so on.

Figure 2.1 is an enormous oversimplification of the actual dynamics of competitive college admissions. Schools do not, of course, rely solely on academic indices or their equivalents to select students; therefore, their student bodies are somewhat more academically heterogeneous than our model suggests. Nor do all or even most students attend the most elite school that will have them. Nor would a law requiring race-neutrality produce the tiny representation of blacks at the most elite schools that our model suggests, because other mechanisms of increasing diversity (such as socioeconomic or athletic preferences) would offset race-neutrality to some degree.

These caveats notwithstanding, the cascade effect is a dominant aspect of racial preference systems. It clearly does multiply the scale on which preferences are used and effectively forces second- and third-tier institutions (however defined) to use larger preferences than do the schools at the very top.

Thus, the most elite schools are thrice blessed. Because they are the first movers in this process, they can (a) enroll larger numbers of minorities than their less elite counterparts; (b) harm them less, because the credential gaps at those schools are more modest than they are at the next few tiers; and (c) often boast excellent outcomes for their minority students who are, after all, coming in with very impressive credentials.

Although academics at very elite institutions generally don't appreciate this dynamic, it does help explain why many of the most ardent defenders of racial preferences hail from those very schools. Looking around their own campuses, they simply do not see anything like the full magnitude of the problem that their use of racial preferences creates for the broader pool of students and schools.

5. It's not so easy to make up lost ground, and it's more common to fall behind.

Two interrelated myths pervade affirmative action discourse. One is that standardized tests like the SAT I and the ACT or other measures of achievement like high school grades are biased against minorities and understate their academic ability. The other is that when colleges and universities use preferences, they are finding and selecting minorities who, despite their low academic indices, have such strong academic potential that they will perform at levels comparable to other students at the college if only given the chance.

FIGURE 2.1. **The Cascade Effect**

College diversity goals create gaps in academic preparation between students who receive racial preferences and those who do not. And since nearly all elite and selective colleges use racial preferences, they end up competing for the same black and Hispanic students. This creates the little-understood "cascade effect" and shapes the contours of the mismatch problem in important ways.

The diagrams on the next few pages explore the workings of racial preferences and the cascade effect through examples that are simplified, but which in key respects mirror real-world data closely. For instance, in our example we simplify by considering just two groups, "blacks" and "non-blacks," even though colleges apply differing racial preferences to several distinct groups.

The Setup

 Colleges are divided into eight tiers

The top five tiers use explicit racial preferences. These schools account for perhaps one-quarter of all college students. The most elite (Tier 1) schools seek to enroll students from the top fortieth of all college applicants. Tier 2 schools generally enroll students from the next fortieth, and so on through Tier 5, which seeks to enroll students between the 80th and 85th percentile of all college applicants.

Tiers 6, 7 and 8 are, in contrast, minimally selective schools. Tier 6 schools enroll any student who is above the 20th percentile of college applicants; Tier 7 schools enroll anyone above the 10th percentile, and Tier 8 schools accept all comers. The bottom three tiers are larger, and account for roughly three-quarters of all college enrollment.

(Continues)

2 **The students: academic index varies by race**

In 2008, blacks constituted about one-tenth of all college applicants. But their grades and test scores (here combined into an "academic index") were, on average, much lower than those of non-blacks as a group. If we divide applicants according to their academic index rank, blacks are severely underrepresented at the top levels, and overrepresented at the bottom.

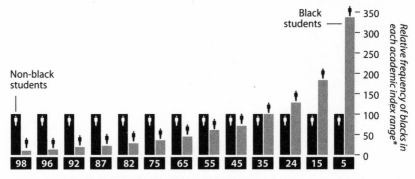

Median percentile of academic index in each cohort   *non-blacks = 100*

Thus, for example, blacks are one-tenth as likely as non-blacks to have an academic index in the top academic cohort (roughly, the top fortieth) of all students, and they are three times more likely to have an academic index that puts them in the bottom cohort (the bottom tenth). This fundamental imbalance drives racial preferences.

3 **The college competition**

We make three more simplifying assumptions to illustrate how students are sorted across colleges. First, we assume that the five selective tiers of colleges admit the strongest students they can. Second, we assume that students enroll at the most selective college that admits them. And third, we assume that colleges would like to achieve an enrollment as close to 10% black as possible, subject to concerns about admitting black students with much lower academic indices than other students (and perhaps poor changes of graduating).

4 The Resulting Mismatch

The most elite schools in Tier 1 can admit all their non-black students from the top cohort of applicants (those with academic indices in the 98th percentile and above), but very few blacks are in that cohort. These schools therefore also admit all the black students in the second, third, fourth, and fifth cohorts. This produces a class that is not quite ten percent black, and which has a significant but not huge academic index gap between blacks and non-blacks.

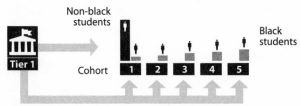

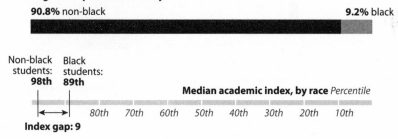

Resulting makeup of student body:

90.8% non-black   **9.2%** black

Non-black students: **98th**   Black students: **89th**

Median academic index, by race *Percentile*

80th 70th 60th 50th 40th 30th 20th 10th

Index gap: 9

5 How the Cascade Affects Tier 2 Schools

Tier 2 schools come next; they seek to admit students who are in the top twentieth of the applicant pool (roughly the 95th percentile and above). The non-blacks at these schools will come from the second cohort (median academic index percentile = 96), but the top available blacks are in cohorts 6 and 7. Even if the schools settle for a class that is only 8% black, blacks at those schools will face a much larger academic index gap.

Resulting makeup of student body:

91.9% non-black   **8.1%** black

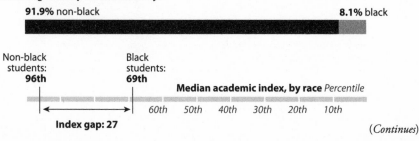

Non-black students: **96th**   Black students: **69th**

Median academic index, by race *Percentile*

60th 50th 40th 30th 20th 10th

Index gap: 27

(*Continues*)

6 The Cascade Continues

This pattern continues through the rest of the selective schools: they must reach progressively further down in the black applicant pool. Thus, the cascade effect creates very large academic index gaps between blacks and non-blacks at schools in Tiers 3, 4, and 5, while at the same time schools in these tiers are unable to achieve their target enrollments of blacks.

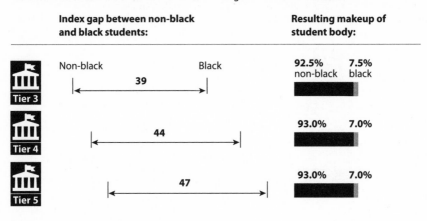

7 Cascading Affects Even the Non-Selective Schools

The larger, non-selective schools have no particular diversity goals, but they are also affected by the cascade effect because the elite schools have absorbed many of the academically strongest blacks. Even the schools with essentially open enrollment (Tier 8) still face a significant academic index gap between blacks and non-blacks.

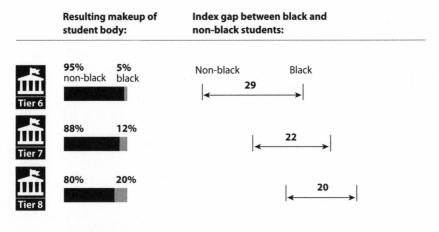

NOTE: A fuller description of this model, and the underlying data used, can be found at http://www.mismatchthebook.com.

These myths are cultivated by many higher education leaders, who often make the sort of gauzy, misleading observations that Duke president Richard Brodhead made in March 2012 when responding to evidence that blacks at Duke were dropping out of science majors at a high rate. "When we offer admission to a student," Broadhead said in a prepared speech, "we do so in confidence that the student will succeed and thrive. We pay attention to test scores for what they are worth but we know they are an imperfect measure: at the end of the day, Duke's goal is not to reward high test scores, but to recruit and train the level of talent that will make the highest degree of contribution to the university community and our future society."

In fact, Duke and virtually all other elite universities admit students primarily on the basis of student grades and scores (which is why, for example, nearly all whites and Asians at Duke have SAT scores at the 90th percentile or above). They do so because of the predictive power of these academic credentials (and because the eliteness of a school is largely gauged by the credentials of its students). And no knowledgeable scholar contends that students who receive racial preferences routinely outperform those credentials—although, of course, some students do. On average, the academic index of black and Hispanic students admitted with large preferences *overpredicts* their academic performance in college; in other words, students tend to do somewhat worse than whites with the same academic index.

No one can know in advance whether a particular individual will succeed or fail. But university leaders know that when they admit a group of students with large preferences, the average grades of those students will be well below those of their peers. Depending on the size of the preference, most members of the group will end up in the bottom quarter, bottom fifth, or even bottom tenth of their class. Nor do students with preferences who start out badly tend, on average, to catch up during college; their class rank remains static or declines further. If you are grouped with students who generally have stronger academic preparation, it's likely that you will struggle and often you will fail.

We cannot reiterate too often: *The vast majority of students who are admitted with large racial preferences are talented people who are well equipped to succeed in higher education.* The issue we examine in this book is not whether these students should go to college but rather which college environment will best promote their success. If they attend somewhere based on preferences, they will be at a relative disadvantage. The biggest question—and the hardest one to answer with confidence—is Will this relative disadvantage in the classroom turn for many into an absolute disadvantage in life?

* * *

The points we have just discussed are foundational in that they shape the way racial preferences operate through much of higher education. On some other important matters there is less consensus, so we pose these as questions rather than settled statements.

6. How far down the hierarchy of schools do racial preferences cascade?

We frequently use the terms "elite" or "selective" in describing colleges and other academic programs that apply racial preferences. But what does that mean? Are preferences limited to a small fraction of schools, or are they fairly pervasive?

Perhaps the most thorough published studies of this issue were done in the 1990s by Thomas Kane, now a policy scholar at the Harvard Graduate School of Education. Using 1982 data on a national sample of high school and college students, Kane found that race played a decisive role in admissions only at the most selective fifth of four-year colleges (which translated into about four hundred institutions out of two thousand in his sample). At these schools the size of racial preferences was quite large (equivalent, for blacks, to about two hundred points on our academic index), but Kane found that the vast majority of four-year colleges were not selective at all, thus making race (or other individual characteristics) irrelevant.

Our analysis of more recent and more comprehensive data suggests that the proportion of four-year colleges using racial preferences has probably grown to perhaps a quarter or 30 percent of the total. Examining data from the 2007 and 2008 admissions cycles at a wide range of public universities, we consistently found racial preferences across nearly all institutions that have a median SAT of 1100 or higher. This includes most or all of the very large, flagship state universities. Taking institutional size into account, perhaps as many as 30 to 40 percent of all undergraduates attending four-year colleges are going to schools that use large racial preferences.

Moreover, as Figure 2.1 shows, the cascade effect pushes the mismatch problem across the whole spectrum of colleges. Even if only the most elite quarter of colleges (the top five tiers in the figure) use preferences, they still leave a large preparation imbalance between whites and blacks attending nonselective colleges. The cascade thus means that mismatch is a potential issue for nearly all blacks, and a great many Hispanics and undergraduates.

Preferences are even more pervasive at law schools and medical schools, perhaps because the competition for spaces at these schools is much greater. Our research has shown that more than 80 percent of law schools make significant (and often massive) use of racial preferences; a variety of evidence suggests the proportion is about the same at medical schools. We suspect that most doctoral (e.g., PhD) programs use racial preferences as well, but the information here is too scattered to draw a firm, quantified conclusion.

7. How do racial preferences compare with other sorts of preferences used by colleges, such as those for athletes and legacies?

Liberal arts colleges extend admissions preferences to all sorts of applicants for a wide variety of reasons. At least some scholars have argued that athletic and legacy preferences are comparable in size to racial preferences. If preferences cause mismatch, why are we focusing on *racial* preferences?

The reasons include the long-standing visibility of racial preferences as a hotly contested political and legal issue that has roiled state and national politics and repeatedly engaged the Supreme Court, the nation's tortured history on issues of race, plus the unavailability of much reliable data on legacy and athletic preferences. The vast majority of datasets about higher education and college students—including nearly all those we draw from for this book—identify the race of students but do not identify whether a student is a legacy or received an athletic preference. We therefore know a great deal about the operation and effects of racial preferences but relatively little about athletic and legacy preferences. The limited data we have seen and the secondary sources that discuss legacy and athletic preferences often tell contradictory stories as to the size and pervasiveness of these preferences. Such data as we have seen plus much anecdotal evidence suggest, if inconclusively, that legacy preferences and many athletic preferences affect many fewer students, and are on average significantly smaller than racial preferences.

What does seem true is that the mismatch operates in much the same way across racial lines. Whenever we have documented a specific mismatch effect, we have found that it applies to all students who have much lower academic indices than their classmates. One can imagine reasons why mismatch might be mitigated in the case of some athletes (because the school provides them with targeted academic support) or some legacies (because they received a stronger secondary education than their numerical indices suggest), but our limited evidence suggests that these groups, when they receive large preferences, are vulnerable to the same mismatch effects we document for racial minorities.

As the reader will see, we believe that a key antidote to mismatch is a dramatic increase in the transparency of information from colleges and universities on the size and effects of all preferences. We argue that this would go a long way toward corralling harmful practices in all preference programs.

8. Do universities even attempt to use racial preferences to create pathways to opportunity for the disadvantaged?

Much of the rationale for racial preferences lies in their putative capacity to improve social mobility, make America a more just society, and bring diverse life experiences and perspectives to university campuses. In the early years of racial preferences—the late 1960s and early 1970s—the main beneficiaries were African Americans who were the first in their families to attend college. As time has passed, however, college and university admissions preferences have become more and more diffuse in their targeting. A wide range of racial groups now receive preferences, including American Indians, Pacific Islanders, Hispanics, and southeast-Asian Americans. A very high proportion of blacks—in some cases 70 percent—receiving preferences at elite colleges are either mixed-race Americans or foreign-born blacks. And a majority of African Americans receiving preferences at elite colleges and law schools themselves come from affluent families, usually with two college-educated parents.

Indeed, all or almost all recipients of large racial preferences are elevated over the large supply of less-affluent Asian and white students with stronger academic credentials. Scholars also have found that "because elite private colleges and universities have access to enough white students in other ways, they intentionally save their scarce financial aid dollars for students who will help them look good on their numbers of minority students." One result is that "the low SES (socioeconomic status) benefit at private colleges is reserved largely for nonwhite applicants" and that "for white students, admissions chances . . . are smallest for low and high SES applicants and largest for white applicants from middle- and-upper-middle-class backgrounds."

The reasons for this shift are complex. In part, we believe, it is because of the mismatch problem itself. College officials often observed that early cohorts of affirmative action admits had disastrous outcomes, and they found themselves caught between their commitment to diversity and the need to improve success rates. They solved this dilemma by creaming the most accessible and talented minorities they could find, who were generally not those with the greatest disadvantage.

It is important to note, too, that there is some disagreement about just how affluent the typical racial-preference beneficiary is. As we shall explore in more detail in Chapter Sixteen, it is hard to deny that at elite law schools the overwhelming share of blacks receiving large preferences come from relatively affluent backgrounds. However, some liberal arts colleges pay close attention to socioeconomic disadvantage, and the data is more mixed. There is no question, however, that one of the most telling critiques of contemporary racial preferences is that they do little to bring in students of modest means.

9. Do racial preferences single out Asians for particularly unfavorable treatment?

As we discussed earlier (point 2), racial preferences vary with the size of the test score gap: blacks receive larger preferences than do Hispanics because in the typical applicant pool, blacks have lower average academic indices. We do not think experts dispute this. But a corollary of this point is hotly disputed: Because East-Asian Americans and Asian-Indian Americans in most applicant pools have higher average academic indices than do white applicants, do schools discriminate against Asians to keep their numbers down?

At most undergraduate schools for which we have data, students with marginal credentials (by the school's admissions standard) are significantly less likely to be admitted if they are Asian. When such findings are pointed out, university officials often respond that this occurs because Asian American applicants tend to have weaker "soft" credentials than do similar whites.

Perhaps. But Princeton sociologist and affirmative action supporter Espenshade and his coauthor Chang Y. Chung concluded that if racial preferences were eliminated at highly selective schools across the nation, "Asian students would fill nearly four out of every five places in the admitted class not taken by African-American and Hispanic students, with an acceptance rate rising from nearly 18 percent to more than 23 percent."

In later chapters, we will occasionally note evidence of discrimination against Asian American applicants. We suspect that discrimination against Asian Americans is spreading. In our view, a system that makes fine racial distinctions among groups that have weaker credentials than whites will inevitably tend to do the same thing with groups that have stronger credentials than whites. The instinct to pursue racial balancing across the board is almost irresistible.

10. Would credential disparities disappear if admissions preferences ended?

A central argument in this book is that when students are surrounded by peers with much stronger academic preparation, their learning suffers and their outcomes are usually worse. Some commentators respond that this mismatch is inevitable—that even if schools abandoned all racial preferences, minority students' lower credentials would still show up in student bodies selected through race-neutral methods.

Simulations show that this argument is not true if schools select students strictly on the basis of academic credentials. For example, in Figure 2.1 we show data on "slices" of the applicant pool based on academic credentials. We see that it is easy to demonstrate that black students in most of these academic slices have average credentials identical to whites even though the overall black distribution is lower.

But that is not quite the end of it. Most academic programs take factors other than measurable academic preparation into account, such things as family background, leadership skills, community service, and writing ability. To the extent that these other factors do not correlate with academic credentials but do shape admissions, race-neutral admissions will not eliminate race-related gaps in preparation. For example, if a school bases half its admissions decisions on quantifiable factors like SAT score and high school grades and half on factors completely unrelated to academic preparation, then race-neutrality will eliminate only about—you guessed it—half of the black-white gap in preparation. Few institutions place this much weight on nonacademic factors, but some do, and more would be tempted to modify admissions to consider nonacademic factors more heavily if they were legally barred from explicitly considering race. This has actually happened in at least some states that ban universities from taking race into account.

Thus, it is the case that eliminating racial preferences will largely eliminate racial disparities in student preparation if an academic program selectively admits students based primarily on their academic credentials. But it is also the case that programs that use extensive "race substitutes" or other nonacademic criteria in admissions will preserve significant disparities in preparation across racial lines, even if those programs are formally race-neutral. The moral is that, to the extent mismatch is a serious problem, it cannot be solved entirely by something as simple as a ban on racial preferences. We think there are better, smarter solutions.

II.

STIRRINGS OF MISMATCH

CHAPTER THREE

THE DISCOVERY OF
THE MISMATCH EFFECT

ARTMOUTH COLLEGE, nestled in the mountains of central New Hampshire, is the smallest and, in some ways, most idyllic of the eight Ivy League schools. Though it has at times been
associated with fraternity hijinks and the conservative *Dartmouth Review*,
faculty and alumni tend to see the campus as a nurturing environment for
future leaders and intellectuals, particularly in the sciences. Dartmouth also
has a tradition of seeking out and enrolling American Indian students (its
eighteenth-century founders had been particularly interested in training
Indian missionaries), and in the 1970s and 1980s Dartmouth had undertaken
significant efforts to increase its black and Hispanic enrollment. These efforts
had produced somewhat dispiriting results; nonwhite students often complained of an off-putting campus culture and tended to self-segregate in particular dorms. But by the end of the 1980s Dartmouth could claim to be a
fairly integrated place, as college campuses go.

Yet to Dartmouth psychologists Rogers Elliott and A. C. Strenta, one
facet of racial integration at the college seemed seriously deficient: Dartmouth
was not producing very many black or American Indian scientists. Elliott was
a longtime faculty member at Dartmouth who worked largely in the fields of
educational and forensic psychology; Strenta was the administration's

institutional research officer. Over the years they had seen a surprising number of cases of black students in particular who had arrived on campus keenly interested in science but ended up in other fields. Wondering if there might be something more general and systematic going on, they approached scholars and administrators at several other Ivy League schools. With support from the Sloan Foundation and the National Science Foundation, they assembled admissions and transcript data on some five thousand students—virtually the entire graduating classes of 1992—from four of the nation's most elite private colleges.

The data made it clear that, whatever else might be happening, the poor minority representation in science did not reflect these students' precollege aspirations. As seniors in high school, blacks were somewhat *more* likely than whites to report an interest in majoring in science, technology, engineering, or math majors (collectively known as STEM). Forty-five percent of blacks wanted to pursue STEM majors, compared to 41 percent of whites; similar rates along with a higher level of interest among blacks and Hispanics relative to whites have since been confirmed in national studies. Once at college, however, the students in the Elliott-Strenta study experienced high and rapid rates of attrition. Blacks who entered these elite schools pursuing STEM majors were only slightly more than half as likely as whites to finish college with a STEM degree. Yet when Elliott and Strenta looked closely at the data, they realized that the distinguishing characteristic of students who fell away from science was not their race but rather the weakness of their academic preparation. Students who entered these schools with a math SAT score under 550 were only about one-fifth as likely to graduate with a STEM degree as students with a math SAT score over 700.

This might indicate that what was occurring was simply a necessary weeding-out process. Rigorous science curricula are in general well known for their high rates of attrition. Perhaps students with weak preparation could not survive the rigors of STEM and were better off learning this sooner rather than later. But this idea conflicted with other evidence. In particular, many historically black colleges and universities (HBCUs), such as Howard, Fisk, and Clark Atlanta, enrolled students who were on average significantly weaker academically than the black students at Dartmouth and the other Ivies. Yet these schools were producing large numbers of STEM graduates; in fact, among the top twenty-one college producers of future blacks with science doctorates, seventeen were HBCUs and none were Ivies.

All of this suggested to Elliott and his colleagues that the problem was not absolute levels of academic preparation but instead relative levels. Students getting A grades in high school science and a 580 on their math SAT might not set the scientific world on fire but had perfectly good prospects for succeeding in a STEM career. At Dartmouth, however, they would be starting in a weaker position than 90 percent of their classmates, meaning that unless they somehow made up for lost time, they would end up near the bottom of the curve. Then there was the teaching: Professors at any school tend to teach to the middle (or to somewhat above the middle) of the class. A freshman physics class at Dartmouth would presume that students were comfortable with calculus and fairly complex, realistic models of natural phenomena; a freshman physics class at Fisk—or at the University of Tennessee—would probably start with algebraic approaches to more classical concepts. Under these circumstances a Dartmouth student starting at a disadvantage would be more likely to fall further behind than to catch up. Mix in the lockstep sequencing of STEM classes: Physics 2 starts where Physics 1 leaves off and professors of organic chemistry presume that students have mastered inorganic chemistry. A student who performs only passably in the first course of a sequence will be at a still-bigger disadvantage in the second and third courses. Finally, there is the particularly challenging STEM grading; in an era of general grade inflation on college campuses (particularly at elite private schools), science and engineering departments often stand out as the last bastions of mandatory curves that tail off with low grades.

Every one of these factors operates on *relative* academic weakness, not absolute weakness. A student who starts as a chemistry major and whose preparation puts her roughly in the middle of her class will probably do fine and will gain a greater sense of mastery and confidence with each passing semester. A student whose preparation puts her near the bottom of the class can easily feel progressively more lost, and the poor grades that take her to the bottom of a STEM curve add insult to injury. Unsurprisingly, students at the Ivies who come in with comparatively low credentials and an interest in the sciences tend to stream for the exits—and into less challenging courses—after their freshman year.

Elliott and Strenta's hypothesis, that low relative credentials hurt students' ability to persist in science, explained a whole array of observed facts. It accounted for the small number of black science graduates from the Ivies that they examined, despite their high initial interest in science. It explained why blacks attending HBCUs were far more likely not only to get bachelor's degrees in science but also to move on to doctoral programs.

To check the hypothesis further, the researchers examined a dataset provided to them by Warren Willingham, a psychometrician at the College Board. It included the test scores of students of all races graduating from nine different liberal arts colleges of varying selectivity, scores that Elliott and Strenta augmented with data from two additional elite colleges. Figure 3.1 shows data from three colleges that illustrate the pervasive pattern.

Elliott and Strenta divided the students at each school into three equal groups, according to their scores on the math portion of the SAT (the SATM), and then determined what proportion of the STEM degrees that each school granted were earned by students in the top, middle, and bottom thirds of the SATM score distribution. Simple inspection reveals that at each school over half of the STEM degrees went to students whose SATM scores put them in the top third of their class; those in the bottom third earned about one-sixth of the degrees. This pattern holds across schools with very different levels of student credentials. Thus, for example, students at the "bottom" of the class in School A have roughly the same math SAT credentials as the students at the "top" of School C, but dramatically different rates of obtaining STEM degrees. What seems chiefly to determine students' chances for a science degree is not their absolute but *relative* credentials. Figure 3.1 indicates that a student with a 580 SATM who aspires to become a scientist is far more likely to achieve her goal at School C rather than at School A.

All of this would seem to imply that large racial preferences, applied broadly to the entire crop of promising black high school seniors, could have the large-scale effect of placing the strongest potential scientists in the settings where they were least likely to achieve their goals. Historically black colleges and universities (HBCUs), as one part of the system where blacks would be well matched with their peers, might be expected to play a disproportionate role in producing black scientists, and indeed this seemed to be the case; HBCUs produced 40 percent of the blacks with bachelor degrees in science and engineering, even though they accounted for only 20 percent of black college enrollment. As one professor at an HBCU observed ruefully, "The way we see it, the majority schools are wasting large numbers of good students. They have black students with admissions statistics [that at the HBCU would be] very high, tops. But these students wind up majoring in sociology or recreation or get wiped out altogether." Elliott and Strenta had found some rigorous support for this intuition. Their research did not, by itself, demonstrate that the racial preferences did more harm than good—one would want to know more about the long-term, postcollege lives of those students. But it did appear to cast great doubt on the common presumption that minority preferences were intrinsically benign.

When Elliott and Strenta finally published their analysis in 1996, they hoped it would spark a robust debate among both scientists and those concerned with higher education policy. After all, the problem of minority

FIGURE 3.1. **The Importance of Relative Position**

Students who enter college with high math SAT scores are much more likely to end up with science degrees, but one's relative math SAT, compared to one's classmates, has a much more powerful effect than one's absolute level. For example, the top third of the entering class at the least elite schools have lower SAT scores than the bottom third of the entering class at the most elite schools, but very high rates of science degree attainment.

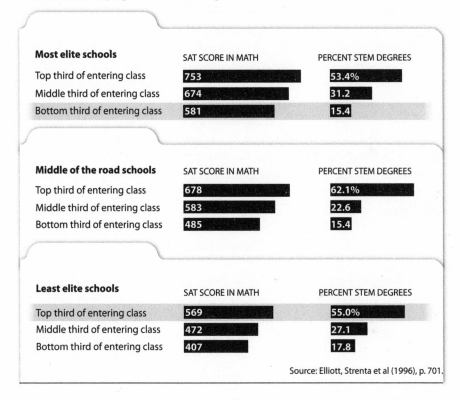

Most elite schools	SAT SCORE IN MATH	PERCENT STEM DEGREES
Top third of entering class	753	53.4%
Middle third of entering class	674	31.2
Bottom third of entering class	581	15.4

Middle of the road schools	SAT SCORE IN MATH	PERCENT STEM DEGREES
Top third of entering class	678	62.1%
Middle third of entering class	583	22.6
Bottom third of entering class	485	15.4

Least elite schools	SAT SCORE IN MATH	PERCENT STEM DEGREES
Top third of entering class	569	55.0%
Middle third of entering class	472	27.1
Bottom third of entering class	407	17.8

Source: Elliott, Strenta et al (1996), p. 701.

underrepresentation in the sciences had been much discussed in both communities for years. Relative to their numbers in the general population, blacks were about one-seventh as likely as whites (and Hispanics about one-fourth as likely) to get a doctorate in the sciences. A number of federal programs had been started as early as 1971 to foster minority interest in science and to provide scholarship and fellowship support for promising minority scientists at various stages in the PhD pipeline. University racial preference systems themselves were, at least purportedly, aimed at improving the pipeline of minorities to leadership positions in society. Now Elliott and Strenta were suggesting that preference programs might be utterly counterproductive in their intended effects. Surely this would stir intensive interest and demands for further research or outright reform?

What followed would be one of the first clear examples of a phenomenon we will see often: the unwillingness of the academic and broader intellectual community to engage research that demonstrated a mismatch problem. The psychology and science communities not only failed to make a big deal of Elliott and Strenta's findings; they pointedly ignored them. Science societies did not hold panels on the new research; science journals did not sponsor symposia. None of the popular science media wrote about the work, nor did the mass media report it. Not a single article, pro or con, appeared on the work in the five years after its publication. The higher education establishment was equally unmoved. Indeed, when in 1998 the former presidents of Princeton and Harvard, William Bowen and Derek Bok, published *The Shape of the River*, their widely hailed and supposedly definitive 459-page work on the effects of affirmative action, they did not even mention Elliott and Strenta's work. (We will return to Bowen and Bok in Chapter Six.) This cold reception surprised and disappointed Elliott. On reflection, he wondered if the higher education establishment already intuitively sensed and, thus, instinctively shunned science mismatch. "Everybody knows it but it's the elephant in the room," he recalls. "They just won't talk about it. They see it but they can't say it. It's a taboo subject."

The idea that relative disadvantage might be a bad thing in a college environment had not always been taboo. In the 1960s sociologist James Davis had written the article, "The Campus as a Frog Pond" (alluding to the choice between being a big frog in a little pond or a little frog in a big pond). Davis had found evidence that a student's aspirations were influenced by his level of achievement *relative* to his or her college peers. Students' aspirations for "high-achievement careers" were whetted when they were big frogs and diminished when they were little frogs. Davis's work generated great interest and discussion and became something of a classic in the field of sociology.

But the simple intuition behind the "frog pond" hypothesis became combustible when race was added to the mix. In 1970, at the dawn of the affirmative action era (only a few years after Davis's article appeared), law professor Clyde Summers spelled out in detail the potentially self-defeating aspects of aggressive racial preference programs. His article was not well received, and the idea disappeared from discussions in legal academia for decades. Around the same time, economist Thomas Sowell laid out the same idea in the context of elite college affirmative action and gave the problem its most durable name: mismatch. Sowell and Summers not only pointed out the potentially counterproductive effects of racial preferences but also deduced many of the likely characteristics of affirmative action systems, as detailed in Chapter Two. The fact that Sowell was black and that a handful of other black analysts agreed with him only seemed to increase the virulence and unanimity with which establishment leaders dismissed his warnings.

In these very early years of preference programs, amid campus unrest and urgency to admit more minorities, many colleges and professional schools largely set traditional academic measures aside in admitting minorities, and flunk-out rates were high. But administrators argued that they simply needed to fine-tune the programs, and faculty were often loath to criticize preferences, lest they be seen as racially insensitive. In the late 1970s, as the pool of minority students improved somewhat and schools became more selective in choosing "diversity" students, outcomes improved to a point at which the problems were less obvious to a casual observer. But most of those involved in affirmative action programs, from admissions officers to faculty supporters, were unfriendly to close scrutiny, in part for legal reasons, as we shall examine in Chapter Thirteen. This code of silence explains why an entire generation passed before, in the 1990s, studies like Elliott and Strenta's even began to look at the effects of preferences and helps to explain why there was so little discussion of their findings. The taboo Elliott came to perceive was very real.

* * *

In 2004, eight years after Elliott and Strenta's work appeared, two more psychologists weighed in on the issue of "relative preparation" and success in science. Frederick Smyth and John McArdle of the University of Virginia obtained access to the carefully guarded "College and Beyond" dataset—a longitudinal study assembled by the Mellon Foundation during the 1990s with extensive information on tens of thousands of elite college students. This dataset was not only much larger than the one Elliott and Strenta had used, covering twenty-eight colleges rather than four, but it also covered schools with varying degrees of eliteness. This meant that Smyth and McArdle could directly examine how students with particular credentials performed at schools where those credentials would put them at the middle or nearer the bottom on the academic preparation spectrum of their respective classes.

Smyth and McArdle found, as they expected, that one's overall level of academic preparation was closely associated with STEM success; students with stronger high school records were more likely to go into the sciences and more likely to graduate with science degrees. But their second hypothesis, that STEM success would be greatest at the most elite schools, "was not supported." On the contrary, they found that students with low academic indices realtive to their classmates were at much greater risk of not persisting in

STEM. Their findings were entirely consistent with Elliott's and Strenta's. Indeed, because they had detailed comparative data, they could actually measure the mismatch effect. They found that, had all the black and Hispanic students in their sample enrolled at schools where their credentials were close to the class-wide averages, 45 percent more of the women minorities and 35 percent more of the men minorities would have completed STEM degrees.

Given these large effects, Smyth and McArdle concluded in their paper that "admission officers . . . [should] carefully consider the relative academic preparedness of science-interested students," and they encouraged students aspiring to science and engineering careers to "compare their academic qualifications to those of successful science students" at the colleges they considered attending. Their advice was not given lightly. Smyth had spent years as both a high school and a college counselor before becoming an academic, and his concerns about how to advise promising minority students being courted with offers from elite schools had partly motivated his interest in the topic.

Smyth and McArdle hoped that their fairly definitive findings would change practices or at least generate significant discussion. It did not. Like Elliott and Strenta's work, their article "seemed to vanish without a trace," Smyth noted. His fellow psychologists generated scores of articles on the politically hot question of whether "stereotype threat" undermined minority achievement in college (see Chapter Six), but greeted with glacial indifference the more politically sensitive question of whether relative levels of preparation hurt minority achievement. Even with the mounting and unchallenged evidence of a "science mismatch" problem, no university took seriously the concerns that these scholars raised.

* * *

A concrete way to think about the size of the science mismatch effect (although none of these four authors put their findings quite this way) is to recall the academic index mentioned in Chapter Two, in which the student credentials one brings into college are measured on a scale of 0 to 1000; 550 might mark the range at which students frequently attend at least minimally selective schools, and 850 to 900 would capture the median student at the most elite schools. In this range every 10-point increase in an academic index increases by about 1 percent the chance that a student will attain a STEM degree. This is hardly mysterious: academically stronger students tend to cluster more in the sciences and are more likely to complete their intended degree program successfully. But a 10-point increase in the index of *a student's classmates* (holding his own index constant) *reduces* his chance of getting a STEM degree by about one-half of a percent. This reduction is the mismatch effect.

Attending a school where your classmates have, on average, an index 140 points higher than you do (a fairly typical racial preference size at selective schools) is equivalent, in terms of your likelihood of achieving a science degree, to knocking 70 points off your index score.

Science mismatch came up again and again in interviews conducted for this book. One interviewee happened to be a Dartmouth graduate, a young black woman who grew up in what she described as a rough neighborhood in a large Midwestern city and overcame significant challenges in her home life—domestic violence, a drug-addicted father, and frequent moving around. In spite of all this, she was sufficiently industrious and bright to succeed in high school, and she entered Dartmouth hoping to major in biochemistry and go on to medical school.

As she described it, things went south almost immediately: "I was with classmates from nationally ranked private and public schools . . . it is not until you meet the best that you realize that you are in a whole other playing field. . . . At first I thought I could handle it, but then as freshman year rolled along, I got hammered academically. People in my class had had science since grammar school, but I wasn't even introduced to science until my sophomore year of high school. . . . I had never developed any of the skills that I needed to achieve." She struggled through her freshman year but felt more and more convinced she would not be able to keep up. She switched to a major in the humanities for which she still felt unprepared ("I could never read fast enough") but that was survivable.

A young black administrator who has worked on minority recruitment and retention at universities in the Northeast spoke to us about the frustrations of many students he counsels: "They have these big dreams of being a doctor, but many pre-med students just aren't up to the demanding courses, so they get weeded out very early on and become *extremely* discouraged." So much so, he says, that many mismatched aspiring scientists and other students at one college where he worked "become miserable and end up leaving. And of those that stay, by the time that they graduate, some students have told me that they don't want the institution to contact them for at least five years, because they feel that they had been used as a poster child for diversity. And so they are just worn out when they leave."

This administrator adds, "You'd be lying if you said that mismatch didn't exist. It's the elephant in the room that nobody wants to talk about. . . . If an institution is just implementing these programs so that they can say that they have these diversity numbers, and they know that they are bringing in kids who are not prepared academically—yet still don't provide the necessary resources for them—then they are definitely doing these kids a disservice."

Dr. William Hunter passed through his own ordeal, although he was not academically mismatched in the same sense as many of the students we discuss. Graduating at the top of his predominantly white public high school class in the small town of Uncasville, Connecticut, he enrolled in Wesleyan. On arrival he found himself woefully unprepared for courses that stressed critical thinking. "I will never forget one of my first science exams," he recalls. "I studied hard, as I always did. And I was used to it paying off: You memorized these thirty facts that you will be tested on. No problem. Well, this test was handed out, and . . . the first question was, 'Based on what you know about chemistry and biology, design a theory of life based on silicone instead of carbon.' . . . It was the first time that I had ever gotten a D-minus." By his junior year he feared he would fail physics and another course. "I was worried that I would never get into medical school," he recalls. "*What am I going to do with my life?* I had what I can only describe as a complete nervous breakdown."

In the end, after moving out of Wesleyan's self-segregated "Black House," Henderson—whose outstanding high school record would probably have qualified him for admission to Wesleyan without any racial preference—overcame his struggles, graduated with honors, won other accolades, and went on to medical school and a highly successful career as an internist at a major medical center. Others, he emphasizes, weren't so determined— or lucky. "There were four black and Latino students that were pre-med when we started that program. As of today, only two of us became physicians. There were a couple of people that were so far out of their element. And then there were Negro urban kids who clearly, clearly, clearly had no business being there. They were not prepared educationally, emotionally. . . . I think that the quota system was well intended but ultimately misguided in some ways. Because it was designed to give advantages to people who were not always ready to take advantage. So as a result, they were in over their heads, and instead of giving them a path to success, it was a doorway to failure."

* * *

When we explain science mismatch to friends, they sometimes suggest that this might simply reflect an unpleasant but ultimately healthy weeding out of the unprepared. "If these students are unable to compete in a tough science curriculum," they ask, "would you really be doing them a favor by putting them someplace less demanding? They might get a science degree, but will they be good scientists? Isn't it better to find out earlier that they aren't cut out for a science career?"

These questions are often asked by nonscientists who themselves went to elite schools and underestimate the depth of strength in American higher education as well as the many paths that lead from a solid STEM education. Elite scientists we have interviewed agree that although a strong *graduate* program is important for a high-level science career, at the undergraduate level it is most important that students get a solid education, learn the fundamentals, and discover their passion. If they go to a school where they are well matched, these things are more likely to happen, and if they excel, they will have access to top graduate programs. If they are well matched and their performance is middling, they will still have a solid education and a valuable degree; every source we have examined confirms that across the broad spectrum of American colleges, graduates with STEM degrees have significantly higher earnings than non-STEM graduates with otherwise similar characteristics. These patterns are, so far as we can determine, just as true for blacks as for whites. This would help explain why a disproportionate number of black MacArthur Prize winners have attended historically black colleges; at those schools they avoided mismatch.

Science mismatch tends to reduce learning, damage self-confidence, and divert students from their tentative path for reasons having little to do with their ability to succeed in a STEM career. We can see no silver lining here.

Another side effect of science mismatch is stereotyping. Colleagues tend to be taken aback when we point out that black and Hispanic high school seniors are, all other things being equal, significantly more interested in science careers than their white peers. People are surprised to hear this because they know relatively few minority scientists. But a large dataset from the University of Michigan (UM), shown in Figure 3.1, helps to illustrate the disconnect. UM is a particularly interesting case because, even though it used large racial preferences in selecting its 1999 freshmen (the cohort analyzed here), its outstanding reputation and low cost also attracted an unusually large number of blacks who could be admitted without preferences.

As before, we illustrate the data using the 0-to-1000 academic index, which measures student preparation at the end of high school; the great majority of UM students are in the 700–900 range of the index. We see that blacks are significantly more likely than are whites with the same index scores to obtain science degrees. But at UM, students with credentials below 660 will almost never obtain science degrees (we think because of science mismatch), even though those students are still quite strong and even though the data at Figure 3.1 suggests that at a less elite school they would be quite likely to obtain science degrees. Because of preferences, a disproportionate number of UM blacks are in this "under 660" range; thus, the overall proportion of blacks at UM achieving STEM degrees is lower than the white proportion.

FIGURE 3.2. **Preferences Can Hide Black Achievement**

Even when blacks are outperforming whites, preferences tend to mute their achievement. Consider, for example, the rate at which University of Michigan students complete challenging, so-called "STEM" degrees, in science, engineering, technology, and math.

*For both blacks and whites, higher relative credentials at Michigan increase one's likelihood of getting a STEM degree. In fact, among students with similar academic credentials, blacks are **more** likely to achieve STEM bachelor degrees.*

Academic Index range   Achieving STEM degree

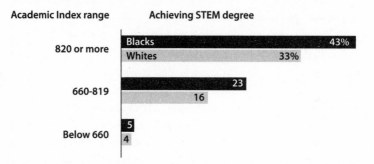

820 or more	Blacks 43% / Whites 33%
660-819	23 / 16
Below 660	5 / 4

But overall, 22.6 percent of blacks earned STEM degrees to whites' 23.1 percent. Why? Some UM blacks are admitted with large racial preferences, which dramatically mutes STEM achievement for those individual students, and pulls average black achievement down below the white level.

Recall from Figure 3.1 that students in the lower score range of an elite school have higher science attainment rates at a school where their relative academic index is higher.

Distribution of students by credential range

	820 or more	660-819	Below 660
Blacks	21%	54%	25%
Whites	45	45	3

Source: Authors' analysis of data provided by the University of Michigan on students matriculating in 1999.

* * *

Over the very same years that Elliott and Strenta and Smyth and McArdle were uncovering and diagnosing the problem of science mismatch, an entirely independent strand of research was developing along parallel tracks. This second strand had its origins in the early 1990s with Harvard's president, Neil Rudenstine. Harvard in the 1990s had a highly diverse student body; its traditional WASP constituency no longer made up even a majority of students.

But pursuing diversity on the faculty had been much less successful, there and elsewhere. At most colleges blacks and Hispanics were less than half as represented in regular faculty positions as they were among the undergraduate student body. In the 1970s and 1980s many assumed that once blacks and Hispanics began to catch up with white rates of college attendance, many more would go on to become professors. By the mid-1990s it was evident that this wasn't happening.

A key problem, it was clear, was that Hispanics and especially blacks were not entering the academic pipeline. Few non-Asian minorities were earning doctorates in most academic fields; indeed, few non-Asian minorities were even entering doctoral programs in the vast majority of fields. Although blacks and Hispanics were attending professional schools in substantial numbers and were getting many doctorates in fields like education and psychology (leading to careers outside the academy), few were pursuing paths that led to academia.

In 1995 black doctorates in all the sciences, engineering, humanities, and social sciences (excluding psychology) accounted for only one-fifth of all black doctorates, compared to three-quarters of white and Asian doctorates. In many fields—not just the sciences—minorities were scarce indeed. For example, blacks made up 8 percent of new law students in 2000, but only 3.5 percent of those earning doctorates in the humanities and less than 1 percent of those earning doctorates in economics.

Rudenstine had discussions about this issue with Elinor Barber, an analyst in the provost's office at Columbia who had herself conducted research on the issue. They developed the idea of a study that would focus on the pipeline to academia, trying to understand what sort of students became interested in academia, what sort of college environments fostered their interest, and what kinds of support helped them to persevere. They wanted to understand why some aspiring minority scholars failed to get into the pipeline and how others slipped out. As her collaborator, Barber brought aboard Stephen Cole, a distinguished sociologist at SUNY Stony Brook, and Rudenstine arranged a seed grant from the Council of Ivy League Presidents.

Barber and Cole conducted focus groups and pretested a survey of high-achieving undergraduates. Then, with additional funding from the Mellon Foundation, they created a large sample of nearly eight thousand students, drawn from the Ivy League, small liberal arts colleges, flagship state universities, and historically black colleges, all of whom were on course to graduate in the spring of 1996. By design, they chose students with strong academic preparation and "oversampled" strong minority students, so nearly all blacks and Hispanics at the selected institutions who had done well were included in the sample. They wanted more than just the aggregate data, so they followed up the written surveys with personal interviews of over one hundred students.

Barber and Cole were immediately struck by the effect that large racial preferences had on minority students' choice of college and, hence, on student performance. At some of the large state universities they studied, very few blacks had college GPAs above 2.8, reflecting the fact that the strong black students who would have excelled at the state university had been recruited away by elite college preferences. Barber and Cole suspected and soon verified that low grades translated into low academic self-confidence and that students with low academic self-confidence were very unlikely to pursue a career in academia or to even pursue a doctorate in the field of their college major. Indeed, they tended to lower their overall career aspirations. Barber and Cole confirmed that a very large number of well-prepared, underrepresented minority students came to strong schools hoping to become college professors. But getting mediocre-to-bad grades tended to kill those aspirations. Few students who, in their own eyes, did not do well in college wanted to fight uphill battles to become professors and spend their careers in colleges.

In sharp contrast, minority students who attended schools where their academic index put them at or above the average entering freshman had a very different experience. They tended to get much better grades. Their academic self-confidence tended to grow rather than wither. And they maintained their enthusiasm about pursuing doctorates and academic careers. Controlling for other factors, these "well-matched" students were about twice as likely as their "ill-matched" peers to sustain their plans to join academia.

Though they knew nothing of the science mismatch research, Cole and Barber had thus, by 2000, found another area in which large racial preferences appeared to backfire on intended beneficiaries. Empirical research—that is, *the facts*—had led the two scholars to conclusions that were profoundly unwelcome to most if not all their sponsors. Cole and Barber used the "frog pond" metaphor to articulate their finding, but the mechanism was essentially identical to the "relative deprivation" concept advanced by Elliott and Strenta and the "fear of failure" identified by Clyde Summers. The intended beneficiaries of preferences in all these situations seemed to face a serious mismatch effect.

Importantly, Cole and Barber (and Elliott and Strenta for that matter) found that Hispanic students at elite schools experienced much less mismatch than did blacks. This might be because Hispanics generally received significantly smaller racial preferences; perhaps there was a "sweet spot" where preferences expanded opportunities without generating mismatch. More work was (and is) necessary on this point.

Cole and Barber's project stretched a decade from conception to publication (not an unusual period for an academic project involving extensive data collection). Then, before the manuscript was finished, Barber tragically developed cancer and died. Their book, *Increasing Faculty Diversity*, was published by Harvard University Press in 2003 and contained a host of prescriptions to increase minority participation in the pipeline to academia. But it also contained a clear statement of the problem of mismatch, offering this advice to student counselors:

> Instead of recommending that minority students go to the most prestigious school they can get into, high school guidance counselors should recommend that each student go to a school where he or she is likely to do well academically. An HBCU may be such a school. Guidance counselors, in short, should try to reduce some of the lack of fit between the level of academic preparation of minority students and the schools where they enroll.

These words were published at almost the exact moment that Smyth and McArdle were giving the same advice to counselors as a way of reducing science mismatch.

Despite the extraordinary involvement of Ivy League leaders in the conception and funding of the project, despite its publication by the Harvard University Press, and despite the careful, richly documented, dispassionate way in which Cole and Barber presented their conclusions, the arrival of *Increasing Faculty Diversity* was greeted mostly with silence. Even though the book came at the height of a national debate on racial preferences in higher education, catalyzed by momentous Supreme Court cases decided in the summer of 2003, the book received virtually no mention in the press. One of the few was in the *Chronicle of Higher Education*, which suggested that the book's primary funder, the Mellon Foundation, was trying to distance itself from the findings. Mellon need not have bothered; the book sold few copies and generated no discussion. As with Elliott and Strenta, Cole could feel a palpable chilling of academic and funding connections. "It was really ignored," Cole recalled in an interview. "The leaders of higher education institutions have their political views and they adhere to them regardless of the evidence."

So far as we know, no scholar has made a case against the findings of Elliott and Strenta, Smyth and McArdle, or Cole and Barber; their work, however challenging to the conventional wisdom, has gone utterly unrefuted. The failure of the academy to take account of the problems these scholars identify is serious. To be sure, none of these works sought to assess affirmative action as a whole or tried to weigh the various benefits of racial preferences against their aggregate costs or to explain whether other forms of preferences, like legacies or athletic scholarships, might produce the same harms as large racial preferences. But these three major studies had each provided compelling evidence that the intuitively logical mechanisms of mismatch were real and were hurting large numbers of minority students. This should have spurred massive concern and discussion about corrective strategies or at least an organized effort by higher education leaders to verify or refute the findings. Instead, higher education leaders along with the reporters covering them chose to pretend the studies did not exist.

CHAPTER FOUR

LAW SCHOOL MISMATCH

THOUGH THE EARLY RESEARCH *on mismatch described in Chapter 3 was dramatic, it focused on very discrete phenomena in which "relative disadvantage" played an obvious, almost intuitive part. Law schools provide a very different window into mismatch. Because law graduates take bar exams, it is possible to see whether mismatch directly affects learning itself. And due to the breadth of data developed on law students and lawyers over the past generation, it is possible to look at the effects of legal education more comprehensively. One of us (Rick Sander) pioneered this work, and because his experience in studying mismatch was in many ways a personal journey, this chapter and the next are told from his perspective.*

The first thing that struck me when I arrived as a junior member of the law faculty at UCLA in 1989 was how different it was from Northwestern, where I had received my law degree. During my years in graduate school, Chicago and its communities had passed through some dramatic events (some of them memorably recounted in Barack Obama's memoir, *Dreams from My Father*), but the university and my overwhelmingly white classmates seemed largely sealed off from the city. UCLA Law School felt very different. Nearly half of the student body along with many of the faculty were nonwhite; student organizational life was vibrant, and many students spent their precious free time engaged with pro bono organizations in Los Angeles neighborhoods. Classroom discussions reflected the diversity of the students, though not in a particularly self-conscious way. Cross-racial interaction was ubiquitous and cross-racial friendships were common. After the racial tension of Chicago and the sequestration of Northwestern, UCLA seemed too good to be true. Of course, in a sense, it was. Like a hundred fictional travelers to new worlds that seemed at first to be utopias, I was gradually to discover that the law school had some disturbing hidden secrets.

One discovery was that race was closely linked to law school performance. Almost all classes other than seminars used anonymous grading, but after grades were turned in, professors could get a "matching sheet" that linked exam numbers to names. After my very first semester I was struck that my Hispanic, black, and American Indian students were mostly getting Cs in a class in which the median grade was a B-. The pattern repeated the next semester—including even students who had impressed me in class. Puzzled, I asked a senior colleague about the pattern. Oh yes, she replied, shaking her head. The minority students come in with weaker preparation. It was a tough problem.

But this answer puzzled me more. How could it be, I asked, that 80 percent of the black students had weaker preparation than 80 percent of the white students? Weren't they all admitted through the same process? No, the colleague replied. Admissions were done separately for each racial group. And though there were lots of blacks in the pool who would shine at UCLA, they were generally attending Stanford, Harvard, and Yale.

This was intriguing. I wanted to find out more, and I soon became a sort of technical adviser to the admissions office, learning for the first time many of the sorts of basic facts about racial preferences that we discussed in Chapter Two. The law school's admissions officers used an index (which I soon persuaded them should run from 0 to 1000) that combined information about an applicant's LSAT score, her undergraduate grades, and the difficulty of her college. An applicant's index score determined whether she was a presumptive admit, a presumptive reject, or a borderline case meriting closer scrutiny. But these thresholds were completely different for each racial group. Whites would be presumptively admitted with an index of 820 and presumptively rejected with an index of 760. For blacks and American Indians, the corresponding numbers were 620 (admit) and 550 (reject).

Most remarkable to me was the role of law students in this process. Through a series of protests and confrontations over the years, including sit-ins, student takeovers of the records office, and smashed windows, the administration and the major student groups had reached an accommodation. The Asian, black, and Hispanic student organizations would each be allowed to appoint students to race-based admissions committees. The students would review their same-race applicants and make recommendations; usually the students favored lower-index applicants with more "authentic" or activist backgrounds. Faculty and admissions administrators would try to pay reasonable heed to these suggestions while screening out the academically weakest candidates.

Once I understood the system, what I observed in the classroom no longer surprised me. The reason I was seeing relatively little racial overlap in academic performance in the classroom was that there was virtually *no* overlap in academic indices across racial groups. UCLA was achieving an extraordinary level of racial integration in the classrooms through a racially segregated admissions process in the basement.

And although the admissions process was generally unknown to students, the performance gap in the classrooms seemed to be well known. Once, when a student told me about his course load, I observed that he was in a lot of tough classes graded on mandatory curves. That was true, he responded, but a couple of them were "safeties." I asked him what that meant. A little embarrassed, he said that was a term for a class that had enough black and Hispanic students to absorb the low grades on the curve. His remark was breathtakingly cynical—and an oversimplification too. (The correlation between race and grades was by no means perfect.) But it was hard to blame him, and I gradually learned that many students thought in these terms.

UCLA's racial diversity, it was clear, had both wonderful and chilling elements. But I was quite prepared to believe that the good predominated. My colleagues had the very best of intentions. We had produced some outstandingly successful minority alumni. There was that magical air of successful integration. And, as several colleagues had told me, the underlying trendlines were producing steadily strong minority candidates. How could we make it better?

Alongside its diversity program, the law school had tinkered with a wide variety of academic support programs to help students who were struggling. I had taught in one of these programs and was impressed with the work of Kris Knaplund, the charismatic coordinator of the law school's academic support. From a series of early conversations we embarked on a three-year (1992–1995) study of the school's many different experiments in academic support. We assembled a database that covered some three thousand recent law students, with information on their academic index, the courses they took, their performance at the law school and on the bar, and, of course, what type of academic support (if any) they had received. We interviewed the various faculty who had been involved in academic support and read the comparatively scant literature evaluating other programs.

Our findings were clear. Students doing poorly in their first year of law school were often those admitted with large racial preferences. They tended

to struggle at the very basic level of understanding what professors were trying to accomplish in the classroom. If a professor, for example, posed a hypothetical that slightly changed the facts of a case, these students might have a
good idea of the answer but no idea why the question was being asked. Consequently, academic support that consisted of merely reviewing material was
singularly ineffective. The approach that worked, at least to some degree and
for some students, was to "decode" the classroom—that is, explain in detail,
and with examples, exactly why professors were asking the questions they
did, what they were trying to teach, and what they expected students to
deduce on their own.

Academic support programs that didn't build on these insights could be
very resource intensive (e.g., individual tutoring of students by faculty) and
yet essentially useless. Programs that were well designed made a real difference. But even here, we found no cure-all. The most effective academic support programs at UCLA had a lasting, positive influence on many students'
grades, but the effect was small and we were uncertain that it carried over to
success on the bar exam.

According to the bar's published reports, UCLA's law graduates typically
had a first-time bar passage rate of around 85 percent, and everyone dreaded
the idea of being part of the 15 percent who failed. Failure on the bar could
mean getting fired from one's job (especially if one failed on the second
attempt) or not getting a job if one didn't have one lined up by graduation
time. Retaking the bar was expensive and time consuming. And a large percentage of those who failed the first time never did pass.

Consequently, nearly every UCLA graduate signed up for a "bar review"
course. These were privately run, very expensive, eight-week courses that
covered all the major topics on the bar, administered practice exams, and
offered insider tips on how to pass the bar. So powerful was the faith in
these bar review courses that the law school's academic calendar ran on a
different schedule from the rest of the university so that graduates could,
upon receiving their diplomas, immediately dive into the review class. It
was—and is—a very strange system that exists throughout legal education
and seems built on the idea that law school provides no useful preparation
for the bar exam.

But, as shown in Figure 4.1, when I found data linking law school grades
with bar exam results for UCLA students, quite a different story appeared.

Law school performance was by far the best predictor of bar exam outcomes. If you were in the top third of the class, you had more than a 99 percent chance of passing the bar; if you were in the bottom tenth of the class,
you had only a one-in-four chance of passing.

FIGURE 4.1. Grades and Bar Passage

A student's law school performance is by far the strongest predictor of success on the bar exam.

UCLA Bar Passage Rates, By Class Rank, 1998–1999

† Passed on first attempt   † Did not pass on first attempt

CLASS RANK	NUMBER TAKING THE CALIFORNIA BAR / NUMBER PASSING ON FIRST ATTEMPT	
Top quarter		(64/63) **98%**
Second quarter		63/62 **98%**
40th to 50th percentile		25/24 **96%**
30th to 40th percentile		25/23 **94%**
20th to 30th percentile		26/18 **69%**
10th to 20th percentile		25/13 **52%**
Bottom tenth		25/8 **32%**

Source: UCLA Records Office, "Bar results per GPA Range, First-Time Takers," July 1998 and 1999. Values shows are an average of the two years.

The obvious implication of this data was that law school *did* matter to bar performance (and, as we shall see later, to one's actual success as a lawyer). A secondary implication was that bar review courses were greatly overrated—a conjecture that was proven several years later in a study Steven Klein and Roger Bolus did for the Texas Bar, in which they found that completely skipping any bar review course would affect bar passage for only two or three graduates out of every hundred.

There were, of course, innumerable other factors that necessarily influenced how one did on the bar exam: the courses one took, how hard one studied, whether one could stay focused during three grueling days of examination, and so forth. But all of these put together appeared to be less important than law school grades.

Such an unexpectedly high correlation fascinates social scientists like me. It naturally suggested that law schools and law students had been overlooking something important about the way things work.

In one sense this correlation was not so mysterious. If one thought of the bar exam as, essentially, a gigantic law school exam, wouldn't one expect its results to correlate with the results of all the little exams one took in law school? If one was good at writing essays and answering multiple choice questions about legal topics, wouldn't that simply translate from one's law exams to one's bar exams?

This was certainly true, but there was more to it than that. The California Bar Exam had introduced in the 1980s a one-day component known as the "performance exam" that was not at all like any conventional law school exam but rather like the sort of practical task a young lawyer might be given by her boss. Students sat down in the exam room and opened a packet of materials from a mythical client with a legal problem. The packet included an introductory memo, various types of evidence, relevant cases, forms, and statutes. The candidate had to sort this all out, figure out a strategy for the client, and explain it in a memo.

It turned out that law school grades predicted scores on the performance exam virtually as well as they predicted scores on the more conventional parts of the bar exam. If nothing else, this meant that law school grades (LGPA) were a *very* powerful predictor both of one's ability to demonstrate an understanding of a wide array of legal issues and one's capacity to assemble legal materials and do conventional legal analysis.

Why would this be? One possibility was that a student's character and personality traits—such as drive, determination, self-discipline, memory, and hard work—are reflected both in LGPA and in bar exam performance. But if this was the main explanation, then why were undergraduate grades nearly worthless as a predictor of bar exam results?

The only other possible explanation—and the more likely one—seemed to be that law schools taught and tested a wide array of legal knowledge and skills that were also tested on the bar exam and that some students learned much more than others. Students who consistently got As or even high Bs in their law school classes were developing a much more powerful and relevant skill set than those who got low Bs or Cs. That would explain both the general bar results and the performance exam results. It might also explain why—after long experience—almost all big law firms looking for the students who would make the best lawyers and almost all judges looking for the best law clerks placed so much weight on the LGPA of law students applying to them for jobs. (Many firms, I knew, had informal rules that they would hire UCLA graduates only if their LGPAs were above a certain threshold.)

A problem with this hypothesis was the conventional wisdom among many law students and even professors that good law school grades had nothing to do with whether one would be a good lawyer. Most students see law school as a "credentialing" exercise: jump through the requisite number of hoops and get the diploma with the all-important name of the school on it. And many professors feel that a fair amount of law school teaching is too theoretical (especially at more-elite schools) to help students pass the bar or practice law and that grading (at least grading by *other* professors) is rather arbitrary. Indeed, in 1995, just as I was discovering the predictive power of LGPA, my UCLA colleagues were voting to abolish numerical grades as being artificially precise and to greatly reduce the number of students with low grades by raising the median grade to B.

The official disdain of the school for its own grading system was even more pronounced in its dealings with employers. Brushing aside the law firms' far better vantage point for assessing the importance of grades, UCLA, like most other law schools, refused to reveal the class rank of its students, which employers considered the single-most important piece of information. And UCLA, like most other elite law schools, stipulated that if an employer wished to be provided an on-campus office for interviewing students for jobs, it would have to interview students selected by UCLA itself through a grade-blind lottery. These egalitarian gestures reflected the school's official ethos that winning admission to the school would always be more important than doing well there.

* * *

By 1997 I had observed the following:

- About half of UCLA Law School's black students were ending up in the bottom tenth of the class; about half of the Hispanic students were ending up in the bottom fifth. Their poor performance seemed to be mostly due to the fact that they were arriving at the school with much lower credentials (and implicitly weaker academic preparation) than most of their classmates.

- Low grades meant poor bar performance. The school's first-time bar passage rates were about 50 percent for blacks, 70 percent for Hispanics, and 90 percent for whites.

- Academic support could slightly improve outcomes for our students, but it had at best only a marginal effect on bar passage rates.

- Yet our minority students were plainly smart, and similarly qualified students attending less elite law schools in Southern California seemed to have much better outcomes. That is, students at other law schools who had academic indices similar to UCLA blacks passed the bar 75 to 80 percent of the time. Students at other schools who had academic indices similar to UCLA Hispanics passed the bar 80 to 85 percent of the time.

Or so it seemed, from the aggregate level data available for entire schools. Without good data comparing individuals attending different schools, I could not really test ideas that I did not yet quite recognize as a mismatch hypothesis.

In 1998 I was invited to a conference organized by the American Bar Foundation to plan an ambitious, unprecedented study of a national sample of lawyers through the early stages of their careers. The proposed study was funded and became known as the "After the JD" study (AJD); I became one of its leaders from 1999 through 2004. The project put me near the center of the legal education community.

There is more on the AJD study below, but of more immediate significance was that one of my AJD colleagues helped me to get access to a massive dataset that documented such matters as racial gaps in bar exam passage. It was known as the Bar Passage Study (BPS), and it had been developed by the Law School Admissions Council (LSAC), the nonprofit organization that administered the LSAT exam. In the late 1980s LSAC had commissioned a major investigation of bar passage rates, primarily aimed at understanding whether (as was rumored) blacks and Hispanics nationally had poor bar passage rates, and if so, whether bar exams were somehow biased against minorities. LSAC was able to enlist nearly 90 percent of all accredited law schools in the BPS, and those schools, in turn, persuaded some 80 percent of their students to participate. A total of more than twenty-seven thousand students starting law school in the fall of 1991 completed lengthy questionnaires and gave LSAC permission to track their performance in school and later on the bar exam. A subsample of several thousand students also completed follow-up questionnaires in 1992, 1993, and 1994. The BPS itself continued to collect data until 1997.

Despite this broad involvement and the massive cost of the BPS, by 2001 almost nothing had been heard of its results. I attended a presentation at which the study's leader, Dr. Linda Wightman, flashed a series of slides with not-very-revealing information on them. Yes, she announced, there was a racial gap in bar passage rates, and it was worrisome, but it was not as large as some had feared. LSAC issued a follow-up report, which was also remarkably bland and opaque.

Surely there had to be much more in a dataset reported to have cost $5 million that spanned all of legal education! I dove into it, sorting through the hundreds of variables on tens of thousands of law students, with a growing sense of disappointment. Wightman and the other LSAC administrators had suppressed the identity of every individual law school in the study. Law schools had been put into clusters; state bar results had been grouped into regions. And the bar data told only whether a candidate had passed or failed the bar exam; there was no specific information on scores either on the exam as a whole or on its various component parts. I will return to the significance of these omissions. For now, suffice it to say that I felt like an art student who journeys to Florence to see Michelangelo's *David* only to find a fuzzy two-dimensional photo in its place.

Despite its weaknesses, the BPS had enough information to answer many questions. For example, if one set aside the historically black schools, the BPS data showed that nearly every American law school was using very large racial preferences (a finding since confirmed with other data). UCLA's racial preferences were by no means unusual. The data also vividly illuminated the "cascade effect" illustrated in Chapter Two. Indeed, Dr. Wightman was soon to publish an article showing that the vast majority of minority law students would still be admitted to a selective law school (albeit a less elite one) if racial preferences suddenly disappeared.

These pervasive racial preferences had the same effect on performance nationally as I had observed at UCLA. The median black at all of the schools using substantial racial preferences had an LGPA that placed her within only the sixth percentile of the white students. In other words, 94 percent of whites were getting better grades than the median black. Conversely, only about 10 percent of all black students were making it into the top half of their classes.

Still—and this is an important point—low grades from blacks or other students receiving preferences did not prove *by themselves* that these students were mismatched in the way we discussed in Chapter Three. The fact that a student might get Cs at Harvard but would get Bs at a twentieth-ranked school (e.g., George Washington University) or As at a fiftieth-ranked school (e.g., American University) does not necessarily mean that the student at Harvard is learning less or will end up being a less effective lawyer than the student with higher grades at a less-elite school. Being a little fish in a big pond is not, a priori, a bad thing. It might be harmful or it might be helpful, or it might make no difference at all to one's medium- and long-term success.

But with the BPS data, one might be able to assess the actual effect (if any) of racial preferences on learning by using bar exam results. Legal education was one of those rare places in higher education where the graduates of all schools had their knowledge tested in a fairly uniform, systematic way. And the BPS did record bar exam outcomes, though there were those data blurring problems mentioned earlier. Since the BPS only had bar outcomes, not scores, first-time bar passage was the best available way to compare learning outcomes across law schools. Because one could not identify specific schools in the BPS, one could not directly measure each student's degree of potential mismatch.

However, there was another approach: to use the race of students as a proxy for admissions preferences. Unlike colleges, law schools granted very few admissions preferences for reasons other than race; if one excluded the historically black schools, then the vast majority of blacks in the BPS data received large admissions preferences, and the vast majority of whites did not. I could, therefore, use black students as a collective proxy for preferences, generally low grades in law school, and hypothetical vulnerability to mismatch. I could use white students as a collective proxy for the absence of these things. Given the type of analysis I planned to do, the fact that these were inexact categories with some overlap (i.e., there were a fair number of successful black students and unsuccessful white ones) was actually an advantage because the overlap would help to assure me that the same statistical patterns applied to both groups.

Taking the twenty-odd thousand white and black students in the BPS, I used regression analysis to see how well the prelaw academic indices of students (e.g., their LSAT scores and college grades) predicted their bar outcomes. The associations were strong but not overwhelming. Of particular interest, though, was the effect of "race" on outcomes:

Blacks were much less likely to pass the bar exam than were whites with the same academic index coming out of college.

So clearly *something* was depressing black performance. But what could it be? Why would black and white students who came out of similar colleges with very similar academic qualifications end up with dramatically different bar passage rates? The potential differences in social background, high school education, or reactions to the pressures of college—all of these would plausibly be reflected in the academic index itself. Why, controlling for academic index, would blacks be doing so poorly on the bar? This turns out to be a fundamental question to which no plausible answer other than mismatch theory has ever been suggested.

Then I ran a second regression, adding law school class rank into the analysis. (The BPS measure of law school grades was a relative measure—that is, a measure of class rank—that mooted differences in grading scales across schools.) This second equation predicted bar passage *much* more powerfully (recall my earlier finding that law school grades at UCLA strongly predicted bar outcomes). This meant that, in general, relative performance in law school was the single-best predictor of bar results. Just as importantly, *in the second regression the "race" effect disappeared*. When one controlled for law school class rank, blacks and whites had the same success rates on the bar.

This second analysis had enormous implications. As in the case of SATs, there had been rumblings that blacks did badly on bar exams because the test was biased. My regression result—that when one controlled for law school grades, blacks did just as well as whites—matched the results of Dr. Wightman (using the same data) as well as the results of highly respected psychometricians who had done analyses with more detailed data from individual states.

In other words, the reason why blacks "underperformed" on the bar relative to whites with similar pre-law school credentials did not lie in the exam itself; it somehow lay in the law schools. In particular, the bad grades that the vast majority of blacks were getting in law school were foreshadowing bad performance on the bar.

These results were exactly what would be predicted by mismatch theory, though it is a subtle point that even some specialists have had trouble grasping. Consider two hypothetical students in New York, one black and one white, who finish college with identical records—say a 3.3 college GPA and a 160 on the LSAT. Those numbers are good but not outstanding. Both apply to law school. The white student is admitted to a thirtieth-ranked school (say, Fordham Law School) whereas the black student is admitted to Columbia, ranked fifth. The white student ends up with grades that put her in the middle of her class; the black student, facing much stiffer competition at Columbia, ends up with low grades that put him in the bottom tenth of his class. Now the mismatch effect: suppose the black student's low grades signify not only that he learned less than his Columbia classmates, *but less than his counterpart at Fordham*. And consequently, the black Columbia student is three times as likely to fail the New York bar as his white Fordham counterpart.

Now suppose this illustration typifies the operation of racial preferences in law schools. Then one would expect that (a) black students would do much worse on the bar exam than white students with the same LSAT scores and college grades because the black students are being "preferenced" up into much more competitive schools, where they learn less (hence the results of my first regression), and (b) when one adjusts for the mismatch these preferences cause (by controlling for law school class rank), the racial differences in bar exam performance disappear (as shown by my second regression).

So the BPS analyses fit the mismatch story exactly. Though weaknesses in the data made it hard to be precise, the analyses implied that *mismatch in law schools was roughly doubling the rate at which blacks failed bar exams.*

There was, however, one alternative theory. What if law school was somehow undermining black performance, independent of mismatch? What if, for example, the use of the harsh Socratic method of interrogating first-year law students came off to black students as an implicitly racist pedagogy and that this undermined their performance?

This argument was pretty implausible—law schools prided themselves on their racial sensitivity—but there was, in any case, a way to test this hypothesis: do a third regression to determine whether it was preferences, or race, that produced lower law school grades among blacks. One couldn't do such an analysis with the BPS data because of its lack of granularity. But the LSAC had done several studies with other data sources, and I was able to do an even better analysis—controlling not only for the college grades and LSAT scores of undergraduates but also the quality of college they attended—with data I had collected with several colleagues from twenty law schools in the mid-1990s. All of these analyses showed very much the same thing: Preferences explained at least 80 percent of the low grades blacks received. Race probably explained nothing, but, in any case, no more than 10 to 20 percent of the grade gap.

The mystery was apparently solved. Blacks graduating from law school indisputably had a terrible time passing the bar. Ever since the advent of racial preferences, there had been an undercurrent of muttering about the large racial disparities in bar passage. Were blacks somehow being discriminated against? Was there something wrong with them? But now it appeared that mismatch could almost entirely explain this phenomenon. Blacks were doing badly on the bar not because of test bias or because of invisible weaknesses they brought to law school or because law schools were somehow unwelcoming. They were doing badly, it turns out, because the law schools were killing them with kindness by extending admissions preferences (and often scholarships to boot) that systematically catapulted blacks into schools where they were very likely not only to get bad grades but also actually have trouble learning. It was thus about race only to the extent that schools based large admissions preferences on that factor.

As my work progressed, many different methods of testing and exploring the mismatch phenomenon in law schools arose. For example, one of my students wondered whether older white students (whom law schools often gave admissions preferences to in pursuit of a different kind of diversity) might also encounter mismatch problems. The BPS allowed us to identify the age of students and confirm that, indeed, a large percentage of older white students were attending schools with credentials a good deal lower than their classmates. Yes, they had disproportionate trouble on the bar. And yes, when we controlled for mismatch, the difference in performance disappeared. Poor outcomes were not a function of age, race, or any other group characteristic—it was about large preferences.

The larger the preferences were, the more severe the mismatch effect would be. My rough estimate was that in the early 1990s, without preferences, about four in five blacks entering law school would pass the bar and become lawyers; with preferences, a large majority of blacks were entering more competitive law schools and only three in five would become lawyers. By 2003, when I was reaching these conclusions, bar exams had become harder to pass in most of the United States. It appeared that for contemporary black law students starting law school, about 47 percent were becoming lawyers (and one-third of these were having to take the bar two or more times). By contrast, 83 percent of entering white students were becoming lawyers, and only one in twenty of these whites required more than one attempt on the bar. Without mismatch, I estimated that the black success rate might be as high as 70 percent. Indeed, the effect was big enough to suggest at least a strong possibility that racial preferences and their resulting mismatch were reducing the number of black lawyers.

It wasn't hard to see why this might be the case. Even though nearly all schools used racial preferences, most of these preferences were simply (through the cascade effect) moving around students who were clearly qualified for *some* law school. An analysis by LSAC's Dr. Wightman suggested that in 2001 all law school racial preferences increased the pool of black students admitted to the nation's law schools as a group by only 14 percent. These 14 percent—who could not get into any law school but for racial preferences—were particularly weak students. Indeed, the evidence suggested that less than a third of them were becoming lawyers, which meant that the loss of these students would have a minimal impact upon the number of lawyers passing the bar each year—even assuming hypothetically that the other

86 percent would continue to have the same aggregate bar passage rate as under the current preference-ridden regime.

But that hypothetical assumption, of course, considerably understates the potential rate of black success: Mismatch appeared to reduce the other 86 percent's chances of becoming lawyers by nearly a third. Admittedly, these were estimates; nonetheless, the negative effect of mismatch on the success of black law students was clearly much larger than the positive effect of racial preferences in expanding the pool of blacks admitted into law schools.

And setting aside the aggregate effects, the "pool expanding" effects of law school racial preferences combined with the mismatch effects were causing a great many minority law students to spend many years and large sums of money pursuing a career that would never materialize. If these results were correct, then law school mismatch was damaging thousands of lives each year.

These findings did not come all at once; I would puzzle over the data, set it aside for a few months, and come back to it again, trying to think through the idea of mismatch and how it might be tested. And as we shall see, there were better ways of using the BPS data that remained to be discovered by others. But by June 2003—ironically, just as the Supreme Court was issuing two big decisions about admissions preferences—the broad conclusions I have sketched were all fairly clear.

There was still one central issue that I wanted to understand: how did law school preferences affect blacks on the job market? Obviously, preferences were harmful for law graduates who never passed the bar. But it was very widely believed that legal employers (especially elite law firms) cared greatly about hiring graduates from the best law schools. Increasing the number of blacks at top-ten or top-twenty law schools was thus seen as essential to giving the strongest blacks better opportunities and helping to integrate not just the legal profession but especially its upper reaches.

Still, if it was true that low grades indicated less learning and that law school learning was related to being a good lawyer, then mismatch would undermine legal skills, and employers would soon catch on.

As it happened, the best place to get some insight into these questions was the AJD, the project that I had helped to coordinate since 1999. By 2003 we had gathered data on a national sample of nearly five thousand recently minted lawyers, including information on their academic indices, the law school they attended, their law school grades, and their jobs as lawyers.

With the AJD, it was possible to compare similar law students attending different schools to measure what effect their degrees—and their grades—had on their job prospects, both immediately after law school and over the first few years of their legal careers. My analysis of the data found that law school eliteness did have a positive effect on early career earnings, but the effect was small. Law school performance was generally as important as and often more important than law school eliteness. A student who went to thirtieth-ranked Fordham and ended up in the top fifth of her class had jobs and earnings very similar to a student who went to fifth-ranked, much more competitive Columbia and earned grades that put her slightly below the middle of the class. I found that in most cases like this, the Fordham student had the edge in the job market. This suggested that although firms cared about the eliteness of one's law school, it was largely seen as merely a signal—to be weighed with other signals, like grades—for identifying intellectual horsepower and strong legal training.

Why, then, were so many law professors convinced that school eliteness was crucial to career success, when I was finding it played a secondary role? I would later explore this question further and find a simple explanation. For much of the twentieth century elite law firms had indeed focused their hiring only on elite law schools. Social background during that time was nearly as important to the relatively small and stuffy law firms as intellectual ability, and these firms had almost a clubby relationship with the elite schools. However, all this had started to change in the 1960s. Many forms of legal activity, from tort litigation to environmental regulation, took off during the 1960s; the number of lawyers as well as the size and profitability of the elite firms began to grow with astonishing speed. The gentlemanly world of old "white shoe" law firms gave way to the bruising competition of "big law." Old inhibitions at law firms about hiring Jews, women, and blacks began to slip away at just this time, and the need for more lawyers caused the firms to start considering candidates from a much broader range of law schools.

These factors and others produced a revolution in hiring by legal employers—away from a focus on school and social breeding and toward algorithms that weighed law school eliteness against law school performance. In the period from 1950 to 1965, 91 percent of the young lawyers at elite New York law firms came from the top ten law schools (Figure 4.2). By 2000 that percentage had fallen to 39 percent. And nationwide in 2000 the largest firms hired only 22 percent of their associates from the top ten law schools.

Somehow, this fundamental paradigm shift had escaped the attention of the elite schools themselves, many of which were led by professors who had come of age long before and who, in any case, tended to think of their institutions as the center of the universe. And so they accepted uncritically the idea that admission via large racial preference to their schools would give blacks and other underrepresented minorities huge advantages in their future careers.

FIGURE 4.2. **Many Roads to Success**

Elite law schools were once the only path to a career at an elite law firm, but not anymore. The top New York firms drew only 39 percent of their new hires from the top-ten law schools in 2002, down from 91 percent in the 1960s.

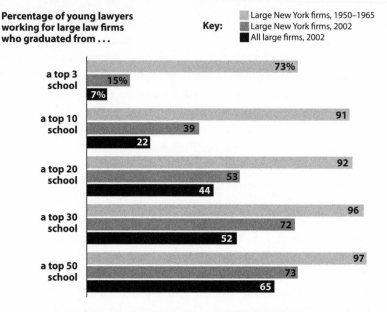

Percentage of young lawyers working for large law firms who graduated from . . .

Key:
- Large New York firms, 1950–1965
- Large New York firms, 2002
- All large firms, 2002

a top 3 school	73% / 15% / 7%	
a top 10 school	91 / 39 / 22	
a top 20 school	92 / 53 / 44	
a top 30 school	96 / 72 / 52	
a top 50 school	97 / 73 / 65	

Sources: Statistics for 1950–1965 are derived from the 1965 Martindale-Hubbell listings for elite New York firms that went on to be members of the Am Law 100 in 2001. We counted each listed lawyer who had graduated from law school in 1950 or later. These 2002 figures are based on AJD data. The same set of schools are classified as "Top Ten," "Top Twenty," and so on, for all three columns. "Top Three" includes Harvard, Yale, and Columbia, the latter because it has long been a principal feeder of New York elite firms.

In Chapter Six we shall return to the question of whether elite schools conferred any long-term career advantage upon students receiving preferences, but my analysis of AJD data pretty much demolished the idea that there was any short-term advantage. Employers had started paying more attention to grades right around the time that racial preferences were coming into wide use at law schools (the late 1960s and early 1970s), and employers were, therefore, well aware that preference recipients were generally not performing well in school. Indeed, my analysis found that although most big legal employers used racial preferences to diversify, they paid particularly close attention to black candidates' grades. Just as I was finishing these analyses, a small factoid provided an "aha!" capstone to this line of reasoning. It seemed that among all law schools, Harvard University attracted the largest number of law firms to its campus to interview students—no surprise there. But the number-two school was low-ranked Howard University—the historically black law school in Washington, DC—that produced more high-GPA black law graduates than any other school.

The stories the many datasets told merged into a larger story that seemed, at every point, to overturn the conventional wisdom. A great deal remained conjectural, but four basic findings struck me as indisputable. First, law schools were using very large, race-based preferences, and even nonelite schools were effectively constrained to use these preferences because of the cascade effect. Second, many and perhaps most black law students (and, to a lesser extent, Hispanics) were saddled with lousy grades, mediocre graduation rates, and terrible prospects for passing the bar. Third, the mismatch effect was the most plausible explanation for the high failure rates on the bar, and confirmation of that hypothesis would mean that affirmative action was systematically lowering the learning of its recipients. And fourth, the major supposed benefits of the affirmative action system—that it boosted the number of minority lawyers and helped propel them to successful careers—were at best unproven and at worst completely wrong.

By the fall of 2003 the various elements of this research were complete. I had decided that the parts of the story were so interconnected that it should all go into one very long article. I began to show drafts to a few colleagues. Reactions were immoderate. "This is 9/11 for law schools," observed one prominent scholar, somewhat enigmatically, over the phone. "The best law review article I've ever read," commented a sociologist friend who taught at a law school. Another colleague invited me to her house after reading it. "It's very powerful," she said. "I'm so glad you have tenure."

CHAPTER FIVE

THE DEBATE ON
LAW SCHOOL MISMATCH

B Y THE TIME MY RESULTS on law school mismatch were published by the *Stanford Law Review* in January 2005, the very powerful work of Elliott and Strenta, Smyth and McArdle, and Cole and Barber had already been published and greeted with essentially total silence by the academic community. That was not to be the case with my article, which I rather grandly called "A Systemic Analysis of Affirmative Action in American Law Schools." Two months before its planned publication date, a reporter for the *Chronicle of Higher Education* called, asking for comment on a thirty-page attack on my article from four critics. I had neither seen nor heard of the critique. I pointed out to the reporter that media coverage was premature; my article had not even been finalized, and surely I could not meaningfully comment on a critique I hadn't even seen. The reporter was brisk. My article was "newsworthy," and the *Chronicle* intended to cover it promptly.

Thus began a period of extraordinarily intense debate over the "law school mismatch" theory. Bootleg copies of my article began to circulate on the Internet, and once I posted a final version in December 2004, it was downloaded tens of thousands of times. Every legal academic I met over the next two years claimed to have read the piece, and scores of professors at law schools and colleges assigned the article to their students. The *New York*

Times, National Public Radio, Fox News, and dozens of other media outlets covered the debate, sometimes carefully. Dozens of academics wrote and often published responses to my article, and I was invited to give talks attended by, collectively, many thousands of lawyers (especially black lawyers), college students, and law professors.

This was the stuff of an academic's fantasies, and I was, of course, pleased by the attention. But disappointingly, the quality of the debate surrounding the article showed the worst sides of academia, not the best. There are several hallmarks of healthy academic discourse: When new work is published raising original and potentially important claims, other scholars try to replicate the work (i.e., check its results), acknowledge what is and is not disputed, clarify the hypotheses under debate, obtain and share new data relevant to shedding further light on the contested issues, engage in careful debate, and help the broader academic community understand the progress of knowledge on the issue.

Little or none of that was evident here. Important academics and institutions in legal academia often reacted as though my work was simply evil—a demagogic, mortal threat to one of their proudest achievements. The thrust of their responses was that my ideas were so flawed that they did not merit serious discussion. A recurring subtheme from both academics and reporters was that I was mentally unbalanced; one law review published an entire article devoted to analyzing what in my psychological makeup could have caused me to write "Systemic Analysis." Regardless of the motive for many of these attacks, their effect was both to discredit me and to warn off the many reasonable observers in the middle: Stay away, or you, too, will be caught in the crossfire. No new data was forthcoming; instead, major institutions clamped down on what data was available, opposed the release of new data, and the ABA instituted *more* aggressive requirements for law schools to engage in affirmative action.

This chapter has two purposes. One is to give the reader some sense of how the debate on law school mismatch unfolded and to reflect on why it took the unhealthy forms it often did. In recounting what happened, I will try to resist the temptation to engage in score settling and instead to capitalize on my unique position at the center of the controversy in order to understand and comment on what happened.

My second purpose is to evaluate the substance of the debate. Many prominent analysts concluded that my findings were unsound. To what extent were they correct? Did their criticisms extend to other mismatch work? Where can we fairly say the debate stands today? This part of the chapter contains perhaps some of the most technical discussions in the book, which may try the patience of some readers. I can only urge those readers to forge ahead, for this sometimes-challenging material is crucial to understanding the debate.

* * *

An important threshold question: Why did "Systemic Analysis" receive so much attention when earlier mismatch research was completely ignored?

Each of these earlier works had been written for a fairly narrow audience, focused on very specific problems, and couched its findings in rather muted terms. "Systemic Analysis," as its title implied, attempted to look at the entire system of law school preferences: It documented how large they were, how they cascaded across schools, and how they affected grades, graduation, bar passage, and the job market prospects of preference recipients. This was much more challenging to the status quo than, say, an article purporting to show that mismatch caused blacks to fail bar exams at higher rates. I was arguing that the entire structure of preferences for blacks at law schools *failed as a system*. There was no silver lining.

On top of this was the fact that this research was about *law schools*. A law school had been at the center of the recent Supreme Court battle on affirmative action (*Grutter v. Bollinger*, which had upheld the use of preferences at the University of Michigan Law School). Law schools and law professors stand astride both the political world and the academic one (after all, two of our most recent three presidents are former law professors) and legal scholarship often enters public debates in a way not true of most social science.

In other words, many proponents of affirmative action probably saw the article as much more than an academic study; they saw it as work that could dramatically undermine support for racial preferences in law schools, and in that sense it amounted to a serious political challenge. As we discussed in Chapters One and Two, many academic leaders as well as affirmative action proponents feel very defensive about racial preferences because, even on the limited basis they are known to the public, these preferences tend to be extremely unpopular. They probably concluded that my piece could not be ignored and must be confronted.

Before getting into the details of how this happened, it is important to note at the outset that all the factual claims and the data presented in "Systemic Analysis" withstood all scrutiny. All of its tables, models, and analyses were replicated. Though this point was often obscured, the debate (such as it was) concerned only the inferences I drew from the facts and models I presented.

* * *

One of the first intimations of the rocky ride ahead came from the *University of Pennsylvania Law Review* (UPLR). UPLR was an important, well-respected journal; I had sent them "Systemic Analysis" in early March 2004, and within a couple weeks they got in touch with news that the piece had been accepted for publication. But a few days later a very embarrassed editor called back. Word about the article had spread to the entire *Law Review* membership, and a battle had erupted over whether UPLR should be associated with something so controversial. The membership had eventually voted to rescind the offer.

This was only a small setback; almost immediately I received two offers from journals better known than UPLR, and I accepted the one from *Stanford Law Review*. Editors at both of those journals also told me that they considered the article so important that they, too, wanted to run a response to the piece in a later issue and a reply from me. This initially seemed to me a flattering honor, but I soon realized that it actually emerged from internal negotiations at the journals. The institutional politics at each of these reviews would allow them to publish "Systemic Analysis" only if the article's opponents would be given a chance to respond.

This quickly became a predictable pattern. At the vast majority of lectures or talks given by academics, including law professors, there is a host who introduces the speaker, the speaker herself, and then a Q-and-A session with the audience. But in nearly every talk that I was invited to give, it would be framed as a "debate," and some local personage would be invited to rebut my claims. Often these rebuttals were absurd. One law school in New York held a well-publicized event that drew an audience of some two hundred faculty and students. After I spoke about "Systemic Analysis," the school's admissions director rose and said that none of my findings applied to *this* law school. At *this* law school, he said, students of all races earned the same grades and had the same rate of success on the bar. I, of course, had no way to respond to these claims; my data came from databases that did not identify individual schools. But at dinner afterward another administrator leaned over with a confidential smile and said, "I hope [the admissions director] didn't nettle you too much. He just made all that stuff up to placate our students."

The general idea seemed to be that the ideas in "Systemic Analysis" were too explosive or dangerous to be presented without some filtering, some sanitizing process. Of course, debate is a good thing, but many of my opponents had no grasp of the underlying arguments and merely served the purpose of assuring the audience that the work should not be taken too seriously. And they generally had the last word.

Once, I received an invitation from the Harvard Black Students Association (HBSA) to give a talk at which my "debate partner" would be Shanta Driver, the director of By Any Means Necessary (BAMN), a civil rights group that had been particularly active in defending affirmative action. The date was in early December, and my flight from Los Angeles landed at Logan Airport late, in the midst of a heavy snowfall. The snow also slowed Boston's subways, and so I felt triumphant to arrive at Harvard a full ninety minutes before the debate. The HBSA organizer then approached me to say that Ms. Driver would be unable to make it because of the weather. When I suggested that we could just have a longer Q-and-A section, she smiled apologetically and said that because there would be no one to respond to me, the event had been canceled. I flew back to Los Angeles the next morning.

This episode, along with many similar examples, were only mildly inconvenient. More consequential were the analogous pressures placed upon the *Stanford Law Review*. The *Review* had accepted my article in April 2004, and word about it started to spread in the professional community by June. At the end of June the *Review* received a letter from two scholars, Richard Lempert and David Chambers. Lempert and Chambers were no ordinary scholars. Lempert was head of the Directorate for Social, Behavioral and Economic Sciences at the National Science Foundation—in a sense, the federal government's chief social scientist. Chambers had been president of the Society of American Law Teachers, perhaps the leading voluntary association of law professors. Their letter to the *Review* read in part:

> [We] have had a chance to read [a draft of "Systemic Analysis"] and believe that at crucial points Professor Sander's analysis and conclusions are seriously flawed. We have also consulted with Timothy Clydesdale, who has been working with the same dataset that is at the core of the Sander article and who has reached results that are in some respects quite different.

In other words, Lempert and Chambers were warning the *Review* that they were about to publish a highly controversial article that was simply wrong. The implied message was that the *Review* should withdraw its offer of publication. Their explicit argument was that, if they did publish "Systemic Analysis," great damage would be done if it was not published side by side with a detailed rebuttal.

Even I found this letter intimidating, and the *Review* editors were obviously concerned. However, Lempert and Chambers were quite vague about just what "errors" I had made. One of the editors was technically proficient and had checked and confirmed many of my results. They turned down Lempert and Chambers's request. They did, however, agree to a request from Stanford's administration that they publish *multiple* responses to "Systemic Analysis." A national competition was announced, and they received dozens of proposals. What neither the entrants nor I knew at the time was that the *Review* editors, again under pressure from their school administrators, would only publish *critiques* of "Systemic Analysis." Commentators who found my analysis persuasive and important were effectively excluded from the competition.

This meant that regardless of actual content, the *Stanford Law Review's* follow-up issue would, *by design*, feature four articles (with a total of eight well-known authors, as it would turn out) all arguing that "Systemic Analysis" was wrong. The idea of always giving equal time to my opponents had reached, in this most crucial instance, the level of caricature.

Meanwhile, the institutions and leadership of legal academia were doing their best to contain the damage they saw flowing from "Systemic Analysis." As I discussed in Chapter Four, I had been one of the leaders of a national study, the "After the JD" (AJD) project, since 1999. The AJD was officially housed at the American Bar Foundation (the research arm of the American Bar Association), but it had been funded by other key institutions in legal academia, such as the National Association of Law Placement and the National Conference of Bar Examiners. The largest single funder—and by far the richest of all these organizations—was the Law School Admissions Council (LSAC).

In July 2004, almost at the same time that Lempert and Chambers were warning the *Stanford Law Review* about the mistake they were about to make, LSAC's president wrote a long letter to all the leaders of the AJD, including me. LSAC's leadership had heard of my article and was dismayed that it was being put into the pipeline to publication. LSAC officially demanded that all scholarship coming from AJD be "cleared" with it before publication.

This was an obvious violation of the principles of academic freedom. LSAC had made no such stipulation in its grant to the project, and it was universally understood within AJD and among our other funders that the purpose of AJD was to create a dataset that the academic community could use. In any case, all of the leaders of the AJD, including me, were independent scholars coming together to do research. None of us had any contractual relationship with LSAC—or, for that matter, with AJD. We were not paid for our work, and we participated in the AJD so that we could conduct research with the data the project generated and then publish our results. Several members of the coordinating committee pointed this out.

The AJD formally responded to LSAC that it could not restrict the scholarly work of its members. I pointed out to the project's then-director, Bryant Garth, that once we finished our report on Phase I of the AJD, I would be leaving AJD and working on other projects. This might provide helpful "cover" for the project in its future funding requests from LSAC.

Oddly, I received a call from Garth and Paula Patton, another coordinator of the project, nearly a year later, long after I had stopped attending AJD meetings or participating in decisions, explaining that LSAC had made it clear that AJD would receive no further funding if I were on the Coordinating Committee. Would I resign for the good of the project? I replied that I already had. Garth and Patton said they just wanted to make it formal. I replied that was fine, so long as I would continue to have access to the data generated in Phase II.

It seemed that the real purpose of this second phone call was to tell LSAC that I had been in some sense "fired" by the AJD. My name was removed from all parts of the AJD website, giving the impression that I had never been part of the project. I was not given access to the Phase II data. And several colleagues told me of rumors that I had "stolen" data from the project or from LSAC or *someone*—an obvious fabrication. But when I asked the new AJD director, Robert Nelson, whether the AJD had made such claims, he briskly refused to confirm or deny.

Around the same time LSAC fired a senior staff member who had been contentiously accused of being too sympathetic to my work. LSAC did, however, resume its funding of what could be fairly called the ideologically purged AJD.

It is worth reflecting a moment on the conduct of both of these institutions. LSAC's predominant activity was developing and administering the LSAT entrance exam for law schools. Its senior staff was predominantly composed of psychometricians. These folks fully understood the statistics in "Systemic Analysis" and, I was often told informally, largely agreed with my conclusions. But LSAC had felt ideologically vulnerable throughout the era of affirmative action because the poor performance of blacks and Hispanics on its exam was a key reason for their weak competitive position in law school admissions. It had borne the brunt of accusations in the 1970s that the LSAT was biased against minorities. It had thus evolved an institutional posture of out-flanking its critics; it created advisory boards on diversity issues and appointed strongly pro-affirmative action law professors to the titular position of president. Going after "Systemic Analysis" seemed like yet another way of proving LSAC's bona fides.

The AJD provided a different but equally interesting prism. In 2002 the eight-member Coordinating Committee had been a tight-knit group. We were volunteers on an innovative, challenging, and often fun project. We met and socialized every couple months; the four of us in the inner core had almost daily phone calls and a strong sense of camaraderie. In 2002 I had written an obviously deeply felt memo to the group about the importance of testing the mismatch hypothesis with AJD data and the consequent need for certain types of additional data; they had supported me fully and we obtained the data. Part of our closeness and harmony came from our seeming ideological and cultural homogeneity; we were all liberal academics who believed success is conditioned by structural opportunities in the real world, and they, at least, all saw affirmative action as an important counter to these structures.

I don't think any of my colleagues expected my analyses actually to find *support* for the mismatch hypothesis. When I first showed them my results they were literally speechless, but some, at least, were prepared to rethink their views. As the research became public, however, and institutional resistance loomed, the mismatch research became not only intensely controversial but an actual threat to the continuation of the AJD. By small steps that varied for each member of the AJD, I changed in their perceptions from an energetic leader and team player to an irresponsible troublemaker. These days, when I talk to members of the AJD, even those who are most fond of me have reconstructed events in their minds—in ways easily refuted by the documentary record—to cast me as someone who was subversive and contemptuous of rules all along.

Before moving on to the substantive discussion of mismatch, one further example helps to illustrate the challenges I faced in seeking an honest debate of the mismatch issue. In October 2004 various websites reported that Lempert and Chambers (introduced earlier) had joined forces with several others to help organize a broad response to my work. One of the others was Chris Edley, the dean of Boalt Law School, a prominent civil rights leader, and Bill Clinton's former adviser on civil rights issues. On October 17, Edley sent a note to *Stanford Law Review* about my upcoming article:

> I commend you for publishing an important piece of scholarship, and thank you for making the data [underlying the analyses] available. I believe, however, that the delay in doing so has seriously interfered with the ability of scholars around the country to engage Professor Sander's article in a timely fashion. You and he appear to be engaged in a game of

ensuring that there is widespread media attention for his very important critique of affirmative action, while creating obstacles to those who
seek to provide thoughtful comment in a contemporaneous way. In
short, you and Professor Sander have been playing politics with a
volatile, divisive issue. I'm confident that this will be a part of "the
story" in the media and academia, to the detriment of Professor Sander
and *Stanford Law Review*.

Edley's note was puzzling. I had made my data available weeks before—
months in advance of the publication of "Systemic Analysis"—to facilitate
Stanford Law Review's national effort to seek out the strongest, responsive critics. This degree of transparency was without precedent. Indeed, when Lempert and Chambers had written an article in 2000 arguing that affirmative
action *helped* minority students at the University of Michigan, they had
refused to make any of their data available for years, even to scholars (including myself) who had been asked to comment on *their* article.

Almost simultaneously with Edley's note, I heard from legal counsel for
the Law School Admissions Council. LSAC wanted me to stop making my
data available and, in particular, to take the data off my website. Was this a
coordinated strategy by Edley and LSAC to put me in an impossible whip-
saw? It was impossible to know. But LSAC's position struck me as ultimately
untenable. I responded that if they publicly posted the data themselves, I
would take my version of the data off my website; otherwise it would stay.
Ultimately LSAC agreed and posted the complete dataset.

Then, a week or two later the thirty-page critique I mentioned at the
beginning of the chapter—the one that prompted a reporter's call and started
the wave of media attention for "Systemic Analysis"—began to circulate. The
critique was by Lempert, Chambers, and two other coauthors, and it was sent
to every law school dean in the country two months before my article was even
published. Especially in the early stages, the attention to "Systemic Analysis"
was driven largely by the Lempert-Chambers piece. Yet it turned out to be a
"faux" critique. It was filled with obvious errors and gross misrepresentations.
When I sent them a lengthy, paragraph-by-paragraph rebuttal, their piece disappeared, to be replaced by a considerably milder version, with no acknowl-
edgement of error or apology. Its only purpose seemed to have been to
preempt a more serious academic discussion. The irony was biting, for Lempert had published an article fifteen years earlier urging the authors of policy-
relevant research to show special restraint and care in fostering honest public
debate; it was particularly improper, Lempert had suggested in 1989, to talk to
reporters before important work was vetted by the publication process.

THE SUBSTANTIVE DEBATE

As the politics surrounding "Systemic Analysis" alternatively boiled and simmered, a substantive debate unfolded as well. Several distinguished social scientists teaching at law schools won the competition to write critiques of "Systemic Analysis" for the *Stanford Law Review*; many other critics jumped into the fray. To date, some two dozen critiques have been published, and many others have been given at talks or posted to websites. I cannot respond to all of them here, but this section discusses those that most engaged the data and that other critics usually point to as the strongest rebuttals of my work.

CLYDESDALE. Two months before "Systemic Analysis" appeared, the journal *Law and Social Inquiry* published "A Forked River Runs Through Law School" by Rutgers sociologist Tim Clydesdale. Clydesdale's work was not a direct rebuttal to "Systemic Analysis"—Clydesdale hadn't seen it when he wrote his article—but it dealt with some overlapping issues and was often cited (as in the letter by Lempert and Chambers quoted above) as evidence that "Systemic Analysis" must be wrong.

Clydesdale, like me, had used the LSAC dataset to evaluate how minority law students did in school and the bar. When he analyzed bar passage outcomes, he had found, like me, that race did not measurably affect bar passage when one controlled for law school grades. But unlike me, he had found that race had a devastating impact upon law school grades. Based on this key finding, Clydesdale constructed a theory in which discrimination and alienation caused blacks and other minorities to do badly in law school and, hence, on the bar.

The problem with Clydesdale's theory was that his crucial finding—that minorities had much worse law school grades than did whites when one controlled for academic index on entering law school—was based on a subtle but undeniable error. The BPS dataset, readers will recall, collapsed law schools into large tiers, some of them with fifty or more schools. The dataset calculated a "class rank" for each student, which measures and calibrates each student's grades relative to her fellow students. But the academic index and its components (LSAT and college grades) are not standardized in the BPS (which, as I discussed in Chapter Four, is one of the key reasons it is hard to measure "mismatch" with the BPS directly). This means that Clydesdale's model would evaluate each student's academic index relative to all other students in the BPS—including those in much less competitive law schools—not relative to other students at the school attended by that student. This mistake would tend to inflate the academic indices of blacks and deflate those of whites, biasing his regression so severely as to make the results meaningless. In my own analysis (as discussed in Chapter Four) I had used other data sources that *did* standardize academic indices for each law school, and this, readers will recall, showed that *race qua race* was a very minor factor in determining law school grades.

Clydesdale's error is not a matter of opinion; I have discussed it with a number of social scientists who, as soon as they grasp the point, immediately and unanimously agree that the error is fatal to his analysis. Clydesdale more or less conceded the error in subsequent, unpublished work. The error escaped the peer reviewers at *Law and Social Inquiry* because Clydesdale did not describe the BPS dataset in sufficient detail or point out this limitation. There is no doubt that, had the peer reviewers known of the problem, they would not have allowed the article to be published in anything like its final form. Yet a surprising number of commentators still list "A Forked River" as an important rebuttal of "Systemic Analysis."

AYRES AND BROOKS. The single-most widely anticipated response to "Systemic Analysis" came from Ian Ayres and Richard Brooks of Yale. Both were sophisticated empiricists with doctorates in economics, and Ayres was one of the most famous social scientists at any law school.

Ayres and Brooks first used the BPS to replicate the main analyses in "Systemic Analysis," and they publicly confirmed that all the factual claims they checked were correct—a nice thing for them to do, which quelled some of the claims that my article was wrong on its facts. They then tried to use the BPS to create an independent model that could test the mismatch hypothesis. This was an excellent idea. In my article's discussion of the racial bar passage gap, I had essentially posed a logical puzzle that mismatch could explain and supported it with an array of circumstantial evidence. Ayres and Brooks wanted to try to test the mismatch hypothesis directly by comparing students who had experienced differing degrees of mismatch.

The biggest challenge facing a direct test was something called "the selection effect"—a common analytic challenge that comes up in many types of behavioral research. To give an example unrelated to racial preferences, selection effects pervade health research. When observational studies conclude that some activity—say, eating lots of green vegetables—produces better health outcomes, they often fail to adequately control for all the ways that avid green-vegetable eaters are different from the rest of the population.

Those who eat a lot of green vegetables are often health conscious, so they drink less, smoke less, exercise more, floss their teeth, and do all sorts of other things that improve their health. So it is hard to know whether particular outcomes are the result of eating green vegetables, or the result of other health activities that are not included in the scientists' data.

In many types of mismatch, research selection effects are a major challenge. Suppose one is comparing two black students, whom we'll call Student X and Student Y. X attended the "most elite" group of BPS law schools, and Y attended a "middle range" law school. We know that the two students have the same academic index. We also know that these credentials suggest that X received a large preference to his school (as most students in that cluster have significantly higher LSATs and grades) and Y probably received a much smaller preference to his middle-range school (as most students in that cluster have LSATs and grades more similar to Y).

But when we simply match students based on academic index, it is likely that we are missing other important characteristics that explain why students are at schools of differing eliteness. Datasets more complete than the BPS show that Student X (at the more elite college) is much more likely, on average, than Student Y to have attended a difficult school, to have majored in a difficult subject, to have secured a master's degree, or to have distinguished himself academically in any number of ways. *That, of course, helps explain why Student X was admitted to and enrolled in the more elite school.* But in the BPS we cannot observe (and, therefore, control for) these other achievements, just as in the medical example above, we cannot observe (and, therefore, control for) all the minor ways the green-vegetable eater pursues a healthy lifestyle.

Thus, any time important unobserved characteristics are correlated (i.e., associated) with a characteristic we want to measure, we face the problem of selection bias. Comparisons of the health of green-vegetable eaters with others will be biased toward finding a powerful beneficial effect from green vegetables alone; comparisons of students at elite schools with apparently similar students at nonelite schools will tend to show better outcomes for the elite students by virtue of selection bias alone. Because the mismatch hypothesis contends that, in important ways, more-elite schools can hurt students, the evidence is often buried underneath the many other unobservable strengths that separate students at different schools.

Ayres and Brooks came up with a very clever solution to this problem. They noticed that in a lengthy questionnaire completed by all the BPS students when they entered law school, the students were asked several questions about applying to law school. The BPS asked them (a) how many schools they had applied to, (b) how many schools had admitted them, (c) whether they had gotten into their "first choice" school, (d) if so, whether they enrolled in their first-choice school, and (e) if not, why not. The data showed that about half of all students got into their first-choice school, and about 80 percent of these matriculated there. But the other 20 percent went to a lower-choice school, usually because it was less expensive or because they had geographic reasons to be there (presumably such things as being near a significant other or living at home to save on expenses).

Ayres and Brooks reasoned (and this could be confirmed in the data) that for any given student, their first-choice school was more likely to be elite than their second- or third-choice schools. Therefore, students in groups that usually received preferences, such as blacks, needed larger preference to get into their first-choice schools than to get into their second- or third-choice schools. Mismatch—if real and important—would, therefore, be a bigger problem (on average) for blacks who ended up at their first-choice schools than for those who ended up at their second-choice schools. So, controlling for other characteristics, second-choice-school blacks should have better outcomes if the mismatch effect were real.

This first-choice/second-choice analysis sidestepped the selection-effect problem because here we were comparing students who had all been admitted to their first-choice school. It therefore followed that their unobserved characteristics (like where they went to college and what they majored in) were as impressive as their observed characteristics.

So what does the analysis show? Figure 5.1 illustrates the findings in a nontechnical way (the same patterns hold up robustly in more sophisticated analyses). The first- and second-choice students, as groups, had very similar academic indices coming into law school; the first-choice students ended up, on average, at somewhat more-elite law schools, but the second-choice students had *consistently better outcomes*. Moreover, these outcomes were extremely close to those predicted by mismatch theory. The performance problems of these students had not disappeared, but they had generally declined at least in proportion to the reduction in the gap between their academic index and that of their classmates.

These results were stunning—arguably more dramatic than anything in "Systemic Analysis" itself. This was a powerful, independent confirmation that law school mismatch was dramatically hurting minority law students, and had Ayres and Brooks fully and fairly reported their results, the entire course of debate on law school affirmative action might have been quite different. An independent, fully consistent confirmation by respected empiricists would have made it, I suspect, very difficult for the legal education establishment to dismiss mismatch as merely a theory.

FIGURE 5.1. **First Choice, Second Choice**

A Decisive Moment

About half of law school applicants are admitted to their first-choice school, and about 80 percent of them choose to attend those schools. But the other 20 percent turn down the offer and attend one of their second-choice schools instead, usually for financial or geographic reasons. This provides a perfect test of the law school mismatch hypothesis.

These black students were accepted to and attended **their first choice school, usually an elite institution.**

These black students were also accepted to their first choice of law school, but **chose to attend a generally less elite school.**

Both groups entered law school with **very similar academic credentials . . .**

STUDENT CHARACTERISTICS:		
Average undergraduate grade point average	2.97	3.03
Average LSAT score (old scale)	30.6	30.3
Academic index	611	608

. . . but the second-choice students attended slightly less-elite schools, **reducing their academic index gaps** *with their peers by about one-quarter. . .*

SCHOOL CHARACTERISTICS:		
Percent attending elite law schools	33	23*
Percent attending very elite law schools	13	10

. . . and produced proportionate or better **improvements in their outcomes**.

STUDENT OUTCOMES:			Predicted by Mismatch Theory
Average law school GPA (standardized)	-1.01	-.74*	-.76
Percent graduating law school	83	88	86
Percent ever passing the bar who attempted	83	85	87
Percent passing the bar on first attempt	66	79**	74
Lawyer completion (% ever becoming lawyers)	63	68	69
Smooth passage (% graduating law school and passing the bar on their first attempt)	51	63*	59

* Statistically significant at the 5 percent level.
** Statistically significant at the 1 percent level.

Source: Williams, "Does Affirmative Action Create Educational Mismatches in Law Schools?" (2012).

But Ayres and Brooks did not fully report their results, and they gave readers no context with which to interpret what they did report. I will not speculate on motives, but as far as I have been able reconstruct events, this is what happened.

Ayres and Brooks were notified in early November 2004 that they were among those chosen to write a responsive critique of "Systemic Analysis." By the beginning of January 2005 they had preliminary results: their first-choice/second-choice analysis showed no meaningful difference in student outcomes. They made presentations of their results to faculty and students at Yale and claimed to have debunked the mismatch theory. A couple weeks later they sent me a copy of their draft. I found pervasive errors in their calculations (apparently made by a research assistant), which accounted for their reversed results. I got in touch with Richard Brooks, who agreed that the numbers were in error and went back to work. In March 2005 Ayres and Brooks sent me another draft, and once again I found errors that they conceded and agreed to fix.

In the final, published version Ayres and Brooks had corrected all of their numbers. But the wording of their conclusion had barely changed: they would at most concede "mixed" but ultimately unconvincing support from the first-choice/second-choice analysis. How was this possible? Ayres and Brooks examined five outcomes:

- **First-year law school grades**. Ayres and Brooks conceded that second-choice students had a relative advantage here but did not explain that the second-choice students improved their grades in a way that exactly matched the mismatch prediction.

- **Third-year law school grades.** Ayres and Brooks did not find a statistically significant difference here, but that was because they dropped from their analysis students who left law school altogether (which were disproportionately first-choice students).

- **Graduation rates.** Ayres and Brooks noted that there was not a statistically significant difference in graduation rates between first- and second-choice students. *But they failed to note that this was completely consistent with mismatch theory*, which itself predicted that the effects on graduation rates would be too small to be statistically significant, given the sample sizes involved. Nor did Ayres and Brooks note that the improvement in graduation rates among second-choice students was *higher* than that predicted by mismatch theory.

- **First-time bar passage.** Ayres and Brooks conceded that second-choice students had a relative advantage the first time they took a bar exam but did not report the enormous magnitude of this advantage (second-choice students were some 40 percent less likely to fail the bar).

- **Ultimate bar passage.** The only surviving thread of Ayres and Brooks's argument against mismatch was that after many tries on the bar exam, first-choice students came closer to the bar passage rate of second-choice students, so close that the difference between the two groups was not statistically significant. But "statistical significance" is intended to rule out false positives that occur from random fluctuation. Obviously, the consistently strong performance of second-choice students on many different measures was not random. Moreover, it was not very surprising that students might, after years of further, post-law school study, partially offset the effects of mismatch *in* law school.

For none of these outcomes did Ayres and Brooks present their results in a way that would let readers evaluate for themselves the consistency and magnitude of the results.

Ayres and Brooks used a second empirical test of the mismatch effect in their paper, one similar to tests used by several other critics. The strategy of all these tests was to compare students with similar characteristics who attended law schools with differing levels of eliteness. Ayres and Brooks called theirs the "relative tier" test.

As I noted earlier, tests of this type suffered from the "selection effect" problem, which was large and serious. The tests were also undermined by the fuzziness of the six tiers in the BPS—the categories of school eliteness that provided the only clue as to just how mismatched students might be. Both of these biases would cause any test to understate the actual mismatch effect.

Despite this handicap, the relative-tier test, when it has been performed by me or (independently) several colleagues, shows substantial mismatch effects for both blacks and Hispanics. But the reported results of Ayres and Brooks showed no such effect. How is this possible?

The only results Ayres and Brooks reported for their relative-tier test were ones that omitted historically black schools from their analysis. In other words, Ayres and Brooks *left out all of the law schools where blacks were least likely to be mismatched.* When this is done, the mismatch effect goes away.

Now, one might argue that blacks do better at historically black law schools for reasons other than the absence of racial preferences. Perhaps they respond better to black professors or they have tighter social bonds with their classmates. But Ayres and Brooks neither argued this nor presented any evidence that such was the case. Nor did they show what their results looked like with and without black law schools included. They simply excluded from their analysis the data most relevant to examining black mismatch, and they failed to discuss their reported result showing Hispanic mismatch.

The unfolding of the Ayres and Brooks paper was, for me, perhaps the most frustrating part of the mismatch debate. These very smart men had come up with a compelling, independent test of mismatch that, correctly done, produced a stunning confirmation of the theory. But they had first gotten the analysis wrong and then, when corrected by me, had massaged the results in a way that made it appear they had disproven mismatch. Had I given them no feedback at all, I could have easily dismantled their published result by showing its clear mathematical errors. Instead, I had been an unwitting accomplice on what was taken as the most powerful rebuttal of mismatch.

BARNES. Whether I learned anything from the Ayres and Brooks experience may be judged from the resolution of another flawed critique, this one by University of Arizona law professor Katherine Barnes and published in the *Northwestern University Law Review* (NULR). Barnes had a doctorate in statistics and, using the BPS data, developed a sophisticated model for testing mismatch. Perhaps the distinguishing characteristic of her model was that it did not rely, as many statistical models do, on an assumption that causes and effects must relate to one another in a linear way; her model allowed for more complicated relationships. Her model was subject to selection bias, but even so, her results seemed to rebut the mismatch hypothesis impressively. For example, her model suggested that a black student with low credentials would have a 63 percent chance of passing the bar if she went to an elite law school, but less than an 8 percent chance if she went to a historically black school, where she would be better matched. If true, such results would obviously imply preferences improved outcomes for students.

But the results were not true; indeed, they seemed to me to have been completely made up.

Doug Williams, an old friend of mine and chair of the economics department at Sewanee University, tried to replicate Barnes's numbers and got radically different results. In the above example he found that the black student at the historically black law school would have a 67 percent chance of passing the bar, compared to a 49 percent chance at an elite law school. This was not only radically different from Barnes's results; it also fit very closely with the predictions of mismatch theory.

When Williams told me of his findings, my first step was to retain an independent analyst (a psychometrician friend who worked at UCLA), give him the BPS data and Barnes's article, and ask him to do his own replication. His results, a couple weeks later, almost exactly matched those of Williams.

Our next step was to contact Barnes, explain that we had obtained different results, and ask for a copy of her computer code. Barnes promised to send us the relevant code but never did. After multiple requests stretching over many months, we wrote up a note explaining our results and sent it to the editor-in-chief of NULR, the journal that had published her article. The editor did not respond or even acknowledge our letter. I contacted the *Review*'s faculty adviser, who seemed nonplussed and suggested that if we obtained different results, we could publish our own article somewhere else.

This level of indifference by the author, the publisher, and the publisher's academic adviser took Williams and me by surprise. In the scientific world there is no more serious offense than publishing fabricated results. Any scientist would see such a charge as a fatal threat to her career; any journal would take such a charge with the utmost seriousness and spare no effort to establish the facts and correct the record. On reflection, we realized that this situation was different in two respects: First, we were dealing with law reviews and legal academics, who more often published opinions rather than facts and often left the factual details of their papers for law review editors to correct. Second, Barnes's article was a defense of racial preferences; "Systemic Analysis" was controversial, so if NULR found that it should retract Barnes's article, that might be seen as taking a political position against affirmative action.

Williams and I had better luck when we contacted a well-known empiricist on Northwestern's faculty; he saw the seriousness of the issue and made clear to NULR's editors that they should take it seriously too. In time, a conference call was arranged between Barnes, Williams, NULR's chief, and me, and Barnes conceded that her results were incorrect. She contended that her original results had been produced on an old computer and had been lost, and that when she redid the analysis, she obtained very different results. A good deal of wrangling and nearly two years of delay followed, but as the editors became immersed in the issue, they became more and more determined to correct the earlier mistake. They secured the input of two academic referees. And in 2011 NULR published a retraction and apology, a restatement of Barnes's results, and a comment by Williams, two coauthors, and me.

For the substantive mismatch debate, the significance of these events is that when Barnes published her corrected results, she had relatively little wiggle room to pick and choose models and outcomes that fit her side of the argument. Her original piece had specified a detailed model and had presented specific types of results; now she was stuck with that model. For example, her model hypothesized that if schools stopped using racial preferences, the number of blacks entering law school would fall by 21 percent. Her corrected results found that despite this drop, the outcomes of these students would improve so much that 58 percent fewer students would fail to become lawyers, and the overall number of blacks who would became lawyers by graduating from law schools and passing the bar exam would hold steady. Barnes could not bring herself to call these results a demonstration of mismatch, but they plainly were.

THE STATE OF THE LITERATURE. The bottom line of my discussion of the substantive critics is pretty simple: None of these articles could have survived peer review by any expert aware of the facts discussed here. Clydesdale, Ayres and Brooks, and Barnes all used models that, when actually carried out in a reasonable way, provided far more support for than refutation of the mismatch hypothesis. The best of these tests—the first-choice/second-choice analysis, which was both a completely fresh approach and one that avoided selection bias—generated results almost identical to my predictions, to a degree that's actually quite unusual in something as imprecise as educational theory.

Moreover, these were not three exceptionally weak or vulnerable articles; on the contrary, partisans in the debate often cited them as examples of the best evidence against mismatch. And the Ayres and Brooks article—certainly the most insightful of the three—exemplifies weaknesses that apply to the other empirical critiques of law school mismatch. For example, political scientist and now–Stanford professor Dan Ho used a "matching" model to compare students who had similar academic indices but attended schools of differing eliteness. This approach is similar to the relative-tier analysis in Ayres and Brooks, discussed earlier, but had some methodological advantages. However, in Ho's analysis he compared students attending schools very close to one another in their eliteness (and, thus, presumably very similar to one another in the level of mismatch facing black students). This is an obvious design flaw in Ho's approach; when this flaw is removed, the matching test shows levels of mismatch similar to those produced by other tests.

A similar problem affects the analysis of Jesse Rothstein and Albert Yoon; Rothstein was then an economist at Princeton (now at Berkeley), and Yoon is a political scientist and law professor at Northwestern. In a broad review of law school mismatch Rothstein and Yoon offered a candid and fair discussion of the selection-bias problem and conceded that this problem weakened their main evidence against mismatch. But this research, like that of their colleagues, showed evidence of having been carefully massaged. When one made simple improvements in their models—improvements that aimed only to make the measurements more precise—the results were entirely consistent with other mismatch findings. Rothstein and Yoon were aware of the first-choice/second-choice method—the best available solution to the selection-effect problem—but inexplicably did not discuss what that method showed.

At the end of the day the evidence points overwhelmingly toward a large law school mismatch problem, one that affects Hispanics as well as blacks. It is hard to dispute that the first-choice/second-choice model provides the soundest direct empirical test of mismatch with available data, and it strongly confirms the hypothesis. In my view all of the other tests also support mismatch when they are modeled in a reasonable way; at the very least an honest critic would have to concede that they provide mixed support for mismatch. Wherever we have actual data comparing similar students at two specific schools (a point we will explore in more detail in Chapter Fourteen), the comparison suggests very large mismatch effects; that is, black students who had been admitted via large preferences into a more elite school but who had chosen to attend a less elite school that could admit them without such large preferences were failing the bar less than half as often as similarly credentialed black students who had entered the more elite school.

Then there is this fundamental point: Not one of the critics has articulated—let alone tested—an alternative theory to explain the patterns that are plainly there. Blacks in law school get roughly the law school grades their academic indices predict and have the bar passage rates that their law school grades predict. Yet they do dramatically worse on bar exams than do whites who enter law school—usually less elite schools—with the same academic index. Mismatch theory contends that this is because blacks disproportionately receive large preferences and, thus, disproportionately end up with lower grades and less learning. If it takes a theory to beat a theory, as George Stigler once famously observed, then mismatch wins by default.

In the summer of 2006 the US Commission on Civil Rights (USCCR) held a hearing on law school mismatch. Because half of USCCR's members are appointed by the president, six of the eight commissioners at the time were Republicans and generally affirmative action skeptics; this would necessarily taint whatever they did in the eyes of many academics and reporters. But the USCCR actually had an impressive record of investigating and documenting important civil rights problems, and on the mismatch issue it took pains to proceed in a fair and deliberate way. Testimony came equally from both supporters and critics of mismatch, questioning was not curtailed, and staff made significant efforts to gather a wide range of material on both sides of the issue. The Commission's background report was authored by an affirmative action critic, University of San Diego law professor Gail Heriot, but Heriot wrote an extraordinarily even-handed analysis of "Systemic Analysis" and its most serious critics. The Commission itself concluded in its 2008 report that some problem was clearly producing unacceptable outcomes for minorities, and mismatch was the most plausible culprit. It urged greater transparency, including a call for Congress to mandate disclosures from law schools that would allow prospective students to assess their likely outcomes across a range of schools.

The legal academic community utterly ignored the USCCR report. At the annual meeting of the American Association of Law Schools (AALS), which sponsors hundreds of panels every year on an array of topics but is most fundamentally responsible for informed deliberation on legal education, not a single panel at its meetings addressed the Commission's briefing or its finding that legal education was failing minority students. Throughout the official world of law schools, mismatch did not exist. Even a national conference in 2008 that was called to discuss the problem of low minority bar passage rates failed to have any serious discussion of mismatch issues. Self-deception in official circles was seamless and complete.

* * *

If the formal law school debate was Orwellian in its resolute disregard of the obvious, "Systemic Analysis" nonetheless stirred enormous interest and reflection in unofficial circles. Dozens of professors and former deans contacted me to share mismatch stories. Frequently these were shared circumspectly; even tenured faculty feared the consequences of any public knowledge of their concerns. One of the best came not long ago to my coauthor. A veteran law professor, whom we will call Kim, recalled a painfully awkward visit from two young African American women when Kim was teaching at a top-ten law school. The women could not understand why Kim had given them such low grades on a first-year exam. It appeared that other professors had also given them low grades. "They were crushed," reported the professor. "You could just see their self-confidence at an ebb. You could see that they were at sea. It's a terrible thing to behold."

Such exams were blind-graded, as is common, so that professors would not know which student wrote which exam until after the grades were in. But these two students wondered whether Kim might somehow have discerned who they were from their penmanship or writing style. The professor assured them that this was not the case. Kim was aware of the likeliest explanation for the low grades—large preferences and mismatch—but thought that sharing such speculations would only further undermine their self-confidence. "I had a very strong intuition," Kim reflected, "that they would be better off at a less selective law school." Then they would probably be in the middle of their class or better and emerge with "much more self-confidence and better job offers." But Kim could not say that, either.

Another lawyer—who has taught at an elite law school and also has practiced at law firms—seethes with anger when explaining how schools like his admit poorly prepared minority students. "They don't tell them before they enroll," says this teacher, whom we will call Jason, that based on their grades and scores, they are expected to rank near the bottom of the class and to have trouble passing the bar exam.

Worse, says Jason, most schools provide little remedial help when such students struggle. "The faculty," he says, "they talk a diversity game, they'll admit black and Hispanic students with low entering credentials, but they're just not that into them. They don't take the time to help them master the skills necessary to pass the bar. You are sacrificing their professional careers. It's immoral . . . to admit people with much lower credentials and keep them in the dark."

Jason, who is white, adds that "the law schools lie a lot about all this. They think of it as a 'noble lie.' They lie about how well minority students do; they lie about job prospects their law students will have. They are teaching by example."

Some black law students—after coming to understand how poorly prepared they were to compete with their classmates—have told Jason that they are nonetheless glad to be at an elite law school. But they have also said things like: "You and I both know how I got in here," and "I'm not competitive here." In addition, they tend to take the easiest courses to get their GPAs up, as advised by peers. But, says Jason, this is "massively counter to their interests. It does not help to avoid hard courses that give you the competencies to succeed professionally."

Of course, says Jason, almost all elite law firms use large racial preferences in hiring—like "putting a twenty-pound weight on one side of the scales." But once the new hires are in place, "What really drives partners' behavior is you want to keep the young lawyers who make you money." Those are the ones who, for example, quickly show an ability to draft in a hurry nearly flaw-less "deal documents." It doesn't take the partners long to figure out which new hires can do outstanding work, which cannot—and which ones they want working on the most important cases.

Scores of colleagues have shared similar stories with us. And at the time so did many admissions officers working at law schools. But ultimately more important and interesting were stories from blacks themselves. I heard from and spoke with dozens of African Americans—prospective law students, cur-rent law students, law graduates who had failed the bar, bar passers who had gone on to successful careers—all of whom were intensely interested in the idea of mismatch and many of whom felt it intuitively to be true. A senior black partner at a major firm reported that in his broad experience "affirma-tive action programs do nothing but (1) place certain students in schools which are well above their abilities—which any parent will tell you is a recipe for disaster, and (2) leave the message with many in society (both minority and white) that most minorities can only make it through the help of others rather than their own merit and hard work."

In the months after "Systemic Analysis" appeared, the audiences who were most eager to invite me to speak—and from whom I learned the most—were predominantly black audiences. I spoke at a panel of the National Bar Associ-ation (the national association of black lawyers) and the minority affairs sec-tion of the American Bar Association. At one of these panels a black lawyer approached me to report that of the first thirty blacks admitted to his moder-ately elite law school in the early 1970s, after large preferences had been insti-tuted, he was the *only* one to pass the state bar exam. I spoke at conferences of black law students and wrote abstracts of "Systemic Analysis" for undergradu-ate guidance counselors, who wished to pass on the findings in advising undergraduate minorities considering law school. I never experienced at these gatherings any of the hostility that often greeted me at academic events. Black students in particular were serious, interested, and concerned.

Meanwhile, as the law teacher who we call Jason above told coauthor Tay-lor, "I've had two professors say to me, 'You don't want to be seen talking to Rick Sander.'"

Did all of the sound and fury over "Systemic Analysis" have any practical effect? There is one very intriguing piece of evidence. Something unusual happened during the 2004–2005 law school admissions season, when my article was being most widely discussed, admissions officers were shaping their incoming classes, and black college seniors applying to law schools were choosing among competing offers. As Figure 5.2 below shows, the number of blacks entering law school did in 2005. The number and academic strength of blacks taking the LSAT did not change noticeably, but the number who ended up choosing to go to law school dropped sharply. Moreover, the black students who started law school in the fall of 2005 appeared to be at least somewhat less mismatched than in other years. Many relatively elite law schools experienced particularly sharp drops in black enrollment that fall, often as much as 50 percent. These data suggest that admission offices in 2005 were extending fewer large racial preferences, and black applicants were choosing schools with an awareness of potential mismatch problems.

I noticed these changes in 2006 and wondered whether blacks entering law school in 2005 might end up having noticeably better outcomes. They did. The matriculants of 2005 went on to have, by far, the lowest rate of attrition from law school during their first year (when academic failure is most common) of any cohort of black law students in the historical record (which goes back several decades). They had the highest graduation rate of any black entering law school cohort on the record. And in California—the only state to publish bar passage rates by race—they had the highest bar passage rate of any black cohort in California's records. If the California pattern held nation-wide (and the fragmentary available evidence suggests that it did), then the smallest cohort of blacks entering law school in many years appears to have produced the largest number of blacks passing the bar on their first attempt—ever. In every measurable respect the black students entering law school in 2005 dramatically narrowed the black-white gap.

Of course, all of this might have been coincidence. It might be coincidence, too, that by 2006, when interest in "Systemic Analysis" had died down and when the official word was that it had been refuted, patterns reverted largely (but not quite) to what they had been before. We do not—and cannot—know for certain until the official bodies of legal education open their records and allow objective research to go forward.

FIGURE 5.2. **A Natural Experiment for Law School Mismatch?**

The intense public debate about law school mismatch in the winter of 2005 may have produced actual changes in behavior that reduced mismatch for the class entering law school in 2005, but with a diminished effect afterward.

Black law students in U.S. accredited law schools, 2000–2007

First year of law school	Enrollment	Percent who left school before second year	Percent passing bar exam in California	Estimated number of black lawyers*
2000	3,402	15.7%	39%	1,081
2001	3,474	17.2	46	1,282
2002	3,491	13.8	40	1,138
2003	3,300	13.0	53	1,439
2004	3,457	12.7	42	1,229
2005	3,107	8.7	61	1,652
2006	3,516	13.2	50	1,455
2007	3,486	11.1	50	1,480

* Estimated number of those who passed the bar on their first attempt, based on California rates; not adjusted for law graduates who decided not to take the bar.

Sources: ABA Legal Education Statistics; General Statistics Report on the California Bar Exam (annual series).

CHAPTER SIX

THE BREADTH OF MISMATCH

SANDER'S NARRATIVE ON LAW SCHOOLS and the evidence for "science" and "aspirations" mismatch from Chapter Three offer some particularly powerful examples of how mismatch can derail lives. These examples collectively affect many thousands of minority students each year, and even if we stopped here, we think we would have made a case for reform. But one might argue that these are special cases—that in law school and science curricula, students must race along a narrow path, and if they fall off, they are in trouble. This is a fair point; we examined law school and science curricula closely largely because in those cases it is easier to observe the consequences of mismatch directly.

In this chapter we consider higher education more broadly. What is the evidence that mismatch affects the general learning environment in college for those who receive racial preferences? Do black and Hispanic students end up flourishing in college and graduating at high rates despite whatever mismatch problems may exist? Are the benefits of getting a preference into a more elite school in the end worth the costs?

These are big questions—and honestly contested ones. One way of answering them is to look at an entire system of higher education that used large preferences for many years and then suddenly reduced them sharply. The two hundred thousand–student University of California did just that, and in Part III we examine closely what happened when racial preferences became illegal. In this chapter we take a different approach, using a range of evidence to understand, as best we can, how mismatch plays out across the broader college experience—how (and whether) it affects learning, graduation rates, and even long-term earnings. And importantly, we will introduce some of the people who spoke with us and our research associates about their experiences with mismatch. Though many questions we ask still await better data and further research, we think the chapter makes the general nature of mismatch far more tangible.

LEARNING

Mismatch is fundamentally about learning. Students who have much lower academic preparation than their classmates will not only learn less than those around them, but less than they would have learned in an environment where the academic index gap was smaller or did not exist.

It is hard to test for mismatch directly because colleges and universities rarely try to measure the learning of their students in ways that can be compared across classrooms or institutions. What we would most like is a controlled experiment, in which students are randomly assigned to classes where they are more or less mismatched and their rate of learning is observed. This sort of "randomized trial" is rare in education, and we know of only one attempt to study mismatch this way. Several years ago the World Bank helped to fund an experiment in Kenya in which thousands of elementary school children were randomly assigned to two types of classes: one that grouped students with a broad range of academic skills together, and one that separated them into high-preparation and low-preparation halves. Three distinguished American economists participated in the experiment's design, observed its outcomes, and concluded that the "tracked" students (in both the higher and lower classes) learned more—suggesting that teachers taught more effectively when they calibrated their teaching to a narrower range of student preparation. Here, at least, reducing mismatch seemed to benefit students across the board.

We can only look in envy at research of this type. In American higher education the closest thing we have to a broad measure of student learning is a relatively young initiative known as the Collegiate Learning Assessment (CLA). Started by the Council for Aid to Education in 2001 as an effort to develop simple, generalized tests of college-level skills that would not rely on memorized facts or multiple-choice questions, CLA has grown rapidly and has to date been used by some five hundred colleges. CLA tests ask students to write essays about complex, somewhat real-world problems based on packets of background material they are given at the test. They integrate this information into a solution and describe it in their own words; the results are evaluated for verbal ability as well as analytic content. Nearly a quarter million students have taken these tests to date, and for researchers, the most useful information comes from CLA's "longitudinal" component, in which the same student at a college takes the test shortly after arriving as a freshman, again at the end of sophomore year, and a third time as a senior. The longitudinal testing, if done systematically to a large random sample of students, would make it possible to measure both their progress and the general rate at which cognitive skills are acquired at their college. But the CLA is controversial because it is funded by the colleges that participate in it and lacks many of the hallmarks of careful research: Colleges sometimes choose which students participate in the tests, and an unusually high number of students who take the initial tests never take the follow-ups.

In a 2011 book that attracted wide attention, education scholars Richard Arum and Josipa Roksa used the CLA to assess the general effectiveness of college education in America. As the title of their book—*Academically Adrift*—implies, they concluded that student learning on college campuses was disappointingly modest. They did not directly test mismatch ideas, but their findings about black learning were particularly bleak.

In their national sample Arum and Roksa found that entering black freshmen had average CLA scores that were at about the 16th percentile of white freshmen—not good of course, but in line with the results of other tests like the SAT (see Chapter Two). But when students were retested at the end of their sophomore year, whites had moderately improved their performance as a group; the white sophomores were at about the 58th percentile of the white freshmen. Blacks, meanwhile, had barely budged; black sophomores were at about the 17th or 18th percentile of white freshmen. Blacks were not only lagging further behind; they were barely registering any improvement in skills during the first two years of college.

Note that this is in sharp contrast to high school. Although black scores on national achievement tests are far below white scores at both eighth- and twelfth-grade levels, both groups make steady progress during high school, and the gap does not significantly widen. The CLA data on blacks also contrast with the data on Hispanics; Arum and Roksa find that Hispanics improve their learning in college at roughly the same rate as whites. Because Hispanics receive racial preferences less frequently than blacks do and are much less likely to have academic indices far below those of their college classmates, each of these pieces of evidence is consistent with the idea that large college preferences for blacks, and the accompanying cascade that spreads the effects of preferences, are undermining their learning. Given the weaknesses in the current CLA (which could be overcome by increased funding) and the lack of any direct test for mismatch, we should not over-read these findings. But the findings to date suggest that there is indeed a crisis of black learning in college.

GRADES

As we noted in Chapter Two, students who receive large preferences tend to get low grades. Every academic study on the subject confirms this, though much of the available data captures this by using "race" as a proxy for prefer-ences rather than measuring preferences directly. So, for example, a number of studies have shown that blacks at elite colleges have GPAs that place them somewhere between the 15th and 20th percentile of white students; only 5 percent of blacks and less than one-tenth of Hispanics end up in the top fifth of the class, and blacks are four or five times as likely as whites to end up in the bottom tenth. But of course, such statistics somewhat confuse the issue, because some blacks at elite colleges have received small preferences or none at all, whereas some white and Asian legacies and athletes undoubtedly *have* received preferences. An unusually careful study at Duke University found that when one looked simply at *admission preferences* and not at race, the race effect disappeared; that is, as Sander found for law school, blacks get low grades in college not because they are black but because they disproportion-ately receive large preferences.

The Duke study also tracked students through college and found that when one controlled for student majors and the different levels of grade inflation that exist in different parts of colleges, the students who received preferences did not catch up with their classmates. Indeed, as we discussed in Chapter Two, as the CLA study implies and as many other studies have found, as college progresses, students receiving preferences often fall further behind academically. Princeton scholar Thomas Espenshade and his coau-thor Alexandria Walton Radford find that "Black students, for example, lag behind comparable whites by about nine percentage points after one year, but the gap grows by an additional eight percentage points by graduation time, resulting in a total deficit of more than 17 points relative to compara-ble whites." Something similar happens on a smaller scale to Hispanics. There are a number of possible reasons for this, but the existence of mis-match—and the social effects of mismatch we will examine shortly—are certainly consistent with it.

STEREOTYPES AND STIGMA

Over the past twenty years an outpouring of literature has come forth on the claimed benefits of preferentially engineered campus diversity, driven in large part by Supreme Court decisions (explored in detail in Chapter Thirteen) that permitted racial preferences as a means to foster the virtue of "educational diversity." The general questions such research raises are whether racial diversity encourages more interracial contact, a greater ability to work with people of different backgrounds, more understanding of differing perspectives, and higher racial tolerance.

Much of this research has been heavily and justly criticized as little more than propaganda. To see some of its intrinsic difficulties (and sometimes enormous silliness), consider a well-known study by Gary Orfield and Dean Whitla that surveyed law students at Harvard and the University of Michigan. Students were asked to report how many close friends they had (implicitly at the law school) who were of another race. Nearly all (92 percent) of the white students reported they had "three or more" such friends; only 37 percent of the black students and 29 percent of the Hispanic students reported "three or more" interracial friendships. Because both law schools had predominantly white student bodies, these answers created a mathematical impossibility: Whites appeared to be claiming at least six "close interracial" friendships for every one such friendship claimed by a minority student. Yet the authors soberly concluded from this finding (and other similar ones) that "white students appear to have a particularly enriching experience" from a racially diverse law school. A similarly profound finding from the study was that over 70 percent of the law students thought that "having students of different races and ethnicities" at the law school was a "clearly positive" thing.

Surveys of this type mostly tell us that students—especially white students—are eager to display their racial cosmopolitanism and their understanding of the official diversity line that university leaders promote at nearly all school events. Studies of student opinion that fail to control for the automatic desire of students to provide the "correct" response are almost worthless. A good deal of diversity research has these weaknesses and amounts to a sort of happy talk about interracial utopias on college campuses.

Thus, when white students are asked how many of their five closest friends on campus are of another race, they give impressively high numbers in response. But when, without any racial prompts, white students are asked to write down the names of their five closest friends, and the race of these friends is later determined, the number of nonwhites on the list is much lower. Or, to put the issue another way, when we compare the interracial friendships of white college students with those of the average white American, the patterns are not notably different. Carefully considered methodologies, in other words, tend to cast great doubt on the findings of much of the pro-campus-diversity research.

We think it goes almost without saying that, especially in a diverse society like the United States, students can benefit from an environment that is diverse in many ways—racially, socially, economically, religiously, and politically. But "diversity" research almost always fails to consider a critical question: What happens when students who bring diversity to a college or graduate program are both easily identified (by their skin color) and struggling to survive academically at very disproportionate rates?

It is not hard to imagine or to find some evidence for a whole interrelated series of consequences (which our discussions with experienced, sympathetic administrators bear out). Minority students—blacks in particular—may struggle heroically during the first semester but will very often be dismayed by their grades. As they start to see the gulf between their own performance and that of most of their fellow students, dismay can become despair.

"Their egos can take a big hit," explains a black administrator, whom we will call Douglas, at a university in the Northeast. "All of a sudden they aren't the top student anymore. And they are confronted with the notion of, 'Hey, I'm not as smart as I thought I was.' Some of them get here and right away start to think that they just can't cut it. They are afraid to talk in class. They say that their classmates just seem so much better prepared. And so they very well may end up leaving."

"I've been watching this happen for twenty years," says Gary Hull, director of the Program on Values and Ethics in the Marketplace at Duke's undergraduate school. "The paralyzing premise is 'I must, but I can't.' That is, the students experiencing these mismatch obstacles arrive at Duke thinking that 'I must' succeed academically because 'they have been told by everyone they trust' that they are well qualified to succeed. The 'I can't' realization comes after they arrive on campus and learn that they simply don't have the preparation or academic ability to be successful students *at Duke*."

So, to paraphrase Hull, they will not be able to live up to the high expectations of their families and friends. No matter how hard they work, they will get low grades and often feel lost during classroom discussions if they take tough courses. The reason is not that they are bad students; it is that the vast majority of their classmates at the highly competitive school have a huge head start in terms of high school education, academic ability, or both. They would be fine at a lower-tier school. But at Duke, "I've seen many of them withdraw into shells," says Hull. "This causes some of those students to take on an unearned guilt, which then triggers a host of psychological maladies." Researchers have come to similar conclusions about racial preference recipients developing negative perceptions of their own academic competence, which in turn harms performance.

Meanwhile, university administrators, who have typically misled (at least by implication) many black and Hispanic students during the recruitment process about their prospects for academic success, often take the position that the best way to build their academic self-confidence after they arrive on campus is to continue misleading them. The university thus *never* tells individual students who run into academic difficulty either that they were admitted via large racial preferences or that this put them at a great competitive disadvantage academically. So the students receiving large preferences may blame themselves and conclude that they are failures.

Beyond feeling self-doubt, sooner or later mismatched students are likely to notice that other students of color are having difficulty too. Their personal academic struggle takes on a collective, racial cast. They may not associate the problem with preferences, as they have been repeatedly assured that everyone admitted to the school is fully qualified and has only to seize the opportunities before them; they may turn to more sinister explanations instead, such as a hostile learning environment or even discrimination by their professors. Whatever explanation they settle on, the natural reaction is to withdraw into a racial enclave within the campus, seeking to foster a separate community in which the minority student can, in some sense, feel more confident and consider herself a better "fit." Many universities encourage this by creating black dormitories and assigning entering students to them.

Indeed, it was no coincidence, we were told by Dr. William Hunter, whom we introduced in Chapter Three, that his disastrous early experience at Wesleyan turned around only after he moved out the "Black House," formally known as Malcolm X House. Hunter had never wanted to be there in the first place. He had applied to room with a white friend from home, but Wesleyan informed him that he would be living in the Black House. There Hunter—a very strong student who had needed no racial preference to get into Wesleyan—lived amid many academically struggling inner-city kids. "I was astounded by how self-segregated they were," Hunter recalls. "Even in the dining hall, there was a 'black section,' where all minorities were expected to congregate, at the risk of being ridiculed or ostracized. There was a great deal of peer pressure in this regard. Leaving the Black House was an essential part of my reasserting and rediscovering myself."

Such harm from self-segregation is common, says Brian Corpening, assistant provost at the University of Oklahoma Health Sciences Center, who is black and is a veteran of four other colleges. "That just further isolates," he says. "The whole point is for them to learn how to interact with people who are different from them and come from a different background. [Self-segregation] not only stratifies the students but, with the black kids, replicates what they came from at home."

Corpening adds, "The existence of African American student advisers, Latino student advisers, Native American student advisers, and multicultural advisers tends to create a segregated environment within the overall college/university setting. It lets the overall infrastructure off the hook through the existence of separate 'advisers,' and it stunts the development of minority students—and, for that matter, white students—because the opportunities for dialogue and interaction become limited." Schools should have a single "chief diversity officer," not a diversity bureaucracy, he says, and the job should be "fostering interaction and sharing/learning among diverse groups on the campus rather than creating structures that maintain a sense of separation."

For their part, white students may find the minority students' behavior off-putting and clannish (even if the whites are clannish themselves). And plausibly, white and Asian students will notice that minority students often have weaker academic preparation, that they struggle academically, and that they often miss key points made in small classes. In other words, large preferences (and consequent, corresponding large gaps in college performance) could easily contribute to negative stereotypes about minority performance and perhaps minority ability in the minds of students of all races. None of these effects are quite what we have in mind when we talk about a healthy racial diversity on campus.

The danger that the widespread use of large racial preferences could reinforce—not dispel—negative stereotypes about blacks, American Indians, and, to a lesser extent, Hispanics would seem so obvious and so awful as to make this the foremost topic that scholars doing diversity research should address carefully. However, we are not aware of a single study that has addressed this topic. This seems incredible until one remembers the politics of diversity research and the broader politics of race on campus. The political cost of carrying out such research, as we illustrate in Chapter Eleven, would be high indeed.

Yet the interaction of preferences with racial attitudes is perhaps the most pervasive theme that has emerged from our interviews with former students who received preferences.

Jareau Hall breezed through high school in Syracuse, New York. In the top 20 percent of his class, he had been class president, a successful athlete, and sang in gospel choir. He was easily admitted to Colgate University, a moderately elite liberal arts college in rural New York; no one pointed out to Hall that his SAT scores were far below the class median. He immediately found himself over his head academically, facing far more rigorous course-work than ever before. "Nobody told me what would be expected of me beforehand," he recalls. "I really didn't know what I was getting into. And it all made me feel as if I wasn't smart enough." But just as surprising and upset-ting was the social environment in which he found himself. "I was immedi-ately stereotyped and put into a box because I was African American," said Hall. "And that made it harder to perform. It may have been somewhat inter-nalized, but people often made little derogatory comments or they would do things like come up and touch your hair. There was a general feeling that all blacks on campus were there either because they were athletes or they came through a minority recruitment program and might not really belong there. That was just assumed right away." Hall dropped out after his freshman year, though he eventually returned to Colgate and obtained his bachelor's degree.

"People thought I was only there because of affirmative action, so I tried to make myself invisible," recalls the young Dartmouth grad we mentioned in Chapter Three. "You just felt that people resented affirmative action because they thought it led to students being accepted to college unfairly. They may not always have said that directly to me, but their remarks certainly implied it. And you would hear them say that about other minority students behind their backs—the idea that they didn't belong there. So you just knew."

"At elite institutions, the walls seem to whisper, 'White males are supe-rior. . . . African-Americans and Hispanics are inferior.'" So wrote Carol Swain, an African-American professor at Vanderbilt, in a book that often touches on mismatch themes. Swain suggests that her own rise to academic success occurred in part because she was not mismatched as an undergradu-ate. She started at a community college and received her bachelor's, magna cum laude, from Roanoke College, eventually getting a doctorate at the University of North Carolina and an L.L.M. at Yale. Many black under-graduates whom Swain has encountered at elite schools, however, "seemed immobilized by the belief that they were incapable of reaching the high aca-demic standards of the institutions. Many seemed to have internalized notions of black inferiority as well-meaning college advisers and other minority students contributed to their insecurities. At one college I attended," Swain recalls, "a well-meaning advisor warned me during my first semester not to expect to perform there as well academically as I had in other settings. . . . I cannot see . . . how affirmative action policies which routinely place black students in institutions where whites and Asians are more academically accomplished can fail to engender this type of condescending mentality."

Jocelyn Ladner-Mathis, a veteran college administrator who is now associate dean of liberal arts at Cuyahoga Community College in Cleveland, brought her own long experience with mismatch to bear on helping her own son choose a college in 2007. "I would think, 'Thomas can get into this school, but can he get out?' That is the first thing you pose to students. 'You can get in, but can you get out?' I have just seen so many kids stumble and get derailed along the way.'"

Ladner-Mathis, who herself had almost no contact with white people before becoming one of the first blacks to enter Mundelein College in Chicago, struggled academically but survived, and she considers herself a beneficiary of affirmative action. But she recalls, "A lot of my fellow African American students didn't make it and dropped out." Now as then, says Ladner-Mathis, many of "our students are coming completely unprepared, and it is really, really scary. . . . Affirmative action places you in situations where you can ultimately be successful. But it does come with a price. You can lose so much. You can lose your mind basically."

Esther Cepeda, now a successful journalist, did well in school and college. Her mismatch experience began when she was given a scholarship to enter a math-intensive MBA program at Northwestern. "I think affirmative action helped me get in," she recalls in a home interview. "It doesn't feel good to know that I was not as qualified as other people for that program and I got in anyway." And, as she elaborated in a 2012 op-ed, "I was not academically equal to my peers and woefully unprepared for the math-heavy statistical analysis needed to complete the basic courses in data mining." Her low first-quarter grades put her on academic probation; she ended up leaving without a graduate degree, and "I left with serious bruises on my psyche and ego." She spoke of the "sting that never seems to go away" from being "seen as someone who succeeded only because of affirmative action" and as "the official Hispanic, routinely called upon to enlighten my white classmates about Latino consumers' struggles in the barrio with English language acquisition, gangs, and discrimination—none of which I'd ever had any experience with." When asked about her "tough upbringing," she would respond, "I didn't have a tough upbringing. I didn't grow up in a dump."

Professor Phillip Richards, an African American English professor at Colgate, has sought to conceptualize broadly the systematic ways that racial preferences can harm black students and lead to "liberal re-segregation" of "marginal, academically inferior blacks" and to "an exceptionally self-destructive form of alienation." We quote Professor Richards's manuscript, with gratitude for his permission:

> Colgate . . . creates a façade of racial diversity, while socializing blacks in an "integrated" world where they are implicitly prepared for a subordinate role in a globalized multi-ethnic sphere. The most recent Campus Climate Survey [at Colgate showed that] a majority of black and Hispanic students report that they are not pursuing the professional goals for which they came to Colgate. By any measure, these students are not being served in an educational sense by the university. And by implication they are not part of the community of scholars, teachers, and students at Colgate. . . .
>
> [D]eparting cohorts of black students . . . rarely returned with their classmates for Colgate's festive reunions. They did not wish to celebrate the assumption of their racial inferiority which underlies the institution's central social knowledge.
>
> The dull, lifeless work I receive from these black students tells me that they have not undergone Colgate's special variant of elite socialization comprised of (for the most part exclusively white) fraternity and club life, as well as an ambitious academic regime. Unlike the upper class white majority of students, my black seniors do not show the analytic and expressive skills gained not only in class but also in the school's wide range of extra-curricular activity. . . . And nothing so much characterizes the black American students' essays than an anomic tone, the shadow of an eradicated selfhood set down in prose. Their failures are not only the consequence of academic inadequacy, but also the particular academic ethos at the heart of the school's economically, socially, and politically flourishing life. No one could expect high academic performance from individuals so self consciously inadequate and consequently miserable as they.

Not all of these voices are singing exactly the same note. Certainly among the memoirs we have read and the people we have interviewed there are differing—sometimes widely differing—interpretations of *why* campus climates on elite colleges leave so many black and Hispanic students feeling like outcasts. But a remarkably pervasive theme that we derive from those we quote—and many other former students and administrators we have interviewed—is that a healthy social diversity across racial lines is extraordinarily difficult to build on a foundation of large racial preferences.

As we pointed out, diversity research rarely takes preferences into account. But when it does, the findings fit the experiences of our interviewees. For example, several studies have found that large racial preferences are directly associated with more negative self-images among the recipients. And then there is a study by three economists that should be considered the gold standard in the field—one that had actual data on the friendship networks of tens of thousands of students attending a range of colleges from moderately selective to the most elite and that explicitly attempted to understand the role of academic indices and relative academic position on cross-racial interaction.

In "Representation versus Assimilation" economists Peter Arcidiacono, Shakeeb Khan, and Jacob Vigdor found that *students are much more likely to form friendships at college with other students whose level of academic preparation is similar to their own* and that this is true both for same-race friendships and cross-racial friendships. Where racial preferences are large, this directly dampens the number of cross-racial friendships. The authors point out that, given the patterns they observe and the consequences of the cascade effect, our current racial preference system sharply reduces the number of cross-racial friendships that would occur if schools used smaller preferences.

Another suggestive example comes from law schools, where "study groups" have been a traditional survival strategy for first-year students. Anecdotal evidence—and common sense—suggests that students will tend to form study groups with students of similar academic strength. Our interviews have found that whereas Asians and whites often form study groups together, blacks and Hispanics often end up in same-race groups, plausibly because whites and Asians do not consider students regarded as "affirmative action admits" desirable study group members. Analyses of data on the effects of study groups shows that whereas Asian and white law students raise their grades by participating in a study group, black and Hispanic law students who do the same achieve no comparable benefit, even though they spend just as many hours studying as their white and Asian classmates. This is a result we would expect if "minority" study groups are almost entirely composed of students who are struggling academically.

One of the most widely discussed but often misunderstood strains of research in the diversity field explores something called "stereotype threat." The idea is that people perform at their best when they are confident; factors that erode self-confidence, which often operate on a subconscious level, also erode performance. Hearing or being reminded of a negative stereotype about a group one belongs to hurts short-term performance; hearing a credible positive stereotype helps. If women are reminded before taking a math test that women tend not to do as well in math as men (a common but increasingly inaccurate stereotype), the average performance of women on the test goes down. Blacks are particularly vulnerable to negative stereotypes about black intelligence. In a famous series of experiments at Stanford that first established the idea of stereotype threat, Claude Steele and Joshua Aronson found that when black undergraduates were given a very challenging set of verbal puzzles to solve, their performance suffered significantly if, before starting the puzzles, they were told that the test would evaluate cognitive ability.

These results are often taken as evidence that black academic difficulties are merely an artifact of a hostile environment—make some simple modifications to the environment, and the "test-score" gap between blacks and whites might largely disappear. But that's not quite what the research shows. Steele and Aronson found in their lab that when the test administrators did nothing to artificially "activate" stereotype threat, blacks and whites did as well on the complex verbal puzzles as would be predicted by their verbal SAT scores. When stereotype threat *was* activated, blacks did worse than their SAT scores would predict. In other words, the preexisting test-score gap is real, but performance gaps can be worsened (creating the so-called black underperformance problem) by activating stereotype threat.

Although there is a vast literature on stereotype threat, very few scholars in the field have considered what is probably obvious to most readers of this book: Selective colleges' use of large racial preferences will very plausibly cause or aggravate stereotype threat. As we have seen, at these schools blacks are immersed in an environment not only where they are at a substantial academic disadvantage but also where their race often marks them as someone at an academic disadvantage. If a malevolent force wanted to establish a breeding ground for negative stereotypes of minority academic ability, it would be hard to come up with a more fertile petri dish.

One of the best studies of social interaction in college, undertaken by Harvard psychologist James Sidanius and three colleagues, examined intergroup relations at UCLA over a period of several years. They did not find that black and Hispanic students automatically performed worse simply by believing they had benefited from affirmative action. But they did find that "when black and Latino students were also concerned that negative stereotypes about their group's intellectual ability could be true of them or that their academic performance would shape others' views of their ethnic group . . . then their suspicions about having been admitted through affirmative action hurt their subsequent academic performance." Given the difficulty of measuring the effects of subtle psychological processes on actual real-world grades, this is a powerful and remarkable finding. Stereotype threat is probably real, and it plausibly will be most severe for students admitted with the largest racial preferences.

GRADUATION

Probably the most famous book in the affirmative action literature is *The Shape of the River*, a magisterial 1998 study by William Bowen and Derek Bok, respectively the former presidents of Princeton and Harvard. Bowen was also the president of the Mellon Foundation, and with Mellon resources they created an extraordinary database known as the College and Beyond study (C&B), which gathered data on tens of thousands of students in three college cohorts, including colleges ranging from the "super-elites" to good state schools and historically black colleges. Bowen and Bok were both strong supporters (and implementers) of affirmative action, and their book was generally triumphant about the virtues and achievements of racial preference programs in college. For years, many took their work as definitive proof that blacks and other minorities benefited greatly from large admissions preferences into elite schools.

In fact, *The Shape of the River* had some notable flaws as a work of scholarship, many of which were detailed in an eviscerating 1999 essay by historian Stephan Thernstrom and political scientist Abigail Thernstrom. As we discuss in Chapter Fifteen, Mellon refused as a matter of policy to make the College and Beyond data available to other scholars to replicate and check Bowen's and Bok's findings. The Mellon Foundation *did* make the data available to scholars who passed through an arduous screening process, and many of these scholars—though not engaging in the forbidden acts of replication—have arrived at findings that are significantly inconsistent with Bowen and Bok's original claims. Bowen and Bok also tended to be quite coy about directly testing the effect of preferences (on which they had incomparably good data) as opposed to examining relative outcomes of groups that benefited from preferences to differing degrees (e.g., blacks and whites). This along with many other research choices tended to blur and obscure their results.

One of most salient findings from Bowen and Bok was their claim that racial preferences bolstered the college graduation rate of black students. They demonstrated this by dividing the colleges in their database into three tiers of selectivity and showing that, other things being equal, blacks were more likely to graduate if they attended the top tier of colleges. This, they suggested, cut heavily against the mismatch hypothesis.

However, as others have argued, the Bowen and Bok findings can be just as easily read as a confirmation of mismatch. As we explained in Chapter Two, the peculiar workings of the cascade effect mean that racial preferences are smaller at super-elite colleges than they are at very elite colleges, and they are smaller at very elite colleges than they are at plain elite colleges. The black students for whom Bowen and Bok found the highest graduation rates—those attending super-elites—were, very plausibly, students who were on average substantially less mismatched than were black students at less elite schools. The authors could have greatly increased the power of their analysis had they examined how graduation varied with the size of a racial preference rather than by how it varied with school eliteness.

There were other, more technical but equally important problems with the Bowen and Bok analysis of graduation (we examine this further in an appendix posted to the website, www.mismatchthebook.com). But in a broad sense, they simply missed the point. The super-elites have such strong students and such deep support that their graduation rates are not far below 100 percent; even struggling students are given many opportunities to come back and finish. But these schools represent a tiny, tiny fraction of blacks receiving large preferences in higher education. As Figure 2.1 in Chapter Two suggested, perhaps the greatest harm done by the racial preferences used at the very elite schools is their cascading effect on somewhat less elite schools, which are effectively forced to use even larger preferences, and so on down the line, greatly aggravating the overall scale of the mismatch problem.

Studies that examine broader swaths of American higher education often find strong evidence that racial preferences produce lower college graduation rates. Economists Linda Loury and David Garman found that students who were mismatched had significantly lower graduation rates than those who were not. Economists Audrey Light and Wayne Strayer got the same result from their own cross-sectional analysis; sociologist Marta Tienda, in contrast, found little evidence of mismatch. All of these studies are, in our view, biased by the same "selection effect" that we discussed in detail in Chapter Five. These studies rely on comparisons of students who are at schools of differing eliteness; the analyst can observe only a few characteristics of each student (e.g., their SAT score); the "unobserved" characteristics in any particular dataset tend to favor the students who have (perhaps because of them) been admitted to the more elite school. These students will thus have higher graduation rates because of their unobserved characteristics, and that will skew the analysis to favor students attending more elite schools. It is, therefore, reasonable to assume that each of the studies mentioned above understated whatever mismatch effect actually exists. Taking this bias into account, these studies as a group provide substantial—if not definitive—evidence that mismatch reduces minority graduation rates. In Part III we will see a test of graduation mismatch that neatly avoids this selection effect and thus yields more definitive results.

EARNINGS AND OUTCOMES

Ultimately, a central purpose of racial preferences is to increase the presence of successful minorities in the economy and especially among the ranks of leaders in the professions, the sciences, business, and politics. How does mismatch affect these long-term outcomes? This is notoriously difficult to measure, and many of the issues are fairly technical, so we have relegated a full discussion of this question to the appendix posted on the book's website, www .mismatchthebook.com. Here we content ourselves with a few key points.

We concede at the outset the *possibility* that the super-elite colleges and professional schools are sui generis, in a class by themselves. Going to Harvard or Yale confers lifetime reputational advantages and opens doors both at school and afterward that might make important differences in careers. Moreover, as noted earlier, the cascade effect means that the typical black at Harvard or Yale has received a smaller admissions preference than the typical black at a second-tier school and, thus, will be less harmed by mismatch.

Conversely, the hard evidence that elite schools really do confer important career advantages, especially to those entering with preferences, is surprisingly weak. Bowen and Bok present analyses that purport to show such advantages, but as we discussed in the earlier section on graduation, those results are susceptible to exactly the opposite interpretation that they offer. And Bowen and Bok's analyses also show that ending up in the bottom third of one's class (as do most students who receive large preferences) has a large, negative effect on long-term earnings.

Stacy Dale and Alan Krueger (the latter currently chairs President Obama's Council of Economic Advisers) obtained access to Bowen and Bok's data and performed a clever analysis similar to the first-choice/second-choice discussed in Chapter Five. That is, they found pairs of students who had been accepted by similar or identical pairs of colleges, with one student ending up at a more elite college than the other student. They then examined the earnings of these pairs fifteen years out of college. Their models suggested that students attending less elite schools earned as much as and perhaps more than similar students attending more-elite schools. Dale and Krueger did not examine mismatch specifically, but their results powerfully suggest that school eliteness is far less important to career outcomes than is generally thought. A wide array of other research suggests the same thing. When we control for the inveterate "selection effect" problem and look at a broad range of schools, there is no decisive advantage to attending a more elite school.

This implies a second generalization: Attending nonelite schools is not harmful to one's career. Students with modest credentials who are interested in science and avoid mismatch by attending a less elite school have excellent long-term outcomes, with earnings well in excess of otherwise similar students who did not obtain science degrees. Students who attend historically black colleges also have very strong outcomes on a whole array of measures. Strong law students who attend nonelite schools regularly get better grades in law school and go on to outearn similar students who attended more-elite schools.

Some people find such statements counterintuitive. After all, a huge proportion of American elites have degrees from elite institutions, including a large fraction of congressmen and senators, most presidential nominees of major parties, most chief executives of large corporations, and most partners at the most elite law firms. Does that not imply that these schools are seeding grounds for greatness? Actually, it does not. The fallacy lies in the fact that top schools invest a good deal of time and effort in selecting the most talented applicants in the nation. For example, careful analysis shows that if we examine the proportion of the most talented law school applicants who go to the super-elite schools, and then examine the proportion of elite law firm partners thirty years later who attended those schools, the second proportion is lower than the first. A remarkable proportion of American Nobel Prize winners attended nonelite colleges.

A key reason behind these relationships—and this takes our discussion back to mismatch—is the effect of grades and, thus, learning on long-term outcomes. Doing well in school helps long-term outcomes, and doing badly hurts them. Again, there is a vast literature on this subject; we will highlight here one particularly interesting finding.

Starting in the mid-1980s the University of Michigan Law School began sending surveys to all of its alumni who had graduated fifteen years before, asking them detailed questions about their careers since law school. About half of the school's graduates responded, and the school then matched these surveys against its own records to determine each graduate's grades.

In Figure 6.1 we show the fortunes of nearly twenty years of Michigan law students who entered relatively large law firms after they graduated. This figure splits these graduates into ten equal "deciles" according to their law school grades. We can see two clear patterns. First, students with higher grades were much more likely to enter the highly sought jobs at big firms because the big firms preferred to hire students with strong academic records.

FIGURE 6.1. People with Good Law School Grades Succeed as Lawyers

A long-term study of many thousands of law graduates suggests that good grades not only help students get jobs at large firms, but also predict promotion to partner.

Hiring to and attrition from large law firms among white University of Michigan Law School graduates, by self-reported class rank

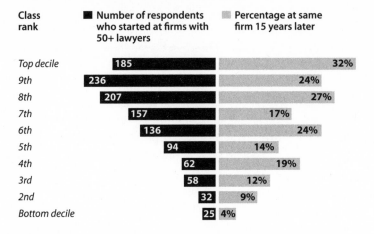

Class rank	■ Number of respondents who started at firms with 50+ lawyers	▨ Percentage at same firm 15 years later
Top decile	185	32%
9th	236	24%
8th	207	27%
7th	157	17%
6th	136	24%
5th	94	14%
4th	62	19%
3rd	58	12%
2nd	32	9%
Bottom decile	25	4%

Source: UMLS fifteen-year surveys of alumni for classes of 1972–1985; see text for details.

But second—and this is the key point—the law firm associates who had high law school grades were far more likely to still be at the firm fifteen years later, which, in this world, means that they survived the associate competition and became partners at the firm. Some associates leave because they don't like the work (or the intensity of the work), and many others are fired if they fail to make partner. But the association between high grades and successfully obtaining a highly coveted partnership at these firms is, well, staggering. The associates with high GPAs were *seven or eight* times as likely to stay and become partners as those with low GPAs. As with the bar passage data we discussed in Chapter Four, these are correlations one rarely observes in human affairs.

There are a couple things that make the link between partnership and grades particularly impressive. Although law firms almost always take law school grades into account when making hiring decisions, they almost never look at grades when they make promotion decisions. Why should they? After all, they have plenty of their own internal information about how these associates have performed. Thus, looking at partnership decisions here is like conducting a "blind taste test": The firms overwhelmingly promote people who happen to have had high grades without knowing or caring that they did. Moreover, the people with *low* grades in this analysis are exceptional people; they were able to get big firm jobs against the odds, despite their low grades, suggesting that they were more likely to have other important qualities, such as a magnetic personality, leadership skills, or a blood relationship to a senior partner. Yet despite these qualities, they did miserably in the competition for partnership. The strong implication is that law firms, routinely criticized for giving too much importance to grades in hiring decisions, may in fact be putting less weight on grades than perhaps they should.

This figure includes only white graduates from Michigan's law school. We excluded minority graduates because many of these have lower grades, and one might then argue that the association between high grades and promotion was simply capturing, indirectly, racial discrimination by law firm partners. But when we do a similar analysis for minority lawyers, the pattern looks just the same. Indeed, these data help to explain another type of mismatch phenomenon, this one in the workforce. From the 1970s onward, law firms faced both internal and external pressure to use increasingly aggressive racial preferences in hiring to diversify their firms. By the 1990s the vast majority of large law firms were using explicit double-standards in hiring, and most black law graduates they hired (because of law school mismatch) had low grades. Few of these hires ever became partners at the firms they joined; most left after a few years, often with considerable bitterness at the lack of opportunity they encountered within firms. But these data along with much related research imply that the problem was low grades, not outright discrimination.

This research as well as a good deal of related work compellingly suggests that learning in school and the grades that measure that learning matter greatly for one's long-term career success. We have tried to illustrate in this chapter how large racial preferences create a campus environment that is not conducive to learning and that in many ways undercuts the intellectual self-confidence that is the vital handmaiden to learning. It is harder to show with data the effect of mismatch on college English majors compared to students in more rigid curricula like college chemistry majors or first-year law students. But from what we can tell, the effects of mismatch are pervasive indeed.

III.

THE CALIFORNIA EXPERIMENT: WHAT HAPPENS AFTER A LEGAL BAN ON RACIAL PREFERENCES?

CHAPTER SEVEN

PROPOSITION 209

The High Road and the Low Road

URING THE FIRST HALF OF THE 1990s, leaders of both US parties spoke of the need to reform or scale back racial preferences. This was not because of concerns about mismatch; as we saw in Part II, empirical mismatch research did not start to appear until 1995 and 1996 and was generally ignored until much later. Rather, it reflected a broader debate about whether, after a generation of preferences, the benefits of what had always been conceived of as temporary efforts to jump-start racial progress still offset the admitted disadvantages of preferences, such as stigma for the beneficiaries, unfairness to whites and (increasingly) Asians, and the general departure from race-neutral ideals.

This debate would come to an unprecedented boil in the searing battles of 1995 and 1996 in California. They led to votes in 1995 by the Board of Regents of the University of California (UC) to end racial and gender preferences across the nine-campus system and in 1996 by California voters to adopt an initiative called Proposition 209, which affirmed and extended the preference ban to all state programs. As we describe in this chapter, those who advocated a ban on racial preferences had a relatively easy time of it; preferences were unpopular with the public. But that same fact drove many opponents to extreme strategies, contending that Proposition 209 would legalize discrimination against women (which was plainly false) or that supporters had a hidden, racist agenda. Other opponents pointed out, correctly, that racial preference bans would sharply lower black and Hispanic enrollments at UC's flagship campuses.

The remainder of Part III shows how the sudden and dramatic change in policy starting in 1998, when all admissions at UC were, by state law, supposed to be race-neutral, turned the massive UC system into what social scientists call a "natural experiment." The research described in Part II tried to infer what might happen to able black and Hispanic college students if they received smaller or no racial preferences. By looking at the UC system, one can directly observe what happened. The preference ban produced some extraordinary effects—and not always the ones we expected. The remainder of Part III chronicles and analyzes these effects. In Chapter Eight we look at whether the sudden end of racial preferences heightened or chilled the interest of affected minority students to attend UC. In Chapter Nine we examine how the preference ban affected mismatch and the outcomes of tens of thousands of black and Hispanic students in the UC system. Chapter Ten considers how the university itself adapted to the ban and, increasingly over time, decided to work around, over, and through it.

The politics of the story covered in this chapter are interesting in their own right, but they are also important for their national consequences. The fervor of affirmative action supporters and the ugliness and extremity of the anti-Prop-209 campaign did not ultimately change the popular outcome in California. Nor have similar tactics worked in other states that have considered preference bans. But we think the campaign changed in an enduring way the willingness of political leaders to talk about preference reform. After 1996 that topic would be relegated to referenda and the courts.

* * *

Before Prop 209 not only conservative Republicans but also a few leading Democrats had begun to suggest that it might be time to wind down or at least reform racial preferences. In 1992, in speeches at Yale and in Washington, liberal Massachusetts senator John Kerry, a future Democratic presidential nominee, said that although affirmative action had achieved many positive results, it "has kept America thinking in racial terms" and fostered both a "culture of dependency" and "a reality of reverse discrimination that actually engenders racism." In March 1995 Connecticut senator Joseph Lieberman, who chaired the moderate Democratic Leadership Council, said that "you can't defend policies that are based on group preferences as opposed to individual opportunities, which is what America has always been about. . . . They're patently unfair. . . . Not only should we not discriminate against somebody, we shouldn't discriminate in favor of somebody based on the group they represent."

In April 1995 Congress eliminated a small preference program that had allowed the sellers of broadcast or cable services to defer taxes on the profits if the buyer was a company at least partially owned by a minority. Although the impetus came from Republicans, the measure enjoyed bipartisan support, perhaps because the funds saved would be allocated to a popular health insurance deduction. It seemed likely that "Gingrich Republicans" would introduce more sweeping measures. In June, in *Adarand Constructors v. Peña*, the US Supreme Court held, 5–4, that racial preferences in federal contracting would have to pass an extraordinarily high hurdle to be constitutional. With trends on the political and legal fronts alike seeming to run against racial preferences, President Clinton ordered a review of federal preference programs and announced his conclusions in a major speech on July 19, 1995. Clinton said that he was against "reverse discrimination" and went on to state, "Let me be clear about what affirmative action must not mean and what I won't allow it to be. It does not mean—and I don't favor—the unjustified preference of the unqualified over the qualified of any race or either gender. It doesn't mean—and I don't favor—numerical quotas. It doesn't mean—and I don't favor—selection or rejection of any employee or student solely on the basis of race or gender without regard to merit."

There was less to these vows than met the eye. No institution anywhere had admitted in years—if ever—to "preference of the unqualified over the qualified" or to "quotas," especially given the malleability of concepts like "qualified" and "quotas." And no university had ever admitted students "*solely* on the basis of race or gender without regard to merit" (emphasis added). In other words, Clinton said nothing that explicitly opposed the use of very large racial preferences to prefer weakly qualified minorities over much *more* qualified Asians or whites. Clinton, who had direct power over only federal programs, said his policy on affirmative action was to "mend it, don't end it" and promised to root out excesses—an almost zero set, given his extremely narrow concept of excesses. The only specific abuses Clinton mentioned in his speech were cases of fraud in which companies used "fronts" to claim minority status. The speech was a political success, creating an appearance of judicious action against racial-preference excesses.

But though Clinton did not lay out any clear path to reform, widespread national discussion of racial preferences accompanied his speech. Talk of reform was in the air and showed signs of moving toward some crescendo. Enter California.

* * *

It was two years before the November 1996 vote on Prop 209 that Ward Connerly, the man whose name is most associated with it—and with opposition to racial preferences nationally—began his rise to prominence on the California and national scenes. Connerly was a self-made, independent-minded, black businessman from Sacramento with a strong libertarian streak and formidable political, rhetorical, and organizational skills. He was also a friend and financial supporter of Republican governor Pete Wilson, who appointed Connerly to the University of California Board of Regents in 1993. Wilson was considered a moderate and was often mentioned as a presidential contender. He had long been a supporter of affirmative action. But Connerly himself had for some time expressed opposition to racially preferential programs, citing both unfairness to whites and dislike of being pigeonholed based on his race, even for favorable treatment. (Connerly's ancestors included French Canadians, Choctaws, Africans, and Irish Americans.) According to his autobiography, Connerly didn't want to be known as Wilson's "black regent" and, thus, was not eager to get into racial issues at UC.

A meeting in August 1994 made a big impression on Connerly, however. The parents of a young white National Merit Scholar came to tell him that their son had been turned down by all five UC medical schools before finally getting admitted by just one when he reapplied a year later. The father, suspecting that his son had been passed over to admit less-qualified applicants, had created a computerized scatterplot with admissions data from three of the UC medical schools. The data showed that almost all of the blacks and Latinos who had been admitted had grades and test scores well below his son's. Connerly was "dumbfounded" by the size of these preferences. And, he recalls in an interview, "the same university administrators who would later defend preference policies as vitally necessary to build a just society were not even willing to acknowledge the existence of such practices"—even to a regent.

Indeed. At the time UC routinely included in its publications and other official documents a statement that "in accordance with applicable Federal and State Law and University policy," UC "does not discriminate on the basis of race, color, national origin, religion, sex, disability" or certain other characteristics in "admission." UC was telling applicants, students, and the world that its admissions policy was colorblind. The policy statement did not even mention "affirmative action" in admission, let alone racial preferences.

At the November 1994 regents' meeting, Connerly asked for detailed information about the apparent use of very large but covert racial preferences in admissions. "I will never forget the pall that fell over the room after I finished talking," Connerly recalled. He had violated a taboo. But although university officials dragged their feet and provided only fragmentary responses, it soon became clear that preferences were large wherever one looked. Even the university's core public admissions policy—that students became "UC eligible" by placing among the top one-eighth of all California high school students—was widely circumvented through "special admissions" that enrolled hundreds of black and Hispanic students who were not UC-eligible. As data came before the regents that contradicted earlier statements from administrators, other regents began to join in the sharp questioning. As Connerly observed a few months later,

> At the beginning of this evaluation [of UC admissions] there were those who said no one is admitted to the University of California who is not eligible. We now know such a statement is not true. We were informed that no one was automatically admitted to the University of California solely on the basis of race or ethnic background. We have now confirmed the inaccuracy of that statement. We were told that race was never a major factor; it was only a "bump." Again, we have confirmed that on at least four of our campuses such a statement is blatantly false.

The university's deception of its own regents transformed the issue; this was no longer merely about preferences per se but also about the university's integrity and the regents' governance role. Connerly began to feel he might win an outright vote to ban preferences.

Two-thirds of the regents were appointed to twelve-year terms by California's governor, and since 1983 Republicans had held the governor's seat. Other regents were ex officio (but voting) state officials, including the governor himself, the lieutenant governor, the speaker of the state assembly, and a few university officials. The lieutenant governor, Gray Davis, and the speaker, Willie Brown, were the state's two most prominent Democrats and would almost certainly oppose a ban. So would university officials.

Although Wilson had in the past voiced moderate support for affirmative action, as noted above, during the winter of 1994–1995 he became an opponent. It is not quite clear what drove this change. According to Connerly's autobiography, he helped to persuade Wilson that preference programs throughout state government had taken on too much a life of their own and were being abused. Wilson may also have shared what seemed to be an evolving bipartisan sentiment toward curtailing preferences.

Another, not necessarily inconsistent interpretation is that Wilson was embracing a political philosophy that combined important moderate elements (for example, on fiscal policy, social programs, and abortion) with appeals to social conservatives on issues like crime and immigration. In his 1994 reelection campaign for governor, Wilson had pushed two ballot measures reflecting these ideas: a "three strikes" law, which imposed life sentences on three-time felons, and Proposition 187, a measure that largely excluded illegal immigrants (including children) from access to public services, including emergency room treatment and public education. Both measures passed easily and probably contributed to Wilson's own victory. Taking on racial preferences would be a logical extension of this approach and would probably help quell doubts about Wilson among conservative Republicans if he ran for president in 1996.

Based on his subsequent actions, we think Wilson's support for a UC ban on racial and gender preferences was both sincere and aimed at securing political benefits. We see signs of sincerity in the fact that he not only agreed to support Connerly but also began issuing executive orders to restrict the use of racial and gender preferences in other state programs. These moves appealed to some of his base, but they also carried significant political risks for him. Although many Republicans did not like racial preferences, they feared that any effort to curtail them was likely to boomerang. John Ellis, a retired professor at UC Santa Cruz (and friend and admirer of Connerly's) recalled, "My sense was that it took courage for Wilson to go against [preferences]" at a time when, as Ellis put it, "in the atmosphere that then prevailed [I doubt] anyone thought of this as an electoral plus."

Whatever the politics, Wilson not only endorsed Connerly's proposed UC preference ban but also lobbied the regents hard to adopt it. This quickly changed the proposal's chances from improbable to odds-on favorite. The regents agreed to vote on the issue at their July 20, 1995, meeting. There were actually two proposals (known as SP-1 and SP-2), one to prohibit the university from considering an individual's race, ethnicity, or gender in admissions, and the second to apply a similar ban in contracting and hiring.

The chancellors of all nine UC campuses opposed Connerly's proposals, stressing with some reason that they would cause big drops in UC's numbers of black and Hispanic students, which were already low relative to the number graduating from the state's high schools. So did UC's president, vice presidents, academic senate, and the student leadership. When it became clear that Connerly might well get the votes he needed, the UC president's office gave the regents an analysis predicting that eliminating race as an admissions criterion would reduce by two-thirds the number of blacks and by nearly one-third the number of Hispanics entering three representative campuses. At

Berkeley the potential effects were much larger: an 85 percent drop in blacks and a 50 percent drop in Hispanics.

At this point, however, UC administrators were in an impossible bind. The doomsday predictions emphasized even more the scale of their earlier deceptions. Which was true? That preferences were so large that ending them would cause a catastrophic drop in minority enrollment, or that preferences were modest and only for highly qualified students? Either answer would anger many regents. And any honest answer would have included such carefully concealed facts as that in 1988, a year for which data are publicly available, the median white-black gap in SAT scores at UC Berkeley was 288 points, at the high end of preferences used by any major college.

Both the buildup to the July 20, 1995, regents' meeting and the meeting itself were high political theater. Jesse Jackson, who was threatening to enter the primaries against President Clinton if he failed to support racial preferences, suggested days before the regents' meeting that he would disrupt it. Wilson retorted, "Then I think he will succeed in being detained." Wilson also warned against "allow[ing] our country to be infected with the virus of tribalism." The day before the meeting Clinton gave his "mend it, don't end it" address. That same evening Jackson declared to a packed crowd at a church rally in San Francisco that "we are willing to offer our bodies and offer our lives to save our children."

The regents' meeting room, at the UC San Francisco campus, was jammed with 250 people while 500 chanting demonstrators massed outside. With seventy politicians, chancellors, faculty members, and students lined up to speak, it went on for more than twelve tumultuous hours of emotional testimony and debate, accompanied by several dramatic sideshows, including a bomb threat that forced evacuation of the meeting room for forty minutes, arrests of six anti-209 demonstrators outside, and heat from TV lights that made the room an inferno. Two potential presidential candidates were there—Wilson and Jackson—both playing to their political bases. Wilson was also lobbying his appointees and other regents, described by the *Los Angeles Times* as "an anxious board uncomfortable with its spot at the center of a national controversy."

The gist of Wilson's speech, as quoted by the *Los Angeles Times*, was to ask, "Are we going to treat all Californians equally and fairly? Or are we going to continue to divide Californians by race? . . . It takes all the state taxes paid by three working Californians to provide the public subsidy for a single undergraduate at [UC]. The people who work hard to pay those taxes and who play by the rules deserve a guarantee that their children will get an equal opportunity to compete for admission to this university regardless of their race or gender."

Wilson, who chaired the meeting, then gave Jackson, the most eagerly awaited speaker, almost forty-five minutes (three times longer than anyone else) to say his piece. Jackson began by urging all to stand and join hands in prayer. Wilson kept his seat. Jackson joined several other speakers in comparing Wilson to former Alabama governor George Wallace, who stood in the doorway of the University of Alabama to block black students from entering. He assailed Wilson for using words like "tribalism." He said that "the consequence of going backwards is the loss of hope, the furthering of despair, the hardening of cynicism we can ill afford." Later, when regents were trying to vote, Jackson led a chorus of "We Shall Overcome."

Finally, after moving to another room when protesters stood on their chairs, the regents adopted the bans on preferences in employment and contracting as well as in admissions by separate votes of fifteen to ten and fourteen to ten, respectively. "What we are seeing tonight is a blatant act of racism," responded Jackson, who also carried on a protest outside with two hundred others, yelling, "We will go to jail tonight" and "No justice, no peace!" Lieutenant Governor Gray Davis, who would succeed Wilson as governor in 1999, compared the regents' vote to the Japanese bombing of Pearl Harbor.

The regents' action was national news and quickly became seen—and feared by many—as the harbinger of a broader rollback of preference policies. Connerly found himself suddenly famous. In just under a year he had cannily broken a taboo, exposed hidden university practices, and mobilized a coalition that acted in the face of considerable pressure to back down. It was a skillful performance by any measure. But in most of the coverage he received, the salient fact was Connerly's race. Though Connerly in fact had a mixed racial background, his symbolic stature as an African American opposing racial preferences made him a fixture of fascination: a hero to some, a villain to others. And as for other black critics of affirmative action, the nastiest comments about Connerly came from African Americans. He was called "strange fruit" by Jackson, a "freak of nature" by black congresswoman Corinne Brown, and an "Uncle Tom" and even uglier epithets by many others. He was burned in effigy and shouted down by protesters in public appearances around the state.

There were efforts in 1995 and afterward to show Connerly himself to have been a major beneficiary of racial preference programs. These were largely unavailing. But he has come under more damaging fire in recent years from former allies and other opponents of racial preferences for paying himself over $1 million a year, more than half of the revenue that he has raised for his American Civil Rights Institute (ACRI), an "organization created to educate the public about racial and gender preferences." ACRI is reportedly under investigation by the Internal Revenue Service and the attorney general of California. There were no such complaints about Connerly during the California battles of 1995 and 1996, for which he drew no salary.

* * *

As the 1995 battle over the regents' vote was raging, the proposal that was to become Proposition 209 was languishing. Two obscure Bay Area academics, Glynn Custred and Tom Wood, had dreamed it up several years before. The voluble, enthusiastic Custred, tall with a fringe of white hair, was then a self-described political independent who taught linguistic anthropology at Cal State Hayward (now Cal State East Bay). The more cerebral, less flamboyant Wood was an itinerant philosophy scholar who told us that he was then a nominal Republican but "quite apolitical."

Custred and Wood told us that they were motivated by alarm at what they saw as raw, ever-expanding racial discrimination against whites and males in faculty hiring, admissions, and many other walks of life. Custred, son of a Birmingham, Alabama, steelworker, had seen oppression of African Americans close up. He was all for ending discrimination and improving conditions facing blacks—but not for discriminating against whites to make amends. Wood had similar views. The main victims of racial preferences at UC, as they saw it, were the white and Asian applicants who were rejected in favor of blacks and Hispanics with far less academic preparation and lower high school grades and test scores. Wood also saw himself as a victim of racial discrimination in faculty hiring.

Both considered the use of preferences to be inconsistent with the letter and the spirit of the federal Civil Rights Act of 1964 and other state and federal laws that, on their face, prohibited discrimination against members of any race or gender. They also thought the US Supreme Court had grossly misinterpreted the 1964 Act when, in 1978 and 1979, it approved limited use of racial preferences in state university admissions and private employment. Before they had met, Custred and Wood independently decided that a ballot measure prohibiting both discrimination and preferential treatment would vindicate the language and intent of the nondiscrimination laws and would have broad popular appeal—an idea captured in the name they eventually adopted for the "California Civil Rights Initiative" (CCRI). When they met through mutual friends, they decided to join forces.

By 1993 they had agreed on the heart of their proposal: "The state shall not discriminate against, or grant preferential treatment to, any individual or group on the basis of race, sex, color, ethnicity, or national origin in the operation of public employment, public education, or public contracting." The "shall not discriminate" part was already embedded in the 1964 Act and state laws. But because the Supreme Court had okayed what seemed to them discrimination against whites and males, Custred and Wood added "or give preferential treatment" (which was not in the 1964 Act) to make clear CCRI's intent to ban state programs favoring blacks, Latinos, other minorities, and women over equally or better-qualified whites, Asians, and males.

They did not include in CCRI the phrase "affirmative action" (which also was not in the 1964 Act). This decision would later become a major point of contention, with pro-preference advocates complaining and claiming in a lawsuit that the omission was deceptive. Wood, who drafted the language, and Custred had both legal and strategic rationales. Though more familiar than "preferential treatment," "affirmative action" was sufficiently ambiguous that universities, governments, and courts would have to guess at what it meant if a ban were to be adopted. Besides, as we discuss below, "affirmative action" had a gauzy, more widespread appeal than did "preferences."

In 1993 Wood and Custred submitted a ballot initiative to the California attorney general, along with the $200 filing fee. But to actually get it on the ballot they needed supportive petitions with around seven hundred thousand valid signatures. Neither had any political base or experience. Their first fateful step toward making CCRI a viable idea came in late 1993 when they met Arnold (Arnie) Steinberg, a highly successful, well-connected Republican political strategist and pollster with a strong libertarian streak. Steinberg liked the concept of CCRI and believed in its potential appeal; he agreed to serve as an unpaid consultant with the proviso that the campaign would retain him if sufficient funds were raised. Now Custred and Wood had a sophisticated insider in their camp. However, even the fast-talking, wiry, red-haired Steinberg had no luck raising enough money to put it on the 1994 ballot. The three decided to shoot instead for 1996.

This second effort was better organized and better funded; still, by the fall of 1995 CCRI had obtained only some two hundred thousand signatures and seemed a lost cause. But CCRI was now at least on the radar screen of California politics and generating concern on the left. Then came Ward Connerly. Fresh from his triumph at the July 1995 regents' meeting, he initially turned down an invitation to become chair of the CCRI campaign, but after a few months he became concerned that a visible failure of the CCRI campaign would be taken as a public repudiation of the regents' bans on racial preferences at UC. Connerly conferred with Wilson. Both realized that the confrontational regents' meeting was just a foretaste of what they could expect, but both agreed to jump in. Connerly became CCRI chairman in December 1995.

Within a few weeks Wilson helped Connerly raise $500,000, some of it from the California Republican Party but most of it "from ideologically conservative donors, including tens of thousands of small donors who contributed by mail," recalls Steinberg. With the aura of a winner, Connerly was also invited to do dozens of radio interviews. Signed petitions rolled in. And on the February 21, 1996 deadline, accompanied by Wilson and two legislators, Connerly deposited with the secretary of state's office petitions including 1.2 million signatures—many more than enough to qualify for the ballot.

Once CCRI was on the November 1996 ballot, eventually titled Proposition 209, a fundamental political reality drove the politics on both sides: Racial preferences were unpopular throughout the United States, and for decades before and since the CCRI campaign, public opinion polls showed lopsided majorities against the use of racial preferences in both university admissions and public programs more generally. Polls tended to show that the more specific the description of the preference, the larger the majorities were against it, including near-majorities of blacks. "Affirmative action" as a concept drew much broader support—sometimes majorities—but here, too, polls showed less support for the concept when pollsters gave preferential programs as examples of its meaning.

For the proponents of Proposition 209, then, the electoral strategy was simple: They emphasized that racial preferences had been widely used in California university, state, and contracting programs (certainly true); that these preferences amounted to discrimination; and that CCRI was a civil rights measure. Custred, Wood, Steinberg, Connerly, and Wilson all agreed upon this simple approach.

For opponents of Prop 209—who early on included such groups as the American Civil Liberties Union (ACLU), the National Organization for Women (NOW), the NAACP, the Mexican American Legal Defense Fund (MALDEF), and the Feminist Majority—the broad strategy was to make the argument about "affirmative action" while claiming that CCRI was racist and would legalize discrimination against women. Several of the groups filed a lawsuit seeking to force the state (in the person of Dan Lundgren, the Republican attorney general) to change the name of CCRI and the summary of it that would be sent to all voters to describe it as a ban on affirmative action. Lundgren said no. There was no evidence that CCRI would prevent efforts by state entities to engage in outreach and "pool-expanding" forms of affirmative action. Indeed, the University of California had announced that it would substantially expand outreach after the regents banned racial preferences. Anti-209 forces challenged Lundgren's decision, won in lower court, but lost, on appeal, in August 1996.

This failure left the anti-209 forces quite pessimistic. They were way behind in the polls. An August 1996 poll by a pro-209 group found that when pollsters read CCRI's language to voters, they supported it by a 77 percent to 17 percent margin. Increasingly, the anti-209 strategy and campaign turned toward aggressive demagoguery. Los Angeles city councilman Richard Alarcon likened CCRI to Hitler's *Mein Kampf.* Bob Mulholland, longtime top strategist for the state Democratic Party, said of Custred and Wood, "These two professors may have white shirts on now, but by the time we're done with them they'll be pretty dirtied up." Assembly speaker Willie Brown told Custred, "I don't care about your idiot kids" during a public debate in Sacramento. (He would apologize later in the debate.) On another occasion Brown was asked by a student during an appearance at Custred's campus what should be done about this anti–affirmative action professor. Custred recalls Brown's answer clearly: "You know what to do. Go and disrupt his class."

A unique perspective on the anti-209 campaign comes from Joe Hicks, a leading black civil rights activist in California. Hicks was in his midfifties in 1996. After serving for more than five years as director of the Los Angeles office of the Southern Christian Leadership Council, he had recently moved to become executive director of the similarly liberal Multicultural Collaborative. Hicks regularly attended meetings with other anti-209 leaders to plan strategy.

In this company, Hicks recalled in a 2011 interview, any threat to affirmative action preferences called forth

> this assumption that blacks and women were under assault, that the old guard forces of racism were at the barricade, that we were losing ground, that blacks are going to be excluded from higher education, that employers will feel free not to hire blacks and women, that black contractors would get no business from the government. We denounced it as right-wing bigotry, and we portrayed Custred and Wood as bigoted kinds of guys who had an anti-black attitude, even though there was no evidence of that—and believe me, if we'd have found any evidence, we'd have used it. We called Ward Connerly a willing tool of Pete Wilson who was allowing himself to be used—a more polite way of saying that he was an Uncle Tom.

Hicks began to feel uncomfortable about the dogmatism of his allies, but he kept his doubts mainly to himself. "I cannot recall a single meeting where a single person—including me, by the way—said that the other side has legitimate points that we need to consider in a serious way," he recalls. "What about the notion that it stigmatized black people? What about the issue of fairness? Is it really okay to discriminate against white men? It's like a faith-based belief system that society is perpetually out to get minorities and women, and they will always need the protection of the state." And, says Hicks, "Political correctness required that we say women were catching hell too, though nobody believed that."

And indeed, a major prong of the anti-209 campaign was to argue that CCRI would roll back women's rights. The argument was partly premised on the incorrect idea that women benefited substantially from preferences and partly premised on the idea that clause C of CCRI, which permitted employers to take account of gender if it was a "bona fide occupational requirement," would relegalize sex discrimination.

Prominent public figures jumped on the clause C concern. Patricia Ireland, head of NOW, argued that under Clause C, "Women could get fired if they had children or if they got pregnant." California Democratic Party chairman Art Torres contended that Clause C would lead to the end of athletic programs for girls. And legal scholars Erwin Chemerinsky and Laurie Levenson wrote that Clause C was an "insidious provision" under which "[s]ex discrimination by the government will be expressly allowed."

But the language of the provision and the uneventful history of the very similar provision in the 1964 Civil Rights Act made this a frivolous argument. Courts had applied the parallel federal law very narrowly to permit, for example, movie studios to discriminate against men in casting women's roles.

As the anti-209 campaign began fielding advertisements, one of its two major themes focused on the assertion that CCRI would move women's rights back a generation. One TV ad showed male hands stripping a woman of a diploma, stethoscope, a medical lab coat, a police officer's cap, and a hard hat. "Want to be a doctor? Police officer? Hard hat? Forget it!" said a narrator, while male voices chanted, "Take it off. Take it all off." Radio ads that featured celebrities such as Candice Bergen and Bruce Springsteen claimed that 209 could cut maternity benefits and funding for rape crisis centers, "legalize discrimination against women and girls," and "stop girls from playing softball." None of these claims were even remotely plausible.

A second major theme arose from an event staged by liberal student leaders at Cal State Northridge, who offered $4,000 in student activity fees to bring David Duke to the campus for a Proposition 209 debate. Duke was a Louisiana politician and the nation's most famous overt racist, having been a Grand Wizard of the Ku Klux Klan. He had been elected to Congress in 1989 and came in second in runs for Senate and governor in Louisiana in 1991 and

1992, respectively, attracting national media coverage both times. He advocated policies such as white separatism and wresting the Federal Reserve from "Jewish" control. The idea behind inviting Duke was, of course, to associate CCRI with his notoriety and program. As a student stunt, it was unsavory. But many leading opponents of 209 were quick to praise it.

Joe Hicks was chosen to go up against Duke as the anti-209 debater. It "was almost an out-of-body experience," Hicks recalls. "I'm sitting on the stage with the best-known bigot in America. It was an effort by our side to link 209 to white sheets and Klan bigotry and bring in the guy who represented all those things to attack affirmative action." Hicks debated ably, and the crowd was on his side. But his heart was no longer in it.

Later, the Democratic National Committee ran a television ad in California that Hicks still recalls with unerring precision: "I'm sitting at home, and this thing comes across my television screen. The ad starts with a burning cross, sheet-wearing Klan members, and goes to David Duke talking on the stage about Proposition 209. I was stunned and outraged." This ad, Hicks recalls, "was kind of for me the capper. It consolidated my thinking about who these people were, my allies, about how unscrupulous they could be." The ad also said preposterously that 209 would "close magnet schools," "lock women out of government jobs," and "end equal opportunity."

Such tactics taxed the tolerance even of many fervent believers in racial preferences. "When I asked an African American woman working for the opposition how she felt about the Duke ad," reported anti-209 journalist-author Lydia Chavez, the woman said, 'I wished we had nicer ads. . . . Theirs, you know, had that nice line at the end, 'bring us together.'"

Of course, there were many very reasoned voices in opposition to Prop 209. Professor Vik Amar, a leading constitutional law scholar and now associate dean of the King School of Law (University of California, Davis), felt that Prop 209 "would significantly reduce the number of black and Hispanic students at the four or five most competitive UC campuses and also at professional schools throughout the system. This would both impoverish the learning environment at these institutions, and also renege on a social justice remedial obligation." Amar was concerned that, in an effort to counter these effects, the UC system might dilute its academic criteria and thus experience a general decline in excellence. Amar and many others were concerned about the symbolic effect of Prop 209 on national debates about issues affecting racial justice, another way of saying that America's work on race was finished. Among others sharing similar concerns were both of this book's authors, and one of us (Taylor) said so in print. But these ideas played a decidedly subordinate role in the public debate.

Meanwhile, some tensions were arising on the pro-CCRI front. Connerly, Custred, Wood, and Steinberg stuck consistently to their themes: that CCRI would end racial and gender preferences and would move California toward the ideal of a color-blind society. "I wanted a highbrow, positive, uplifting campaign," recalls Steinberg. But CCRI leaders had a difficult relationship with national (and some state) Republican leaders, even at times with Wilson. For a long time national Republicans were wary of CCRI, seeing it as a peripheral issue with a large potential downside. But as Bob Dole lagged in the summer presidential polls, he decided to endorse Prop 209, and Republicans announced plans to run a $3 million advertising campaign. Designed to help Dole, not CCRI, the ad would attack President Clinton for opposing the CCRI and imply, by featuring his "I Have a Dream" speech, that Martin Luther King Jr., like Dole, would have supported the CCRI (a doubtful claim).

According to Connerly and Steinberg, this was done without consulting CCRI's leadership, and it struck all of them as a deliberate effort to drag 209, which was very popular, into the presidential campaign alongside Dole, who was not. "Those bumbling Republican fools made a half-witted effort to politicize the [209] campaign," recalls Steinberg. The plan generated so much media criticism that the commercial was abandoned before it ever aired, and in the process it probably fueled some of the vitriol on the anti-209 side and narrowed 209's margin of victory. Meanwhile, through most of the Proposition 209 campaign, the media lined up heavily on the side of the anti-209 forces and adopted their vocabulary in describing the issue in news stories and editorials alike. Nearly all media coverage of Prop 209 focused on "affirmative action" and only rarely on "preferences."

Although initiative campaigns in California are often partisan and routinely feature ads that seek to push buttons rather than discuss issues, the nastiness of the anti-209 campaign stands out; it offended many thoughtful opponents of 209—especially Joe Hicks. He recalls that the zealotry of his camp disturbed him so much that he began to read more widely on the affirmative action issue and to reexamine his own views. On the morning of election day, November 5, 1996, he called Connerly (whom he had debated three times during the campaign) to wish him luck. Flabbergasted, Connerly said it sounded as though Hicks wanted his own side to lose. Hicks responded, "I do want to lose. Between us, I've changed sides."

By and large, the elected officials who opposed Proposition 209 won on election day—most notably, President Clinton, who won California by a landslide. But 209 still won easily, carrying more than 54 percent of the vote. Although whites and Asians supported CCRI in larger numbers than did blacks and Hispanics, the vote was far less racially polarized than, say, the usual split between Republicans and Democrats.

One might think that this would have energized more Democratic defections from the racial-preference camp and would have tempted Republicans to exploit the issue by pushing for legislative bans on racial preferences in other states and in Congress. But the opposite happened. Although the opponents' bruising campaign fell short of winning the vote, they (as well as the much-denounced Republican ad) probably narrowed 209's margin of victory. Far more important, they appear to have helped convince national leaders in both parties that racial preferences were so toxic and dangerous an issue as to be best left untouched.

Leading Democrats like Kerry and Lieberman would still any doubts they had about racial preferences. Indeed, James Traub reported in the *New York Times Sunday Magazine*, when Lieberman's "equivocal praise" in 1995 for Prop 209 prompted denunciations by the civil rights establishment, "Lieberman reeled in horror. 'It was just about the first time in my public life that I was not on the civil rights side,' he says. 'Jesse Jackson spoke out against me.' Lieberman quickly came to the conclusion that Clinton's 'mend it, don't end it' policy met his concerns, though the policy had the effect of keeping the entire apparatus of affirmative action intact."

On the Republican side enthusiasm for taking on racial preferences largely evaporated; two major antipreference measures before Congress died in 1996. During the Prop 209 campaign a federal appellate court in Texas issued a ruling invalidating racial preferences used by the University of Texas Law School and broadly holding that such preferences were impermissible. The Supreme Court in July 1996 declined to review the Fifth Circuit's decision, effectively leaving intact a ban on racial preferences in universities in Texas, Louisiana, and Mississippi.

Henceforth, it seemed, political leaders would be happy to leave the dangerous issue of racial preferences to state referenda (several states followed California) and court decisions. We cannot think of a single major political figure who has forcefully taken on racial preferences since the adoption of Prop 209.

CHAPTER EIGHT

THE WARMING EFFECT

A S UNIVERSITY OF CALIFORNIA administrators fretted over the first steps toward implementing Prop 209, they shared a common fear: that race-blind admissions would dramatically reduce minority enrollments. It stood to reason that fewer minorities would be admitted, especially at the most selective campuses, and that fewer would apply because once a talented black high school senior realized that her chances of getting into Berkeley had fallen from, say, 60 percent before Prop 209 to 30 percent after, it was reasonable to suppose that she should devote her energies to more promising alternatives. There was also much talk of a "chilling effect," the idea that black and Hispanic students who *were* admitted might refuse offers from campuses where their numbers were in free fall. It was at least plausible that many of these students would see the UC system generally and the most selective campuses in particular as hostile places for minorities and, thus, look more favorably upon the scores of private colleges and other state universities that were waiting in the wings with offers of generous scholarships. And finally it occurred to administrators that a vicious cycle might ensue, in which minority enrollment drops would produce still greater chilling and that the cycle might end in a virtually complete disappearance of blacks and Hispanics from the most elite campuses.

It is hard to overstate how pervasive this fear was among affirmative action supporters, particularly within the university. As we mentioned in Chapter Seven, a careful estimate presented to the regents in 1995 projected that Berkeley would lose 85 percent of its black freshmen in the first year alone if the university did not institute large-scale socioeconomic preferences to offset the loss of racial ones. And that, many feared, would only be the beginning. UC Berkeley chancellor Chang-Lin Tien observed in 1996, "I've visited urban inner-city schools . . . many students feel, 'Why should I work anymore? I'm a second-class citizen.' I think 209 will have that kind of impact." A senior administrator at Mills College, a selective private college in Oakland, commented just after the Prop 209 election that "I've heard that educators are worried that qualified minority students are not applying to the UC system because they feel they will be rejected or don't like the environment." In early 1998, pro-preference advocates pubished an entire book called *Chilling Admissions*, which spoke of "campus resegregation" and the "return [of our campuses] to almost total domination by the most privileged racial and ethnic communities."

Race-blind admissions for undergraduates began with the 1997–98 season, and officials watched nervously as applications began to trickle in during the early fall of 1997. By November officials at several schools noticed unusually large numbers of incoming applications. At first glance, this was not a surprise: It made sense that lots of white and Asian high school seniors with good but not outstanding records would conclude that the end of racial preferences had significantly improved their chances. But actual counts of applications from whites and Asians did not show an increase for either group. The biggest jump in applications was coming instead from "none of the above," applicants who declined to give any racial identification.

By January 1998 it was clear that this was turning into a banner year for the university. Applications rose at all eight UC campuses; total applications were up nearly 12 percent. This was partly because more students applied to multiple campuses, but the number of unique applicants was still up by nearly 7 percent. Because the university generally considered applications only from students who were "UC eligible" (something that a high school senior could figure out in consultation with a counselor), this meant that a much larger fraction of California seniors eligible to apply were actually doing so.

Even more astonishing was the race count. The change in total unique UC applications from 1997 to 1998 broke out like this:

Whites: down 13 percent
Asians: down 3 percent
American Indians: down 1 percent

Blacks: up 1 percent
Hispanics: up 7 percent
"Other" and "Unknown": up 214 percent
Total: up 7 percent

It seemed likely that most of the new "unknown" race persons were whites and Asians, which would mean that applications went up for every racial group. But regardless of the true race of the "unknowns," the message of these figures was startling. California high school seniors had applied to UC campuses in unprecedented numbers, and applications from blacks and Hispanics, rather than dropping precipitously, had *gone up*.

The more closely we look at these patterns, the more remarkable they become. We were able to obtain data from the College Board (which administers SAT and AP exams) on all California high school students in the years immediately before and after Prop 209 went into effect. They show that in 1997, the last year of race-conscious admissions, about 58 percent of the academically strongest blacks in California applied to Berkeley, the most elite school in the UC system and one of the top colleges in the nation. In 1998 this percentage went up to 70 percent. In 1997, with racial preferences still in place, black high school seniors in California who had a 50-50 chance of getting admitted to Berkeley had a one-in-three chance of applying there. In 1998, with no racial preferences, those who had a 50-50 chance of admission were an academically stronger group, with many more options at non-UC schools. That might lead one to suppose that fewer than one in three of this 50-50 chance group would apply to Berkeley. But in fact, one in two applied —a remarkable surge. Much the same thing happened, though not quite as powerfully, for Hispanics.

Looking across the entire pool of black and Hispanic potential applicants, race-blind admissions cut their chances of being admitted to Berkeley and UCLA by about half. Other things being equal, that should have produced a substantial drop in the likelihood of any given black or Hispanic high school senior applying to these top schools—arguably a decline on the order of 20 to 30 percent. Instead, total black and Hispanic applications to these schools went up. This means that, if we control for the "likelihood of acceptance," black and Hispanic seniors in California became *much more* likely to apply to Berkeley and UCLA after race-neutral admissions began.

Similar patterns occurred at the less elite campuses. Black applications rose at seven of the eight UC campuses, and Hispanic applications rose at all eight. But it is harder to draw inferences from applications to, say, the UC Irvine campus, since minority students may have applied in higher numbers simply because they were less confident of being admitted to Berkeley or UCLA.

The implication of these application patterns is that Prop 209 did not "chill" the interest of minorities in attending the University of California; rather, if anything, Prop 209 "warmed" their interest. We cannot be sure why. But the most plausible inference from their actions is that the prospect of attending schools that admitted them without regard to their race attracted and even excited them.

An even better test of this hypothesis is the so-called yield rate—the rate at which blacks and Hispanics accepted offers of admission from the various UC schools. As college admissions officers well know, black yield rates tend to be much lower than white yield rates when we control for things like academic index because racial preferences give blacks many more options. This pattern had traditionally held across the UC campuses. *In 1998, however, the black yield rate at Berkeley was nearly 52 percent, by far the highest in many years and probably an all-time record.* The white rate that year was under 40 percent, slightly higher than the white average. The black yield is particularly astonishing because the black students admitted that year had, on average, far stronger academic records than their predecessors (and thus more numerous college options); race-blind admissions had greatly reduced the number of admissions of blacks with only moderately strong qualifications. More modest but still substantial improvements in yield occurred for blacks at other campuses and for Hispanics as well.

The jump in minority yield rates reinforces our impression from the application data: Blacks in particular and, to a slightly less extent, Hispanics, showed an extraordinary increase in interest in the University of California, especially in its most elite campuses, the year race-neutral admissions went into effect. Race-neutrality did not chill their interest in the UCs; instead, it drew them like a magnet.

The upshot of these shifts is that the various campuses experienced a much smaller drop in enrollment than administrators had feared. Black freshman enrollment at Berkeley in 1998 fell by 52 percent; Hispanic freshman enrollment fell by 43 percent. At UCLA the drops were 31 percent for blacks and 23 percent for Hispanics (many strong minority students cascaded from Berkeley to UCLA). For the UC system as a whole, the drops were 19 percent for blacks and 6 percent for Hispanics. And the declines in minority enrollment did not set off their own "chilling" chain reaction; in 1999 both black and Hispanic enrollment numbers rebounded modestly.

Something extraordinary seemed to be happening, but one would never know it from either the official reaction of UC officials or the media coverage.

In May 1998 the *New York Times* ran a story entitled "Fewer Minorities Entering University of California." The story noted that it appeared minority enrollments would "drop only slightly throughout the state system" and that "university officials . . . were heartened that the drop at [Berkeley and UCLA] had not been steeper, but they expressed concerns that the numbers foreshadowed a racially divided system." The *Times* quoted UCLA's vice chancellor, Theodore Mitchell, observing that "if this trend continues over the next five or six years," the "University of California . . . will become a segregated system." Another May 1998 *Times* story was devoted almost entirely to the anger of minority students—especially African Americans—at the post-209 policy. The reporter explained that black faculty and students, especially at the more elite campuses, "feel betrayed and insulted by what happened, and have told prospective students to beware of what could be an isolating experience." The *Los Angeles Times* observed in April 1998 that "though coveted at the top two UC campuses, many high-achieving blacks and Latinos are likely to take their gifts to Stanford, the Ivy League, Michigan, and other campuses where the freshman classes intentionally will be more diverse." Other California papers echoed the same themes.

Almost no one in either the UC administration or the media seemed to notice that, from a learning perspective, the unfolding developments of 1998 might signify a triple win for minority students and the UC system. Race-neutral admissions meant that students previously admitted to Berkeley and UCLA would "cascade" down to schools where they were likely to do better academically. (Students who previously got into less-selective UC campuses only through race-based "special admissions" would cascade into the excellent Cal State system.) At the same time, increased minority interest in the UC schools was strengthening the quality of students at every UC campus, and the rise in yield rates suggested that minority students now found the UC campuses more appealing.

* * *

We think the story we have just told is compelling, but there is a difference between highlighting impressive facts and analyzing a problem thoroughly with social science tools. For example, although black yield rates surged in 1998, they fell back some in 1999 (though still well above pre-209 levels). As minority applicants learned more about how race-blind admissions would work, those with particularly low chances of admission became progressively less likely to apply. It is worth standing back and asking whether a rigorous analysis of all the available data supports our hypothesis that minorities were "warmed," not "chilled," by Prop 209.

David Card and Alan Krueger, both renowned labor economists, published an analysis in 2005 using the College Board data mentioned above (Card generously helped us access the data as well). The College Board dataset includes detailed information on the academic background of each student and lists the schools to which she sent her SAT scores—a fairly good proxy for a student's decision to eventually apply. Card and Krueger were interested in whether Prop 209 would cause some sort of chilling effect. They also realized that it was important to factor in the lower rate at which blacks and Hispanics would be admitted in the race-neutral regime. Their solution to this problem was to look at very strong applicants, whom they believed would be virtually certain to get into top UC schools both before and after Prop 209. They analyzed the relative probability of blacks and Hispanics, compared to whites and Asians, applying either to UC schools in general or specifically to the most selective UC schools, for 1994–1996 and 1999–2001. (They left out 1997 and 1998 on the grounds that these were transitional years, when students might be uncertain of whether racial preferences were being used, and by 1999 any "chilling effect" should have set in.) Their finding was that after the ban on racial preferences took effect, applications to UC schools from these very highly qualified blacks and Hispanics rose slightly, relative to whites and Asians. When good social scientists have a finding like this, they subject it to a variety of tests to see how "robust" it is. Card and Krueger's finding was indeed robust.

Card and Krueger's results actually understated the resilience of minority applications in an important sense. Even the sort of very strong minority students Card and Krueger examined faced much more competitive admissions under the race-neutral regime. To see this, suppose we divide all applicants to Berkeley and UCLA into ten equal groups (deciles), based on their academic index scores. The top three deciles are all very strong students, similar to those examined by Card and Krueger. In the three years before Prop 209's implementation, whites and Asians in those deciles had a 75 percent chance of admission; blacks and Hispanics in those deciles were admitted 90 percent of the time. With applications going up after Prop 209, everyone faced more competitive admissions. Whites and Asians in these three deciles were admitted to Berkeley and UCLA 61 percent of the time after Prop 209, a 14 percent decline. Blacks and Hispanics were admitted 66 percent of the time, a 24 percent decline (and a more than threefold increase in the likelihood of being rejected). This means that the increase in highly qualified minority applications documented by Card and Krueger rose faster than white and Asian applications increased, *even though* these minority applicants were facing significantly diminished chances of admission.

So the evidence that blacks and Hispanics became more likely to apply after Prop 209, holding other factors constant, is quite strong. But what about the yield rate—their likelihood of actually attending a UC campus?

After very protracted negotiations, the relevance of which will become clearer in Chapters Nine and Ten, the University of California Office of the President (UCOP) reluctantly released to us in 2008 a fairly comprehensive dataset on students who applied to or entered the University of California as freshmen from the early 1990s through 2006. The dataset contains information on the academic characteristics of every applicant, their family background, which UC schools they applied to, which ones accepted them, and which one they chose to enroll in (if any). Though the UCOP data allows one to examine individual behavior and outcomes (critical, for example, in looking at yield issues), the data is blurred in some ways: Blacks, Hispanics, and American Indians are lumped together in a single "minority" group, and enrollment years are grouped in three-year aggregates.

Kate Antonovics, a labor economist at the University of California, San Diego, collaborated with one of us (Sander) in using UCOP's data to study how yield rates were affected by Prop 209. Antonovics realized that gross yield rates alone could be misleading. Because stronger students would have lower yield rates (as they have more options), it was important to control for the significant strengthening of admits of all races during these years. Even trickier was the problem of adjusting for the other options students would have. For example, the black yield rate at UC San Diego might go up after Prop 209 simply because those black applicants would be less likely to get into Berkeley or UCLA. To deal with this problem, Antonovics and Sander controlled for the "choice set" that each student faced—that is, they compared similar students who had been admitted to the same set of schools before and after Prop 209.

Their analysis yielded statistically powerful results. Students of all races, (including those who did not identify their race) were somewhat more likely to accept an offer from most UC campuses in 1998–2000 (after the implementation of race-neutrality) than in 1995–1997. Yield rates generally went up by around 5 percent in the later period. But the increase was much larger for minority students (defined, as noted above, as blacks, Hispanics, and American Indians). Minority yield rates went up two or three times more than those of everyone else.

Moreover, as Figure 8.1 suggests, there were some interesting patterns across the campuses. It is hard to draw a firm statistical conclusion with only eight campuses to observe (rather than, say, one hundred). But the four most elite campuses all had big increases in black and Hispanic yield rates, whereas

FIGURE 8.1. The Warming Effect

The announced end of racial preferences at the University of California coincided with a jump in the rate at which blacks and Hispanics accepted offers of admission from UC schools. This "warming effect" was particularly large at the more elite schools, which had formerly used the largest racial preferences, and seemed unaffected by drops in total minority enrollment at three elite campuses.

		Comparing 1995–1997 with 1998–2000	
Campus	**Campus eliteness** (mean academic index of students on 0 to 1,000 scale, 1995–2000)	**Change in likelihood that Underrepresented Minorities would accept admissions offers**	**Change in absolute minority enrollment**
🏛 Berkeley	805	+15% ▶	◀ -42%
🏛 UCLA	776	+10 ▶	◀ -33
🏛 San Diego	752	+14 ▶	◀ -9
🏛 Davis	702	+14 ▶	◀ -1
🏛 Santa Barbara	682	+5 ▶	◀ -1
🏛 Irvine	680	0	+22 ▶
🏛 Santa Cruz	647	+9 ▶	+18 ▶
🏛 Riverside	631	+13 ▶	+65 ▶

Source: Antonovics & Sander, "Affirmative Action Bans and the Chilling Effect" (2012), and calculations by the authors.

three of the four less-elite campuses had much smaller increases. The four top campuses, especially Berkeley and UCLA, had generally been using the largest racial preferences before Prop 209, so the change to race-neutrality was particularly dramatic for them. These patterns reinforce the general implication of our findings, that UC schools became much more appealing to minority students after preferences ended. It is plausible that the bigger the change in policy at a particular campus, the more powerful the attractive effect might be.

Figure 8.1 shows, too, the change in black and Hispanic freshman enrollment that occurred at each UC campus after Prop 209. What is striking about this pattern is its seeming irrelevance to the warming effect discussed here. Although it is possible that the aggregate effect of Prop 209 on minority enrollment on each campus mattered to black and Hispanic students assessing admissions offers, such concerns certainly do not seem to have affected cross-campus yield rates.

Another interesting barometer of sentiment comes from out-of-state applicants. After Prop 209, the number of academically gifted, out-of-state minority high school students sending their SAT scores to UC campuses jumped. From 1995–1997 to 1998–2000, score sending by academically gifted, out-of-state Hispanics to UC schools went up 12 percent. The number of gifted blacks sending scores went up 48 percent. Over 90 percent of the increase in black interest was focused on the three most elite UC schools, Berkeley, UCLA, and UC San Diego.

* * *

The warming effect is the sort of powerful finding one can obtain from a natural experiment like Prop 209. The passage of Prop 209 stoked all sorts of powerful emotions, and its implementation was undoubtedly upsetting in particular for black and Hispanic students on UC campuses who had been admitted under the old regime. But the implementation of the policy and the availability of data that lets us observe actual decisions to apply or accept an offer of admission lets us rely on people's actual behavior to infer their fundamental attitudes. Undoubtedly, the end of preferences dismayed some blacks and Hispanics considering the UCs. Some may have decided to go to other schools with traditional preference programs. Some undoubtedly participated in protests against the very idea of Prop 209. But as high school seniors making individual decisions about what colleges were most appealing, it seems that the aura of race-neutrality attracted many, many more black and Hispanic students than it repelled.

This conclusion is strengthened when we consider what else was going on at the same time. Financial aid is important to students; could more minorities have been lured to UC campuses after Prop 209 by increased financial aid? Actually, no: Prop 209 forbade race-based scholarships as well as race-based admissions. A significant number of race-based scholarship programs halted in 1998. Administrators worked to move some funds "offshore," contending that if the university merely provided information about minority admits to private donors, those donors could confer race-based scholarships. But this process took time and never came close to offsetting the loss of earlier race-based programs. Thus, the warming effect occurred despite a probably sizeable loss of financial aid for black and Hispanic admits, relative to whites and Asians.

What about recruitment? The chancellor at Berkeley received some media attention for his efforts to stave off the feared chilling effect by telephoning black and Hispanic admittees personally to urge them to attend Berkeley. But even if this strategy was effective, a few dozen phone calls cannot account for the breadth and depth of the warming effect over several years and many campuses. And, as we saw earlier in the chapter, many UC minority students and faculty actually engaged in "antirecruiting" after race-neutral policies arrived, warning students away from a university that they saw moving toward segregation. For example, a black Berkeley senior who served as director of the campus Black Recruitment and Retention Center reported that her message to prospective students was "It's a very hostile environment and . . . we're not welcome here, and they don't want us here because they're not letting us in. We weren't pushing them to come to [Berkeley]."

The University did develop new and ambitious outreach plans in 1997 and 1998, and it eventually spent tens of millions of dollars trying to strengthen the pipeline of disadvantaged and minority students into college. But these were generally long-term strategies that did not meaningfully get underway before 1999 and could not plausibly have had an effect upon the first few freshman classes admitted after Prop 209. Moreover, increasing applications through "outreach" would tend to depress yield rates because those applicants are likely to have the weakest preexisting interest in attending a UC school. The simultaneous increase in applications and yield rate, which, if anything, was strongest in the first year of Prop 209's implementation, show that long-term outreach programs cannot explain the warming effect.

The imagined chilling effect that so many supporters of racial preferences believed in (and continue to believe in) was based on the idea that black and Hispanic students would find the University of California a less welcoming place without preferences. But, of course, another possibility was at least equally plausible: that students of color would welcome the chance to attend a school without the stigma of being a suspected "affirmative-action admit." They may have anticipated that under a race-neutral regime campus life would be easier and that white and Asian students would be less likely to stereotype them as academically weak and more likely to be friends. As we documented in Chapter Six, the perception of stigma is widespread, and the increased likelihood of cross-racial friendships in a race-neutral environment is empirically demonstrable.

Then there is the likely long-term benefit of winning a college degree that will be more valuable because it is untainted by any affirmative action stigma. A Berkeley degree is considered valuable in part because it shows to potential employers and future professional associates that one was smart and able enough to *get into* Berkeley. But when employers logically assume that one was admitted through a large preference, then that very credentialing effect is muffled. If it is much easier for black or Hispanic students to get into Berkeley, then won't employers be less impressed by their Berkeley degrees?

There is empirical evidence for this idea too. Three scholars of organizational behavior conducted a series of experiments a few years ago to assess the effect of credentialing. They created and gave to a hundred business school students a series of "pitch books" describing a variety of hypothetical venture-capital investments. Each book was crammed with financial information about the investment and about the key player. The students were asked to estimate the value of the ventures. Controlling for other factors, the interaction of the educational background and the race of each key player affected in a nuanced way the valuation students gave to the venture. Companies led by white key players from elite schools received higher valuations than those led by black key players from elite schools—except that when the pitch book specified that the school in question did not use racial preferences in admission, the black-white valuation difference disappeared. The scholars concluded that their test subjects downgraded the presumed skill of black businessmen not based on their race but instead based on the assumption that their elite school credentials had been won in part by admissions preferences.

It's true that the subjects in this study were business students rather than actual investors or employers. But that makes the study all the more relevant to the question before us. If business school students have these perceptions, it is very plausible that other students do too and that prospective black students would be aware of them.

It makes every aspect of our warming effect finding fit. Getting into Berkeley is good; getting into Berkeley without any taint of a preference is *really* good. The size of the warming effect should be, as it is, closely related to the reduction in racial preferences after Prop 209. Preferences fell dramatically at Berkeley and UCLA, and this had particularly impressive warming effects; they fell much less at the less-elite UC campuses.

One other manifestation of the warming effect is worth at least a brief mention: its possible influence on the ambitions of minority high school students. Many thoughtful critics of affirmative action suggest that young blacks with academic promise realize that they are a scarce commodity and that even a reasonably successful high school career will gain them entrée into a fairly elite college. An interesting question, as John McWhorter has put it in describing his own youth, is whether

the maintenance of affirmative action . . . hinders the completion of the very task it was designed to accomplish, because it deprives black students of a basic incentive to reach for that highest bar. . . . I can attest, for example, that in secondary school I quite deliberately refrained from working to my highest potential because I knew that I would be accepted to even top universities without doing so. Almost any black child knows from an

early age that there is something called affirmative action which means
that black students are admitted to schools under lower standards than
white; I was aware of this at least [from] the age of 10.

Might, then, a ban on racial preferences produce some change in the behavior
of minority high school students?

A few scholars have studied this question, and some interesting work is
still in progress that specifically examines the effect of Prop 209 on minority
high school achievement. The evidence thus far suggests to us that, overall,
black and Hispanic high school performance (relative to other groups) may
have improved in some modest ways but by no means dramatically. There
does seem to be one interesting exception at the top of the achievement distribution. The College Board data described earlier allows us to track the proportion of blacks taking the SAT in California whose overall academic index
in high school put them at a level comparable to the top eighth of all students—a pool similar to those ordinarily eligible for race-neutral UC admission. From 1994 (when our data begins) through 1997 the proportion of
California and US blacks in this elite range tracked exactly in the neighborhood of 2.5 percent of blacks. But in 1998 the proportion of California blacks
with high academic indices jumped by 20 percent over the national rate, and
an upward trend begins. In 2001, the last year for which we have complete
data, California blacks were achieving high academic indices at a rate 35 percent higher than the national average (meaning that 3.5 percent of blacks
reached the top eighth of academic indices). This is just one piece of evidence,
not "robust" in the sense of the very powerful evidence for the warming effect.
But it is at least plausible that Prop 209 has stimulated black high school students aiming for the University of California to raise their sights on their own
performance.

* * *

The existence of the warming effect calls into question many of the core
assumptions of racial preference policies. It suggests that many talented black
and Hispanic high school seniors are aware of the potential side effects of
large preferences—enough so that a great many talented high school seniors
would prefer to avoid them, other things being equal. That doesn't mean that
a black student will choose the local community college over Princeton simply to avoid a preference, but it certainly implies that black and Hispanic students would like to have choices among elite colleges that use smaller
preferences or none at all.

CHAPTER NINE

MISMATCH AND THE SWELLING
RANKS OF GRADUATES

THE WARMING EFFECT we documented in Chapter Eight was an unexpected development. Although administrators feared that an end of racial preferences would produce disaster, the University of California instead experienced an upsurge of interest among California high school students of all races and record applications and yields from black and Hispanic seniors. The various UC campuses were able to admit stronger students and mitigate the enrollment drops produced by the loss of racial preferences. The warming effect fostered a virtuous cycle in future years that, with improved outreach to low- and moderate-income communities, further augment black and Hispanic enrollment.

This leads us to the question of what happened to the new classes of black and Hispanic students after they enrolled. For reasons we explore below, the new admissions regime did not eliminate racial gaps in academic preparation—far from it. But to the extent it did, the results were extraordinary: Black and Hispanic students improved their academic performance, stuck more successfully to STEM majors, and graduated at stunningly improved rates. Indeed, the overall improvements were so large that graduation improvements tended to swamp declines in enrollment. These happy developments would be generally ignored or minimized by administrators focused only on resisting Prop 209. However, they provide compelling evidence that reducing mismatch is crucial to improving minority outcomes.

* * *

The University of California is a large, complex system. Its ten campuses enroll well over two hundred thousand students and an almost equal number of staff. In the mid- and late-1990s eight campuses enrolled undergraduates. They range widely in eliteness, as Figure 8.1 in the last chapter suggests, from Berkeley and UCLA at the top, which rank on most lists of top twenty American universities, to UC Santa Cruz and UC Riverside, which are important research universities that rank probably among the top two hundred American schools in student strength and faculty reputation. These schools together comprise the first of three tiers in California higher education. Under the "Master Plan" adopted by state authorities in 1960, the eight UC campuses were each envisioned as research universities that would have graduate programs and would collectively make room for any California high school student whose academic index placed her among the top eighth of all students (these top students would come to be called "UC eligible"). A broader pool of students—those in the top third of the academic index—would be eligible for one of the twenty-plus campuses of the four-hundred-thousand-student Cal State system. Those who qualified for neither the UCs or Cal State could attend one of the dozens of community colleges operated by the state (some of them quite good). And, importantly, students who did well in community college nor at Cal State could transfer after their freshman or sophomore year to one of the UC schools.

This background is important for a few reasons. We focused on freshman admissions in Chapter Eight; but in addition to the roughly twenty-five thousand freshmen enrolled at the eight UC campuses collectively each year in the late 1990s, there were also some ten thousand transfer students who arrived as sophomores or juniors. At Berkeley and UCLA, which were sought after by transfers in particularly large numbers, they often made up between 30 and 40 percent of the senior class. Before Prop 209 many UC campuses applied very different standards to transfer students depending on their race. But in an era without overt racial preferences, transfers were an important mechanism to identify strong students of all races who, in early adulthood, were on a trajectory of rapid academic improvement. Managed properly, a transfer system was a good way to elevate talented students when they were ready rather than gambling on their success as freshmen.

UC eligibility also played a crucial role in shaping the effects of Prop 209. Because of the racial test-score gap, far more than one-eighth of Asian high school students in California qualified for UC eligibility, whereas far fewer than one-eighth of black or Hispanic students qualified. For many years before Prop 209 university administrators had sidestepped the "top eighth" rule through "special admissions," but still, even before Prop 209 effectively shut down race-based special admissions, the UC system as a whole did not have anything comparable to the racial proportionality that one could find at most elite colleges. In the years before Prop 209 blacks made up just over 4 percent of UC freshmen and Hispanics made up 13 to 14 percent of UC freshmen—both numbers far below their relative numbers in the pool of high school graduates.

This meant that before Prop 209 the various UC campuses were competing intensely among themselves for the limited supply of black and Hispanic freshmen. Not surprisingly, Berkeley and UCLA often won this competition: In 1997 nearly half of all UC blacks and nearly a third of all UC Hispanics were at the Berkeley and UCLA campuses. The constraint UC eligibility created also meant that a substantial proportion of UC freshmen had academic indices that already qualified them for admission to at least one of the lower-tier UC schools. This is why, before Prop 209, racial preferences at Berkeley and UCLA were very large (and close to national norms), whereas preferences at the less elite UC campuses were generally modest.

How did Prop 209 change all these dynamics? As we have already observed, UC officials were very anxious about the prospective drop in minority enrollment, which they expected to be very large. They could not openly defy the ban on racial preferences, so instead they instituted a variety of ostensibly race-neutral measures intended to stem the decline. Some created or expanded socioeconomic preferences. Some began to favor applicants from inner-city schools. We suspect from our statistical analysis of admissions decisions at the time that some campus admissions offices, aware of the intense concern about diversity numbers, looked for signs in applications for minorities they could favor. So, for example, in the three years before Prop 209 a black or Hispanic applicant with an academic index in the low 600s had a 63 percent chance of being admitted to Berkeley or UCLA, compared to an 8 percent chance for a similar white applicant and a 7 percent chance for a similar Asian applicant. In the first three years of putatively race-neutral admissions, the black or Hispanic applicant's chances fell sharply, to only 27 percent. But that was still far higher than the chances faced by whites (7 percent) or Asians (9 percent) with the same academic index.

These measures significantly moderated the effect of Prop 209. Without them, the cascade of blacks and Hispanics to less elite campuses would have been more severe; more students probably would have been displaced from the UC system altogether and into the generally less elite Cal State system. The use of race substitutes gave race-neutrality a less severe feel.

But the same race substitutes also preserved substantial gaps at every campus between the average academic index of whites and Asians on the one hand and blacks and Hispanics on the other. True, after Prop 209 there was much more overlap at every campus in the academic qualifications of students of different races, and both ends of the qualification spectrum were more racially heterogeneous. But overall, the academic index gaps between whites and Asians on the one hand and blacks and Hispanics on the other shrank by only 20 to 30 percent.

* * *

Perhaps the most important mismatch question we can consider from the UC move to putative race-neutrality is this: Did even a modest reduction in the net preferences received by blacks and Hispanics improve their graduation rates?

The simple answer is an emphatic yes. Minority graduation rates rose rapidly in the years after Prop 209, and on-time (four-year) graduation rates rose even faster. For the six classes of black freshmen who entered UC schools in the years before race-neutrality (i.e., the freshman classes of 1992 through 1997), the overall four-year graduation rate was 22 percent. For the six years after Prop 209's implementation the black four-year graduation rate was 38 percent. Thus, even though the number of black freshmen in the UC system fell almost 20 percent from 1997 to 1998, the number of black freshmen who obtained their degrees in four years barely dipped for this class, and the entering class of 2000 produced, four years later, a record number of blacks graduating on time. The increase in black six-year graduation was less dramatic (63 percent before and 71 percent after Prop 209) but still substantial.

The improvement in Hispanic graduation rates was striking too, though, as always, the smaller initial racial preferences Hispanics receive imply that we should see smaller improvements from the new admissions regime. The four-year graduation rate for entering Hispanic freshmen averaged 27 percent in the six years before Prop 209 and 40 percent in the six years after. Six-year graduation rates rose from 69 to 74 percent. Because the Hispanic drop in enrollment after Prop 209 was smaller and because the underlying demographics of California produced steadily larger numbers of strong Hispanic applicants, the absolute numbers of Hispanic graduates rose at a stunning rate. The entering Hispanic freshman classes of 1992, 1993, and 1994 produced a total of 2,005 on-time graduates. The three classes of freshmen entering from 1998 through 2000 produced 3,577 on-time Hispanic graduates from the university.

Not all of these gains, however, should be attributed to the narrowing of racial preparation gaps. The early 1990s were difficult financial years for the university; improving fortunes in the late 1990s allowed the university to provide more student-support services and expand course offerings, both of which improved on-time graduation across the board. And, of course, reducing the number of academically weak black and Hispanic students would tend to boost the average graduation rates of the remainder. Is it possible to isolate these various effects from one another? The UCOP data (a dataset described in Chapter Eight) contains extensive information on every UC freshman enrolled in the years before and after Prop 209—not only on their high school record, test scores, and applications to UC schools but also on their performance and outcomes after they enrolled at UC. A team of economists led by Joe Hotz (a labor economist at Duke and former chair of economics at UCLA) and Peter Arcidiacono (also of Duke) examined Prop 209's effect on UC undergraduate graduation rates for blacks, Hispanics, and Native Americans, using a wide range of controls to compare similar students attending campuses where their academic indices were closer to or further away from the median student in the entering class at that school—in other words, they compared students with varying degrees of academic match with their classmates. *They found that Prop 209 had the effect of raising five-year minority graduation rates from 3 to 7 percent points.* They also concluded that the effect would have been significantly larger had the university more rigorously implemented race-neutrality and thereby further reduced disparities in the academic preparation of students on each campus.

These findings perhaps do not settle the issue of whether mismatch always hurts black and Hispanic graduation rates, but they should weigh heavily in the debate. There is simply no other study that has so effectively handled the difficult problem of "selection effects" that we discussed in detail in Chapter Five. In this case, we can for once be confident that we are comparing fundamentally similar students experiencing different levels of mismatch.

Moreover, there are three reasons to think that Hotz and Arcidiacono are, if anything, underestimating Prop 209's true effects. First, the impact of mismatch on four-year graduation appears to be larger than the effect on the five-year graduation rates they studied. Four-year graduation is generally the ideal, and students who avoid academic difficulty or who stay with their original major are more likely to finish in four years. Second, it is plausible that the better graduation outcomes for better-matched students will contribute to a broader academic climate of success, helping to propel the general increase in graduation rates. But third and most importantly, Hotz and Arcidiacono did not have data on and therefore could not take into account the positive effect of reduced racial preferences on transfer students.

As we noted earlier, an open transfer policy—that is, one that makes it relatively easy for students who do well at nonelite public schools to transfer up to elite ones—offers an ideal way to avoid mismatch while capturing what we would view as the true spirit of affirmative action. If high school seniors with good but not excellent academic records are able to attend colleges where they will not be overwhelmed, if they are able to demonstrate at those colleges that they can do excellent work, and if excellent students are able to transfer easily to more elite schools, then we are providing effective access without inviting the painful consequences of mismatch. We think California's university system came somewhat closer to this ideal as it eliminated formal racial preferences, and the data on the outcomes for transfers supports this view.

During the four years before Prop 209's implementation, less than 19 percent of black students who transferred into a new UC school as juniors graduated on time. That rose to 34 percent in the first four years after Prop 209, and 38 percent in the four years after that. (These are impressive numbers, as transfers often face especially great challenges in meeting new requirements.) The corresponding rates of eventual graduation for these black transfers were 61 percent before the new admissions regime and 74 percent after. The on-time graduation rate for Hispanic transfer students rose from 26 percent before race-neutrality to 42 percent afterward; eventual graduation rates rose from 74 percent to 81 percent. The number of black and Hispanic transfer students dipped for a few years after the change in admissions practices but then began to rise steadily. The number of blacks receiving bachelor's degrees from the University of California as transfer students was more than 40 percent higher in 2007–2009 than it had been before Prop 209, an average of three hundred students per year. Most of these students started their college careers at community colleges or at Cal State. For Hispanics, the increase was over 60 percent.

These surges in successful transfer students further amplify our earlier point: *The elimination of formal racial preferences led to increases—not decreases—in the numbers of blacks and Hispanics earning bachelor's degrees at the University of California, and even more dramatic increases in the numbers earning bachelor's degrees on time.*

* * *

Of course, Prop 209 had many other effects on black and Hispanic undergraduates. One of the most persistent claims by critics, often echoed by journalists and even UC officials, was that race-neutrality was "segregating" the UC campuses. Their argument was that fewer underrepresented minorities were getting into the elite schools; those that got in at all were clustered at UC Riverside, the least elite of the eight UC campuses. UC Riverside (which, relevantly, has a less idyllic campus setting than most of the UC schools) was henceforth to be the "minority" campus, and UC would enter into a sort of Jim Crow era.

The claim was ridiculous. As we discussed earlier in the chapter, the constraining rule of UC eligibility had always imposed limits on the number of blacks and Hispanics in the UC system, and before race-neutrality began Berkeley and UCLA lured a disproportionate number of these students to their campuses. Before Prop 209 Berkeley and UCLA had substantial numbers of black and Hispanic students, but many campuses had few indeed. Race-neutrality cascaded many blacks and Hispanics to less elite campuses, producing a more even distribution of students of all races across the campuses. Although UC Riverside did end up with the largest share of Hispanics of any single campus (it is, after all, located close to the largest residential concentration of Hispanics in the United States), it was still less than a quarter black and Hispanic after Prop 209.

We can objectively measure the degree of "segregation" across campuses with something called the "index of dissimilarity," a measure often used in studies of urban segregation. For blacks entering as UC freshmen in 1997, the last year before Prop 209's implementation, the index was .20, a very low number, indicating that the distribution of blacks vis-à-vis other races was only 20 percent off perfect proportionality. In 1998 the index fell to .18, and it dropped further in subsequent years. For Hispanics, the index of dissimilarity fell from .20 in 1997 to .15 in 1998. Substantively, this meant that many campuses that had very few blacks and Hispanics before Prop 209 (e.g., UC Santa Barbara and UC Santa Cruz) were significantly more integrated afterward.

* * *

The Prop 209–induced decline in academic disparities across racial lines generated other important benefits for black and Hispanic students in the UC system. To a degree almost perfectly predicted by mismatch theory, these students had better academic outcomes during their college careers.

For example, black and Hispanic grades improved, both in absolute and relative terms. As with graduation, there was already a trend in the UC system (and in American higher education generally) toward higher grades unrelated to Prop 209. But gains for blacks and Hispanics outpaced those of other groups. In the three years before the end of formal racial preferences blacks and Hispanics system-wide had freshman GPAs that put them at the 20th percentile of whites and Asians. As the credential gap between the races narrowed, GPA gaps narrowed by amounts that were identical or slightly larger; in 2001–2003 freshman GPAs for blacks and Hispanics had risen to the 30th percentile of whites and Asians. Academic probation rates for blacks and Hispanics declined commensurately.

Science persistence improved. For many years blacks and Hispanics applying to UC schools had been as likely to indicate that they planned to major in the natural sciences or engineering as white applicants did. But once they enrolled, students admitted with large preferences tended to have the same sorts of very high attrition rates that we saw documented in other settings in Chapter Three.

UC-wide, the number of black and Hispanic students graduating with STEM degrees steadily increased after the admissions reforms of 1998, and the number of science-interested students never graduating steadily fell. The share of black and Hispanic students majoring in STEM fields rose as well. Black and Hispanic engineering graduates rose by nearly 50 percent from 1997 to 2003, whereas the number of blacks and Hispanics majoring in ethnic studies and communications fell 20 percent.

As with the issue of graduation mismatch, the natural experiment of suddenly reducing the preparation disparities among different groups of students provides an excellent test of the science mismatch hypothesis. Marc Luppino, Roger Bolus, and one of us (Sander) completed an analysis of the UCOP data to measure the effect of science mismatch upon student persistence in science over a period from 1995 to 2003. We measured substantial mismatch effects for a variety of science outcomes, with magnitudes similar to those found by Smyth and McArdle (see Chapter Three).

Note how each of the accomplishments we have discussed—higher grades, higher graduation rates, and higher science-completion rates—is particularly remarkable in light of the others. Science courses grade harder, so it's harder for the grades of a group of students to go up when more of them are studying science. Lower drop-out rates mean that the average final GPA of a group includes more students who hung in there, even if they struggled. It is remarkable that at the University of California, blacks and Hispanics in the post–Prop 209 era managed to simultaneously lift their achievement levels in multiple ways.

* * *

Thus far we have focused entirely on undergraduates. It is hard to say a lot about graduate schools because graduate programs across the University of California are so numerous and heterogeneous, and the available data are spottier and harder to interpret. But some striking effects of Prop 209 seem unmistakable here as well.

Preference programs at the doctoral level are much more subjective and ad hoc. Scores on such tests as the Graduate Record Examination (GRE) and college grades often provide a rough screen for admissions, but a history or physics department is likely to be much more concerned about whether an applicant has interesting ideas and has shown an ability to engage in independent research. Doctoral programs were much slower in the 1960s and 1970s to adopt preference programs, and because they rely on soft criteria and report little systematic data on admissions and performance, it is hard to measure the extent of preferences. But when they did, preferential admissions sometimes lacked any coherent standards, perhaps because many graduate admissions committees felt that even their subjective criteria might be unfair when applied to blacks and Hispanics.

John Ellis, a retired professor of German literature at UC Santa Cruz, provides an interesting window into the origin, operation, and effects of doctoral-level preferences on a UC campus. From the 1970s until 1986 he was dean of the school's graduate division, and it was during his tenure that UC Santa Cruz began significant efforts to use preferences in recruiting graduate students. Ellis recalls that new federal programs in the 1970s provided rich incentives for schools to use preferences; the initial cost to the school of providing fellowships to black and Hispanic students was minimal, and he encouraged various departments to make active efforts to find promising candidates.

As Ellis tells it, his recruitment and outreach programs morphed in the hands of others into racial and gender preferences. The preferences were particularly large for black recruits, with a variety of harmful results. Often, the recruits were woefully "under-qualified students who were then psychologically harmed by their lack of preparation" and whose academic difficulties aggravated stereotypes about blacks' academic abilities. Although Ellis felt that far less damage was done to the white and Asian candidates who, because of the preference programs, were displaced to slightly less elite schools, the loss of those strong-but-not-stellar students widened the preparation gulf between the highly qualified students admitted without preferences, and the preferentially admitted blacks and Hispanics.

Ellis observed few success stories and many cases in which black students were devastated and embittered, seeing the school and its generally very liberal professors as racist: "Even those who oppose affirmative action generally don't grasp the full extent of the damage to underqualified and unqualified black students."

Ellis is unusual for his passion on the issue, but the problems he identifies come up again and again when other UC faculty share their stories about the efforts of graduate programs to recruit black and Hispanic graduate students with large preferences and fellowships. As we discussed in Chapter Three, mismatch at the undergraduate level creates an extremely slender pipeline of black talent into doctoral programs. When schools aggressively compete for the small number of interested students, serious mismatch problems often ensue.

Again, the post–Prop 209 era at UC provides a chance to check the mismatch hypothesis with some admittedly imperfect data. Most graduate programs in the UC system were instructed to adopt race-neutral admissions for classes entering in 1997 and beyond. Total black graduate enrollment (not first-year entries but students in all years of study) began to fall in 1997, and from 1999 to 2004 it averaged about 25 percent below pre-209 levels. Yet the number of doctoral degrees granted to blacks crept upward and, taking into account the lagged time to degree, averaged about 20 percent *higher* in the post-209 era than before. Black graduate degrees in STEM fields held steady. Similar patterns occurred for Hispanics too, except that the overall decline in Hispanic admissions was smaller, and the growth in STEM graduate degrees was larger.

Once again we see a startling pattern: A reduction in racial preferences led to modest declines in black and Hispanic enrollment but an increase in black and Hispanic degrees. In the graduate school case it is plausible to conclude that Prop 209 caused two things to happen: Particular departments phased out the most aggressive preferences, and the aura of race-neutrality may have attracted some very strong black and Hispanic students.

* * *

One final development in UC's post–Prop 209 era deserves mention. The improvement in black and Hispanic performance was particularly noticeable among the best students. Across all the UCs during the 1995–1997 period, less than one-tenth of blacks and Hispanics had GPAs of 3.5 or higher (compared to over one-quarter of whites and 30 percent of Asians). Both the number and proportion of blacks and Hispanics achieving high GPAs jumped after Prop 209, rising for them at a much faster rate than for whites and Asians.

It is not surprising that many more blacks and Hispanics would have had high academic achievement after formal racial preferences ended. Because, starting in 1998, the entire distribution of black and Hispanic academic qualifications moved up relative to whites and Asians, a larger proportion of black and Hispanic students were able to compete at the highest levels.

But other factors might well have bolstered this effect. Blacks and Hispanics at putatively race-neutral UC campuses may have felt more intellectually self-confident and less (if at all) stigmatized, and were thus less likely to withdraw from academic competition.

Diversity advocates have widely argued that blacks and Hispanics will perform better academically if they constitute a "critical mass" on campus. A recent, careful attempt to test this idea empirically found no support for the critical-mass hypothesis and some evidence that just the opposite was the case. The reshuffling of racial composition across the various UC campuses after Prop 209 provides an interesting opportunity to study this question. When we compare similar students across the various UC campuses and adjust for the racial composition of each campus, we find that black and Hispanic students earned slightly higher grades when the proportion of blacks and Hispanics on their campus *fell*. Strikingly, the effect is strongest for those black and Hispanic students arriving on campus with the highest academic indices. They are primed to do well, but they are also most likely to exceed the predictions of their academic indices on UC campuses with smaller minority populations.

This is only one finding, and we do not claim it has the rigorous support that lies behind findings like the research on undergraduate graduation rates at UC. But the finding makes sense in the context of the other research we have discussed. Many black and Hispanic students on UC campuses continued to be at a serious preparation disadvantage relative to the typical student on their campuses even after Prop 209. They were subject to some of the same pressures to withdraw from the academic competition that appears to occur at so many universities that use large racial preferences. But a smaller presence of academically struggling blacks and Hispanics may have made it more likely that they would, as individuals, have cross-racial networks and feel part of the broader campus community. That, very plausibly, helped to maintain their academic engagement.

* * *

The post–Prop 209 aggregate picture is nothing short of remarkable. If we compare minorities entering the UC system in 1995–97 (the final years of explicit racial preferences) with those in the post-209 cohorts, everything seems to be moving in the same direction:

- The number of blacks entering UC as freshmen in 2000 through 2003 is, on average, only 2 percent below pre-209 levels, and black enrollment jumps when we take into account transfers and lower attrition.

- The number of Hispanic freshmen is up by 22 percent over the same period, and again more when we include transfers.

- The number of blacks receiving bachelor degrees from UC schools rose from an average of 812 in 1998–2001 (the final cohorts entirely comprised of pre-209 entrants) to an average of 904 in 2004–2007 (the first cohorts entirely comprised of post-209 entrants). For UC Hispanics, the numbers rose from 3,317 to 4,428.

- The number of UC black and Hispanic freshmen who went on to graduate in four years rose 55 percent from 1995–1997 to 2001–2003.

- The number of UC black and Hispanic freshmen who went on to graduate in four years with STEM degrees rose 51 percent from 1995–1997 to 2001–2003.

- The number of UC black and Hispanic freshmen who went on to graduate in four years with GPAs of 3.5 or higher rose by 63 percent from 1995–1997 to 2001–2003.

- Doctorates and STEM graduate degrees earned by blacks and Hispanics combined rose by one-quarter from cohorts starting in 1995–1997 to cohorts starting in 1998–2000.

What is wrong with this picture? Only one thing: Academics and administrators across the university were determined to ignore good news and were increasingly restive over the ban on racial preferences. The covert dismantling of race-neutrality would soon move into high gear.

CHAPTER TEN

THE HYDRA OF PREFERENCES

The Evasion of Prop 209 at the University of California

IN THE SPRING OF 1999, on assignment from the *New York Times Magazine*, James Traub visited some campuses of the University of California to assess Prop 209's implementation. What he saw, he generally liked. The campuses seemed to be flourishing and at peace. As Traub reported, "When I asked Kenya Coleman, a black student [at UC Riverside] who was majoring in business, whether she felt that students denied admission to Berkeley would be losing out on something at Riverside, she bristled slightly and said, 'If they end up here it would be a blessing in disguise.'" Another black Riverside senior told him, "I think I am more prepared in terms of graduate school than I would have been if I had gone to UCLA." Traub also noted that

> Ending affirmative action has had one unpublicized and profoundly desirable consequence: it has forced the university to try to expand the pool of eligible minority students. Outreach programs have . . . proliferated; the State Legislature authorized $38.5 million for such efforts last year and has required the public schools to spend an additional

$31 million on similar initiatives. UC campuses are now reaching down into the high schools, the junior highs, and even the elementary schools to help minority students achieve the kind of academic record that will make them eligible for admission.

Traub pointed out that a 1996 poll of Berkeley students showed that most of them opposed racial preferences, but they were happy to vote for a $3 per student increase in student fees to support improved minority outreach. He also observed that UC administrators, like Chancellor Robert Berdahl of Berkeley, did not think that students necessarily knew what was good for them. Those running the UC system remained overwhelmingly convinced of the goodness of the racial preferences they had been forced to give up.

Our research found the same patterns. On the ground, students were adapting well. The warming effect strongly implied that black and Hispanic high school seniors embraced the opportunity to attend a university that had accepted them without regard to their race. Once they arrived at UC, as we saw in Chapter Nine, they performed exceedingly well. Unprecedented outreach efforts were expanding the base: By 2001 black applications to the university would be 10 percent above the previous, pre-209 record, and Hispanic applications would be more than 30 percent above pre-209 levels.

Yet top UC administrators were virtually unanimous in viewing the post-209 landscape with disgust. They deeply resented the intrusion of the regents and the voters into their realm, and they felt continually on the defensive in their dealings with the rest of the academic world. They condemned what had happened, and their condemnation took on a self-fulfilling character: Their expectation of disaster made them incapable of seeing anything else.

Consider, for example, a report prepared several years after Prop 209's implementation by Susan Wilbur, the university-wide director of admissions. Wilbur was asked to examine the impact of Prop 209 on minority enrollment patterns. As we discussed in Chapter Eight, the formal adoption of race-neutrality was accompanied by rising applications and record rates of acceptance among blacks and Hispanics given offers of admission. But Wilbur described the situation differently:

> I will demonstrate that the loss of talented African American and Latino students who are admitted to the university [i.e., by turning down offers of admission] has contributed to the decline in diversity experienced at the UCs. Underrepresented minority students (and especially African American students) are more likely than others to decline an

offer of admission from the UC in favor of an offer from a top-tier institution . . . in a post-209 world, underrepresented minority students are
taking advantage of alternative offers of admission. . . . The loss of
diversity incurred by 209 may have a more negative effect on the educational opportunities of those who attend the UCs than it does on those
who do not.

How did Wilbur reach this powerful conclusion? How could she miss
the startling surge in yield rates that followed Prop 209? It was easy: Wilbur
completely ignored data from the pre-209 era. She only examined yield patterns among UC students admitted long after Prop 209 had been implemented. Her findings were based on the simple fact that academically
strong blacks (and, to a lesser extent, Hispanics) were more likely than
whites and Asians to turn down a UC offer in favor of a competing offer
from another elite school. But of course, because blacks (and, to a lesser
extent, Hispanics) are much more likely, other things being equal, than
whites and Asians to *have* a competing offer from an elite school, Wilbur
was measuring nothing more than the continued existence of racial preferences at other schools. Had Wilbur done the exact same analysis of, say, students offered admission by Harvard or Stanford, she would have found the
exact same patterns.

Wilbur's analysis might have been wildly misleading, but it was prepared
for an audience of UC colleagues who very much wanted to be misled. UC
officials regularly made public statements about the harmful effects of Prop
209 upon the university; to our knowledge, they made no comparable statements about the many ways in which black and Hispanic performance surged
during those years, the more even distribution of minority students across
campuses, or the steady rise of black and Hispanic enrollment numbers UC-
wide. The dominant mindset was that Prop 209 was harmful. The question
that nagged at administrators and many faculty, in a way that increased over
time, was whether Prop 209 was so illegitimate that there was an affirmative
duty to evade it.

One of us (Sander) was active in the university community throughout
the period of Prop 209's implementation. Over the years he discussed with
many other UC faculty and administrators how race-neutrality operated
within their schools and programs. It was exceedingly rare for any of his colleagues to wonder whether the new era might actually benefit blacks and Hispanics. Sander's colleagues contended either that Prop 209 was an
unavoidable evil that must be accommodated or that it was an evil that must
be resisted. In terms of admission policy, these two schools of thought argued,

respectively, for admissions methods that would produce disproportionate racial dividends or for the covert violation of the law.

In December 1996, just weeks after Prop 209 won at the polls, Sander was invited to a UC system-wide meeting in Oakland to discuss ways that graduate programs would adapt to race-neutrality. The meeting was dominated by a discussion of the feasibility and merits of evasion versus the "indirect racial dividend" approach. For many small programs (e.g., graduate programs in areas like psychology, history, or German literature) faculty spoke of the feasibility of evasion: The number of students was so small, and the criteria for selection so subjective, that outside investigators could not easily detect racial discrimination. For larger programs, such as law schools or business schools, that would obviously be more difficult. Sander advanced the notion that socioeconomic (SES) preferences were a viable and desirable alternative to racial preferences and would yield a particularly strong racial dividend if they took into account not only family circumstances (e.g., parental income and education) but also neighborhood conditions (e.g., the level of poverty in the applicant's neighborhood). The others listened with interest, but there was a good deal of skepticism that SES preferences would really produce the desired effect because, it was repeatedly pointed out, there were a lot of low-income whites and Asians.

Soon after, a colleague from a UC medical school told Sander that the medical schools had the ideal antidote to Prop 209: interviews. Because medical schools have very large faculties relative to the number of students admitted each year, it is feasible to interview finalists for admission and to give as high a mark as necessary to black and Hispanic interviewees to produce the desired level of racial diversity.

Boalt Hall Law School, on the Berkeley campus and the most elite of the university's four law schools, appeared to play things completely straight in the first year of race-neutrality. Unlike UCLA's Law School, which adopted a version of Sander's socioeconomic strategy and ended up with ten black first-year students (down from nineteen in 1996), Boalt seemed to focus narrowly on its own version of the academic index and enrolled only a single black student in 1997 (down from twenty in 1996). This became an emblematic moment for the university; the "single black" received national news coverage and *Doonesbury* did a long riff. Even Prop 209 proponents criticized Boalt for the precipitous drop in black enrollment, suggesting that Boalt had neglected its outreach responsibilities.

The decline at Boalt was, however drastic, a foreseeable consequence of race neutrality. Unlike the undergraduate colleges, UC's top law schools operated in a national market. Most of Boalt's students came from outside

California, and nearly all of them believed that the best path to career success was to attend the most elite law school that would have them, wherever it might be located. (As we saw in Chapters Four and Six, the evidence for this view is shaky at best.) Any black student admitted to Boalt without a racial preference would probably have a strong enough academic index to be admitted to any other law school in the country *with* a racial preference, and often with a race-based scholarship as well. Boalt had actually admitted eighteen black students in 1997 (down from seventy-seven in 1996), but these eighteen were generally the very strongest black applicants, with other highly attractive offers, and few if any of them would have accepted Boalt even in the pre-209 era.

Nonetheless, Boalt's students were unhappy, and some of its faculty felt humiliated by negative attention focused on its "one black" class. The next year a committee was established to review many admissions files and exercise more "subjective" judgments. Black admissions rose by over 40 percent, and eight blacks enrolled at Boalt in 1998. By 2002 Boalt was admitting forty-four blacks and enrolling twelve. There was little doubt that Boalt decision makers had reinstituted racial preferences. In some ranges of the academic index, blacks were ten times as likely as whites to be admitted. According to a colleague from Boalt, when asked how the admissions committee managed to admit so many blacks, a faculty member of the committee smiled and said, "No one can know what's in my head."

In the 2000–2001 academic year, faculty at UCLA's law school followed Boalt's lead down the race-conscious road, voting to create a special admissions path for students interested in "Critical Race Studies" (CRS). CRS, in legal studies, is a school of thought that contends that racial categories are deeply embedded in the reasoning and underlying policies of the law. The CRS path was seen by some faculty as a more subtle way to sidestep Prop 209 than Boalt's approach because the school would not overtly be choosing students based on race but based on their substantive interest in a program that would have the effect of producing more students of color. There was also a plausible argument that by admitting students into a substantive program, the CRS admissions path would contribute to intellectual diversity at the school. Subtlety, however, went out the window when, during the program's first full year of admissions, nearly as many whites as blacks applied to the program. The program's special admissions committee admitted eight of the black applicants and none of the white applicants, even though many of the rejected whites had higher academic indices than any of the accepted blacks. The CRS students received preferences very similar to the racial preferences that UCLA used before Prop 209.

Meanwhile, the political climate in the state and on the UC Board of Regents was changing. Pete Wilson stepped down as governor at the end of 1998; his successor, Democratic governor Gray Davis, had been a vocal opponent of Prop 209. His appointments to the regents gradually changed its politics. In May 2001 the regents voted unanimously to rescind its 1995 bans on preferences. These precursors to Prop 209 (as discussed in Chapter Seven) had been made largely moot by it, or so university officials argued. By repealing the measures and reaffirming the university's commitment to diversity, UC administrators suggested, the regents could help dispel the impression that the university was somehow hostile to minorities—in other words, to dispel a "chilling effect" that seemed to exist mostly in administrators' imaginations. The repeal did have one important substantive effect, however: It ended a requirement that between 50 percent and 75 percent of the students on each campus be selected primarily on "academic" grounds. This opened the path toward less formulaic and more "holistic" admissions, under which each student could be rather mysteriously assessed based on "all" her characteristics—much as Boalt Law School was now doing.

Accompanying the repeal of SP-1 came a new path to "UC eligibility" called "Eligibility in the Local Context" (ELC). As the reader will recall, students had long become UC eligible by taking a particular regimen of courses and achieving a combination of test scores and high school grades that placed them in the top eighth of California seniors. In the years leading up to Prop 209 administrators had used a back door, "special admissions," to increase on a case-by-case basis the number of blacks and Hispanics eligible for UC admission. The end of race-conscious special admissions had been the main reason for the drop in minority enrollment after Prop 209, a drop that had since vanished for Hispanics and was now (by 2000–2001) only about 10 percent below pre-209 levels for blacks. ELC would expand UC eligibility by making students UC-eligible if they ranked among the top 4 percent of their own high school class. The main beneficiaries of ELC would be students who had attended weak high schools, had done badly on standardized tests, but had studied conscientiously and received strong grades.

ELC was appealing as a social justice measure; it reached out to many of the state's poorest communities and reduced the emphasis on test scores. Because high schools participating in ELC essentially had to "partner" with the university in determining eligibility, it fostered UC's growing connection to the K-12 pipeline. But it also had an obvious potential to increase mismatch problems. It meant, in effect, that one's high school became a major predictor of admission, but in a way negatively—not positively—related to high school quality. This was exacerbated when some of the more elite

UC campuses began to use a measure of California high school quality as an explicit factor in admissions, with students attending weak high schools having much higher chances of admission to Berkeley and UCLA than otherwise similar students who had attended strong high schools. In other words, ELC became a pipeline not just to the UCs but often to the most elite UCs, who were most worried about their low black and Hispanic numbers.

The following year Berkeley decided something more was needed. In 2003 it announced that the admissions process would be reorganized into a "holistic" system. In the past, admissions officers had used a variety of academic screens to narrow the applicant pool. Under the holistic system, two specially trained readers would examine an application in its entirety, considering every aspect of a student's background and qualifications, and would assign an overall score to that applicant. If the two readers came up with a similar holistic score, then the average of their scores would be the final evaluation of the applicant and would determine his or her place in line for admissions. If the reader scores diverged, a more senior reader would help to determine which "read" would be determinative.

In principle, holistic admissions was far from a radical idea. This was pretty much how admissions had always been done at small liberal arts colleges. In the context of Prop 209, however, holistic admissions was seen—by both supporters and critics—as another way of getting around the ban on racial preferences and increasing minority enrollment. The reader could guess the race of the applicant and let that influence the holistic score, while the admissions office could further hone the correlates of race and instruct readers to give those correlates special weight. As we will see in Chapter Thirteen, the Supreme Court would, in its June 2003 decision in *Grutter v. Bollinger*, contemporaneously endorse holistic admissions as a constitutional method of weighing the overall diversity contributions of individuals (including their race) to academic programs.

The effect of holistic admissions at Berkeley was very modest, both in its racial impact and its academic effects. There was only a slight uptick in black enrollment, and the general level of academic disparity between blacks and Hispanics, compared with everyone else, increased only slightly.

Holistic admissions would soon take on an entirely different cast at UCLA. In the spring of 2006 the *Los Angeles Times* published a front-page story headlined, "A Startling Statistic at UCLA." According to the story, UCLA would be enrolling only 96 blacks among the incoming freshman class, down from 118 the year before. (In the end, 95 blacks would matriculate.) The article quoted Professor Darnell Hunt, a UCLA sociologist and head of the Bunche Center for African American Studies, who contended that Berkeley's "holistic" system was fairer than those used at UCLA and UC San Diego (the next-most elite campus) and produced larger minority—and, in particular, black—enrollments. Hunt criticized the school for using factors of "questionable validity" in rejecting blacks, and the article seemed to endorse his suggestion that something sinister and harmful to minorities was afoot at UCLA.

Over the next several months the issue of declining black enrollment at UCLA became a low-boiling crisis. A widely expressed feeling among faculty, students, and black alumni was that the school had gone from race-neutrality to a regime in which blacks were gradually fading away. Administrators reacted defensively, agreeing that the numbers were alarming and promising to do better.

In reality, there was no crisis. Far from neglecting black applicants, UCLA admissions officers performed elaborate gymnastics to keep black numbers as high as they were. Despite the ban on racial preferences, black freshmen in 2006 entered with a mean SAT score of 1091, compared to 1311 for whites. True, black freshman enrollment at UCLA had fallen from 118 in 2005 to 95 in 2006; but black transfer enrollees had risen by essentially the same amount (from 85 in 2005 to 104 in 2006). True, Berkeley enrolled 148 black freshmen in 2006, but its average black freshman enrollment since Prop 209 had been virtually identical to UCLA's, and UCLA consistently beat Berkeley in the number of black transfers it attracted. Throughout the post-209 period UCLA had the highest aggregate black enrollment of any of the three elite UC campuses.

Much more importantly, black outcomes at UCLA had improved dramatically since the implementation of Prop 209. From 1992 to 1997 entering black freshmen had an average four-year graduation rate of about 20 percent and a six-year graduation rate of about 55 percent; those rates had risen to nearly 40 percent and 70 percent since Prop 209. Indeed, despite the very large impact Prop 209 had on black freshman enrollment at UCLA, the number of blacks actually receiving bachelor degrees from UCLA had declined rather modestly—around 20 percent—from pre-209 levels, and the number of UCLA bachelor degrees going to blacks and Hispanics combined had remained essentially unaffected. And it was true at UCLA, as at the UC campuses generally, that rising graduation rates among blacks and Hispanics were accompanied by rising GPAs and higher concentrations in STEM fields. This was a wonderful story: It meant that UCLA was doing a dramatically better job than before of turning minority students into college graduates with promising futures.

In short, the *Los Angeles Times* story, misleading as it was, provided a perfect learning opportunity for the UC community—a chance to reveal and

FIGURE 10.1. **Minority Enrollment Falls While Graduation Numbers Hold Steady**

Number of black and Hispanic enrollees and B.A. recipients at UCLA, before and after Proposition 209

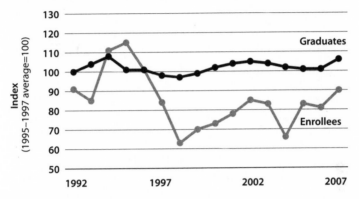

Source: UC Office of the President. Note that the number of graduates is adjusted to parallel freshman cohorts; thus, graduates for the 1992 cohort is an average of those receiving B.A.s in 1996 through 1998. For all years, B.A.s include those received by students transferring to UCLA.

explain how the prohibition on explicit racial preferences had become on the UC campuses a way of preserving and enhancing opportunity; how, of all groups affected by Prop 209, the greatest beneficiaries had been blacks and Hispanics in substantively improved outcomes; how rising yield rates among those groups provided implicit confirmation of this truth.

But the leaders of UCLA did not do this. Though one of us (Sander) knows many of these leaders personally and truly admires the wisdom and moral purpose of each of those he knows, the leadership exercised in this case fell seriously short. UCLA leaders sought to ally themselves with those accusing the campus of racism and promised to make reforms.

We have an unusual window into what happened next because of an aide-memoire produced in 2008 by Tim Groseclose, a political scientist at UCLA and a member of its admissions committee from 2004 until 2007. Groseclose is right of center and therefore sometimes at odds with his more liberal colleagues, but he is an eminent scholar and his account remains, so far as we know, completely undisputed.

According to Groseclose, UCLA's chancellor Norman Abrams asked to meet in the early fall of 2006 with UCLA's Committee on Undergraduate

Admissions and Relations with Schools (CUARS). Groseclose reported
Abrams's opening remarks as follows:

> First, I want to say how much I favor and respect faculty governance. I
> don't want to pressure you. But at the same time, we worry about many
> of the same things. I want to report to you what we are hearing from the
> outside world. Several constituencies of UCLA are distressed and upset
> about the very low numbers of African American freshmen. The politi-
> cal angst and concern is enormous. I don't feel the pressure. I sublimate
> very well. But there is pressure exerted upon me. The numbers of
> underrepresented minorities on campus are too small. . . . I ask that you
> make the whole admissions process holistic. Not only that, I have a fur-
> ther request: This is that you do it quickly and adopt the exact same
> process that Berkeley currently uses.

Soon afterward CUARS voted to move UCLA toward the Berkeley holistic system. Groseclose (along with an African American colleague) voted
against the proposal. Groseclose argued that holistic admissions, especially in
this environment, would open up opportunities to engage in forms of discrimination prohibited by Prop 209. In relatively short order, the admissions
staff had started setting up the mechanisms for holistic admissions, including
the hiring of many part-time readers to do the intensive "holistic reads" of
individual files. Groseclose soon learned that of the 160 readers hired to
handle the job, 40 were African American (in a labor market where black college graduates made up about 7 percent of the total pool). Asian readers were
underrepresented.

Six months later, in the spring of 2007, UCLA announced a dramatic
increase in African American freshman enrollment for the coming year—an
exact doubling, from 95 to 190. The mood of campus administrators was cel-
ebratory; it was not generally pointed out that Hispanic freshman enrollment
at UCLA, which had been at or close to pre-209 levels for several years,
slightly dipped. Clearly other forces besides the change to holistic admissions
had played a role. Abrams and other campus leaders had mobilized black
alumni to help improve recruitment among talented black high school students and to develop private funding sources that could channel recruitment
scholarships to blacks accepted by the campus.

Still, the question remained what role admissions had played. In another
New York Times magazine article, this one in September 2007, David Leonhardt generally praised UCLA's efforts to foster opportunities for blacks, but
noted, "The big question that hangs over UCLA's success, of course, is

whether the university broke the law. Looking at the numbers, it's hard not to conclude that race was a factor in this year's admissions decisions." The key numbers Leonhardt pointed out were the SAT scores of admitted students, which fell sharply for blacks while holding steady for other racial groups. This, along with the dip in Hispanic enrollment and the 50 percent jump in the black admission rate, was damning indeed. If the purpose of the holistic process was to do a better job of considering one's success in overcoming personal disadvantage, how could it produce huge jumps in black admissions while leaving Hispanics—who, in California, are fully as disadvantaged as blacks—untouched?

Groseclose wanted to look closely at the numbers, and he asked the staff director of admissions to provide him a sample from the university's admissions data covering several hundred students from before and after the "holistic" era. He received a variety of deflecting responses. The director expressed his view that "we should not study or do any analysis of holistic admissions at UCLA until we have at least four or five years of the outcome to avoid normal annual fluctuations." The faculty chair of CUARS suggested that although a study was a good idea, it would be best if done by CUARS as a whole rather than by individual faculty. This implied that no individual faculty member would actually get the raw data. Groseclose brought matters to a head by introducing a formal motion that all faculty members of a workgroup on the consequences of holistic admission be given an anonymous database of a sample of applications. His motion failed on a 3–3 vote.

Eventually, the committee determined (in consultation with campus administrators) that UCLA should retain an empirical specialist to study the effect of the holistic process. The administration offered to fund the study at $100,000. Groseclose, who was a distinguished empiricist and thought the key analytic questions were quite simple, offered to do the study for free on condition that the entire CUARS committee could have access to the data. His offer was declined. Groseclose's inference was that the university was unwilling to have a skeptical faculty member of its own admissions committee scrutinize a process that had produced suspiciously discriminatory results. Groseclose resigned in protest over this lack of transparency in September 2008.

Groseclose's resignation made local news, and Sander was keenly interested in the story. Soon afterward they met for the first time. Sander had just had some success (in collaboration with others) shaking loose pre- and post-209 data on student outcomes from the UC Office of the President; perhaps the two of them could secure data on holistic admissions through a public records request? They did and, in due course, secured a dataset in many ways superior to the one Groseclose had initially sought (e.g., it included all applicants, not just a sample). UCLA provided Groseclose and Sander with a dataset containing roughly twenty variables on every applicant to UCLA during the three years before holistic admissions began (2004–2006) and the first three years of its implementation (2007–2009).

The admissions data files did indeed show that UCLA had restored explicit racial preferences with the introduction of holistic admissions in 2007. Blacks were admitted under standards different not only from those applied to whites and Asians but even from those applied to Hispanics. But the actual mechanism of discrimination was surprising. The holistic process helped black and Hispanic applicants because, other things being equal, students who went to weaker public schools or had less affluent parents received stronger evaluations. It helped them further in ways that our data could not capture—perhaps through the stories of disadvantage told in their essays or from the holistic readers' subjective evaluations of letters of recommendation. All told, blacks and Hispanics with a particular academic index were twice as likely to get a holistic score strong enough for admission as were whites and Asians with similar academic indices.

But as it turned out, the holistic system had been oversold. The preholistic system had already been capturing the same sorts of "soft" factors—sympathetic personal histories, family hardship, and so on—that conferred racial dividends in the holistic system. The special readers UCLA hired to do the holistic scoring were not—at least to any measureable degree—"cheating" in favor of black applicants. As at Berkeley, holistic admissions by itself would barely budge UCLA's admissions rate for black applicants. This was not an acceptable outcome for those running the admissions system. They had been urged in the strongest possible terms to produce more black freshmen.

We cannot say exactly what happened next. We can say two things with certainty. First, blacks with middling or poor holistic scores were admitted at rates far higher than those of any other racial group. Second, the particular black applicants admitted tended to be those who had attended UCLA outreach sessions.

Here is our speculation about what happened. UCLA admission officers found the results of the holistic method disappointing. The holistic process generated some racial dividend, but no more than the preholistic system and certainly not enough to produce the dramatic increase in black freshmen they wanted. So as they reviewed files in particular holistic ranges, they set aside those of blacks and, to a lesser extent, Hispanics that they remembered from outreach sessions. These students would be admitted despite their modest holistic scores.

The upshot was that over a quarter of all blacks admitted to UCLA during the holistic period had *holistic* scores that were ordinarily disqualifying. The same was true for only about 4 percent of East Asian admits and about 6 percent of the white admits. Of the total increase in black enrollment produced by all of the extraordinary efforts launched in 2006, it appears that perhaps one-quarter came from recruiting a stronger applicant pool, one-quarter came from more effectively wooing those who were accepted, and one-half came from explicit racial preferences. These last tended, of course, to be applicants with particularly weak academic preparation and, thus, a particularly acute vulnerability to mismatch.

* * *

UC San Diego (UCSD) is generally regarded as the new "star" in the University of California firmament. Over the past thirty years it has built extraordinarily strong science departments, and in recent years it has often eclipsed UCLA in national or worldwide rankings. It has also become, in admissions, by far the most selective UC campus after Berkeley and UCLA. In racial matters, however, UCSD was seen as the campus least concerned with diversity. Even before Prop 209, UCSD used much smaller racial preferences than did UCLA or Berkeley, and after Prop 209's implementation it had notoriously admitted a class (the freshman matriculants of 1998) in which blacks had virtually the same objective qualifications (and subsequently the same performance) as white students. Characteristically, USCD got no credit for this achievement; it was instead criticized for matriculating only fifty black freshmen. And throughout the decade after Prop 209's implementation, central administrators often regarded UCSD with vague suspicion on racial matters.

The fuse was thus set for ignition in the winter of 2010, when a group of white and Asian fraternity students at UCSD had, off campus, a social event billed as the "Compton cookout." The students had apparently held a series of outdoor picnics featuring and making low-key fun of a variety of cuisines. "Compton" referred to a working-class black neighborhood in Los Angeles that had gained some notoriety during the 1992 Los Angeles riots, and the "Compton cookout" featured both authentic and stereotypical black dishes. The event was both sophomoric and offensive, and when word of it reached campus groups, the reaction was one of predictable outrage and condemnation. Matters were further inflamed when a student discovered a noose lying on a shelf in the university library; although it turned out that the noose had been put there by an Hispanic student trying to make a political statement and seeking to convey her own feeling of vulnerability, this fact was widely ignored, and the two events were conflated into proof that racism was wide-spread and out of control on the UCSD campus.

These events precipitated a reaction among the university-wide leadership similar in nature though much larger in scale and consequence to the reaction at UCLA when the number of black freshmen fell below one hundred. Almost immediately there was talk of requiring UCSD to adopt the same holistic admission system used by UCLA and Berkeley. This broadened into the idea that all the UC undergraduate programs (which, since the opening of UC Merced in 2004, now numbered nine) should adopt holistic admissions—a proposal that UC authorities formalized and adopted in the winter of 2011.

Almost at the same time the university decided to expand Eligibility in the Local Context so that the top 9 percent (rather than the top 4 percent) of students at each public high school would be eligible for UC admission. This meant that the university could no longer guarantee enrollment to other students who placed in the top eighth of high school seniors statewide, and it meant that, for many students, the single-most promising path to UC was to attend a public school with academically weak classmates.

The university had the full support of the UC regents in taking these steps. The personnel of the regents had completely turned over since the mid-1990s heyday of race neutrality, and most of the regents wanted the university to do more—not less—to promote black and Hispanic enrollment. Influential state legislators regularly pressed university officials to be more aggressive in pursuing diversity, and three times the state assembly and state senate passed bills that directed the university to take race into account in UC admissions. (All three bills were vetoed by Governors Schwarzenegger and Brown as in conflict with the California Constitution, as modified by Prop 209.) UCOP leaders knew that they would face minimal resistance and perhaps receive rewards for efforts to use any devices available to increase black and Hispanic representation.

Meanwhile, back at UC San Diego, administrators had determined that an effective way to inject more racial diversity into the school was to lower entrance requirements for transfer students. By the 2011–2012 academic year it was possible to transfer to UCSD with a B average in community college courses. The racial dividend was modest—most beneficiaries of the easier transfer policy were white and Asian—and the lowering of academic standards was disturbing to many faculty. In the fall of 2011 one of us met with a distinguished professor who had been dragooned onto the admissions committee. She was not pleased with the logic of a policy that substantially increased the number of academically weak students at UCSD while having only a small impact on the school's overall diversity. She shook her head and sighed, "One question is whether racial preferences are a good thing. Another question entirely is whether we can get rid of racial preferences without self-destructing as an institution."

* * *

At this writing, the University of California system is still, formally, race-neutral, but in practice it has come very close to a form of racial proportionality. The university still requires all freshman admittees to be high school graduates and to have completed a standard "college-prep" high school curriculum (e.g., at least three years in high school of English and math). When one examines the pool of California public high school graduates who have completed the core curriculum, Hispanics and blacks are as likely as whites to go on to a UC campus, even though the disparity in test scores and grades remains quite large.

The quest for racial diversity without (in general) the explicit use of race means that the university scoops up many academically weak students in the hope that a disproportionate fraction of them will be black or Hispanic. As these devices move from the margins to the center of campus admissions policies, we are starting to observe an even wider academic gulf between the most-prepared and least-prepared students than existed before Prop 209. And because most of the work-around devices are formally race-neutral, they also bring into the system many whites and Asians with weak academic preparation. Students of all races still tend to be sorted across the UC campuses in a way more closely related to their level of academic preparation than was the case before Prop 209. But gaps in academic preparation within campuses are large and resurgent. Mismatch is likely to grow and to be more multiracial now than it was before Prop 209.

We should thus expect in coming years to see at least a partial reversal of the academic improvements for black and Hispanic students that were so notable in the immediate post-209 period. It is difficult at this writing to tell what has happened, partly because the most dramatic steps aimed at producing racial dividends have just been implemented and partly because the university has clamped down even further on its release of information. For example, at UCLA Law School the initial classes admitted to the school's Critical Race Studies program had quite poor bar results, comparable to or even worse than those received by blacks and Hispanics in the pre-209 era. But as of 2006 the school stopped making available detailed information on the school's bar passage outcomes even to its own faculty. The school's total bar passage rate plunged in 2009—clearly in significant part because of the school's covert diversity efforts—but a report analyzing the decline was bowd-lerized before being released to the faculty. Boalt Law School experienced a similar, precipitous decline in bar passage rates as it reintroduced covert racial preferences. Both schools have stonewalled public records requests aimed at making it possible to study carefully the link between large preferences and poor bar outcomes.

* * *

All of this tells us that neither voters nor state officials can end university racial preferences by a single stroke. Like the ancient Hydra of Greek myth, two heads are likely to grow in place of the original.

The University of California is by no means a special case in this regard. In Michigan, voters approved a 2006 referendum that was virtually identical to Prop 209. Mary Sue Coleman, the president of the University of Michigan, announced the next day that the university would not be deterred in its quest for diversity. In the months that followed, university officials spoke of using a new system, called "Descriptor Plus" (developed by the College Board) as a way of preserving the school's diversity. The Descriptor Plus system used techniques similar to those common in the marketing business to divide neighborhoods and high schools into clusters with very similar characteristics. The College Board reported the detailed demography of each cluster along with the neighborhood and school clusters to which each student taking the SAT belonged. A school wanting to admit blacks, for example, could simply assign extra weight to students from black neighborhood or high school clusters.

After a typically lengthy negotiation, we obtained from the University of Michigan admissions data on freshman applicants for 2006, before the passage of Prop 2, and for 2008, after Prop 2 had been implemented. The results were surprising. The university made some use of the Descriptor Plus categories, but not much. So far as we could tell from the data—and in our opinion, the data was strong enough to sustain a suit against the university—admissions officers were simply continuing to use unadulterated racial preferences. Descriptor Plus might be a race substitute, but for the most part it was a screen for business as usual.

* * *

Proposition 209 had three major effects upon the University of California. First, it prompted a rise in applications and yield rates that was particularly remarkable and impressive among black and Hispanic students. Second, the cascading of black and Hispanic students led to campuses where their credentials more closely matched those of white and Asian students lowered their numbers at the elite campuses but led to improved academic outcomes and, most notably, higher graduation rates. But third, university officials generally ignored the good news and instead introduced a series of measures—many of them probably legal but some clearly not—that sought either to produce racial dividends in enrollment or to use racial preferences covertly.

We can now appreciate some of the complexities of the situation that higher education has gotten itself into. Racial preferences produce perverse consequences—not only mismatch but also stigma and many other problems we have discussed. However, a simple abolition of racial preferences produces perverse consequences as well: In particular, it produces evasive maneuvers by universities that can accentuate the mismatch problem. If a school uses large racial preferences to achieve a student body that is 10 percent black, a moment's reflection makes it obvious that any *indirect* method of achieving the same goal will require still larger preferences. A school that is determined to offset a ban on racial preferences fully through racial substitutes will merely aggravate the mismatch problem.

Universities are generally reluctant to make available information on admissions and student outcomes, no doubt in large part because of the large size of racial preferences and the poor outcomes of many students admitted with those preferences. When we add a legal ban on preferences into the mix, the incentives for concealing information grow. Although we and our colleagues did eventually obtain enough data from the University of California to demonstrate many of the findings discussed in the past few chapters, the datasets made available to us were heavily censored. We can see enough to verify that mismatch is a serious problem at the University of California that was somewhat ameliorated by Prop 209, but the data lacks sufficient detail to answer many important questions, such as the point at which preferences are small enough to be academically benign.

Any reader capable of being persuaded by evidence should recognize by this point in our story that the mismatch problem is real. But diagnosing its exact dimensions requires better data, and it is not clear that a simple legal ban on preferences is either a necessary or workable solution. We now turn to an exploration of some of the institutional dynamics—in higher education and among those who are supposed to provide oversight and accountability for higher education—to dig more deeply into the problems.

IV.

LAW AND IDEOLOGY

CHAPTER ELEVEN

WHY ACADEMICS AVOID HONEST DEBATE ABOUT AFFIRMATIVE ACTION

I N PART II WE EXPLORED THE social science evidence on mismatch, and in Part III we saw the effects of Prop 209 in reducing mismatch at the University of California. The evidence is powerful; indeed, the evidence that large racial preferences have counterproductive effects is as powerful as any body of evidence we know on *any* issue in higher education. But as we have seen, that evidence has, to date, had little effect on actual practices. The vast majority of academics and university administrators have seemed determined to look away from the harm done by large racial preferences.

Part IV considers why reform has been difficult and examines in turn how a series of mechanisms that might ordinarily further reform have not worked well in the realm of racial preferences. We begin, in this chapter, with academia itself. The "academy" is supposed to be a realm in which all ideas can be advanced in free and open discourse, in which data matters and smart people struggle toward understanding. Yet these hallmarks of healthy exchange seem absent in debates on affirmative action. Why? It is easy and tempting to put the problem down to "political correctness" and a simple intolerance of dissent. But we hope in these pages to dig more deeply and identify some of the specific mechanisms that contribute to the impoverished dialogue. We start by chronicling a recent episode that captures why the free exchange of ideas on campuses is, in this realm, so terribly constricted.

* * *

In April 2011 three scholars from Duke, Peter Arcidiacono, Esteban Aucejo, and Kenneth Spenner, posted online a paper titled, "What Happens After Enrollment?" They sought to answer a question of great importance to anyone hoping to evaluate the real-world impact of racial preferences on their supposed beneficiaries: Do students who receive large admissions preferences "catch up" with their peers over their college years? If they did, this would obviously strengthen the case for the current racial-preference regime. And indeed, aggregate data at Duke suggested at first blush that the GPA gap across racial groups was narrowing as college progressed, from a black-white GPA gap of over half a point in the first semester to less than three-tenths of a point by the eighth semester.

But the three scholars determined that this narrowing was illusory; it seemed that courses taken by juniors and seniors were graded more leniently than earlier courses, and more importantly, students who received bad grades in their freshman year migrated in large numbers from STEM fields and economics to other majors, which generally had easier grading. When one adjusted for these effects, the relative achievement level of different groups was unchanged over the course of college. Thus, not only was there a significant science mismatch effect at Duke—students with low entering credentials were leaving technical majors in large numbers—but there was also no silver lining of academic "catching up" to offset the science mismatch effect.

Importantly, the authors found that these patterns had nothing to do with race but rather with a student's level of academic preparation upon entry into Duke. White legacies admitted with preferences showed the same patterns as blacks admitted with (usually larger) preferences.

The paper offered no policy recommendations; it simply presented intriguing results in a clear and empirically careful way. Nor were the findings themselves startling; if anything, they showed that earlier research about science mismatch and the persistence of poor performance held up strongly with the new data and methods these authors brought to bear. The paper generated some discussion among scholars in the field and began to wend its way through the peer-review process leading to publication. (It was accepted for publication in June 2012 by the *IZA Journal of Labor Economics*.)

Then, in mid-January 2012 "What Happens After Enrollment?" was lifted from relative obscurity by the *Chronicle of Higher Education*, which ran a story on the study. As news of the study and its citation in a Supreme Court brief (ours) began to circulate at Duke, the reaction was extreme. The university's Black Student Alliance denounced the research, saying in a letter to the state NAACP that the "implications and intentions of this work at the hands of our own very prestigious faculty, seemingly without a genuine concern for proactively furthering the welfare of the black community is hurtful and alienating" and suggesting that the research would tarnish "the image . . . of Duke and its black students." The Alliance also called on Duke's administration to provide a "complete public account" of Duke's "effort to provide an optimal learning environment for black students" and "provide a public affirmation of the university's commitment to diversity as well as its full support for policies and programs that promote the success of black students."

Members of the Alliance staged a protest outside Duke Chapel after the university's annual Martin Luther King Jr. service. Students passed out fliers saying, "Duke: A hostile environment for its black students?" and "Does GPA have a color?" Seventeen black alumni wrote an open letter attacking the research as "misguided scholarship" whose results and methodology were "both flawed and incorrect," though they provided no specifics. "We cannot sit idly by and allow this slander to be (mis)labeled as truth," they wrote.

Local media covered these events, and the Arcidiacono-Aucejo-Spenner paper became a major campus issue. Duke faculty sent angry e-mails to the authors and the economics department, objecting to the insensitivity of the research. Then several top Duke administrators, headed by Provost Peter Lange and Vice Provost Steve Nowicki, declared in a letter to the Duke community that "the conclusions of the research paper *can be interpreted in ways that reinforce negative stereotypes*" (emphasis added). The administrators went on to note that "our goal of academic success for all should not inhibit research and discussion to clarify important issues of academic choice and achievement" and that "there is no 'easy' major at Duke."

Richard Brodhead, the president of Duke, weighed in on the controversy on March 22 at the Annual Meeting of University Faculty. He said he had decided to devote his talk to the issue of race in part because of the controversy the study generated. He extolled the university's progress in moving from exclusionary policies in the 1950s and before to having among the highest proportion of enrolled blacks of any elite university today. Turning to the Arcidiacono-Aucejo-Spenner paper, Brodhead said,

> With respect to this January's controversy I would say the following.
> I hope all members of this community recognize that it is not the
> proper function of the university to block expression from its faculty or

enforce a correct view. Universities live through free and open debate; when someone thinks someone else has come to an erroneous conclusion, the remedy is to criticize it and offer a better account. . . . On the other hand, I can see why students took offense at what was reported of a professor's work. Generalizations about academic choices by racial category can renew the primal insult of the world we are trying to leave behind—the implication that persons can be known through a group identity that associates them with inferior powers. A further insult was that the paper had been included in an amicus brief submitted by opponents of affirmative action urging the Supreme Court to hear [the *Fisher* case].

It was bad enough that Brodhead made no attempt to deal substantively with the problems Arcidiacono, Aucejo, and Spenner had identified. Much worse was the unmistakable import of Brodhead's words, even more than those of Lange and Nowicki, that Arcidiacono and his coauthors had engaged in research that was at best insensitive and at worst reckless and incorrect. Strikingly, Brodhead seemed to invoke academic freedom not to protect the professors—who felt hurt and stigmatized by the university's actions—but Brodhead himself, as if to say that he might like to retaliate against the professors more directly, but academic freedom must stay his hand. His words also implied that research for its own sake would be tolerated but that to actually use research findings in a public policy debate (i.e., a Supreme Court brief) was going too far.

Interestingly, behind the scenes there was no sign of official disfavor toward Arcidiacono, Aucejo, and Spenner. On the contrary, the university had provided the data the authors used in their paper, and administration officials seemed anxious to let them know that there were no hard feelings. Certainly no one ever suggested that there was anything incorrect in their findings or even anything improperly phrased. The public criticism, it seemed, was all for show.

We cite these events not because they are unusual but because they are so quintessentially typical. Research that documents the workings of racial preferences seems to experience one of two fates: It is either ignored or it is subject to ritualistic denunciations. One of us (Sander) could recount experiences at UCLA, following his own research on law school mismatch, that almost perfectly parallel—even in many of the words used—the events at Duke.

It is tempting to write off things like Brodhead's speech as a necessary gesture to campus politics. But politics, in the end, is supposed to be about leadership and about moving from social argument toward institutional solutions. Imagine if Brodhead had said something like this:

Arcidiacono, Aucejo, and Spenner have done exemplary research here. Their data are accurate, and other experts tell me that their analysis is correct on every point. Importantly, they have demonstrated that race itself does not affect outcomes at Duke, validating our efforts to create an environment where discrimination is either absent altogether or so minimal as not to affect academic performance. But they have also demonstrated that relative levels of academic preparation do matter, not for every individual but in a way that is somewhat predictable when we look across large numbers of students. They matter not only for grades but perhaps for learning itself, and apparently they have an influence on one's choice of major and chances of successfully sticking with that major. This merits further research, but assuming these findings hold up, they suggest three things that we in the administration should be doing.

First, we should provide academic support counseling for students who wish to pursue STEM fields but enter Duke with lower-than-average levels of academic preparation. Through careful and rigorously evaluated support efforts, we may be able to improve successful persistence in these fields. Second, we should work with our sister institutions to evaluate how students who struggle at Duke would have fared at other schools, and we should all pool data to evaluate postgraduate outcomes so that we better understand how the tradeoffs that students encounter at Duke affect their long-term success and career goals. And third, as we learn more, we should make those findings transparent to our applicants. If a high school senior we choose to admit hopes to become a physicist, we should help that student have the best possible information about his actual prospects at Duke so that she can weigh the advantages and disadvantages of coming here rather than some other school. This transparency is not only fairer to our students, but I can think of no better way of maintaining accountability among Duke's administrators and faculty.

Words in this vein would be both moral and intellectually honest. Our concern in this chapter is with why, exactly, university leaders find it impossible to say them.

* * *

To begin with, there is a profound and shared awareness among Americans—and especially among American elites—that the United States has successfully passed through a stunning transformation of racial attitudes over the past seventy years. Widespread norms of equality have replaced a racial caste system resting on assumptions of racial inferiority. We are all aware that pockets of racism still exist and that many racial stereotypes flourish, and many—particularly but not only on the left—fear that racism could be resurgent (the feared "counterrevolution" of aggrieved whites, as one sometimes sees in European nationalist movements). Academics and journalists are particularly aware of this as well as of their own roles in helping to foster and solidify the comparatively recent and enormously important norms of racial equality.

But although equality of opportunity has come a long way, even a rough equality of results has proven very elusive. As Peter Schuck has noted, "The cruel legacy of 250 years of slavery in America has proved more stubborn than even Frederick Douglass, a former slave and consummate realist, imagined." The evidence is not hard to find: Black-white segregation is very high in most large cities; black households are more than three times as likely as non-Hispanic whites to have incomes below the poverty line; the black-white test-score gap (as we explore in Chapter Seventeen) is wide and has barely changed over the past generation. Taking race into account to produce diverse college campuses is an intuitively appealing way both to chip away at substantive racial inequality and to create a visible sense that the civil rights revolution has succeeded and that (name the college of your choice) has embraced that revolution.

But once racial preferences exist, how can one discuss them? To acknowledge that they exist, even to hint at how large they are, necessarily brings attention to racial differences in performance. And to acknowledge racial differences in performance can, simplistically, seem like talk about *intrinsic* racial differences. Even when the interlocutor makes an effort to allay this concern specifically, there can lurk the suspicion that the person advancing this thesis harbors a secret agenda.

The label "racist" is the most potent and feared epithet in contemporary American discourse—certainly within the elite and even through much of the general population. It has many of the same effects as did conventional racial epithets in the mid-twentieth century. "Racist" implies intellectual backwardness, an unfitness to live within civilized society, certainly a profound disqualification to hold any institutional role in modern America. And it has considerable psychological power as well—for what self-respecting citizen could live with the burden of wondering if he is, in some inner recess, an unreconstructed racist?

Individual academics, journalists, and other social elites therefore have a profound aversion to saying or doing anything that can bring them anywhere near the "danger zone" of being called or even perceived as racially insensitive or racist. Indeed, many understandably seize opportunities to demonstrate to others (and perhaps themselves?) that they are fully aligned with the racial enlightenment.

For those leading college campuses, then, there are obvious reasons of self-interest, even self-preservation, to steer clear of candidly discussing the consequences of racial admissions preferences—or even to acknowledge their existence. There are other motives as well. Questioning racial preferences—or documenting their effects—will both inflict emotional distress upon minority students and anger them, as the events at Duke illustrate. The emotional distress should be of concern to any feeling person. The anger can threaten racial peace on campus. Nearly all higher education leaders as well as a great many other academics came of age or are keenly familiar with the disruptive campus years of the late 1960s and early 1970s, when many universities essentially lost control of their campuses. The most enduring source of campus strife has been racial grievance, and many affirmative action programs and other racial initiatives (ethnic studies programs, special funding for race-related programs, racially themed dorms, etc.) are seen as ways of maintaining racial peace. University leaders realize that the "peace" is fragile; they see maintaining this peace as a key part of their job.

For a university leader, these sorts of considerations obviously militate against candid discussion of racial preferences and in favor, instead, of passing over their existence or, if that is impossible, at least denying their relevance to academic performance. Emphasizing the talent of each new class and the ability of every student to do great things are understandable ingredients of every welcoming address to new freshmen. As we discussed in Chapter Six, leaving students who receive large preferences with the impression that they have every reason to succeed—and no excuse to fail—can have paralyzing and alienating effects once students realize that they (and other minority students) are having academic trouble. But it is easy for administrators to convince themselves that acknowledging these possibilities would be harmful and destructive to the students.

All of which feeds back into self-interest. In modern university culture the ability to negotiate campus racial politics successfully is highly prized. When the University of Michigan was sued in the late 1990s for two of its racial preference programs, officials managed the crisis so deftly that both the president and the provost were widely praised, and their success was often cited as one reason that both were hired away to still loftier academic posts. Conversely, university leaders who show insufficient skill in promoting affirmative action goals, such as the recent case of a "politically tone deaf" chancellor at the University of Massachusetts, Amherst, often find their jobs in jeopardy.

The confluence of these factors creates a sort of code of silence on campuses about matters related to racial preferences. And the code is self-reinforcing. Surveys have found that half or more of university professors and administrators are dismayed by the workings of racial preferences and would, in principle, be sympathetic to reform. But many of the same people are in practice hostile to even discussing reform because they see it as a nonstarter that has negative consequences (disturbing racial peace) but no positive consequences (because no internal reform is possible).

As if all this were not enough, there is one more set of factors inhibiting discussion about racial preferences: the intellectual and emotional tensions that, for many academics, suffuse the subject. These come in several varieties, but perhaps the most common one is the paradox noted by Justice Harry Blackmun in 1978: "In order to get beyond racism, we must first take account of race. There is no other way. And in order to treat some persons equally, we must treat them differently." But once one legitimizes the process of taking race into account, how does one get past it? As Peter Schuck notes, "Racial essentialization utterly contradicts liberal, egalitarian, legal, scientific, and religious values [holding] that all individuals are unique and formally equal regardless of genetic heritage, and that their race causally determines little or nothing about their character, intelligence, experience, or anything else that is relevant to their diversity-value." Orlando Patterson similarly observes that "When they are not proving that 'race' as a concept has no scientific meaning, most social scientists and even medical researchers are busily controlling away all other variables in a relentless effort to prove that one, and only one, variable explains the condition of Afro-Americans: 'race.'" The internal contradictions in these attitudes perfectly mirror the norm that although racial preferences might be not only desirable but also necessary as a social policy, looking too closely at the inequalities that preferences produce—inequalities *within* the college campus—is taboo.

Then there is what Jonathan Haidt described in an interview as the "sacralization" of historically downtrodden groups:

> I think the New Left, the commitment that was made in the '60s, was toward victim groups. So it was civil rights, women's rights, gay rights. Now these were all incredibly important battles that had to be fought. [But] follow the sacredness. If you sacralize these groups, it makes you, it binds you together to fight for them. So the sacralization had to happen, the sacralization of victim groups had to happen to bring the left together to fight what was a truly altruistic and heroic battle. And they won, and things are now better in this country because of that. But,

follow the sacredness. Once you've sacralized something, *you become blind to evidence.* . . . You can't see it because you've sacralized a group. Anything that seems to be helping that group, anything our group says is going to help them, you go with. [emphasis added]

Finally, there is the awkward position of black faculty, who are often particularly aware of difficulties black students experience but feel a special pressure not to "break ranks" on preference issues. Carol Swain, the Vanderbilt political scientist we met in Chapter Six, recalls that when, as a member of the Princeton faculty, she began criticizing racial preferences: "Everything just shut down. . . . People started distancing themselves from me. . . . The liberals made it very clear, 'How dare you criticize affirmative action when you are a product of affirmative action?' My response was, 'There's not much I can do about that.'"

There are, in short, a whole host of interlocking attitudes and forces that make it extraordinarily difficult for either university leaders or even individual faculty to broach discussion on the effects of racial preferences. "Happy talk" about diversity is favored; critical reflection is downright dangerous. And when critical reflection is absent even from private conversation, it is easy to overlook what would otherwise be patently obvious. This helps explain why even thoughtful and principled people at the University of California often ignored evidence and pushed to evade or repeal a ban on racial preferences that was, in nearly every objective sense, benefiting the black and Hispanic students these people wanted to help.

All of these dynamics are, of course, exacerbated, as they often are when facts are suppressed and dissenters are ostracized by people who are *not* acting in good faith but rather exploiting campus politics for their own personal or ideological reasons. Consider, for example, another recent episode, this one from Wisconsin.

In 2002 the Supreme Court of Wisconsin decided in *Osborn v. University of Wisconsin* that the university (UW) could be compelled, under Wisconsin's Freedom of Information laws, to disclose to members of the public detailed information about the admissions and educational outcomes of its students while maintaining the students' privacy. The Center for Equal Opportunity (CEO) was a coplaintiff and principal funder of the litigation. CEO's general mission is to work against racial classifications in the law, sometimes through policy advocacy and sometimes through investigative research on preference programs.

Data from UW was eventually forthcoming; CEO performed two analyses of the admissions data, essentially finding that UW used the largest racial preferences of any of the many public universities CEO had studied, and in September 2011 CEO's president, Roger Clegg, scheduled a press conference in Madison, Wisconsin, to release the research results. Emeritus UW economics professor Lee Hansen was also on hand to discuss Clegg's findings.

During the press conference, a large number of UW students entered the hotel, overpowered hotel staff outside the press conference room, and stormed the room. Clegg, Hansen, and two members of the hotel staff quickly retreated out a side exit and headed to a hotel elevator, followed by angry students. When an elevator arrived and Clegg and Hansen got on, several of the protestors prevented the elevator doors from closing until hotel staff pushed them back.

Part of what made this scene striking was the role of UW's vice provost for Diversity and Climate, Damon Williams, in fomenting the disturbance. The day before the press conference Williams posted an "Important Invitation to Students" on the university's Creating Community website. The message warned of "a threat to our diversity efforts." At a subsequent rally, Williams urged the students to mobilize and told them, "Don't wait for us to show the way." He also told the students that "CEO has one mission and one mission only: dismantle the gains that were achieved by the civil-rights movement." Williams was not at the hotel when the press conference was disrupted, but he afterward tweeted his praise of the protesters from his official university account: "Students were awesome."

* * *

We see no obvious way of easily or quickly changing the dynamics we've described in this chapter. More than one university leader has confided to us that they feel trapped by a combination of forces that even courageous leadership cannot easily surmount. We therefore cannot expect normal academic processes to produce internal reform of mismatch or the other problems that come with racial preferences. From this, it follows that some external authority must mandate full public disclosure of the role of preferential admissions programs on a sufficiently wide scale and in sufficient detail to make the basic operation and effects of preferences well known and obvious. This would empower a broader community to engage in dialogue about racial preferences and the effects they produce, thereby pushing campus conversations in helpful directions and making the simple denials of reality that are so pervasive today much harder to sustain.

CHAPTER TWELVE

MEDIA, POLITICS, AND
THE ACCOUNTABILITY VOID

IN JUNE 2011 THE *NEW YORK TIMES* ran a long, front-page story about an increasingly common dilemma in college admissions offices: the problem of multiracial candidates. It told the story of Natasha Scott, a high school senior who had an Asian mother and a black father. What racial box should she check on her college applications? She sought out guidance on College Confidential, an "electronic bulletin board for anonymous conversation about admissions." Scott wrote, "It pains me to say this, but putting down black might help my admissions chances and putting down Asian might hurt it. My mother urges me to put down black to use AA to get in to the colleges I'm applying to . . . I sort of want to do this but I'm wondering if this is morally right." As the article noted, "Within minutes, a commentator had responded, 'You're black. You should own it.' Someone else agreed, 'Put black!!!!!!! Listen to your mom.'"

It was an interesting and timely story, highlighting an important moral problem for applicants and colleges alike. Of course, the heart of the dilemma lies in the very large size of racial preferences: Checking "black" versus "Asian" could easily mean the difference between getting into a 5th-ranked or 105th-ranked college. But when it came to specifics about racial preferences, the article faltered. "There are several thousand applicants whose fate might still be in limbo by the committee round because their qualifications can seem fairly indistinguishable from one another. This is when an applicant's race— or races—might tip the balance."

Any reader who has followed our story this far knows that the authors of this story (Susan Saulny and Jacques Steinberg) had, at this point, shifted from the realm of fact to the realm of myth. In failing to report the true magnitude of racial preferences, they were following a well-worn tradition in journalism. But this case is particularly interesting because up to this point the reporters' story had been candid and searching, and in suggesting that racial preferences were a tie-breaking exercise, they undercut the entire point of their article. Saulny and Steinberg had the perfect set-up for identifying a growing and obvious flaw in the racial preference system—making radically different admissions criteria turn on increasingly arbitrary racial categories. The reporters had the opportunity to paint a true picture of how colleges use racial preferences, and instead they painted a false one.

A hallmark of the American system is its supposed ability to create accountability. When an institution seems to lose its moral compass— whether it be a White House creating its own surveillance operations or Apple subcontractors engaging in dubious labor practices—there are a number of more or less effective mechanisms for calling out the bad behavior and documenting problems for all the world to see. The news media, especially print journalism, sometimes play this role well. So, sometimes, do such governmental institutions as the congressional investigation. An obvious question raised by the findings in this book is why the problems we document have not been vividly exposed. If preference systems generate the bad outcomes we claim and if racially segregated admissions are pervasive and actually hurt blacks and Hispanics more than they help them, why isn't this universally known?

This chapter considers why the regime of racial preferences in college admissions seems to enjoy an unusually protected status even among those who make a living exposing wayward people and institutions.

* * *

We argued in Chapter Eleven that despite the university's traditional role as a forum for robust debate and unfettered exchange of ideas, academic discourse on racial preferences is thoroughly dysfunctional. The evidence below suggests that similar mechanisms, pressures, and orthodoxies mute the nature of coverage and ideas in journalism because journalists are part of a leadership corps in society in which the importance of "correct" thinking about affirmative action is a nearly universal given.

A powerful contemporary example comes from the pending Supreme Court case of *Abigail Fisher v. University of Texas*, a case the Court will hear in its 2012–2013 term, taking up the issue of racial preferences in higher education for the first time in a decade. (We examine prior Supreme Court decisions on racial preferences in Chapter Thirteen and *Fisher* itself in Chapter Eighteen.) During the spring and summer of 2012 nonparties to the case who wished to bring information or arguments to the Court's attention filed friend-of-the-court (*amicus curiae*) briefs. Many important cases attract only a handful of amicus briefs; in *Fisher* a total of ninety-two were filed. Seventeen came from individuals or groups agreeing with the plaintiff that the University of Texas's use of racial preferences is unconstitutional and goes beyond existing Court precedent; seventy-three came from groups and individuals (with many a brief joined by many people or groups) contending that the use of racial preferences by the University of Texas is both legal and desirable. (Two briefs, including one by the present authors, came from *amici* supporting neither party.)

The seventeen pro-Fisher briefs came predominantly from conservative civil rights groups and think tanks. They were counterbalanced by perhaps thirty pro-University briefs from (generally larger) liberal civil rights groups and think tanks. But there the symmetry, such as it is, ends. On the pro-University side was an amicus brief from the US government as well as briefs from seventeen US senators; sixty-six US congressmen; fifty-seven of the Fortune 100 American corporations; thirty-seven retired military and defense leaders; fifteen states; well over one hundred colleges and universities (filing at least half a dozen briefs making similar points but representing different constituencies within higher education); seventy-six education associations, including leading groups like the American Council on Education; the National Education Association; and the American Educational Research Association; and a host of mainstream organizations, from the American Bar Association to the American Psychological Association. On the pro-Fisher side there was not a single comparable institution: no governments (and only a lone House Republican, Allen West), not one major corporation, none of the principal membership organizations of any profession, no higher education institution.

This makes the issue of racial preferences something that is perhaps unique in America. What could be called the "leadership class" either favors the broad use of racial preferences to promote diversity or is sufficiently neutral or cautious to remain silent. Yet, as we noted in Chapter Seven, racial preference programs are quite unpopular among Americans as a whole. This is a nuanced point worth some elaboration.

When public opinion polls ask respondents direct questions about the desirability of racial preferences, most respondents of all racial groups seem overwhelmingly opposed. For example, a *Washington Post*/Kaiser poll from 2001 asked, "In order to give minorities more opportunity, do you believe race or ethnicity should be a factor when deciding who is hired, promoted, or admitted to college, or that hiring, promotions, and college admissions should be based strictly on merit and qualifications other than race or ethnicity?" Only 3 percent of whites, 7 percent of Hispanics, and 12 percent of blacks thought race or ethnicity should be a factor. When the question is softened somewhat, however, opinion shifts significantly. A Quinnipiac poll in 2009 asked, "In order to increase diversity, do you support or oppose affirmative action programs that give preferences to blacks in hiring, promotions, and college admissions?" Twenty-four percent of whites, 51 percent of Hispanics, and 69 percent of blacks expressed "support." When similar questions leave out the word "preferences" altogether and merely speak of "affirmative action," support levels are even higher. What American respondents do support consistently—by large margins—are college preferences that take economic and social circumstances (but not race) into account, as well as efforts to expand the pool of college-eligible students.

We take from this that Americans strongly support measures to increase opportunity; they are also strongly committed to the idea that actual positions, whether in colleges or workplaces, should be awarded on merit. The polling data suggests that few "average citizens" of any race would support racial preferences as large as those that selective colleges use, especially when they are so strongly associated with poor academic outcomes.

This poses a genuine puzzle: Why are the leaders of American institutions outspokenly supportive of racial preferences when most Americans oppose them? We can think of no other public issue in which the leadership class displays such cohesion in the face of a largely opposite view among Americans in general.

Our hypothesis to explain this disconnect is that institutional leaders in America have coalesced around diversity strategies for reasons that are both pragmatic and ideological. Inclusive practices that focus on the need for an organization to have a respectable level of racial diversity, that emphasize the importance of cross-racial understanding or cross-racial teamwork, and that try to ensure that management levels are as diverse—or nearly so—as the rank and file are seen as having very important benefits. Perhaps the most central of these is the achievement of racial legitimacy; the organization is not seen as reactionary or out of touch with the changing demography of the American workforce but rather as part of the progressive leadership toward a cohesive, multiethnic tomorrow. Organizations that lack racial legitimacy can become targets of civil rights lawsuits or unfavorable media coverage; these can create both morale costs and substantial financial liability. Any organizational leader who is seeking to establish the proper diversity climate within her ranks would prefer to have racial preferences available as at least a tool for shaping the proper structure.

One fascinating analysis of these phenomena is Frank Dobbin's *Inventing Equal Opportunity*, which traces the rise of diversity policies within corporate America from the 1960s to the turn of the century. So far as we can tell, Dobbin is not at all a critic of the use of racial preferences but rather someone trying to understand how business leaders evolved from hostile and defensive reactions to civil rights legislation in the 1960s and early 1970s to the point of supporting the pursuit of diversity through racial preferences in hiring, promotions, and contracting as well as in college admissions. As Dobbin notes,

> **Current diversity measures face little overt opposition in corporate America, in large part because the human resources profession has done such a good job of framing them as promoting efficiency, or depicting the problem as one of outdated personnel systems rather than as one of prejudice, and of making the case that the workforce is in the midst of becoming dramatically more diverse. These successes suggest that corporate diversity programs will continue to flourish even in the absence of new legislation. . . .**
>
> **Yet all of this activity still occurs in an evidentiary vacuum. The workplace has become markedly more diverse since the early 1960s, but how much of that is due to the particular programs that the human resources profession promulgated? We have little hard evidence that employer programs increase opportunity. When companies choose new diversity programs, they rely on "best practices" lists rather than on research findings. Perhaps this is not altogether by chance, for following "best practices" has often protected firms in court.**

The diversity program, including the use of racial preferences that is systematic at the university level and widespread but probably more sporadic in companies, thus acquires its hegemony among organization leaders because it achieves racial peace, protects each individual organization from attack, and is either compatible with or enhances institutional goals. Once "best practices" have been established, empirical evidence could actually be threatening—new facts might push best practices out of equilibrium. Public hostility to prefer-ences is a problem, so talk of preferences is to be discouraged. "Diversity," now more than ever, is the operative term. In this context, the wide, tacit sup-port for racial preferences among the leadership class could be seen as the last example of a "gentlemen's agreement" in America.

* * *

It seems to us plausible that this combination of leadership solidarity on diversity policies and the strong (but not very intense) public dislike of prefer-ences could make the topic of higher education racial preferences one to which the usual rules of journalism do not apply. Of course, claims of media bias are sometimes unfair and almost inevitably subjective—we do not attempt here to prove media bias—but we think a combination of facts, some systematic and some not, are very suggestive.

We conducted a Nexis search of articles published in major newspapers from April 2011 through March 2012; we sought articles that dealt with either affirmative action or racial preferences in higher education. We found 146 articles; of these, about 30 pieces were opinion articles and another 49 used our search terms but really dealt with other topics. That left a sample of 56 news stories.

One notable pattern in these news stories was their terminology. Every one of the fifty-six stories used the term "affirmative action," usually to describe racial preference programs. Less than half of the stories mentioned racial pref-erences at all, and when they did, it was usually on some point of elabora-tion—the central concept relied upon was nearly always affirmative action.

This is significant for several reasons. As we have noted, public opinion polls consistently show that racial preferences (especially when they compro-mise selection based on merit) are intensely unpopular, whereas "affirmative action" elicits more evenly divided responses. Terms are important: As many psychological studies have shown, the way that public policies are described has a powerful effect on the reaction they generate in the listener.

Moreover, in the context of most of these stories, "racial preferences" was the more accurate term. Correctly speaking, court battles like that in *Fisher* or political battles like that over Prop 209 are not about "affirmative action" but rather about prohibiting racial (and gender) preferences. The vast outreach and pool-expansion programs undertaken by the University of California after Prop 209, for example, were never in legal danger provided they did not actually exclude whites and Asians in systematic ways. Certainly these are forms of affirmative action. It's hard to argue that "affirmative action" is not a misleading term in utterly representative story leads like these:

Michigan's 5-year-old affirmative action ban will be debated today before a federal appeals court in a case that pits those who say the law embodies the spirit of America's equal opportunities against those who say it undermines diversity and democracy. (*Detroit Free News*, March 7, 2012)

The U.S. Supreme Court has agreed to consider rolling back university affirmative action programs, re-entering a racially charged debate by accepting an appeal from a rejected white applicant to the University of Texas. (*Chicago Tribune*, February 22, 2012)

Gov. Jerry Brown added his voice Friday in support of a federal lawsuit seeking to have the state's ban on racial affirmative action in public university admissions declared unconstitutional. (*Los Angeles Times*, July 9, 2011)

One might argue that "affirmative action" is more a part of the standard American lexicon than "racial preferences" and that journalists and editors are simply following standard usage. But this is a weak argument. For one thing, media obviously powerfully shapes usage itself. And for another, it is hard to think of other examples in which journalists use broad, inaccurate terms simply to defer to popular customs; it is much more common for journalists and editors to try to avoid terms that could create misleading biases or stereotypes (e.g., witness the commendable trend toward not identifying criminal defendants by race).

None of the fifty-six stories in our sample examined the mismatch issue (though two mentioned it as an issue in the California Bar litigation, which we discuss in Chapter Fifteen). None covered the intense controversy over preferences research at Duke (see Chapter Eleven). None of the stories discussed how black and Hispanic outcomes have improved dramatically at the University of California since the passage of Prop 209 (we believe no such news story has *ever* run). On the contrary, the only article in our sample that discussed the effects of a ban on racial preferences was a March 2012 *USA Today* article about Michigan's ban, which had three sentences about the effect of the ban on the University of Michigan: "Last fall, minorities in the University of Michigan undergraduate schools constituted 10.5 percent of all freshmen, down from 12.7 percent in 2007. 'I'm usually the only black kid in the class,' says University of Michigan junior Margaret McKinney, 20. The campus climate is so hostile, she says, that she plans to transfer to Eastern Michigan University."

It is perhaps understandable that journalists labor under the impression that blacks and Hispanics can only lose if preferences are curtailed. But it is also the case that none of the ninety-three stories gave any hint to readers of the actual scale and operation of black and Hispanic racial preferences. One article (from the *New York Times*) considered whether Asians are penalized, but it examined only whether there was a penalty vis-à-vis whites. And another *Times* article examined the alleged growing practice of colleges to give admissions preferences to applicants who are not seeking financial aid. (This trend is plausible, even likely, but the preferences in question are undoubtedly far smaller than a typical racial preference.)

Many stories gave misleading impressions of preference programs. For instance, a story about a proposed ballot measure banning preferences led off with this:

> **A Republican-backed plan to wipe out affirmative action programs in Oklahoma appears headed for approval by the Legislature, prompting a bitter response from some minority lawmakers that it is merely a political ploy to play on racial fears and draw conservative voters to the polls. . . . Supporters say the measure would underscore an important principle even though the practical effect would be minimal. No preferences are given to minorities or women in state contracts or for admission to state colleges or universities. The measure would abolish a handful of state scholarships that target minority students.**

The flat factual statement that Oklahoma universities do not use racial preferences was based simply on claims by state university officials. But data that we have gathered from the University of Oklahoma School of Law shows a marked pattern of racial preferences, slightly smaller than those most law schools use but still quite substantial. Given the near-universality of preference programs at flagship state schools and law and medical schools, it is striking that the reporters and editors behind this story so willingly treated the university's claims as factual.

The way media cover racial preferences is likely to shape the way the public perceives them. In June 2003 a Gallup poll asked: "If two equally qualified students, one white and one black, applied to a major U.S. college or university, who do you think would have the better chance of being accepted to the college—the white student, the black student, or would they have the same chance?" Respondents were almost evenly divided, choosing "black student" by only 31 to 29 percent. And black and Hispanic respondents chose "white student" by 67 to 5 percent and 44 to 14 percent, respectively. In the real world of selective school admissions, however, there would be no contest: The black student would have dramatically higher odds of admission at nearly every selective school in the country (see Chapter Two)—and we routinely find that reporters who cover higher education or affirmative action are well aware of this. But that basic fact is virtually never reported.

The pattern we describe is, therefore, a national one. But it is worth focusing a bit more on the *New York Times* because its stories are, in general, more probing and in depth than those of many papers and because it has such disproportionate influence on the national policy conversation. It is also, like many other contemporary newspapers, a place that sees itself very much in step with the values of affirmative action described in Chapter Eleven. *Times* CEO Arthur Sulzburger, for one, has repeatedly stressed that diversity "is the single most important issue" facing the *Times*.

The *Times* has devoted a fair amount of coverage to the difficulties students with low SES have in accessing college. For instance, an excellent May 2011 analysis piece by David Leonhardt, a recent Pulitzer Prize winner and now the *Times* Washington Bureau Chief, observed that "for all the other ways that top colleges had become diverse, their student bodies remained shockingly affluent." Highlighting these gross imbalances was important, but Leonhardt's article did not mention (though perhaps it implied) that current racial preference programs predominantly benefit affluent black and Hispanic applicants.

A September 2011 *Times* article, headlined "Why Science Majors Change Their Minds (It's Just So Darned Hard)," reported that "roughly 40 percent of students planning engineering and science majors end up switching to other subjects or failing to get any degree." It went on to quote Mitchell Chang, a UCLA education professor, that "if you take two students who have the same high school grade-point average and SAT scores, and you put one in a highly selective school like Berkeley and the other in a school with lower average scores like Cal State, that Berkeley student is at least 13 percent less likely than the one at Cal State to finish a STEM degree." The article was largely describing the "science mismatch" phenomenon, but it gave no hint that this might especially affect blacks and Hispanics or that, indeed, it was logically intertwined with the broad system of racial preferences—even though only the year before the US Civil Rights Commission had released a several-hundred-page report detailing the problem.

In January 2011 the *Times* ran another long article headlined "Law School Admissions Lag Among Minorities." Relying on a study by Conrad Johnson, a professor at Columbia Law School, the *Times* reported that the number of black and Mexican American students entering law school was in decline even though their college grades and LSAT scores had been improving. The conclusion Professor Johnson and the *Times* reporter, Tamar Lewin, drew was that these minorities were being shut out of law schools and, hence, the opportunity to practice law.

But readily available data directly contradicted the central factual claims of Lewin's article. Using the same reference period as the article (1993 to 2008), accurate statistics show that absolute numbers of blacks entering law school were up and that the numbers of Hispanics were way up. Meanwhile, the improvements in the average college grades and LSAT scores of minority law school applicants had been trivial or nonexistent over this same period. Comparing black and Hispanic admissions rates to those of white applicants with similar grades and test scores at a sample of forty public law schools reveals massive racial preferences for these minorities. The typical preference for blacks was equivalent to roughly 140 points on the academic index we have used elsewhere in the book.

Lewin's article relied uncritically on Professor Conrad's statistical analyses of data coming from the Law School Admissions Council (LSAC), and Conrad had made comparisons that LSAC's website explicitly advised researchers not to make. Indeed, after the publication of Lewin's piece, LSAC sent an e-mail to all law school deans disassociating itself from Conrad's study and explaining why it was likely to be unreliable. One of us (Sander) contacted Lewin, the public editor, and another *Times* editor to ask that the claims in the article be corrected or retracted. The general defense was that the *Times* had not made these assertions directly; it had accurately quoted a third party's study. The only outcome of these efforts was Lewin's promise to "do better next time." A fitting denouement to this story came a few months later when Sander witnessed a law school dean, speaking to a large crowd of federal judges and other prominent lawyers in California, citing Lewin's uncorrected article as proof that law schools were not doing enough to help minorities.

Then there are the stories the *Times* does not cover at all, including Duke University's winter 2012 attack on its own faculty over a careful, dispassionate analysis of how preferences affect major choice and school performance (see Chapter Eleven) and the mobbing of Roger Clegg at the University of Wisconsin (also in Chapter Eleven). In both cases it is hard to imagine the *Times* not covering the events if the racial and ideological polarities were reversed. Suppose that Duke had mounted an institutional attack on a black professor who produced path-breaking research demonstrating that blacks receiving admissions preferences caught up with their white peers by the senior year of college, or if white University of Wisconsin students mobbed a visiting black civil rights advocate who was presenting a report on a pattern of admissions discrimination against black students. Either one of these stories would almost certainly have been major news, probably with many follow-up stories until the perpetrators of intolerance were punished.

Or consider a more classic case of omission. In 1995 the *New York Times Sunday Magazine* ran a cover story about Patrick Chavis, one of the black students admitted under the UC Davis Medical School quota plan that was struck down in 1978 by the Supreme Court (see Chapter Thirteen). In the story, prominent journalist Nicholas Lemann (now dean of Columbia's Graduate School of Journalism) glorified Chavis as a doctor doing noble work caring for poor minority patients and, thus, as serving the public interest better than Allan Bakke, the white plaintiff who had won his reverse-discrimination lawsuit against UC Davis, earned his degree, and went on to become a Mayo Clinic anesthesiologist. The import of the article was that in prohibiting racial quotas at the medical school, the Supreme Court had undermined the cause of improving access to medical care (represented by Chavis) in favor of letting more middle-class whites become affluent doctors.

But this, as it turns out, was not the first media attention Chavis had attracted. In 1993 the *Los Angeles Times* had run a story (unrelated to affirmative action) about Chavis's run-ins with California medical licensing boards. And three years after Lemann's article California's medical board suspended Chavis's medical license for "'gross negligence, incompetence and repeated negligent acts" and "inability to perform some of the most basic duties required of a physician." The immediate reason was that six patients were injured and one died from botched operations in Chavis's liposuction business. He had also been sued for malpractice at least twenty-one times. Not only had Lemann and the *New York Times* overlooked Chavis's documented problems as of 1995; they did not cover the story of his suspension (though several other major newspapers did). Chavis only returned to the pages of the *Times* in a 2002 obituary, which mentioned his suspension and his role as a symbolic affirmative action figure. Does anyone doubt that if Allan Bakke's medical license had been suspended for flagrant malpractice, it would have been a major *Times* story?

* * *

As we discussed in Chapter Seven, 1996 marked a watershed year in the national political dialogue on racial preferences. For several years in the early 1990s many national leaders from both parties were willing to engage questions about the efficacy of preferences, and Republicans showed an interest in legislatively limiting or narrowing their use. Whether the rhetorical intensity of the anti-209 campaign in California was a key causal factor or not, since

1996 political leaders have treated the preferences debate as toxic and dangerous. Calls from the US Commission on Civil Rights for Congress to take steps toward making racial preference systems more transparent have elicited no more reaction from either chamber or either side of the political aisle than they have from higher education institutions.

Asked what explains Republican political leaders' reticence about campaigning against or even criticizing racial preferences, a senior Republican in the House of Representatives told us that "philosophically, Republicans tend to oppose quotas and racial preferences in favor of equal opportunity for everyone. But even though a large majority of Americans agree with our philosophy on affirmative action, quite frankly the intensity of the name calling and vituperation from the other side makes it easy to decide to stay away from the issue."

We can see this tendency in the presidency of George W. Bush. As governor of Texas, Bush endorsed judicial decisions that banned race-based preferences and, as a presidential candidate, noted that he still opposed them. But the Bush administration did not notably disturb existing diversity practices, and when the Supreme Court took up the issue of preferences in 2003, Bush's solicitor general, Ted Olson, stopped short of arguing that the Constitution bars all racial preferences in admissions, though he urged the Court to strike down the specific plans of the University of Michigan Law School and undergraduate college. When the Court rejected the Bush administration's position by upholding the law school's preferences, Bush applauded the Supreme Court for "recognizing the value of diversity on our nation's campuses." One might have concluded that Bush had just won a significant victory.

Barack Obama also sounded at least a modestly skeptical note about racial preferences during his presidential campaign. When asked by George Stephanopoulos in early 2007, "Why should your daughters, when they go to college, get affirmative action?" Obama responded that "First of all, I think that my daughters should probably be treated by any admissions officer as folks who are pretty advantaged, and I think that there's nothing wrong with us taking that into account as we consider admissions policies at universities. I think that we should take into account white kids who have been disadvantaged and have grown up in poverty and shown themselves to have what it takes to succeed." He went on to suggest that "in our society race and class still intersect, that even those who are in the middle class may be first generation as opposed to fifth or sixth generation college attendees. . . . I would like to think that affirmative action becomes a diminishing tool for us to achieve racial equality in this society."

Obama sounded like a reform-minded leader on the issue. He seemed to be suggesting that higher education should move from race-based to class-based preferences. (His aside that socioeconomic class measures should take account of the intersections of race and class is one that we consider conceptually and empirically sound, for reasons we discuss in Chapter Sixteen.) It was possible that Obama was merely espousing a politically popular position—as we noted earlier, class-based preferences, unlike race-based preferences, consistently enjoy substantial popular support in polls. But it also seemed possible that the first black president might be the one to "go to China" on the affirmative action issue.

Obama has not "gone to China." On the contrary, his administration seems to have taken the view that race-based preferences are one area of policy in which it should take great care to placate Obama's most liberal supporters. Obama's attorney general, Eric Holder, has observed in discussing preference programs that the past forty years have been "a relatively small period of time in which African-Americans and other people of color have truly had the benefits to which they are entitled. I can't actually imagine a time in which the need for diversity will ever cease." Many race-based distinctions in existing federal programs have been followed zealously in the Obama administration, and major new pieces of legislation, such as the Dodd-Frank financial reform law and the health care overhaul, have created dozens of new racial preferences. Though some of these have generated Republican opposition, the gradual expansion of racial preferences in federal programs over the past few years has not surfaced as a significant issue.

Obama missed a rare opportunity. As Richard Kahlenberg has noted, "President Obama was uniquely positioned to move the Democratic Party to a better place on affirmative action—one which recognizes that low-income students of all races deserve far better—and instead fell back on stale thinking."

If racial preference programs are to be reformed at all, we see no sign that Congress or the executive branch will be the agent of change.

CHAPTER THIRTEEN

THE SUPREME COURT

Rewarding Opacity

A S CHAPTER TWELVE SUGGESTS, neither Democratic nor Republican politicians—nor even presidents—have shown much capacity to take on the problem of racial preferences in higher education. One might think, at first glance, that the Supreme Court has shown considerably more fortitude. Twice during the affirmative action era the Court has taken on major cases that squarely posted the constitutional dilemmas that these preferences raise. Twice a centrist justice held the balance of power on the central issues, and twice the Court has issued opinions that, on their face, appeared to curtail the ways that colleges and universities could use race in admissions decisions.

Yet, as we will demonstrate in this chapter, in both cases the Court's holdings were half-measures that effectively encouraged schools to obscure the workings of their preference policies. Both opinions emboldened many schools to perpetuate and even enlarge their racial preferences—exactly the opposite of the effect that the two centrist justices purported to seek.

* * *

Mounting a legal challenge to a college's system of admissions preferences is not an easy thing to do. First, there is the question of standing: Under federal law one must be injured by the practice that is challenged. That means one must be a student who was turned down for admission to a college or university because of race. Few students know much about how admissions systems and preferences work; even fewer have enough information to sense whether they could prove that they would have been admitted to any particular school but for its use of racial preferences. And nearly all in this small group would rather get on with their lives than pursue complex, protracted, and demanding litigation over a rejection at one school.

Even if a student with standing does sue and does win, the university will almost certainly appeal. By the time appeals are heard—often several years after the plaintiffs have gone to other colleges—the case has become "moot" because the plaintiff would no longer attend the school that turned her down even if the court ordered her admitted. That happened in the first admissions preference case to reach the Supreme Court, *DeFunis v. Odegard*, and led the Court to dismiss the action in 1974. (Since then, some plaintiffs have avoided mootness by claiming monetary damages or filing class actions.)

But despite these challenges, all the elements came together in California in the person of Allan Bakke. Indeed, he seemed to have been created by central casting to play the role of the sympathetic victim of a preference regime. Bakke was a hard-working, straight-arrow, Vietnam veteran of Norwegian ancestry, son of a mailman and a teacher. He had joined Navy ROTC to help pay for his education at the University of Minnesota, with a major in mechanical engineering. He did a combat tour in Vietnam as a Marine and then went to work for NASA in California. But by his early thirties Bakke had set his heart on becoming a physician. His age counted against him in admissions. But Bakke hoped that he would get an offsetting advantage by better qualifying himself; to that end he took courses in chemistry and biology and worked in a hospital as a candy striper—a rare thing for a man.

After the medical school at UC Davis and some others denied him admission in 1972 and again in 1973, Bakke sued UC Davis for violating his constitutional right not to be subjected to racial discrimination by the state. The school—which was new and had no history of discrimination—had set aside an unusually rigid quota of sixteen of the one hundred positions in the entering medical school class for blacks, Chicanos, American Indians, and Asians. All or almost all of the minority applicants admitted under this quota had much lower test scores and grades than Bakke did. To justify its racial quota, the medical school contended that the Medical College Admissions Test (MCAT) was biased against minority students and that a decision barring consideration of race "would be a return to virtually all-white professional schools." Neither claim was accurate, although *the most selective* professional (and undergraduate) schools would indeed, without preferences, have become much whiter.

Bakke won a ringing, 6–1 decision in the California Supreme Court, written by Justice Stanley Mosk, a much-admired liberal. "We conclude that the program, as administered by the University, violates the constitutional rights of nonminority applicants because it affords preference on the basis of race to persons who, by the University's own standards, are not as qualified for the study of medicine as nonminority applicants denied admission," Mosk wrote. The California court thus banned all state schools from using race as a factor in admissions. The US Supreme Court agreed in February 1977 to hear the state's appeal, captioned *Regents of University of California v. Bakke.* By then, racial preferences were pervasive at the top two hundred undergraduate programs outside the South and in most law and medical schools.

Bakke's case would become one of the most highly publicized judicial battles of all time and the first in which the US Supreme Court would rule on whether governmental preferences favoring minorities were subject to the same virtually automatic judicial invalidation as discrimination against minorities. The case attracted massive media coverage and a then-record fifty-three friend-of-the-court briefs from interest groups, states, the Carter Justice Department, and others. Most of the academic and legal establishments opposed Allan Bakke and supported racial preferences. Prominent Jewish groups, fearful that Jews would now be victimized by affirmative action quotas as they had once been victimized by anti-Jewish quotas, supported Bakke.

The Supreme Court would not achieve anything like the near consensus of the California justices; their June 1978 decision was a 4–1–4 split, with six opinions totaling 156 pages, none speaking for a majority. Four justices—Chief Justice Warren Burger and Justices Potter Stewart, William Rehnquist, and John Paul Stevens—held in an opinion by Stevens that all racial preferences in admissions at universities receiving federal funds (as virtually all do) violate the 1964 Civil Rights Act. Stevens deemed it unnecessary to decide whether such preferences also violate the Fourteenth Amendment equal protection clause. (Burger and Rehnquist privately believed that state-sponsored racial preferences violate the equal protection clause and wanted to so hold, in part because Congress could not overturn a constitutional ruling. But Stevens insisted on avoiding the constitutional issue.) Four other justices—liberal lions William Brennan and Thurgood Marshall plus Harry Blackmun and Byron White—voted to uphold virtually unlimited admissions preferences "as a means of remedying the effects of past societal discrimination," as Brennan said in a dissenting opinion joined by Marshall, Blackmun, and White, who also wrote separate individual dissents.

The 4–4 split left Powell with the deciding vote. A courtly gentleman of the old South and former member of the Richmond, Virginia, school board, Powell had become the Court's pivotal vote on a wide range of issues, including—as Bakke would show—race. And this was not so many decades after "there was *de jure* segregation in the Southern states," as Powell would recall in a tone of wonderment during a 1987 interview by coauthor Taylor, "not only of the schools but of public accommodations, facilities, theaters. I just can't imagine how I grew up and accepted that as a normal way of life in this country."

Powell sought out a middle position on *Bakke* between warring absolutes. He had told his law clerks that outlawing affirmative action—already entrenched in the universities and elsewhere—would be a jarring reversal of direction and "a disaster for the country." But he also feared that "it would be equally disastrous to give carte blanche for racial preferences," which could lead to benefits being "carved up among competing minorities in an ugly game of racial politics" and to "entrenched bureaucracies" administering an "ethnic spoils system" regarded by minorities as "perpetual entitlements." Powell's goal was to allow some racial preferences while keeping them in check "so that race-consciousness would not become the norm."

In his *Bakke* opinion Powell sided with the four antipreference justices by holding that courts must apply the same "strict scrutiny" to affirmative action preferences as to other forms of racial discrimination and by ordering UC Davis to admit Allan Bakke on the ground that numerical racial quotas such as the one before the Court were flatly unconstitutional. Powell also wrote that "distinctions between citizens solely because of their ancestry are by their very nature odious to a free people whose institutions are founded upon the doctrine of equality" (quoting *Hirabayashi v. U.S.*) and that "the Constitution forbids" schools from seeking "some specified percentage of a particular group merely because of its race or ethnic origin" or "preferring members of any one group for no reason other than race or ethnic origin."

But Powell sided with the four more liberal justices in holding that race could be one factor considered in admissions decisions. At the same time, he rejected the liberals' contention that this was justified by the need to remedy the effects of past "societal discrimination" and warned that this was "an amorphous concept of injury that may be ageless in its reach into the past."

Powell wrote, for himself alone, that promoting "diversity" on campus in order to foster a "robust exchange of ideas" was a "compelling" state interest that could justify consideration of race if "precisely tailored" to promote intellectual diversity. "Race or ethnic background may be deemed a 'plus' in a particular applicant's file, yet it does not insulate the individual from comparison with all other candidates for the available seats," Powell wrote. He focused on the supposed (and now, hotly debated) contribution of racial diversity to *intellectual* diversity rather than on racial diversity as such. Thus, Powell stressed, "ethnic diversity is only one element . . . in attaining the goal of a heterogeneous student body" and must be weighed along with "exceptional personal talents, unique work or service experience, leadership potential, maturity, demonstrated compassion, a history of overcoming disadvantage, ability to communicate with the poor, or other qualifications deemed important."

No other justice endorsed Powell's "diversity" rationale for preferences. Indeed, all eight shunned the diversity rationale. Even for Powell himself, in the view of his biographer John Jeffries, "diversity was not the ultimate objective but merely a convenient way to broach a compromise."

Powell explicitly approved by name Harvard College's diversity plan, which Harvard had described in a friend-of-the-court brief, based on Harvard's assurance that race could "tip the balance" in favor of a well-qualified applicant "just as geographic origin or a life spent on a farm may tip the balance in other candidates' cases." The choice of the Harvard example was unfortunate. For one thing, Harvard gave far more weight to race than it did to geographic diversity or an interesting childhood. For another, Harvard's position at the top of the cascade (see Chapter Two) allowed it to achieve significant racial diversity with smaller preferences than other schools would be forced to use when seeking the same sort of numbers.

Powell also suggested that the Harvard plan involved no "facial intent to discriminate," in contrast with the UC Davis quota. "This was pure sophistry," John Jeffries, a former Powell law clerk, later wrote in a generally admiring biography. "Harvard did not—and could not—deny that race was a factor in admissions. . . . Powell simply penalized candor. Stripped of legalisms, the message amounted to this: 'You can do whatever you like in preferring racial minorities so long as you do not say so.'"

Nor did Powell or any other propreference justice suggest any specific limit on the size of racial preferences or identify an end point. Blackmun did express "my earnest hope" that such programs would become "unnecessary" and "only a relic of the past . . . within a decade." But he added that this hope "is a slim one." Indeed, when Stevens said during a confidential Court conference that blacks would not need these special programs much longer, Marshall broke in and declared that it would take another one hundred years. This horrified Powell, who "recoiled from the prospect of generation upon generation of racial quotas."

In the ensuing months and years selective colleges and graduate schools took *Bakke* as a green light to continue quietly using racial preferences as

large as necessary to reach their rough targets for black and Hispanic enrollments. Most went through rituals of individualized assessment and took care
to avoid the overt numerical quotas that *Bakke* had barred—no great loss
from the schools' standpoint, as quotas were not needed to make racial preferences as large as the schools might wish; they were also an inefficient way
of administering a system of racial preferences because the inflexibility of
rigid quotas would not allow a school to admit a few more or a few less preferred-minority applicants depending on variations in the applicant pool
from year to year. But the changes were cosmetic. As one of us wrote in
2005, "Racially separate admissions tracks were draped with fig leaves of various shapes and sizes to conceal actual practices, which changed hardly at all.
Enrollments also remained constant."

One careful study that examined admissions patterns before and after
Bakke found that the decision had no noticeable effect on minority enrollments at either law or medical schools; the preferences they used after *Bakke*
were at least as large as before. This basic fact—that preferences were still very
large and were applied by a rising number of institutions to a widening array
of minorities—attracted almost no notice during the 1980s.

Meanwhile, political and judicial trends during the 1980s and 1990s led
many to believe that the era of racial preferences—unpopular from the start
with the public—would be brought to an end by force of law or politics or
both. Many Reagan and Bush appointees to the executive branch and the
judiciary were clearly hostile to preferences. The Supreme Court, reshaped by
twelve years of Republican appointments starting with that of Justice Sandra
Day O'Connor, took a restrictive view of racial preferences in cases involving
government employment and contracting. In 1991 the Bush Justice Department found that Boalt Hall (the law school of the University of California at
Berkeley) had effectively segregated its admissions by race, using separate
committees that applied differing standards. The department reached an
agreement with Boalt to stop the practice. Anecdotal evidence of massive university racial preferences began to circulate in elite circles, and many of these
examples were gathered and published by Abigail and Stephan Thernstrom in
1997 in *America in Black and White: One Nation, Indivisible*. The weight
given to race at many schools far exceeded that given to all of the other diversity factors listed by Powell combined. Evidence also mounted that students
admitted with weak academic qualifications soon found themselves struggling
with low grades and high dropout rates.

In addition, as we noted in Chapter Seven, influential liberal and moderate public figures, including Democratic senators John Kerry and Joseph
Lieberman and the Democratic Leadership Council, thoughtfully argued that

perhaps the time had come to phase out racial preferences. So did some influential public intellectuals with liberal followings, including Christopher Jencks, who in 1992 published an influential analysis of affirmative action that called into question the continued use of explicit racial preferences.

This was also the period when conservative public-interest law firms emerged as important players in bringing activist litigation; some of these firms were interested in challenging affirmative action practices. When Bill Clinton won the 1992 presidential election, conservative activists were eager to bring further legal challenges to racial preferences before he could fill any Supreme Court vacancies with liberal justices. The first of what would be several challenges against elite state law schools came in Texas, brought by four white plaintiffs who were led by a well-qualified applicant named Cheryl Hopwood. They had been rejected by the University of Texas Law School at the same time that it was accepting preferred-minority candidates with far lower test scores and grades. The libertarian, Washington-based Center for Individual Rights litigated the case on a pro bono basis.

The law school was vulnerable. Not only had it, like Boalt, assigned admissions decision making for black applicants to a separate committee; it was also using very aggressive preferences. Hopwood's suit soon turned up in the law school's records a draft letter addressed to alumna Clara Meek, prepared in 1988 by then-associate dean Guy Wellborn, observing that the law school used "radically different admissions standards" to admit blacks from "the bottom half of the national pool" whereas whites were "overwhelmingly drawn from the very top of the national pool." The draft was written for Mark Yudof, then-dean of UT's Law School (who went on to become president of the University of Texas and, since 2008, president of the University of California). Yudof made many changes in the draft that obfuscated the explosive evidence it contained before signing and sending it to Meek.

The same draft letter also included evidence of mismatch, observing that more than half of UT Law School's black graduates (and fewer than 10 percent of its white graduates) failed the bar exam on their first try, and half of those failed again on their second try—the sort of pattern that Sander would later chronicle in "Systemic Analysis." Thus, a great many affirmative action admits spent three years and went deep into debt studying law at UT—and elsewhere, as it later became clear—without ever qualifying to practice law. But Hopwood and her lawyers made no argument about the effectiveness of the law school's preference policies; they simply argued that the preferences amounted to racial discrimination against whites and were illegal.

In March 1996 a conservative panel of the Fifth Circuit agreed, in a sweeping decision holding that all racial preferences in state university admissions were unconstitutional, effectively banning them in the three Fifth Circuit states, Texas, Louisiana, and Mississippi. In the process the court boldly proclaimed that *Bakke* was not a binding precedent because no other justice had joined Powell's balance-tipping opinion (which was true) and subsequent Supreme Court decisions had effectively overruled the majority's holding (which was debatable). The Supreme Court declined in July 1996 to review *Hopwood,* prompting widespread speculation that a majority of justices were comfortable with the result.

Meanwhile, while *Hopwood* was pending, the UC Board of Regents had banned racial preferences in admissions. And four months after the Supreme Court let stand the Fifth Circuit's ruling against racial preferences in Texas, California's voters adopted Proposition 209. These combined legal and political forces, in the nation's two most populous states, seemed to threaten all racial preferences in university admissions.

But at the same time, as discussed in Chapter Eleven, the devotion to diversity goals was becoming ever more deeply entrenched in the universities. Preference policies and bureaucracies to administer them mushroomed at flagship state universities, elite colleges, professional schools, and many doctoral programs, and they also spread through the South, where preferences had not been much used in the 1970s.

It also became clear that when university leaders spoke about diversity, uppermost in their mind was not the kind of *intellectual* diversity that Justice Powell had seen as the only justification for any kind of racial preference. Higher education diversity—as well as the diversity explicitly pursued by many other American institutions—was, rather, indistinguishable from the racial balancing that Powell had condemned.

Justice Powell had feared that the societal-discrimination rationale embraced by Justices Brennan, Marshall, and their allies would perpetuate racial preferences forever. But in fact that rationale was weakened both by the growth of the black middle class, including millions of students who have never experienced serious discrimination, and by the extension of racial preferences to Latinos and others—descendants not of slaves but of recent immigrants who came to America because they saw it not as a caste-ridden society but as the land of opportunity. The diversity rationale had far greater potential for perpetuating preferences indefinitely.

Faced both with the deepening descent of establishment institutions into the ideology of racial diversity and with an apparently promising legal landscape for challenging racial preferences, a coalition of antipreference lawyers and nonprofits led by the same Center for Individual Rights that litigated *Hopwood* got behind lawsuits, filed in 1998, by disappointed applicants

Barbara Grutter and Jennifer Gratz against the University of Michigan Law School and Undergraduate College, respectively. Both schools used racial preferences on a large scale.

By the time the cases reached the Supreme Court in the 2002–2003 term, an epic battle was joined. Observers on all sides saw the case as the last stand for state-sponsored affirmative action policies. After all, none of the five more conservative justices had ever upheld a racial-preference plan of any kind, and all of them had expressed broad disapproval of racial preferences in cases involving government contract and employment programs. The university commissioned millions of dollars in research and expert testimony on the benefits of the preference programs, media coverage was intense, and amicus briefs from education associations, interest groups, academics, and others poured into the Court in record numbers. Like *Bakke*, *Grutter* and *Gratz* set a new mark for the number of amicus briefs filed, nearly doubling *Bakke*'s 53 with a total of 102, with 78 supporting affirmative action (many of them speaking for twenty or more institutions), 19 opposed, and 5 in between.

Perhaps the most revealing brief of all—coming after decades of depictions of affirmative action as merely tipping the balance between students of nearly equal qualifications—was that of the Law School Admission Council (LSAC), filed by Walter Dellinger, an eminent lawyer and scholar who had headed the Solicitor General's Office under President Clinton. The LSAC brief stressed that "only about 25" black students do well enough in college each year to rank among the more than 4,000 applicants to the most selective law schools with grades and LSAT scores high enough to qualify under the standards applied to most white and Asian applicants. The message to the Court was, We must keep using very large racial preferences or we will have virtually no black students.

Grutter and *Gratz,* as cases, had fundamental similarities. Both UM's College and Law School were among the very top public institutions of their kind and highly selective, though the law school was more so, as is typical of professional schools. Both schools drew many of their students from out of state, though, again, the law school had a more genuinely "national" student body. And in both schools black and Hispanic applicants had much lower average entering academic credentials than white and Asian applicants and could not have been admitted in significant numbers without racial preferences of some kind.

There were also four important differences between the two programs. First, the college had many more students and thus received fifteen to twenty thousand applications each year, five times as many as the law school. Second, the college, like most undergraduate colleges, took account of many distinct factors in its admissions decisions. These included SAT scores, achievement tests, and AP exams as well as applicants' high school GPAs, essays, race, athletic gifts, and interests. In contrast, admissions at the law school, as in most of legal education, were driven predominantly by each applicant's LSAT score, college GPA—and race. Third, given the scale and complexity of the admissions process at the college, it used an explicit point system whereas the law school did not. And fourth, as detailed below—but ignored at the time by the justices and almost all observers—the law school's preferences were substantially larger than the undergraduate college's.

Not that the college used modest preferences. Michigan used a 150-point "selection index" to rank applicants. A perfect 1600 SAT score earned applicants 12 points (only 2 more points than it awarded for a mediocre 1,010); 20 points for each high school grade point average unit (i.e., the difference between 3.0 and 4.0); and 20 points for being black, Hispanic, or Native American. Alumni children received a 4-point boost.

So at the college, a preferred-minority applicant with a B (3.0) average would have had the same score on the selection index as an otherwise indistinguishable Asian or white with an A (4.0) average. The effect was identical to that of a system penalizing whites and Asians by having their As counted as Bs, their A minuses as B minuses, and so forth.

But as Judge Danny Boggs of the Fifth Circuit was to point out in the course of the *Grutter* litigation, at the law school "race is worth over one full grade point of college average." On the 1,000-point academic index we use throughout this book, the college's preference translated to about 120 points, and the law school's to about 140 points.

Yet it was the law school's system that survived. In *Gratz* six justices struck down the college's explicit point system for awarding racial preferences, with Chief Justice Rehnquist writing for himself and four others and Justice Stephen Breyer concurring separately. But in *Grutter* five justices joined an opinion by Justice Sandra Day O'Connor that found the law school's preference system to be constitutional. O'Connor's opinion, then, defined how and when the Court would consider university racial admissions preferences to be permissible.

O'Connor's Powell-like role came as something of a surprise. Though not a colorblind-Constitution absolutist, she had never voted to uphold any system of racial preferences of any kind and had never publicly shown any sympathy for Powell's diversity rationale. Indeed, her 1989 majority opinion in a major affirmative action decision had implicitly rejected the diversity rationale, at least in the context of contract awards, by holding that unless racial classifications are "strictly reserved for remedial settings, they may in fact promote notions of racial inferiority and lead to a politics of racial hostility." O'Connor had also evinced strong distaste for race-based election districting.

In *Grutter* O'Connor embraced Powell's view that universities have a "compelling interest" in pursuing "diversity" if their racial preferences are "narrowly tailored" to that end. At the same time, she jettisoned Powell's focus on intellectual diversity as the compelling interest by holding that the "unique experience of being a racial minority" was all the diversity one needs to win a preference. Without seeking to reconcile this holding with her assertion that "racial balancing" would be unconstitutional, O'Connor endorsed giving diversity bonuses to *all* blacks, Hispanics, and Native Americans on the assumption that intellectual diversity would be furthered by *every* increase in their numbers up to what O'Connor called "critical mass," which she said could not be quantified.

But O'Connor also expressed grave misgivings about racial preferences. Echoing Powell, she declared that for a university to seek a specified percentage of any racial group would "amount to outright racial balancing, which is patently unconstitutional." She also specified that "enshrining a permanent justification for racial preferences would offend" the Constitution, and that "We expect that 25 years from now, the use of racial preferences will no longer be necessary."

Like Powell, O'Connor seemed to be permitting racial preferences only when colleges and universities followed a narrow path. She set out a series of seemingly formidable tests that preferences must satisfy to be constitutional: each student's diversity contribution must be assessed in light of multiple characteristics; race alone must never be "the defining feature" of an application; no racial group can be "insulated" from competition with other applicants; there must be no numerical targets for race representation, although schools can seek that mysterious, unquantified "critical mass"; schools must carefully consider race-neutral alternative methods of furthering diversity before resorting to racial preferences; and schools must phase out racial preferences as quickly as possible.

Moreover, O'Connor held that even this restricted scope for racial preferences would be tolerated only because of the Court's deference to academic freedom and the special autonomy accorded universities in shaping the educational experience of students:

> **We have long recognized that, given the important purpose of public education and the expansive freedoms of speech and thought associated with the university environment, universities occupy a special niche in our constitutional tradition. In announcing the principle of student**

> body diversity as a compelling state interest [in *Bakke*], Justice Powell
> invoked our cases recognizing a constitutional dimension, grounded in
> the First Amendment, of educational autonomy. . . . From this premise,
> Justice Powell reasoned that by claiming "the right to select those stu-
> dents who will contribute the most to the 'robust exchange of ideas,'" a
> university "seeks to achieve a goal that is of paramount importance in
> the fulfillment of its mission."

O'Connor's argument to this point was at least plausible, though the four
dissenters argued that deferring to the judgment of any institution was inappropriate in a case involving racial classifications. But O'Connor's opinion
became completely unmoored when she then broadly deferred to the law
school's assertions that it had met the specific requirements for permissible
preferences. In other words, O'Connor seemed to jump from arguing (a) that
universities could use tightly constrained racial preferences because of the
Court's deference to their academic freedom, to then suggesting (b) that she
would also defer to this particular school's judgment of whether it satisfied the
tight constraints.

For example, O'Connor gave great significance to the idea that the law
school engaged in a "highly individualized, holistic" review of applications,
inferring thereby that the school did not give automatic preference to any
black and considered all the different ways each applicant contributed to
diversity at the school. She accepted the law school's claim that in seeking a
"critical mass" of underrepresented minorities, it had no specific racial targets.
And she took "the Law School at its word that it would 'like nothing better
than to find a race-neutral admissions formula' and will terminate its race-
conscious admissions program as soon as practicable."

This was sophistry beyond anything in *Bakke*. The law school produced
no evidence that it had ever tried using race-neutral methods or experimented
with smaller racial preferences. And independent analyses done with data
available to the Court showed that the law school's racial preferences were not
only larger than those of the college but that they also dwarfed other considerations of diversity, were generally mechanically applied, and, overall, would
render race as more likely to be the determinative factor in a student's admission to the law school than the college.

To insiders already familiar with the way Justice Powell's opinion in *Bakke*
had appeared to curtail preferences but in reality left them untouched, it was
immediately clear that Justice O'Connor's opinion did the same thing—perhaps in a more deliberate way. In a dissent joined by Justices Antonin Scalia,
Anthony Kennedy, and Clarence Thomas, Chief Justice William Rehnquist

wrote, "Stripped of its 'critical mass' veil, the Law School's program is revealed as a naked effort to achieve racial balancing." He said that admissions data showed the law school to be discriminating in favor of blacks over Hispanics as well as over whites and Asians so that "the proportion of each group admitted should be the same as the proportion of that group in the applicant pool." Justice Anthony Kennedy added in his own separate dissent that although he agreed that race could be considered to promote diversity, the majority's broad deference to the law school's judgments abandoned "the essential safeguard Justice Powell insisted upon as the precondition of the approval, [which] was rigorous judicial review." Kennedy also said that "the concept of critical mass is a delusion used by the Law School to mask its attempt to make race an automatic factor in most instances and to achieve numerical goals indistinguishable from quotas."

Supporters of affirmative action immediately got the point too. Even though the Court struck down the University of Michigan's college preference system and articulated facially arduous restrictions on the law school's program, newspapers across the country showed the president of the University of Michigan, Mary Sue Coleman, literally jumping for joy on the steps of the Supreme Court.

Probably interpreting O'Connor's opinion much as Coleman did, Stephan and Abigail Thernstrom had a harsher reaction. The Thernstroms were leading critics of affirmative action who were concerned both about mismatch and about the tendency of university racial preferences, by allowing universities to achieve racial balance despite the large racial gaps in academic preparation, to thereby foster complacency about the serious problems in the K-12 pipeline. Writing of O'Connor's sunny expectation that race neutrality was only twenty-five years away, the Thernstroms observed, "It is criminal to offer complacent optimism about the racial gap in academic achievement. [This] is the most important source of ongoing racial inequality. Those who care about the persistence of that inequality will not engage in such duplicity. Instead, they will say loud and clear, America must get its educational act together. A racially-identifiable group of educational have-nots is morally unacceptable."

The Thernstroms noted that the only basis that O'Connor offered for her we-expect-you-to-stop-discriminating-in-twenty-five-years version of equal protection was her assertion that during the twenty-five years since *Bakke*, "the number of minority applicants with high grades and test scores has indeed increased." But O'Connor must have been aware of the overwhelming evidence that as of 2003 the racial gaps in academic achievement had been level or growing for fifteen years—not shrinking.

Perhaps the most troubling part of O'Connor's opinion was her interest in fostering opacity in college admissions, something that bothered even affirmative action supporters. Ian Ayres and Sydney Foster pointed out that the sort of holistic processes O'Connor mandated would make it difficult—if not impossible—to measure and, therefore, to weigh the relative costs and benefits of preference programs, and this seemed fundamentally inconsistent with narrow tailoring. And the liberal wing of the Supreme Court, though glad to have O'Connor's vote, also seemed troubled by her insistence on hiding the ball. Justice David Souter pointed out that the University of Michigan's college "simply does by a numbered scale what the law school accomplishes in its 'holistic review,'" and Ginsburg tartly observed that "If honesty is the best policy, surely Michigan's accurately described, fully disclosed College affirmative action program is preferable to achieving similar numbers through winks, nods, and disguises." (Of course, the college's policy was not truly transparent; it had only been "fully disclosed" to public view through a professor's Freedom of Information Act request and subsequent lawsuits.)

Further public information requests, both by the present authors and other groups, makes it possible to measure, for at least some higher education institutions, how the *Grutter* and *Gratz* decisions affected the scale and operation of racial preferences. Perhaps the most remarkable example of this is the College of the University of Michigan itself. One might think that, having lost in *Gratz* and been instructed by the Supreme Court to reform its admissions, the university's administrators would have treaded carefully indeed. But when comparing admissions data from under the pre-*Gratz* point system (in 1999) and data from a couple years after *Gratz* (2005–2006), it is clear that the college gave substantially *more* weight to race after *Gratz* than before, more often making it the decisive factor in individual admissions decisions.

UM's college also adopted, after *Gratz*, multiple racial distinctions. Its old point system simply distinguished between "underrepresented minorities" (who received bonus points) and everyone else. Post-*Gratz*, however, it favored blacks over Hispanics, Hispanics over whites, and whites over Asians—the essence of the racial balancing that *Gratz* and *Grutter* alike purported to forbid. The 2006 data also show that many Asians and whites of low socioeconomic status (SES) were denied admission in academic index ranges in which many blacks of high SES were admitted. Further, the data make it clear that black applicants were *not* evaluated individually to determine what special contribution their race might make to UM's educational environment.

In other words, the college's move to a "holistic" system in the wake of *Gratz* and *Grutter* made race a more pervasive and heavily weighted factor, introduced racial discrimination among preferred minorities, and thoroughly

FIGURE 13.1. Unchastened: Admissions at the University of Michigan Before and After *Gratz v. Bollinger*

The University of Michigan's application of racial preferences in admissions actually intensified after the Supreme Court struck down the school's point-system in 2003. Previously, the school had distinguished only between "underrepresented minorities" (who received bonus points) and everyone else. After 2003, it favored blacks over Hispanics, Hispanics over whites, and whites over Asians. And the cross-racial disparities in admission rates, for students with similar academic indices, increased.

Undergraduate admissions rates at the Univ. of Michigan by academic index and race

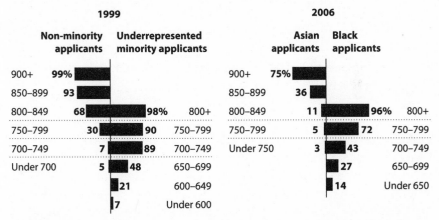

Source: 1999 data was disclosed by the University of Michigan in *Gratz v. Bollinger*, 2006 data was disclosed by the university in response to a public information request. Data analysis from Sander, "Why Strict Scrutiny Requires Transparency" (2012).

subordinated socioeconomic diversity to racial diversity. None of these developments was apparently known to Michigan's voters, who nonetheless approved by a large margin at the end of 2006 a ballot initiative that banned all use of race in state programs (including UM), as had California's Proposition 209 in 1996 and a similar Washington state measure in 1998. The enforceability of the Michigan ban, which has been challenged in court and disparaged by Mary Sue Coleman and other UM leaders, is still unresolved at this writing.

We also looked at data from six law schools to determine how their use of race in admissions changed after the 2003 *Grutter* decision. The University of Michigan Law School is one of those schools, and it is the only one of the six that shows a significant evolution in its admissions in the spirit of *Grutter*'s broad mandates. At four of the other five law schools the size of preferences given to blacks increases, and the apparent weight given to other diversity factors declines. The data also show the schools applying one level of preferences for blacks and another level for Hispanics in ways that invariably calibrate admissions to a close approximation of the relative number of blacks and Hispanics in the applicant pool—again, the essence of racial balancing. Analysis of a larger sample of forty public law schools for 2005–2007, including most of the nation's major public law schools, shows that the recent practices of the six are representative of the forty.

The most reasonable conclusion one could draw from these data is that law schools, the UM undergraduate school, and, in all likelihood, many other selective schools around the country interpreted *Grutter* as a green light to use preferences aggressively and mechanically so long as they did not overtly use "quotas" or "points."

There has nonetheless been one very commendable change in recent years, a move by some of the most elite (and most wealthy) schools to pay greater attention to socioeconomic disadvantage. We shall return to this point in Chapter Sixteen.

* * *

Perhaps the best-known part of Justice O'Connor's *Grutter* opinion was her call for colleges and universities to phase out racial preferences in twenty-five years—by 2028. Although that period is more than a third past as of this writing, we can find no evidence that even a single college, university, or higher education leadership group has taken a single step toward phasing out racial preferences. In short, after forty-five years, during which racial preferences for minorities have become ever more entrenched in virtually all establishment institutions, with no end in sight, we are drifting ever closer to being the sort of quota-ridden society that Powell, O'Connor, and the Court have purported to rule out. Thanks in large part to *Grutter*, this entrenchment has proceeded even as the justifications for racial preferences have shrunk.

Justice Clarence Thomas's blistering dissent in *Grutter* included a bluntly worded passage about the academic mismatch problem, which no justice had ever mentioned before. Thomas had previously spoken forcefully about mismatch (without using the word) in 1982, long before he joined the Court: "To say we are protecting their rights, when in fact they are unqualified, is to create a false hope," he said then. "I watched the operation of such affirmative action policies when I was in college and I watched the destruction of many kids as a result. It was wrong for those kids, and it was wrong to give that kind of false hope."

On most big Supreme Court issues, we find ourselves in agreement with Justice Thomas less often than with any of the eight other justices. But he has been remarkably prescient on the real-life effects of racial preferences in higher education. A growing body of social science research has since confirmed in most of their particulars his assertions about the perverse dynamics resulting from the preference regime, based on his personal experience and observations. Persuading Thomas's colleagues to consider the actual operation and on-the-ground effectiveness of preferences is a key step along the path to reform.

The question remains: Why have both *Bakke* and *Grutter* been so completely ineffective in accomplishing their declared objectives of ending "racial balancing," mechanical use of racial preferences, and efforts to entrench preferences for the long term?

Part of the reason is that Justice Powell and especially Justice O'Connor chose to strike down ostentatiously visible *symbols* of what makes preferences so unpopular—"no quotas" and "no point systems"—while failing to impose any specific requirements that could prevent universities from using preferences as large and mechanical as they want for as long as they want. Having crossed the line into allowing *some* use of racial preferences, both Powell and O'Connor may have assumed that it would be a hopelessly subjective project to draw a new line specifying how large is too large or how long is too long. They may also have feared that more specific prohibitions would lead either to a drastic plunge in minority representation at the most elite schools or to wholesale noncompliance. Relatedly, both Powell and O'Connor were no doubt impressed by the overwhelming and broad support for racial preferences among establishment institutions—and appropriately so, as one of us wrote in 2004.

Sandra Day O'Connor's ruling encouraged opacity. The current justices have seen where opacity leads. The lessons of experience may help persuade them that transparency has to be part of any effort to restrain racial preferences in the future.

CHAPTER FOURTEEN

THE GEORGE MASON AFFAIR

A S WE SAW IN CHAPTER THIRTEEN, the Supreme Court is significantly more deferential to colleges and universities than other spheres of American life when it comes to the use of racial preferences. Under Justice O'Connor's controlling opinion in *Grutter v. Bollinger*, that deference rests on the Court's assumption that racial admissions preference policies emerge from independent, autonomous educational judgments by the universities themselves, without substantial outside intervention. Indeed, O'Connor stressed the importance of college administrators carefully evaluating each individual act of racial preference for its unique contribution to particular educational environments.

This raises some important questions: Do colleges and universities actually exercise autonomy on matters of diversity? Are the premises behind the Court's extraordinary deference to higher education truly warranted? We have seen in earlier chapters some of the difficulties universities experience when the topic of racial preferences comes up: the strong internal pressures administrators face to maximize diversity and the difficulty of engaging in thoughtful discourse on the effects of preferences. But there are broader problems as well. Universities face entirely external pressures and incentives that often constrain their freedom to do as their administrators think best on the issue of preferences.

One of us (Sander) witnessed this firsthand when UCLA Law School adapted to Prop 209 by implementing a system of class-based rather than race-based preferences. In the very first year of the program the school became the subject of an investigation by the Office of Civil Rights of the US Department of Education. The feds were responding to a complaint filed by a civil rights group that alleged that under the guise of race-neutrality, the various UC law schools were discriminating against racial minorities by relying on the LSAT and other measures of academic performance to admit students. Such criteria, the reasoning ran, disproportionately and unfairly excluded blacks and Hispanics if used without the leavening of racial preferences. This argument had little chance of success—LSAT scores were highly predictive of law school and bar performance, and as we discussed in Chapter Two, they are effective and unbiased predictors of black and Hispanic performance too—but the investigation was nonetheless intimidating. It was also more than a little ironic: No federal agency had even asked questions about the law school's pre-209 admissions, under which, for many years, race-based student committees helped determine which applicants would be admitted. The school was, in effect, under federal investigation because it *stopped* discriminating based on race.

Institutional pressures to use racial preferences are deeply embedded in academic culture. A vast array of federal and foundation programs exist to promote and subsidize programs and research that seek to foster "diversity"— which is almost always taken to mean racial diversity. Although the goals of such programs are laudable and although they sometimes lead to important initiatives, many such programs lure universities toward using more aggressive racial preferences—as we saw in John Ellis's experiences in Chapter 9. Most universities have diversity officers who are charged not only with ensuring compliance with equal opportunity laws but also with passing along the latest collective wisdom about prodiversity initiatives; the mingling of these two functions gives the recommendations of diversity officers special force.

Accreditation agencies, which determine whether academic programs will retain the ability to grant degrees recognized by official bodies, assess the extent to which schools provide "equal opportunity" and comply with antidiscrimination laws. Frequently, these standards have evolved into assumptions that schools must use racial preferences to ensure requisite levels of racial diversity. Thus, the University of Colorado Medical School recently freed itself from a long-standing cloud over its accreditation by improving its racial diversity through national outreach efforts and, one suspects, the use of more aggressive racial preferences.

Perhaps the best way to understand how these pressures operate is to examine a single case study in some depth. The rest of this chapter chronicles what happened when the George Mason University Law School (GMU Law) reduced its use of racial preferences in the late 1990s. Through a series of public records requests, we obtained an unusual window into the way accreditation processes—in this case administered by the American Bar Association—operate behind closed doors. The experience of GMU Law suggests a system very different from the autonomous world of academic freedom that received the blessing of Supreme Court deference in *Grutter*.

* * *

George Mason University is one of several state universities in Virginia. Its law school (GMU Law) was very young—it had been founded in 1972 and had acquired its name and a secure funding source only in 1979—but by the late 1980s it had accomplished something essentially unique among American law schools: The school had developed a coherent intellectual specialization. GMU Law became known as a school that fostered the economic analysis of law. "Law and economics"—the idea that efficiency considerations were relevant not only in designing the law but even in understanding how law evolved over time—dated only to the early 1960s but had rapidly gained currency in many judicial and regulatory circles.

GMU Law's focus on law and economics gave it far more prominence than it would have otherwise enjoyed. This was a thriving, booming field. But the law school was well known for another reason: It had a number of faculty well known as conservatives or libertarians. Even though the political center of the school was probably quite close to the American center, that still made it a political outlier among American law schools.

By the mid-1990s GMU Law had begun to accrue the key ingredients needed to rise in the academic rankings—influential faculty, stronger students, and a rising budget fueled by a state in good fiscal health. In the late 1990s the school started construction of a new, modern, and glass-sheathed campus building and then made a few hiring coups. A new dean (eminent scholar Mark Grady, who replaced another eminent scholar, Henry Manne) arrived in 1997 and effectively tapped more new sources of school support and generated a strong sense of GMU Law being a school on the move.

Up until the mid-1990s national rankings like the one produced by *U.S. News* generally ranked GMU Law as a middle-tier school. By 2000, however, it had jumped into the top third of law schools, and this in turn helped the school attract yet stronger faculty, stronger students, and more donors, which led to another rise in the rankings. By 2004 GMU Law was consistently cracking lists of the nation's top fifty law schools—that is, about the top quarter or even top fifth of all law schools. No law school in the country had come so far in so short a period of time.

But the mood in the inner councils of GMU Law in 2003–2004 was not one of celebration. The school seemed to be nearing the climax of an existential crisis. Grady and his boss, the president of George Mason University, had been summoned to a hearing before a committee of the American Bar Association. The subject was to be whether the law school should lose its accreditation over matters of race.

* * *

Accreditation is a part of life for the vast majority of colleges and universities. Its purpose is to ensure that these institutions meet some generally agreed upon standard of basic quality—that faculty have sufficiently high credentials to be legitimate experts in the subjects they teach, that students be able enough to master the material taught, that facilities provide a decent instructional environment, and so on. Institutions of higher education must be accredited for their students to be eligible for federal student loans (an increasingly vital source of tuition funds in recent years). Medical students must graduate from an accredited school to be eligible to sit for licensing exams, and in nearly all states law students must graduate from an accredited school to be eligible to take the bar exam.

After the federal government started financing higher education through the GI Bill at the end of World War II, it began to "certify" private accrediting agencies to act on the government's behalf, and dozens of such organizations now exist in nearly every field of education. The American Bar Association carries out accreditation for law schools through a division dominated by legal academics.

Accreditation is particularly critical for new institutions, which often face the Catch-22 of simultaneously trying to attract good faculty and students, who are reluctant to join the school until it is accredited, which is hard to secure before some critical mass of institutional structure is in place. Once accredited, institutions come up for renewal every five or seven years, but such processes are rarely traumatic (barring a financial crisis at the school). In the hands of a skillful school administrator, the accreditation process can be used as an instrument to push for particular reforms and a means to extract more funding from university or state authorities.

Getting its initial accreditation had been a challenge for the school that became GMU Law. It had twice failed to gain accreditation as an independent

denominational school; only after those failures had it negotiated its absorp-
tion by George Mason University and, in 1980, successfully achieved accreditation. These difficulties were still in the institutional memory a generation
later and meant that re-accreditation site visits were approached with perhaps
more than the usual amount of trepidation.

The ABA's re-accreditation process begins with a self-study by the school.
Several members of the law faculty work with the deans to survey developments at the school over recent years and to address a series of topics identified by the ABA. The self-study is usually reviewed at a faculty meeting,
finalized, and submitted to the ABA, which then appoints a visiting committee to spend two or three days at the school. The visitors are mostly comprised
of faculty (normally including at least one current or former dean) from other
law schools, who review the self-study and schedule a series of meetings with
key administrators, faculty, and sometimes students at the visited school.

For its 2000 re-accreditation, GMU Law had prepared an understandably
glowing self-study. As we have noted, the school had flowered in an extraordinary way. But the visiting committee did not seem impressed. "This was a
particularly . . . liberal group, even for the ABA," one GMU administrator
observed later. "It was like oil and water from the outset."

The visitors were unimpressed by the school's rise in the rankings ("the
ranking systems have well-known flaws," one commented). They glanced
unsmilingly around the new glass-sheathed atrium and seemed to think the
new building was rather cold. They returned to a common theme over and
over during the site visit: Why was the law school so overwhelmingly white?
As the committee would soon write in its official report: "In 1999, there
were only seven entering minority students (6.5 percent) in the full-time
division. In the part-time division, 9.5 percent of the 1999 entering class was
minorities, down from 19.1% in 1998." The numbers were true enough, and
behind them lay an interesting story. In its early years GMU Law had used
fairly conventional racial preferences; admissions standards varied by race,
and the school's admissions roughly approximated the racial makeup of the
applicant pool. In 1995 about 12 percent of GMU Law students had been
nonwhite—a number somewhat lower than national averages but a fair
approximation of its applicant pool and similar to the numbers at other Virginia schools. Given the scale of its preferences, though, the minority numbers were a bit low, perhaps because nonwhite students were more likely to
be put off by its conservative reputation or less likely to be attracted by the
law and economics curriculum.

At the same time, the use of racial preferences was generating growing dissent among GMU Law faculty. Students admitted with large preferences

tended to have academic trouble at the school. Frequently they did not graduate, and many of those who did failed the bar exam. This pulled down the school-wide bar passage rate, which had attracted unfavorable notice for being only a little above the statewide average. Meanwhile, *Hopwood,* along with recent Supreme Court decisions strongly suggested that racial preferences were falling out of judicial favor, especially in the Fourth Circuit, which included Virginia.

Faculty and administrators at GMU Law cannot remember any moment when a collective decision was made to phase out (or at least minimize) racial preferences in admissions, but that is exactly what happened, very gradually, during the admission cycles from 1996 to 2000. In 1995 black applicants had been about eight times as likely to be admitted as whites with comparable credentials, as one can show through a logistic regression analysis. By 1999 there still appeared to be some preference (the coefficient on "black" was positive), but it barely registered statistically. It seems most plausible that by this time the school was merely using race as a tie-breaker for otherwise comparable black and white students.

But because of the cascade effect we discussed in Chapter Two, a reduction of racial preferences at this single school funneled minority students away from it. There were hundreds of blacks who were fully competitive for admission in 2000 to a race-neutral GMU, but those blacks were being eagerly sought after by much more elite schools. And they were being sought out not just with admissions offers but also with offers of scholarship money—the lure was enormously powerful. The only blacks and Hispanics likely to attend GMU Law through a race-blind admissions process would be the very occasional student who had a special interest in the school's curriculum, had a strong reason to be in northern Virginia, or for some reason needed to take advantage of the school's low in-state tuition.

Interestingly, at the same time as it implemented a more or less race-neutral admissions policy, GMU Law was doing something else that made it very unusual among law schools. The school operated a summer program in which students (disproportionately but not entirely minority students) whose academic qualifications fell short in the admissions process could enroll and study an intensive, focused legal curriculum for six weeks—essentially, a miniature version of the first year of law school. At the end of the program students took exams, and those who passed the exams were offered admission to the school.

The beauty of this policy was that it provided a way to increase racial diversity while avoiding the mismatch problem. LSAT scores and undergraduate grades were reliable indicators of law school performance when applied to large numbers of students, but there was a good deal of individual variation. Some people with good academic indices would turn out not to "take" to legal analysis very easily, and the reverse was true for some people with weaker credentials. GMU Law's summer program provided a way to find just those students whose credentials understated their actual ability to do well at the school and benefit from the school's curriculum. And indeed, the students admitted through the summer program had high success rates. This was "affirmative action" in its very best sense.

The visiting committee from the ABA, however, did not see it that way. Its report went on: "The school makes virtually no need-based scholarship grants to minority or any other applicants. The School has not engaged in any significant preferential affirmative action admissions program. One of the School's administrators expressed doubts regarding the legality in the Fourth Circuit of such a program. There appears to no written plan describing the School's current program and the efforts it intends to undertake relating to compliance with Standard 211." Standard 211 was the "civil rights" provision of the ABA's accreditation policy. The Standard provided that "a law school shall foster and maintain equality of opportunity in legal education, including employment of faculty and staff, without discrimination or segregation on the basis of race, color, religion, national origin, gender, sexual orientation, age or disability . . . a law school shall not use admissions policies or take other action to preclude admission of applicants or retention of students on the basis of race [and the other categories listed earlier]." By a fair interpretation of this language, GMU Law was *exceptionally* in compliance. Not only was it the rare school that did not discriminate on the basis of race in admissions; it also had funded an unusual and successful program aimed at identifying potentially successful applicants who would be screened out by a mechanical reliance on numerical credentials.

But in the Orwellian lexicon of law schools—and thus the world of academics participating in ABA accreditation processes—Standard 211 did not mean "be race-blind in admissions"; instead, it meant, in effect, just the opposite: Take what measures are necessary to make sure that your student body looks as diverse as your applicant pool, and if your applicant pool is less diverse than the local population of college graduates, take measures to diversify your applicant pool. This was the classic double-speak of affirmative action. But here it was more than public relations; here it was about to create a direct conflict between the values of GMU Law and the values of the ABA accreditation committee.

The site visit committee barely mentioned the school's summer program. It did not evaluate the outreach efforts of the admissions office. It certainly did not contend that the admissions office discriminated against minorities. The ABA's sole focus was on the actual numbers of minority students—especially black students—enrolled, and the heart of its dissatisfaction lay with the fact that only three blacks were matriculating in the current first-year class. The concluding section of the committee's report laid out a variety of findings and minor admonitions, and it listed two issues on which "the Committee concludes that it has reason to believe that George Mason University School of Law has not established that it is in compliance with the Standards" for accreditation. One issue—a trivial one—concerned whether the head of the school's library had full standing as a member of the faculty; the other concerned the school's lack of racial diversity.

Based on the report, the ABA's section on legal education followed its standard procedure for schools that "might" be out of compliance with accreditation standards: It deferred any decision on re-accrediting GMU Law and asked that the school submit a report by May 1 of the following year, giving its response and explaining any corrective actions.

Dean Grady responded the following spring, showing some level of concern but not great distress. He discussed the various small problems noted in the ABA's 2000 report and the steps GMU Law had taken to clarify or solve them. He noted that the law school had adopted a formal affirmative action policy, which "committed" the school to "the fullest opportunity for entry into and participation in the legal profession. This commitment includes making special efforts to reach out to members of racial or other minority groups which have been victimized by discrimination." Grady elaborated on minority recruitment strategies and conceded that minority enrollment remained "distressingly low."

The ABA's response was more pointed than its prior report. The nondiversity issues were considered settled. The remaining issue was the school's diversity performance and its compliance with Standard 211. Re-accreditation would be deferred again; the ABA asked that the president of the university along with the dean of the law school submit a report by May 2002 reporting both the number of entering minority students in the fall of 2001 and "information regarding the amount of scholarship monies spent for minority recruitment and financial assistance in 2000–01 and 2001–02, as well as the amount budgeted for 2002–03." The ABA's message was unambiguous: We are not interested in process. We are interested in numerical results.

GMU Law felt between a rock and a hard place. Its skepticism about racial preferences had been intensified by the realization that students admitted with preferences over the past half-dozen years had frequently had very poor outcomes. But the school's accreditation appeared to be in genuine jeopardy, and there seemed no way to satisfy the ABA short of reinstituting preferences. If the school lost ABA accreditation, none of its other recent achievements would matter; the school would essentially be out of business.

In the 2001–2002 academic year, then, GMU Law did two things. First, it gingerly waded back into the realm of racial preferences in admissions. Whereas in 2001, again, blacks had been about twice as likely to be admitted as whites with comparable academic indices, in 2002 blacks were *six* times as likely to be admitted. If, for example, a white student with a 158 LSAT and 3.3 college GPA had a 10 percent chance of admission, then a black applicant with the same numbers would have a 60 percent chance of admission. In the more prestigious day program (which drew stronger applicants and was more visible), blacks were *nine* times as likely as comparable whites to be admitted. The school also shifted scholarship funds from merit-based recruitment to race-based recruitment. In 2002 roughly *half* of all scholarship monies were awarded to black students, even though these students accounted for fewer than 3 percent of all incoming first-years.

With these changes GMU Law admitted forty-one blacks to its day or evening program in 2002, ten of whom accepted the offers and matriculated. The first-year class also included six Hispanics and one American Indian—a total of 6.5 percent of the entering class. The ABA remained unimpressed; in the summer of 2003 the accreditation committee observed that the law school's letter "does not report significant progress in complying with Standard 211, and does not differ much from what was reported by the School to the Committee a year ago, in June of 2002." The law school, the committee concluded, had shown a woeful "lack of progress in achieving student diversity. The number of minority students, especially African-American, Hispanic, and Native American students, continues to be extremely low." Moreover, the ABA apparently concluded that it had been overly indulgent to the law school. It decided to schedule a probationary hearing for April 2004 in Baltimore, to which both the law school's dean and the university's president were to appear to "show cause why the School should not be placed on probation or removed from the list of approved law schools."

This was a rather dramatic escalation of affairs. No longer was the ABA merely holding up GMU Law's reaccreditation; now matters were coming to a head, and the law school's continued existence was on the line. To say that the school's administrators were angry and frustrated would be an understatement. GMU Law had abandoned race-neutrality; it was granting very large racial preferences to black applicants; black admittees were receiving financial aid from the school at more than ten times the rate of whites; the number of minorities at the school had sharply increased—what exactly did the ABA want? The ABA would not say.

Strikingly, the ABA showed no interest in any *other* form of diversity. It did not inquire into the socioeconomic makeup of George Mason students (and has not, so far as we can determine, made such an inquiry part of any of its accreditation visits). It did not inquire into whether the school had political diversity or had enough students trained in economics to sustain the school's special mission to pursue the economic analysis of law. It showed no interest in regional diversity (always lower at state schools) or whether students brought a sufficient level of real-world experience into the classroom to enrich discussion.

Faced with what was now clearly a life-threatening crisis, the school acted on multiple fronts. GMU Law again increased the size of racial preferences used for blacks and began using racial preferences for Hispanics as well. The school created a special faculty committee on "Minority Recruitment and Retention" (with members elected by the faculty). It devoted about two-thirds of the school's entire recruitment budget to minority recruitment, including visits to historically minority schools, minority student career fairs, and the like. Commendably, to help deal with the academic fallout of increased racial preferences, the school also invested more resources in academic support, focusing on students with low entering credentials.

In a lengthy prehearing report to the ABA in November 2003, Dean Grady took a more assertive tone. He laid out in relatively stark terms the size of the racial preferences the law school was using (the median LSAT of black students starting in the fall of 2003 was ten points lower than that of any other group) and the academic consequences of these preferences:

> Although we do not treat scores and numbers as the final word on any admissions decision, our analysis of student performance over the past five years has demonstrated that numerical qualifications do place some boundaries around our discretion. Students with LSAT scores below 150 are more than six times as likely to experience academic difficulty . . . more than thirteen times as likely to be dismissed for

academic cause, and almost twice as likely to fail the bar exam on their first attempt.

Grady described in massive detail the evolution of the school's efforts to increase diversity. The law school was now sending its own message: What did the ABA expect it to do? And could it seriously believe more aggressive preferences were in the best interest of the admitted students?

By raising such questions, Grady was implicitly invoking another part of ABA's accreditation criteria—Standard 501, which stipulated that "a law school shall not admit applicants who do not appear capable of satisfactorily completing its educational program and being admitted to the bar."

Although the evidence is sketchier on this point, GMU Law and the university's president also appear to have started making some inquiries. They determined that the ABA's own accreditation authority came from the US Department of Education, which could review the ABA's exercise of its power and revoke its authority. The school made inquiries among other law school deans about how the ABA applied Standard 211 to them.

Perhaps because of a rising sense that further steps against GMU Law would create a major fight, the ABA took a step back. In January 2004 it announced itself pleased by Dean Grady's latest report. It canceled the de-accreditation hearing but still contended that there was "insufficient evidence" to conclude the Law School was meeting its obligations under Standard 211. GMU Law was still in limbo.

Mark Grady had left the deanship by this point—at the end of the 2003–2004 academic year—and another eminent scholar, Daniel Polsby, had taken up the reins. The school continued to adopt more race-conscious policies. Preferences for blacks rose again in the 2004–2005 admissions cycle; blacks applying to the law school's day program were now fifteen times as likely as similar whites to be accepted. The school instituted a special tuition increase (going beyond levels recommended by state authorities) to fund additional recruitment scholarships, again focusing on minority candidates. By 2005 there was no longer much to distinguish GMU Law's preference practices from any other law school, and indeed, Polsby pointed out to the ABA that in the fall of 2005 its first-year class would have roughly the same proportion of nonwhite students as the other Virginia public law schools (around 17 percent, two-thirds of whom were blacks and Hispanics).

There was not much more the ABA could ask, and in February 2006 its accreditation officials notified GMU Law that, after nearly six years, it was "in compliance" with Section 211. It would receive re-accreditation.

FIGURE 14.1. The Fall and Rise of Preferences at GMU Law

George Mason University Law School phased out its use of racial preferences in the late 1990s, but under pressure from the American Bar Association from 2001 to 2006, brought back even larger preferences than before.

Factor by which a typical applicant to GMU Law had her chances of admission multiplied

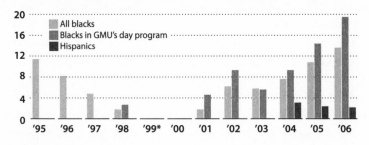

Black and hispanic percentage of 1st year class

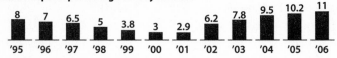

* No statistical differences in 1999, or for Hispanics before 2004. Data unavailable for blacks in GMU's day program prior to 1998, and for all groups in 2000.

Source: Public records data disclosures by George Mason University Law School, and Yakowitz and Sander, "The Fall and Rise of Affirmative Action at George Mason University Law School" (2010).

Still, GMU Law was not quite out of the woods. Later in 2006 the ABA adopted a new Standard 212, which addressed "Equal Opportunity and Diversity." It provided in relevant part that

> Consistent with sound legal education policy and the Standards, a law school shall demonstrate by concrete action a commitment to providing full opportunities for the study of law and entry into the profession by members of underrepresented groups, particularly racial and ethnic minorities, and a commitment to having a student body that is diverse with respect to gender, race, and ethnicity. . . . A law school shall demonstrate [a similar commitment] to having a faculty and staff that are diverse with respect to gender, race, and ethnicity.

The ABA also approved supplemental interpretations of the standard, including this passage: "Through its admissions policies and practices, a law

school shall take concrete actions to enroll a diverse student body that pro-
motes cross-cultural understanding, helps break down racial and ethnic
stereotypes, and enables students to better understand persons of different
races, ethnic groups, and backgrounds. . . . The determination of a law
school's satisfaction of such obligations is based on the totality of the law
school's actions and the results achieved." One of the first law schools to be
evaluated under the new standard would be . . . GMU Law. Because ABA
accreditation occurs on a seven-year cycle, and because the last site visit had
been in 2000, a new accreditation cycle would begin in early 2007.

This site visit was friendlier than the last one. The visitors were prepared
to give the law school considerable credit for its dramatic—indeed unheard
of—rise in the rankings. But the school's black population was still only 4
percent of total enrollment. (And this was George Mason, with a politically
diverse faculty in a world of overwhelmingly liberal law schools.) The visita-
tion committee submitted a report praising many of the school's achievements, pointing out a few technical matters it should address, and criticizing
the school, once again, for its lack of racial diversity.

Polsby concluded that he was in a good position to take the offensive.
Soon after receiving the site visit report and before the ABA accreditation
committee could act upon it, Polsby prepared a lengthy report that conveyed
the frustration that had built at the school over seven years. Recounting the
school's six-year effort to win re-accreditation, he observed,

At no point during this six-year period did the Committee or any other
office of the ABA ever explain how we had failed to demonstrate compliance, or state what more was required in order to demonstrate our
compliance. What did become quite clear to us during this ordeal was
that our efforts to attract minority students would never satisfy the
Committee until they produced some unspecified increase in minority
enrollment, especially of certain groups. But we were never told how
many students of which races and ethnicities we had to enroll in order
to satisfy the ABA. Nor were we ever told what steps we were required
to take in order to satisfy whatever implicit quotas the ABA was seeking
to impose upon us.

With all deference, this process was unfair to us, as well as to some
of the students whom we were pressured to admit, and who later
failed out of the law school at great cost to them in terms of time,
money and emotional distress. It also fails to live up to the ABA's own
commitment to principles of justice and due process. In any case,
there must be no repetition of this adjudicatory opacity in connection

with the current accreditation cycle. We have demonstrated—and will again demonstrate below—full compliance with the Standards. If somehow and for whatever reason, the Committee does not agree with this conclusion, there must be no more guessing games. The ABA must tell us in plain language what we must do in order to demonstrate compliance. I can assure you—and I am confident that you are well aware—that [I am] very far from the only law dean to hold this point of view.

Polsby had correctly taken the measure of the ABA. The specter of losing accreditation was extremely powerful, but if one called the ABA's bluff and demanded to know what specific numbers would satisfy Standards 211 and 212, it was suddenly vulnerable. Any attempt to impose a specific quota on a law school would almost certainly not survive a legal challenge, and President Bush's Department of Education might be moved to revoke the ABA's entire accreditation authority.

The ABA fully understood the import of Polsby's letter. GMU Law faculty had, the year before, helped to persuade the US Civil Rights Commission (USCCR) to hold a hearing on the ABA's use of its accreditation power to push schools toward the use of preferences. The head of the ABA accreditation committee had been summoned and asked pointed questions. The USCCR would soon be issuing a report. The authorities at the ABA concluded that, after all, GMU Law had been curbed in its race-neutral experiments—indeed, it had completely abandoned any hint of race neutrality. It was time for the overseers to move on. The accreditation committee, meeting in early 2008, chose not to cite the law school on either Section 211 or Section 212. Its criticisms focused on such minutiae as the academic status of the school's librarian and the need for clearer procedures in its externship programs. The battle with GMU Law over racial targets was over.

* * *

The academic world described in Justice O'Connor's *Grutter* opinion is one in which schools carefully deliberate about how best to educate their students. Racial preferences are, preferably, not used at all, but if they are, it is only because the school cannot devise any race-neutral method of enrolling a student body that has sufficient racial diversity to accomplish the school's fundamental pedagogical goals. Even then, each applicant is carefully evaluated for the ways in which that student's unique background can contribute to the school's diversity, and the school engages in an ongoing search for ways to phase out any use of race at all.

The academic world that the George Mason affair reveals is entirely different. A school that decides that racial preferences are not essential to its academic mission—and, indeed, determines that conventional racial preferences are hurting the students who receive them—is hauled up before a national body and threatened with the loss of its accreditation, a step that would effectively destroy the school. The national body acts under a system of regulations that law schools collectively adopt, whose specific requirements are murky but whose import is to require each law school to use the same size and scope of racial preferences as its peer schools. The fact that GMU Law was clearly succeeding as an academic institution—even the fact that it had instituted special programs (like its summer program) designed to promote access to legal education for students missed by ordinary preference programs—did not help it at all. In this world the ideas of academic freedom, of searching for race-neutral alternatives, and of phasing out preferences are not simply ignored: They constitute highly dangerous acts.

When we obtained through public records requests extensive data on GMU Law's admissions and its student outcomes over the period from 1995 to 2007, our colleague Jane Yakowitz (now an assistant professor of law at the University of Arizona) analyzed the files and generated the data in Figure 14.1. She also found that black admittees during this period graduated at a 70 percent rate, and (for those who were tracked) had a first-time bar passage rate of about 43 percent. Combining these numbers meant that a black matriculating at GMU Law had roughly a 30 percent chance of graduating and passing the bar on her first attempt. It was hard to argue this was an acceptable outcome. Indeed, students at the historically black Howard University Law School, only a few miles away, had academic indices very similar to blacks at GMU Law but had a graduation-and-first-time bar passage rate of about 57 percent, nearly twice as high. These differences are entirely consistent with the mismatch hypothesis, as most blacks at Howard of course had academic indices close to the class average, whereas blacks at GMU Law, during the years of large preferences (when many more enrolled), had academic indices many, many percentile points below their typical classmate.

Indeed, the GMU Law data made possible a direct test of the mismatch hypothesis. During its rapid rise in the rankings the median academic index of students at the law school had risen rapidly from year to year. Students admitted with preferences in 2006 and 2007 had academic indices similar to students admitted with much smaller or no preferences in the late 1990s. When Yakowitz compared these students, she found that the students with academic indices closer to their classmates had substantially better outcomes. Thus, as with the University of California undergraduate outcomes we considered in Part III, changing internal policies of a school made possible a test of the mismatch hypothesis, and mismatch did indeed exist and harmed student outcomes.

This is strong evidence that the ABA was abusing its authority in two ways. First, Standards 211 and 212 conflicted directly with the strictures of *Grutter* to respect the academic freedom and diversity calculus of individual institutions. Second, it violated Standard 511 by pressing—in effect, forcing—GMU Law to admit students who faced long odds against becoming lawyers and who would have been much better served by attending a different law school.

The US Commission on Civil Rights issued a report following up on its 2006 hearing. A majority of its commissioners concluded that

> [The ABA] should revise the recently adopted Standard 212 to delete the requirement that law schools seeking accreditation demonstrate a commitment to diversity. The standard should instead be revised to permit law schools, consistent with *Grutter v. Bollinger*, the freedom to determine whether diversity is essential to their academic mission. . . . Law schools should voluntarily provide disclosure to the public and, at the very least, to potential applicants on student academic performance, attrition, graduation, bar passage, student loan default, and future income disaggregated by academic credentials. . . . [The ABA] should, pursuant to its accreditation authority, require law schools to disclose the details recommended [above].

The ABA has not adopted these recommendations. So far as we are aware, its leaders have never even considered them.

CHAPTER FIFTEEN

TRANSPARENCY AND
THE CALIFORNIA BAR AFFAIR

ONE OF THE GREATEST ENGINES of social progress in recent history has been the gathering and analysis of data—to help identify causes of and possible cures for diseases, to shed light on the dangers of climate change, to help develop the most effective instructional methods for K-12 schools, and much, much more.

But as we have seen repeatedly in past chapters, the first instinct of racial preference supporters has been to suppress rather than confront and analyze data showing preferences' operation and effects on supposed beneficiaries. Consequently, by far the greatest barrier to diagnosing mismatch—and, more broadly, to reforming affirmative action—is the jealous care with which the proponents of preferences guard the data about their domain. Indeed, the opponents of coauthor Sander's "Systemic Analysis" article on racial preferences in law school admissions were, if anything, more upset about the indisputable data that Sander revealed than about his conclusions as to the import of the data.

Just as the George Mason affair, recounted in Chapter Fourteen, helps make vivid and concrete the pressures on individual schools to conform to broader conventions on racial preferences, so in this chapter we focus on one high-profile battle over access to potentially illuminating data between

233

mismatch scholars (led by Sander) and the State Bar of California. This struggle, which is, as we go to press, before the California Supreme Court, has created an unusual face-off between national media organizations supporting access to government data and civil rights groups supporting secrecy. Before turning to this story, we discuss some of the general contours of the transparency problem and the dilemmas that inhere in it.

* * *

As we will see, opponents of data transparency often cite the threat that databases can pose to individual privacy. Hospital patients have both legal and ethical rights to have information about their medical conditions remain private; students have similar if somewhat less compelling rights to the privacy of their academic records. How do we preserve these rights while making data available for research?

The simplest way to protect privacy is simply to remove what are known as "personal identifiers" from databases, which include not only someone's name but also any other piece of information that belongs more or less uniquely to him, such as his address or Social Security number. This creates a simple privacy screen, but it does not fully protect individuals from a resourceful researcher who can use "indirect identifiers"—such as a combination of one's place of birth, current zip code, race, and height—to infer who somebody is. The feasibility of using indirect identifiers to "crack" individual identities in databases has grown significantly with the Internet, as vast databases have become searchable online, and a wide variety of tidbits about nearly everyone have become relatively easy to access.

To solve these problems, institutions that gather data use one of three mechanisms to protect privacy. First, they may require researchers to use the data only on in-house computers: The researcher is allowed to visit a site where the data (with personal identifiers removed) is kept in electronic form; she may analyze the data with statistical programs already on the computer but can only take aggregated results from her analysis with her. Second, the institution may establish a contract with the researcher that essentially makes her liable for any disclosure of private data. Or third, the institution may "anonymize" the data. In this technique one combines "indirect identifiers" into larger categories, so that no person whose information is included in the data has a unique combination of characteristics. Thus, in the example suggested above, one might provide only the first three digits of each person's zip code and only the region (rather than the city) of birth so that several different people in the database would have these characteristics in common and could not be uniquely identified even by inference.

These methods have proven remarkably effective. Consider, for example, the Inter-University Consortium for Political and Social Research (ICPSR), which is based at the University of Michigan. ICPSR was created and exists in order to help make databases available to scholars. Large data-gathering projects all over the world deposit their data with ICPSR, which makes sure that proper anonymization procedures are followed, takes applications for data use from scholars, and makes data available. ICPSR has custody of thousands of databases on a host of social, economic, and political phenomena; tens of thousands of academics and other researchers receive or download ICPSR datasets every year. Yet at least as of 2009 (when we last checked), there has not been a single incident in ICPSR's entire history when the privacy of study participants has been breached.

Dangers to privacy undoubtedly exist in the brave new world of instant data retrieval. But in the world of academic research, well-established norms and techniques have done the job.

* * *

Because the free flow of information and data in society is truly the lifeblood of academic research, it is more than a little ironic that higher education institutions have been extreme in their secretiveness about admissions and student outcomes. Opacity is evident at every turn—particularly when data touches on race or racial preferences. We saw this in Chapter Ten, when political scientist Tim Groseclose was denied access to even an anonymized version of admissions data—presumably because he expressed concern over the school's use of race in admissions decisions—even though he was a faculty member of the university's admissions committee. The same thing happened to Robert Steinbuch, a professor at the University of Arkansas, Little Rock. When Steinbuch expressed concerns that the university's use of racial preferences might wind up admitting students who would struggle on the bar exam, he found himself unable to get even elementary data linking admissions standards to long-term academic and bar outcomes.

As we discussed in Chapter Four, the Law School Admission Council's (LSAC's) Bar Passage Study (BPS) severely compromised its potential for shedding light on mismatch and other effects of racial preferences by obscuring the identities of the law schools attended by participants and the states in which they took bar exams. The University of California's efforts to keep under wraps the data on which much of Part III of this book is based forced Sander and many colleagues to struggle with the university for over a year to get any data at all; and in the end the university released only data that, for example, combined some forty academic majors into three categories and did not distinguish between blacks and Hispanics. This made impossible many important analyses that could have been done with more complete data. Both the university and LSAC showed a zeal for privacy protection far beyond anything that was either necessary or comparable to the standards used with much more sensitive data—such as medical information—in other areas of research.

Undoubtedly the most valuable information thus far compiled anywhere for the study of racial preferences lies in the "College and Beyond" databases created at the Mellon Foundation in the 1990s (and, since then, significantly augmented). William Bowen, a former president of Princeton University and president of the Foundation from 1988 to 2006, instigated the creation of the databases, secured the cooperation of dozens of universities, and poured millions of foundation funding dollars into the project—all remarkable achievements. Bowen used the College and Beyond data in a series of books, most famously in *The Shape of the River* (coauthored with former Harvard president Derek Bok), which we discussed in Chapter Six.

But *The Shape of the River* is not a dispassionate book, and many of its conclusions are in sharp tension with other research findings using similar data. Unfortunately, Mellon has erected barriers to other scholars who might critically examine Bowen and Bok's conclusions. Indeed—and incredibly— Mellon's explicit policy is to not make data available to check or replicate the results published in *The Shape of the River*. The databases are available only for academics who submit lengthy, detailed research proposals to the Foundation, and these are then reviewed for approval or rejection. In effect, a scholar must go through the laborious process of writing an academic paper, with blanks where the data analysis will fit, in the hope that Mellon's review committee will like the proposal enough to allow limited use of the College and Beyond data. To say this severely chills research is an understatement.

All this prompted Stephan and Abigail Thernstrom, the leading scholarly critics of racial preferences, to observe in a scathing review of *The Shape of the River*,

> If you are inclined to believe that policies are best evaluated by those who design and implement them, Bowen and Bok are superbly qualified for the task they set themselves. They were present at the beginning of preferential policies a generation ago and presided over their implementation in two schools that rank at the very top of the prestige ladder. . . . That the data upon which *The Shape of the River* rests are apparently available only to totally trusted insiders obviously compromises the search for truth. If the only medical records available to determine whether cigarette smoking causes lung cancer had been controlled

by the tobacco companies, and if the companies had given access only to scholars who doubted the link, scientific progress in resolving the issue would surely have been impeded.

In fairness, some professors who can undoubtedly be regarded as independent have gained access to College and Beyond data. But more than one of these scholars have told us of their concerns about how Mellon might react to their actual research findings and whether they might find their access to the data cut off. The broad point is that the Mellon Foundation has no moral or legal justification for limiting access to its data so severely. It would be entirely justified in using any of the anonymization procedures we discussed earlier. It could fairly create strong contractual obligations and severe penalties if users of its data made inappropriate disclosures (such as identifying individual colleges). But creating a demanding gauntlet for access, tingeing it with ideology, and prohibiting replication of Bowen and Bok's results is antiscientific and not in the public interest.

* * *

As we noted in Chapter Five, early in the debate over law school mismatch the LSAC made clear its intention to tighten its grip on its BPS database. Had LSAC maintained a version of the BPS that identified individual schools and made it accessible, for example, under tightly controlled conditions at LSAC's headquarters, many of the intense debates over mismatch evidence could have been easily resolved. But that was not going to happen. So one of us (Sander) began to cast about for a comparable source of data. He found one, but only one: a database compiled by the State Bar of California. Since the 1970s the California Bar had collected unusually detailed information about the more than one hundred thousand law graduates sitting for its bar exams, including the law school that each of them attended, their LSAT scores, law school GPAs, and bar scores. The California Bar was the only one in the nation that had assembled a database of this type; it had used the data as part of an ambitious research program, which included the development of the "performance exam"—a realistic simulation of actual lawyer tasks—described in Chapter Four.

Sander's effort to use the California Bar data to test mismatch theory began with an approach to Stephen Klein, a respected psychometrician with the Rand Corporation who had worked as a consultant for the California Bar for a generation. Klein was respectfully skeptical about mismatch theory, largely because of a study he had conducted in the late 1980s suggesting that mismatch was not a serious problem. But he agreed that it was an important issue worthy of further study and that the California Bar data was ideally suited for testing mismatch because it contained so many relevant variables concerning the relationship between the law school a student attended and her performance on the bar exam. They collaborated on a research proposal to fund a study of bar data (which a private foundation agreed to fund) and to ask the bar to let Klein use the data for the mismatch study in conjunction with his ongoing research.

The California State Bar had been created many generations earlier by the California Supreme Court, which still had ultimate control over the bar's structure. It had delegated power to a board of governors, which included some lawyers elected by members of the bar and others appointed by elected state officials. The board appointed the bar's executive director, who ran day-to-day operations. The incumbent, Judy Johnson, was the bar's first African American director. The board also appointed a committee of bar examiners, which made policy decisions relevant to the bar exam. The staff officer who dealt with the bar—essentially Johnson's second-in-command—was Gayle Murphy.

Klein suggested that I contact Murphy, and in due course I received an invitation to meet with her at the bar's heavily secured San Francisco headquarters. I laid out my proposal: Klein and his principal research associate, Roger Bolus, would undertake a study of mismatch issues using the California Bar data. Outside scholars, including me, would pose specific research questions, analyze results, and have other input—but no access to the database itself and, thus, no opportunity to violate privacy protections even had we wanted to do so. We would collaborate on a report of our findings. Before starting any work we would obtain funding for the entire project. The bar would, therefore, get some free research, conducted by its own experts, examining a problem that everyone seemed to concede deserved careful study.

Murphy seemed agreeable. She nodded and smiled and explained that the Committee of Bar Examiners would make such decisions. Murphy showed no particular interest in the study but no hostility toward it either other than to note that mismatch research had been controversial. Klein and Sander submitted a memo outlining the case for the study and were invited to meet with the Committee of Bar Examiners in early October 2006. Members of the committee—all practicing lawyers—had heard about the mismatch issue, and several thought the study made a lot of sense. The committee voted unanimously to make a formal decision on our proposal at an upcoming meeting, and this seemed a good sign. After the session a couple of committee members sought out Sander and congratulated him on the proposal and on doing important work.

But in the ensuing weeks several law school deans expressed opposition to the study at another bar meeting, and several other deans wrote a letter to the bar (which we have not seen) also urging that no study be done. One recurring theme of criticism was that generalizations emerging from the study might stigmatize black and Hispanic law students. This was an interesting claim. It was already well known that California Bar passage rates differed dramatically across racial lines; the bar posted reports on its website twice a year that documented the disparities. Indeed, one of the motives for originally gathering detailed bar data was to study whether the bar exam itself in some way aggravated these disparities. (Klein had long since concluded it did not; racial disparities disappeared when one controlled for the law school grades of bar takers.) *The mismatch hypothesis had the potential to explain the racial disparities in nonracial terms.*

Of course, if racial stigmatization were widely accepted as a reason not to release information and study data, then all sorts of research could not proceed: AIDS infections, criminal activity, drug use, and welfare dependency all interact with race, and research on any of these subjects could generate racially unfair generalizations. But that is rarely if ever invoked as a reason for not releasing data that can help us understand those phenomena, diagnose causes, and work toward solutions.

There was a far more plausible—if less respectable—reason for law school deans to vigorously oppose the proposed study: It would reveal racial disparities in bar passage rates at individual schools. (Bar reports listed total bar passage rates for schools but no breakdowns within schools by race or any academic index measures.) No dean wanted it known, for example, if whites and Asians at her school passed the bar more than 90 percent of the time but blacks and others receiving very large preferences passed 50 percent of the time or less.

After the law school deans had weighed in, Murphy was conspicuously more skeptical about the study. She indicated to Sander that the decision would depend on the persuasive powers of the constituencies for and against the study. Given the opposition among law schools, she said, Klein and Sander would need to show that there was significant support for our position.

Some support was forthcoming. The US Civil Rights Commission had recently held hearings on the law school mismatch issue, and staff at the commission were preparing a report on the phenomenon; as we noted in Chapter Five, the commission would soon call for greater transparency by law schools on the racial preferences they used and the outcomes of students admitted with preferences. A majority of the commissioners sent a letter to the Committee of Bar Examiners urging that the Klein-Sander study go forward. So did a group of leading legal empiricists, including one scholar, Albert Yoon, who had been a prominent critic of the mismatch hypothesis. A group of former law school deans and more than a score of other academics wrote or signed letters as well. Vik Amar, a constitutional law professor at the University of California, Davis Law School, who had led a constitutional challenge to Prop 209, agreed to join the study as a co-investigator, as did Indiana University Law School professor William Henderson. Amar's and Henderson's involvement sent a strong signal that the Klein-Sander study would carefully consider hypotheses from scholars on all sides of the mismatch issue.

Murphy and the Committee of Bar Examiners scheduled another meeting for early 2007. They brought in several experts who had participated in past bar studies; the experts were either neutral about or supportive of the Klein-Sander proposal. But a new strain of criticism had entered the debate. Some of the scholars and researchers who had argued that mismatch did not exist now began to attack the study on various grounds. William Kidder, a critic of Sander's original mismatch article and now a staff member working on diversity issues at the University of California's Office of the President, wrote a long letter to the bar advancing a variety of arguments against the study. He suggested that bar exams were not necessarily a good measure of student learning, that the study might not produce statistically significant results, that information about bar passage rates at individual law schools might become public, and the like. Kidder's report was accompanied by a letter from Dr. Judy Suzuki, the university's vice president for student affairs, which commended the letter to the bar's consideration. The Society of American Law Teachers, a generally leftish but nonetheless substantial organization of law professors, weighed in with its own view that the Klein-Sander study would give too much significance to bar exams. Larry Kramer, dean of Stanford Law School, and Professor Michelle Dauber of Stanford, an early and vocal critic of mismatch, weighed in with a letter and testimony arguing that the proposed study would violate federal privacy laws—even though the study proposal at the time envisioned no release of data.

Perhaps most striking of all was a very long letter submitted to the bar by Richard Lempert, probably the most prominent of all the mismatch critics. Lempert advanced a convoluted argument suggesting that the Klein-Sander study should not proceed because no "human subjects" process had yet vetted the study to make sure that the research would not harm the research subjects. (In fact, the UCLA Human Subjects Committee held, more or less automatically, that the study did not require any human subjects review because the study merely involved the analysis of already-collected data.)

The opposition of so many mismatch critics to a proposal to use the best available, very powerful data to study mismatch was striking. It is difficult to avoid the conclusion that they wanted to prevent the study—or any step that would make the data available to researchers—because the results might discredit their own work. Consider Lempert, for example. In 2000 he had coauthored a study claiming that minority law students at the University of Michigan Law School (UMLS) had bar passage rates in excess of 95 percent. He had testified in the *Grutter* trial that UMLS blacks virtually always passed the bar. Yet such bar passage rates were unheard of for schools using large racial preferences, as UMLS of course did. A growing amount of other evidence suggested that Lempert's claims were greatly exaggerated and that the actual bar passage rates of blacks at the law school were far lower. If the Klein-Sander study went forward, it would be possible to examine the bar passage rate of nearly one thousand UMLS minority graduates who had taken the California Bar. Someone in Lempert's position would have a powerful motive for keeping this data secret.

Klein and Sander had a compelling response to mismatch critics' arguments that their study design was flawed. In the course of seeking funding for the study, they had submitted their proposal to the National Science Foundation (NSF), which makes limited awards for research on "law and social science" and sends proposals out to distinguished, anonymous, independent reviewers for advice. Although NSF had ultimately not funded the study, the peer reviews had been generally glowing: "I have rarely seen a research proposal that more clearly merited funding"; "On intellectual grounds, one of the strongest proposals I have reviewed—either for the NSF or for any funding agency"; the study would be "of enormous value in advancing knowledge on this difficult subject."

There was, of course, a more fundamental response: If critics believed that Klein and Sander might reach erroneous or misleading results, they could submit their own hypotheses to be tested, conduct their own study, or gather data they considered more relevant. But none of those seeking to stop the study suggested any of those things. They proposed only that no research be done.

Lost amid these protests was the idea that databases created by government agencies belong to the public. It would be reasonable for a public agency like the bar to decide whether to fund its own study based on the perceived value or popularity of the research. But it was not reasonable for a public agency to deny citizen access to a public database and prevent independent research, simply because some other parties did not want the research done.

Perhaps sensing that an overtly political decision would look unsavory, bar officials advanced in June and July 2007 a series of new arguments against the research proposal. Murphy contended (falsely, as it would turn out) that the bar had never made its data available for research by anyone other than the bar itself. She also suggested that the research, because it was not "for Bar purposes," would violate the terms under which the data had been collected from bar applicants and law schools. She further implied that individual identities of bar takers might be inferred from data the bar released (an impossibility, as we were not asking the bar at that point to release any data). Purportedly on grounds such as these, the Committee of bar Examiners voted not to proceed with the Klein-Sander study.

The Board of Governors—the California Bar's highest authority—decided to review the committee's decision and scheduled a hearing for November 2007. Bar officials burnished their legal arguments against the study, and antimismatch scholars submitted their own arcane reasons for stopping the research. But opponents had new allies as well. In October 2007 other critics of the mismatch hypothesis began to spread the word through the California community of minority lawyers that the Klein-Sander study would lead to the release of black lawyers' personal information. A pro-affirmative action advocacy group in San Francisco echoed the same message and alleged that the notoriously conservative Scaife Foundation would fund the study (an entirely false claim). At the November meeting scores of black lawyers and law students created a standing-room-only crowd in the board's hearing room, and their spokespersons argued passionately against releasing the data. The study was not without defenders—the chairman of the Civil Rights Commission, Gerald Reynolds, flew to town to speak in the study's defense, as did Joe Hicks, an important figure in the debate over Prop 209 (as the reader will recall from Chapter Seven) and a former governor of the bar. Still, no one was surprised when the board voted against the study.

The proposal seemed irretrievably dead, but resurrection came from an unexpected quarter. Peter Scheer, a respected attorney and journalist who had founded and directed the First Amendment Coalition (FAC), based in San Francisco, read about the Board of Governors' meeting and vote in a legal newspaper. The FAC's mission was to pursue public interest litigation on behalf of free speech, transparency in government, and related causes. Scheer thought that the suppression of data in the hands of the California Bar, which was clothed with government power, was the sort of conduct he was in business to challenge. The chairman of FAC's board, James Chadwick, was himself a leading litigator in the field of information law. Chadwick and Scheer offered to make our request for the bar data into a test case to clarify the public's right of access to government records in California.

Sander, Hicks, and the First Amendment Coalition filed public information requests seeking key elements of the California Bar's database to be made available to any researcher interested in the data. Jane Yakowitz, a research colleague of Sander and an emerging expert on privacy law, drafted protocols designed to protect the privacy of every bar taker who provided information to the bar. When the bar rejected the request, Chadwick and a team of other pro bono attorneys filed suit in the California courts.

The case gained momentum when discovery showed that bar officials had not told the truth about their past use of the bar database. In the early 1990s, with the advice and consent of the California Supreme Court, the bar had provided thousands of individual bar records to LSAC. Bar documents showed that, among other things, LSAC proposed to use the data to explore the mismatch issue (a study that was never done—perhaps killed for political reasons). Even more damning was the bar's failure to anonymize the data that it provided to the LSAC. And Yakowitz demonstrated that the bar had published hundreds of bar results that could, if anyone cared to make the effort, be traced to individual bar takers. All of the bar's reasons for not doing our proposed study now looked like the flimsiest pretexts, perhaps even willful misrepresentations to the Board of Governors.

In June 2011 the First Amendment Coalition, Hicks, and Sander won a unanimous decision by a three-member California Court of Appeals panel that we were entitled to have access to the bar data.

The California Bar appealed to the state Supreme Court, where, at this writing, the case is still pending. Meanwhile, the case has become something of an open-records cause célèbre. Few cases on the openness of public records reach supreme courts, even though the rise and growing pervasiveness of electronic records create many open issues. News organizations, in particular, are concerned that rights of public access be protected. The *Los Angeles Times* and *San Francisco Chronicle* had been early supporters of the coalition's lawsuit, and in February 2012 a broader alliance of news organizations weighed in with a specially commissioned brief. The Gannett Company, the Hearst Corporation, the *New York Times* Company, the *Washington Post*, the *Newsweek/Daily Beast* Company, NBC Universal, Reuters America, *Forbes*, the Scripps Company, the publishers of the *New York Daily News*, the American Society of Newspaper Editors, the Reporters Committee for Freedom of the Press, and dozens of other publishers and journalists' associations—all of these joined an amicus brief arguing that the plaintiffs have a right of access to the Bar's databases.

This amicus brief was an important development—perhaps as important as the lawsuit itself. This issue of racial preferences was difficult for many in the leadership class to discuss openly. It was a hard subject on which to press for reform. But the importance of data access and transparency—that was a bedrock value for many who transcended the politics of race. For this entire free-speech, open-government community, one value was clear, a value that had once been—and perhaps could again be—pervasive among academics: "Sunlight is the best disinfectant."

V.

THE WAY FORWARD

CHAPTER SIXTEEN

CLASS, RACE, AND
THE TARGETING OF PREFERENCES

A T THE INCEPTION OF THE affirmative action era in the late 1960s, the foremost advocates of action stressed the fundamental goal of social mobility—of using the civil rights revolution as an engine for broadly smoothing the path of opportunity. The 1968 Kerner Commission famously argued that "white racism" was the root cause of urban black riots, but it emphasized the importance of helping the disadvantaged in a race-neutral way. Martin Luther King Jr. also emphasized that "it is a simple matter of justice that America, in dealing creatively with the task of raising the Negro from backwardness, should also be rescuing a large stratum of the forgotten white poor." And indeed, though there is still much debate about the credit due to the Great Society, poverty rates among all races in America declined at unprecedented rates during the 1960s.

The preference programs that rapidly began to spread across American higher education soon after King's death were almost always race based. But they often tried hard to reach low- and moderate-income blacks. The new preference initiatives often had names like "First Generation" and "Legal Education Opportunity Program" to emphasize their orientation toward the most disadvantaged minorities. This was more than rhetoric; available data sources from the 1970s suggest that a very large proportion of those receiving large racial preferences either were from economically modest backgrounds or were the first in their families to attend college.

But as Richard Kahlenberg has pointed out, in the 1980s and 1990s things changed. Justice Powell's balance-tipping solo opinion in the Supreme Court's *Bakke* decision energized the idea that campus diversity rather than social reform was the proper legal basis for racial preference programs. College costs escalated. Though they rarely publicly admitted it, college administrators became concerned about the particularly severe preparation deficits of low- and moderate-income blacks. Outreach efforts atrophied; many colleges and admissions officers became more cynical, viewing preference programs as being about reaching racial enrollment targets rather than a special social mission. All of these shifts made schools more likely to award racial preferences not on the basis of objective disadvantage but rather to those blacks and Hispanics with the strongest academic preparation and the most impressive résumés.

Figure 16.1 captures the dimensions of this shift. In an authoritative series of national surveys of high school students, more than half of blacks entering elite colleges in 1972 came from families that were in the bottom half of the socioeconomic distribution. By 1982 less than a quarter of blacks entering elite colleges came from the bottom half, and by 1992 the proportion was down to 8 percent. Two-thirds of the 1992 cohort of blacks at elite colleges came from the top quartile of the American socioeconomic distribution— that is, the upper-middle class and the upper class. There is little reason to think that things have gotten better since then.

Ironically, racial preferences have become more focused on affluent recipients at the same time that economic inequality has become a more severe phenomenon and a more pressing issue in the United States. Since 1979 the share of consumer income in the United States going to the top 5 percent of the income distribution has doubled, and the share going to the top 0.1 percent has more than tripled. Measures of social mobility show that persons who start life in the bottom fifth of the income distribution are less likely now than they were a generation ago to move to the top half.

Most of this book has focused on whether large admissions preferences work for their intended beneficiaries. In this chapter we consider whether preferences are doing effective work for society. There are four key questions we hope to answer. First, to what extent does our higher education system of preferences give people access to opportunities that would otherwise elude them because of accidents of birth? Does race or class better capture patterns of exclusion? Second, does the general absence of students with low- and moderate-income backgrounds from elite higher education simply reflect a shortage of academically strong students who are potentially admissible? Or is

FIGURE 16.1. **Drift Toward Affluence**

Each decade the federal government funds a longitudinal study that tracks high school students through college and the start of their careers. The socioeconomic background of blacks who attended elite schools has changed markedly since the early years of racial preferences.

Although the sample size is small (a total of 61 black respondents at elite schools) the socioeconomic background of blacks who attended elite schools has changed markedly since the early years of racial preferences, and the shifts are statistically significant.

Proportion of black students at elite colleges whose family background puts them in the . . .

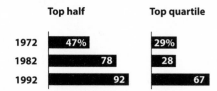

Sources: Authors' calculations of data from National Longitudinal Study (1972); High School & Beyond (1982); National Longitudinal Education Study (1992).

our system overlooking diamonds in the rough? Third, to what extent do class and race intersect and overlap? If we shifted from race-based to class-based preferences and other mechanisms of affirmative action, would racial minorities be shut out? Fourth, given the problem of mismatch, does it make sense to talk about admissions preferences for any group?

* * *

When we talk about class in America, we are talking about a somewhat fuzzy concept; Americans obviously do not sort themselves into clearly distinct social strata based on accent, clothing, or habits. In this chapter we treat social status as a continuum ranging from the poor to the rich, from people with an eighth-grade education to others with doctorates or professional degrees. Social scientists usually measure "socioeconomic status" (SES) with some combination of information about a person's education, her occupation, and her household income. When they analyze the SES of college students, they generally measure the education, occupation, and/or income of each student's parents. An SES index puts these measures into a scale so that we can talk about someone whose parents rank in, say, the bottom quartile of SES or the top tenth. We know these rankings mean something because one can predict with reasonable accuracy many aspects of a person's life by knowing their SES or (before they are independent) the SES of their parents. People tend to marry others with similar SES, live in neighborhoods where their SES predominates, and end up with jobs predicted by their parents' SES.

Measures of the SES of students attending elite colleges and professional schools show that their backgrounds are dramatically skewed toward affluence. As Figure 16.2 shows, roughly three-quarters of students at elite colleges are from families in the top quarter of SES, whereas only 3 percent come from the bottom quarter and under 10 percent come from the bottom half. Put differently, this means that a boy or girl who grows up in a top-quartile family is about twenty-five times more likely to end up attending an elite college than someone from the bottom quartile. The class background of students is even more skewed at elite law schools.

FIGURE 16.2. Not-So-Diverse

Most students at elite undergraduate and law schools come from privileged backgrounds.

Proportion of students in each socioeconomic quartile

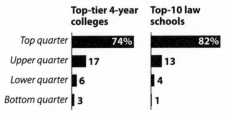

Source: Analysis of elite colleges is from Carnevale & Rose, "Socioeconomic Status, Race/Ethnicity, and Selective College Admissions," (2004); analysis of law schools is from Sander, "Class and American Legal Education," (2011).

We can intuitively sense from this data that low-SES students are much more underrepresented in the ranks of selective colleges than are, for instance, blacks or Hispanics. A random black high school senior is perhaps 30 percent less likely than a random white high school senior to end up at Harvard, but a senior from the bottom quartile of SES is dozens of times less likely to end up at Harvard than a senior from the top quartile or top tenth of SES.

Indeed, even if we consider college education more broadly, the disparity in opportunities is striking. Using the National Educational Longitudinal Study (NELS), the federal government's major effort in the 1990s to study such things as the transition from high school to college, we can compare the chances of different groups of high school graduates advancing to a four-year college. When we control for academic preparation, black high school graduates are about 30 percent more likely than comparable whites to attend a four-year college. But persons of all races from the bottom 20 percent of the SES distribution are about 70 percent *less likely* than otherwise comparable people from the top 20 percent of the SES distribution to attend a four-year college. Ironically, the same data shows that blacks are less likely than comparable whites to actually receive a bachelor's degree—a plausible consequence of mismatch. In other words, racial preference policies (and their cascading effects through the system) have more than leveled the playing field for blacks in *college access*. However, our system does a poor job on two other counts: providing access to able students from the lower SES ranges and helping blacks succeed *after* they get to college.

Especially in the context of our book's other findings, these patterns from the NELS are unmistakable signs of a racial preference system gone badly awry. And the picture becomes all the more distressing when we look closely at who actually receives preferences. As we noted at the beginning of the chapter, 92 percent of the blacks attending elite colleges (in the NELS sample) came from the families in the top half of the American SES distribution (which means the top third of the black SES distribution). The NELS sample is small, but data from the "After the JD" (AJD), a database we discussed in Chapters Four and Five, has detailed SES information on a much larger sample of law students who finished law school in 1999 or 2000. Analysis of this data shows that 89 percent of blacks entering elite (top twenty) law schools—a large majority of whom received large racial preferences—came from families in the top half of the American SES distribution. Sixty-six percent came from families in the top quarter, and 43 percent came from families in the very elite and affluent families in the top tenth. Hispanic law students were more likely to come from working-class backgrounds (and received smaller preferences), but nonetheless, *half* of the Hispanic students at elite law schools came from families in the *top quarter* of the SES distribution.

When we look more closely at students receiving preferences, their "representativeness" dissolves even further. Ten years ago black students at Harvard Law School organized a sort of self-study. They found that only 30 percent of black students at the school had four African American grandparents. Another third of the blacks were from interracial families, and the rest were either foreign born or the children of foreign-born people of West Indian and/or African descent. More systematic studies have found that nearly 40 percent of black Ivy League undergraduates are first- or second-generation immigrants. And for mixed-race students (recall Natasha Scott from Chapter Twelve), the potential for inflated numbers has become so significant that the federal government changed its rules last year, now requiring colleges to report mixed-race students separately. "In the past," reports Jeff Brenzel, dean of undergraduate admissions at Yale, "if a student self-identified as both African-American and white, or both African-American and Hispanic, the student would be counted as African-American."

The temptation for admissions officers to admit, in greatly disproportionate numbers, affluent blacks, mixed-race blacks, and foreign-born blacks arises from three simple facts. First, the academic indices of each of these groups are much higher, on average, than those of American blacks in general. Second, they are easy to find; indeed, the admissions offices don't need to do any outreach at all—students in these groups will tend to seek out and apply to elite schools. Third, if one is focused on a numbers game, then anybody who can be given the appropriate racial identification will serve. (One of us once witnessed an admissions office, particularly desperate to get up its "black" numbers, count someone of Egyptian descent as African American.)

As America becomes more multiethnic and intermarriage grows in popularity, our multiracial population has soared, growing by 36 percent from 2000 to 2009 and projected by the census to grow another 21 percent by 2015, to over 6.4 million. Black immigration continues to grow as well; first- and second-generation black Americans (who tend to be highly educated) now make up close to 20 percent of the black population. Under these demographic circumstances, even admissions officers who want to be racially inclusive face increasingly difficult and arbitrary distinctions. Who should count as black? And these difficulties are even greater when we consider Hispanics, Southeast Asians, or American Indians, all of whom have still higher cross-racial marriage rates.

There are, as well, the increasingly important intersections between class and race. This flows in two directions. On the one hand, middle- and upper-middle-class blacks have increasingly entered the mainstream of American life. They are likely to be college educated, have professional or managerial jobs, live in attractive neighborhoods, and have cross-racial social networks. When we control for measures of learning and academic preparation, blacks with college degrees have the same or higher earnings and are more likely to have professional jobs than are comparable whites. On many matters they have attitudes about a host of social and economic issues similar to those of their middle- and upper-middle-class white neighbors and work colleagues, especially if they live on the East or West coast.

But "intersectionality" occurs in a completely different way for those in the bottom half of the American income distribution. Low-income blacks tend to be substantially worse off than whites with similar incomes. Low- and moderate-income blacks are very likely to live in highly segregated neighborhoods. A very high proportion of their neighbors are likely to be poor. The local school is likely to be terrible. Crime rates are higher; two-parent families are a rarity. As Eugene Robinson powerfully argues in his 2011 book *Disintegration*, social policy needs to (but often fails to) distinguish between America's distinct strata of blacks; for all of the enthusiasm about diversity, lower- and working-class blacks are the ones who need help but are often utterly overlooked.

As matters stand, our racial preference system is poorly targeted. Whether the goal is to achieve a meaningful representation of America's population, to create classrooms that have a diversity of life experiences, or to improve social mobility, we are not doing a passable job.

* * *

Defenders of the status quo who concede these huge disparities often suggest that greater consideration of class might be desirable, but is unworkable because there are simply not enough low-SES students who can cut the mustard.

Not true. As we noted earlier, high school seniors in the bottom fifth of the SES distribution are 70 percent less likely to attend a four-year college than *academically similar* seniors in the top fifth of the SES distribution. That means that when we are comparing two seniors—one low-income and one high-income—who have the same measureable level of academic preparation, the high-income senior is three times as likely to go to a four-year college.

An even more compelling way of seeing this point is captured in Figure 16.1. Using the College Board data described in Chapter Eight, we examined the pool of all students taking the SAT who, under the pre-2006 scoring system, had a combined score of 1200 or more on the math and verbal portions of the test. A 1200 score puts a student into the top 8 or 9 percent of all high school students—well within the pool of students that even the most elite schools consider (under preference programs). This pool is sorted by race and quintiles of socioeconomic status; the number in each cell shows the proportion of those students who applied to any of a loosely defined "top ten" undergraduate colleges (the Ivy League plus Duke and Stanford). These data show that a high-scoring black student in the bottom SES quintile had only a 4 percent chance of applying to any of these schools, whereas a high-scoring black student in the top SES quintile had a 48 percent chance. The disparities are smaller but still striking for white and Hispanic students. Only among Asians, whose parents often have a fierce determination to maximize the educational achievement of their children, are the disparities seriously blunted.

FIGURE 16.3. Untapped Potential

Exceptional students from poorer backgrounds are unlikely to apply to elite colleges. Only 4 percent of low-SES black students who scored a 1,200 or greater on the SAT apply.

Percent of 1999 SAT-takers scoring above 1,200 sending test scores to very elite colleges

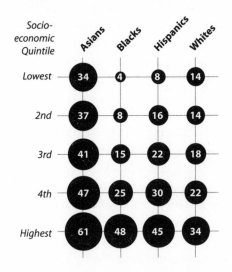

Source: Authors' calculations of data obtained from the College Board.
Top-tier colleges include the Ivy League, Duke, and Stanford.

Figure 16.3 speaks volumes about the landscape of opportunity for promising high school students and about the poor job that college admissions officers are doing in finding "diamonds in the rough" outside prep schools and high schools attended by the upper-middle class. In fact, this analysis understates our point in an important way. An upper-middle-class student who does reasonably well in high school is almost on a default path to college and, thus, automatically in the pool of students who take the SAT or ACT along that path. A student growing up in a poor household is on the default path *not* to attend college—or if college is considered at all, to attend the local community college. Therefore, a substantial number of talented low-SES students never take the SAT and, thus, never make it into the pool this data captures.

Moreover, as we saw in Part III, schools such as the University of California that have been constrained to avoid or minimize racial references end up doing a dramatically better job than their peer institutions in assembling minority cohorts that are far more representative of the populations they purport to represent. Our preference systems are simply missing a very large pool of talented, low-SES students.

* * *

In the wake of Prop 209 one of us (Sander) helped to persuade his law school (UCLA) to adopt a system of race-neutral, class-based preferences. The experiment was controversial within the school, and it was modified after its first year. But by the criteria discussed in this chapter (and to many of its opponents in retrospect), the experiment was a stunning success. With an average preference of about one-third the size of the racial preferences used before Prop 209, the law school assembled a class that actually resembled the socioeconomic distribution in America. More than a third of the students came from the bottom half of the SES distribution; more than a quarter of the students were the first in their family to attend college. The class was nearly a third nonwhite and included more underrepresented minorities than any other race-neutral method that had been adopted at any UC professional school. And, very importantly, the students were academically successful. The cohort admitted through this program (the graduating class of 2000) achieved the highest bar passage rate in the school's history.

All of this was achieved without a significant outreach effort or a very broad awareness among low-SES college students of what we were doing; with such efforts in place, we plausibly could have admitted an even stronger class. (UCLA still uses significant class-based preferences, though in a somewhat retrenched form, and has managed to advance steadily vis-à-vis its law school peers in the average academic index of its students.)

A hallmark of the UCLA experiment was its use of measures that captured the intersections between race and class that we mentioned earlier. Conventional measures of SES—which, as we have noted, usually are limited to measures of income, education, and occupation—understate levels of disadvantage for Hispanics and blacks. A black household in the middle of the income distribution has, on average, only a fraction of the assets held by a typical white household with the same income. Segregation concentrates low-SES Hispanics and blacks in poorer neighborhoods with weaker institutions.

To address those intersections, the law school used eight measures in constructing a measure of socioeconomic status: In addition to the education of each parent and the parent's income, it also measured the parent's assets and several indices of social conditions in the zip code in which the applicant lived during high school, such as the poverty rate and high school dropout rate.

Including such factors meant that blacks and Hispanics with a given level of academic index were much more likely to be admitted than were whites and Asians. Considering only the broadly defined SES of applicants and not their race, UCLA Law School admitted 21 percent of its black applicants and 24 percent of its Hispanic applicants with good but not outstanding academic indices, compared with 7 percent of its white applicants and 7 percent of its Asian applicants in the same academic index range. The school achieved substantial racial diversity, a unique level of socioeconomic diversity, and a high level of academic success for its students.

As we discussed in Part III, the UC system as a whole also experimented with class-based preferences after Prop 209 and had similar successes. At the end of the 1990s the UC system had managed to achieve systemwide black and Hispanic enrollment levels that were close to their pre-209 levels (with many minority students cascaded to less elite campuses), had improved black and Hispanic academic achievement, and had achieved far higher levels of socioeconomic diversity than had comparable schools elsewhere in the nation. More than 30 percent of Berkeley and UCLA undergraduates qualified for Pell Grants (a form of federal educational assistance generally available to students from roughly the bottom half of the income distribution); at other elite colleges around the country the Pell Grant rate hovered around 10 percent. The problem with the UC experiment came after 2000, as the professional schools and eventually the colleges were tempted to introduce more and more aggressive proxies for race itself. Those steps tended to reintroduce or exacerbate the mismatch problem.

+ + +

This leaves us with a vital question: Can we increase SES diversity in American higher education without simply exacerbating the mismatch problem? We think the answer is yes, for two reasons.

First, there is a great deal that universities can do to increase SES diversity without *any* use of preferences. They can do a much better job of finding the talented students excelling at nonelite high schools that are off the radar from outreach officers. They can do a better job of simply recognizing that the applications of students with socioeconomic disadvantage may require a closer, different kind of scrutiny than that applied to affluent applicants. Many admissions officers focus on how "interesting" a student is—how original her essay might be, how many countries she has visited, whether she has done innovative charity work or an unpaid internship with, say, an environmental group. Giving weight to these sorts of experiences may help produce an eclectic entering class, but it is important to keep in mind that low-SES students are far less likely to offer them: They are more likely to work at uninteresting jobs during the summer (to help support their families), and they are far less likely to have some kind of résumé coach.

It is well documented that expensive private colleges have been particularly guilty parties in the pervasive grade inflation that has swept over higher education in the past forty years. In the applications to graduate and professional schools, students who have attended private colleges are more likely to have inflated grades than otherwise similar students who have attended public universities of the same academic quality. If admissions officers do not take this distinction into account—and they generally do not—they will disfavor the low-SES applicants who disproportionately attend public universities. It is plausible that similar mechanisms reward affluent college applicants who have attended undistinguished but expensive private schools.

Higher education institutions can also do much more to make themselves affordable to low-SES applicants. For most of the past forty years college tuitions have risen much faster than the rate of inflation. Some very elite colleges (e.g., Harvard and Princeton) have not only practiced need-blind admissions for a long time but have in the past decade introduced dramatic policies that promise tuition-free education to low-, moderate-, and even many middle-income families. If more schools move in this direction, it would substantially increase enrollments of low-SES students without the use of preferences.

If we again consider law schools as an example, recent data show two disturbing patterns. First, among all students enrolled at a broad cross-section of law schools in the mid-1990s, the white students with the lowest academic indices (compared to others at the same school) were those with the highest SES. The implication is that the law school admissions systems tended, on balance, to favor affluent applicants over others and, thus, admitted more affluent white students with slightly lower academic qualifications over other whites. (These patterns existed alongside much larger racial preferences aimed at blacks and Hispanics.)

Second, high-SES blacks at law schools nationwide receive, on average, four times as much scholarship money as do low-SES whites. This suggests that law schools deploy disproportionate resources toward bidding wars for black students while providing very little need-based aid. (We saw in Chapter Fourteen how George Mason Law School engaged in this behavior while under relentless pressure from the ABA.) Shifting available aid to focus more on need and less on diversity gamesmanship would increase SES diversity.

There is, in short, a great deal that colleges and universities can do simply to make the playing field more level for low-SES candidates. The question of whether they should go further and actually grant preferences based on SES is a harder one that we return to in Chapter Eighteen. We know from the experiments described above that sharp increases in socioeconomic diversity can be achieved with preferences much smaller than those typically used to pursue racial diversity. We also know that mismatch is fundamentally related not to whether preferences are tied to race, SES, or athletic ability but rather to the size of the preference. What we do not know is how large a preference is too large. Small preferences may well be harmless or may even foster positive peer effects. These uncertainties create difficult policy tradeoffs—tradeoffs we will try to navigate in Chapter Eighteen.

CHAPTER SEVENTEEN

CLOSING THE TEST SCORE GAP

Better Parenting and K-12 Education

OUR BOOK HAS BEEN ABOUT THE SYSTEM of large racial preferences in American higher education. As we noted in Chapter Two, the only reason those preferences exist is the gap in academic achievement—the so-called test score gap—across high school seniors of different races. We think we've shown that large preferences are not a good solution to the test score gap, and in Chapter Eighteen we lay out a program for reform of admissions preferences in higher education. But that leads us back to the underlying question: Can America reduce or eliminate the test score gap itself?

It would be tempting to sidestep this issue, because discussing racial achievement gaps inevitably draws one into the debate over public education reform, a controversial subject on which many readers may already have firm opinions that could cause them to doubt our understanding of the issues. And we concede at the outset that neither of us is expert on early education or the elementary and secondary school system (K-12). Still, it seems to us very important to address the test score gap, for three fundamental reasons.

First, the test score gap is not fading away. The early optimism that racial preferences would be a transitory remedy arose from the obvious racial inequities in our K-12 system. Once those were substantially addressed, many observers believed, racial performance levels would quickly converge. And indeed, during the 1970s and early 1980s racial test score gaps did narrow substantially. But sometime around the mid-1980s this trend stopped and even went into reverse for five to ten years (depending on the measure one uses). Since the mid-1990s racial test score gaps among high school seniors have, in general, been extraordinarily stable. That means that this is an issue we cannot ignore.

Second, the test score gap is not rooted in racial genetics. Almost no one mentions this issue because it is perhaps the most explosive of all racial questions. But scholars have been attempting to disentangle the sources of the test score gap for more than a generation, and we believe the evidence now is overwhelming on this point: Racial test score gaps arise from a wide range of environmental factors, not genetic ones. We explore these factors later in the chapter, but for now the important point is this: The racial test score gap is malleable; we *can* do something about it.

Third, we believe there is an emerging consensus among scholars about how to narrow the test score gap and the closely related question of how to reform K-12 education. The work done by enormously respected scholars such as Roland Fryer, Eric Hanushek, and James Heckman tends toward similar diagnoses. A spate of popular works by such thoughtful people as Stephan and Abigail Thernstrom, Steven Brill, Matthew Miller, and Peg Tyre has woven these research findings into case studies of school reforms. Important reformers in both parties, such as Democrat Arne Duncan and Republican Charlie Crist, seem to accept many of the findings of this research while still shying away from those elements most heretical to members of their respective parties. This means that there is some agreement about what, specifically, should be done. Indeed, there are already examples of reformed schools that have had documented success not only in preventing black and Hispanic students from falling behind but also in significantly narrowing achievement gaps.

The test score gap is hugely important. Much of this book has documented the folly of pretending, via large admissions preferences, that academic preparation gaps will not affect the success and outcomes of students in college. These same gaps—through mechanisms we suspect have no relation to mismatch per se—have powerful effects on other life outcomes. Economists June and Dave O'Neill show in an exhaustive 2012 study that, as of 2008, black-white and Hispanic-white differences in earnings disappear when one controls for human capital qualities (including performance on standardized tests). Similarly, Roland Fryer has noted that the educational achievement gaps among fifteen- to eighteen-year-old blacks, whites, and Hispanics explain between 40 to 70 percent (depending on the study) of the black-white gap in wages among men, all of the black-white gap in wages among young women, and all of the Hispanic-white gap in wages among men and women alike. The test score gap also contributes significantly to black-white difference in unemployment and incarceration. We do not think Fryer exaggerates when he says that "closing the racial achievement gap is the most important civil rights battle of the twenty-first century."

We therefore undertake in this chapter to explore these fundamental ideas and suggest what, to us, seem like the most promising strategies for reducing the test score gap.

* * *

Perhaps the most authoritative source for documenting racial achievement gaps is the National Assessment of Educational Progress (NAEP), which has measured reading and math skills among nine-, thirteen-, and seventeen-year-old students for over forty years. NAEP tests attempt to maintain comparability over time and across ages; test results for reading and math are each measured on an absolute 500-point scale. In 2008 (the most recent year with good comparative data) the mean reading score for nine-year-olds of all races was 220; for thirteen-year-olds, 260; and for seventeen-year-olds, 286. Another way of putting this is that a typical seventeen-year-old has reading ability that would place her at about the 80th percentile of thirteen-year-olds. Students thus progress over time, but not very dramatically.

The black-white test score gap among high school seniors in contemporary America is comparable to the gap between thirteen- and seventeen-year olds—in 2008, 29 points on reading tests and 26 points on math tests. This means that the typical black high school senior is performing on math and reading tests at about the 15th percentile of white seniors. This NAEP gap—which is mainly a measure of learning and skills, not some more abstract measure of intelligence—is almost identical to the gaps we observe on the SAT, the ACT, and other national standardized tests.

We don't have good data, comparable to the NAEP, for the 1950s and 1960s, but a variety of circumstantial evidence suggests that black academic achievement was rising rapidly during that period, as blacks migrated to better school systems in the north and the worst disparities in educational funding levels declined. Black illiteracy fell by half in the 1960s, and the proportion of young adult blacks graduating from high school rose from one-third in 1950 to nearly two-thirds in 1972.

This pattern of rapid progress continued in the 1970s and early 1980s. The NAEP black-white reading gap among high school seniors fell from 53 points in 1971 to 20 points in 1988; the black-white mathematics gap among seniors fell from 40 to 21 points. Had these trends continued, the black-white test score gap would have disappeared entirely by the early twenty-first century. Instead, the gaps among seniors widened in the late 1980s and early 1990s and then stabilized around the levels noted above. Over the past twenty years there has been no measurable decline in the test score gap between both black and Hispanic high school seniors and their white counterparts.

The most hopeful sign in the NAEP data is that trends for nine-year-olds are notably better. Since the early 1990s white nine-year-old reading scores have risen by 10 points, Hispanic reading scores have improved by about 15 points, and black nine-year-old reading scores have risen by nearly 20 points. All three groups have also experienced rising math scores (though blacks have not closed any of the math gap). Some observers have dismissed this trend as simply reflecting more "teaching to the test" in elementary school, but the pattern is so broad and steady that it suggests to us genuine improvement. Unfortunately, we have yet to see a cohort of nine-year-olds preserve these gains as they move through junior high and high school. The data provides no basis for complacency.

When the racial test score gap stopped narrowing, social scientists began to look more closely at what could explain the gap. A variety of studies that took advantage of "natural experiments" offered persuasive evidence that the racial gaps were not genetic. For example, black infants adopted by white parents grew up to have test scores that were largely indistinguishable from other whites. Cohorts of mixed-race children raised in Germany, whose fathers were black American servicemen stationed in Germany, tested at the same level as other German children. In 1997 sociologist Meredith Phillips and two coauthors used data on a large cross-section of children and showed that nearly two-thirds of the black-white gap on test scores disappeared when one adjusted for differences in socioeconomic status (SES) and a few parenting practices. Findings like these inspired a larger, more detailed federal study known as the Early Childhood Longitudinal Study (ECLS), which is still ongoing.

In 2004 Roland Fryer and Steven Levitt published an analysis of ECLS data on study participants through age six. Their study produced two very significant findings. First, Fryer and Levitt found that large racial gaps in test scores exist at age five. For blacks, the gaps were about half the size of those that exist among high school seniors; for Hispanics the gaps among five-year-olds were about the same size as those among high school seniors. The gaps did not change much when, instead of using tests, the study asked kindergarten teachers to complete individualized assessments of each student's cognitive skills. These findings imply that although the test score gap may be exacerbated by K-12 education, it already exists in large measure when students start schooling.

Second, Fryer and Levitt found that nearly all differences in test scores across five-year-old blacks, Hispanics, and whites disappeared when one controlled for half a dozen characteristics, including the age of the mother, the birth weight of the baby, SES, and the number of books at home. Some of these factors (like birth weight) probably had a direct effect on children's learning and academic performance; others (like the number of books at home or the mother's age) were very imprecise proxies for a host of parenting practices that influence the child's upbringing and environment. The fact that even such imperfect proxies made the test gaps disappear suggested powerfully that the child's environment, from the womb through age five, could fully explain group differences.

And it appeared that parenting practices during these early years were even more important than such objective factors as household income. While noting that the reasons for this are unclear, Fryer points to evidence suggesting that "parenting practices differ between blacks and whites." For instance, "black college graduates have the same number of children's books for their kids as white high school graduates." Indeed, the racial gap in reading disappears and the math gap is greatly reduced when one compares the test scores of black and white children with the same numbers of children's books. As Phillips and Christopher Jencks argued, "Changes in parenting practices might do more to reduce the white-black test score gap than changes in parents' educational attainment or income."

A host of parenting practices have an enormous impact on cognitive development, and many of these practices vary substantially across racial lines. The depth and complexity of verbal interaction between mothers and children is crucial and favors cognitive development among white and Asian children. Enforced bedtimes and bedtime routines are important; black children are less likely to have these. One of the largest racial disparities lies in the probability that a child's father is in the home. More than 72 percent of black children are born to unmarried mothers, as are more than 53 percent of Hispanic children, 29 percent of white children, and 17 percent of Asian American children. The correspondence among these rates and the average academic preparation of these groups in high school is striking. Scholars examining the effect of single parenthood on the cognitive development of children have reached different conclusions, but there is broad agreement that single-parent households tend to have a variety of disadvantages—not the least of which are much lower incomes—that collectively relate strongly to cognitive development. Conversely, two-parent families have "a profound advantage in income and nurturing time, and [that] makes their children statistically more likely to finish college, find good jobs and form stable marriages."

After a child starts school it is harder to disentangle the effect of the schooling itself from the rest of the child's environment. Common sense suggests that the home environment will continue to have a powerful, if gradually declining, influence. And a host of field research suggests that peer influences become more and more important. For the black-white gap, the most important of these peer effects may be the "acting white" syndrome.

Although the "acting white" problem is hard to measure, it is widely recognized as real. In one of many memorable passages from his keynote address to the 2004 Democratic National Convention, Barack Obama said that "parents have to parent [and] children can't achieve unless we raise their expectations and eradicate the slander that says a black youth with a book is acting white." Michelle Obama later "described the ridicule she faced from neighborhood kids for 'acting white' when she got good grades." Scholars who have written about issues of racial inequality, from sociologist Douglas Massey to linguist John McWhorter, have commented on its importance. Anthropologist John Ogbu, in his ethnographic studies of students in Washington, DC, and Shaker Heights, Ohio, perhaps did more than anyone else to detail and analyze how this process works. Ogbu's research convinced him that most black students in Shaker Heights did not work hard and equated "good school performance with acting white" and that many of their parents paid little attention to their kids' homework, blaming poor academic performance on teachers.

Roland Fryer and economist Paul Torelli, in a fascinating 2010 paper, argue that the "acting white" problem can significantly undermine black achievement but that it is evoked in particular contexts, namely integrated schools with significant populations of both blacks and whites. Fryer and Torelli showed that although white students become more popular on average if they have good grades, the opposite is true of blacks, especially boys, in integrated schools.

In the course of our research for this book we interviewed Rick Nagel, a retired white teacher who taught at Seattle's Franklin High School for many decades—an integrated school of the type Fryer and Torelli identify. Nagel gave us vivid examples of what he sees as phenomenon similar to but distinct from the "acting white" problem: a widespread feeling of intellectual inferiority among black students that is particularly prevalent among those who have received little encouragement from their families for making academic excellence a priority. "Every September," Nagel recounted, "I would hold informational meetings for the mock trial team. Many black students would enter the room every year and, seeing a preponderance of white kids from the school's humanities program, turn tail and head out, often making remarks such as, 'This is for the smart [or white] kids.'" Last summer, Nagel attended a PTA meeting at a predominantly black high school, where he was going to present ideas for enhancing the school's curriculum. In introducing Nagel, the black PTA president observed that there was a move to beef up the school's academic side because "white people expect academic rigor." Nagel felt he "shocked the predominantly black audience by stating that I thought that that is what black parents want for their children, too."

Patterns of this sort can help explain the results of an important paper by Jesse Rothstein and David Card, who found that increased levels of *housing* integration sharply reduced test score gaps between blacks and whites, whereas increased levels of *school* integration (controlling for housing integration) did not. It seems plausible that when black students are attending integrated schools but still live in heavily segregated neighborhoods, their social networks may tend to pull them away from the academic norms of the school. When they live in racially integrated neighborhoods, in contrast, the range of environmental changes is much broader, and "acting white" might become to be seen as a positive good.

What we can say for sure is that racial test score gaps are at least as much due to social and environmental influences as to objective differences in schooling. In one sense, this makes the gaps seem intractable. Changing parenting practices could help, but what social program can undertake that task? Greater housing integration can help, but segregation is a massive problem that has responded only slowly to two generations of fair housing initiatives. The key question, then, is whether there are K-12 reforms that can not only improve schooling but also offset the broader environmental factors that are pulling down black and Hispanic achievement.

* * *

To get a preliminary idea of what can be—and has been—done, consider a few facts about New York City's Success Academy Charter Schools. The students at the four schools are almost all black and Hispanic, and about 75 percent are poor. But in the most recent statewide tests an astonishing 97 percent achieved proficiency in math and 88 percent in English. That's more than 30 percent higher in both math and reading than the average across New York State as a whole. Still more impressive, the Success Academy students are performing at the same level as those in the New York City public school system's gifted and talented schools, which admit students based solely on rigorous tests and have disproportionately few low-income and minority students.

The biggest question facing American education is whether we can reform the regular public schools attended by more than fifty million children—especially African American, Hispanic, working-class, and low-income kids—to be more like these exceptional schools. The answer will turn on whether our leaders can muster the will and political power to overcome the extremely formidable obstacles to reform. Both Barack Obama and George W. Bush took important steps toward reform, but there is a long way to go. As we noted earlier, there is a growing consensus about the most important ingredients for reform.

The problem does not lie primarily in funding—which is fortunate because the growing fiscal crises of governments at all levels are likely to curtail major new spending programs for at least the next decade. Education spending in the United States has, since 1980, steadily risen faster than national income as a whole; during that period spending per student, in real dollars, has doubled. Over the past twenty years—a period during which, as we have noted, the test score gap has not narrowed at all—real, per-student spending has risen 42 percent, but real teacher salaries have less risen than 6 percent. Indeed, writes Eric Hanushek, "The lack of any consistent relationship between more spending and better test scores has been documented time and time again, both in actual practice and in hundreds of scientific studies based on empirical data. . . . In summary, whether one looks at increases in spending over a long period of time or variations in spending between school districts or states, there is little or no evidence that higher spending is related to better achievement."

Nor is spending related in any obvious way to racial differences in performance. "Despite trillions spent," writes Ronald Fryer, "there is not one urban school district that has ever closed the racial achievement gap." Indeed, schools in some areas have spent spectacular amounts of money per student—far more than many or most of the best majority-white public schools—without raising their students' test scores. There is some debate about whether the nation's per capita education spending on blacks is higher or lower than its spending on whites, but there is no debate that the levels are close. Nor does the problem lie in class size. Extensive research and experimentation with class size and educational outcomes has failed to show much improvement in learning outcomes once class size reaches a reasonable range—say twenty-seven students per class at the high school level, and twenty-two students per class in kindergarten through grade three. Meanwhile, special education for students classified as disabled consumes nearly 20 percent of all federal aid to K-12 education. "Programs for gifted children get less than half of one percent, and pre-K education gets almost nothing," according to Philip Howard, head of Common Good, a civic reform non-profit based in New York City. "Is this a sensible allocation of education dollars?" asks Howard. "No one is even asking the question."

There are two factors that show up repeatedly in educational studies that look at cross-sections of students or experiment with particular education strategies. The more important is teachers who are well trained, enthusiastic about their jobs, and, most of all, intelligent. The second is an orderly school environment that motivates students to learn, instills good academic values, and minimizes obstacles to the learning process.

When strong, gifted teachers are placed in well-ordered, learning-conductive environments, education thrives. Both of these qualities are disproportionately absent from even well-funded schools with large black and Hispanic enrollments. When these qualities are achieved, black and Hispanic students—as the Success Academies illustrate—not only keep the test score gap from widening; they substantially narrow it.

Let us first consider teacher quality. A wide range of education studies consistently show that teachers who score better on cognitive tests or perform better on any type of independent evaluation of teaching skills are the single-strongest predictor of student learning in K-12 schools. This is why Bill Gates, who has made K-12 education a major focus of his foundation, observes that "the quality of the teachers in our schools is paramount: no other measured aspect of schools is nearly as important in determining student achievement."

A study by Hanushek found that having a teacher for one year whose performance was one standard deviation above the average of all teachers had a measurable and large impact on the lifetime earnings of the teacher's students. His results imply that "salaries several times higher than those paid teachers today would be economically justified if teachers were compensated according to their effectiveness." Other studies have echoed this finding; still others have shown that the implied counterpart is true as well: A bad teacher can do great harm.

Although there are of course thousands of outstanding teachers in American public schools, there are also many more mediocre ones. A strong argument can be made that the modest average skills of American teachers is the single-largest reason that American students fare poorly in international comparisons: "Although the United States spends considerably more per capita for K-12 education than almost any other country in the world," writes

Hanushek, "large numbers of its students fall below even the 'basic' level in reading, math, and science skills."

In the United States only about half of all teachers score among the top third of all workers in cognitive skills tests. In South Korea the percentage is essentially 100 percent, because high cognitive ability is a prerequisite to entry into the teaching profession. Nearly the same high rates are seen in Singapore and Finland, both of which greatly outperform the United States in student comparisons. In these countries teaching is a venerated profession and accorded high social respect. As Nicholas Kristof has observed, "In South Korea and Singapore, teachers on average earn more than lawyers and engineers."

There are three keys to improving the quality of our teachers. The first is to recruit and carefully screen applicants and raise entering pay for well-qualified recruits enough to draw more of our brightest and most motivated college graduates into the profession while also keeping good teachers by offering generous merit raises and relieving them of mind-numbing paperwork and bureaucratic rules.

Another indispensable step toward improving teacher quality is empowering school administrators to dismiss the many teachers who have shown themselves to be ineffective and unlikely to improve much. In school districts across much of the country most bad teachers enjoy the equivalent of life tenure no matter how execrable their performance. When New York City tried to fire twenty-six teachers last year for gross incompetence, for example, it was blocked in half the cases. The main obstacle to getting rid of bad teachers are teachers unions, which for decades have made it a priority to provide tenure for teachers and tie compensation and other job benefits to seniority. Unless such practices can be changed, the time, money, and political will needed to make school reform work will necessarily greatly increase. Weak teachers not only do direct harm to their students, but they also contribute to an environment that undermines the motivation and staying power of the strong teachers.

The final key to improving teacher quality is effective teacher evaluation. It is important that such processes combine fairness with expedition. Observation by master teachers and principals is important; measuring results is indispensable. And that means evaluating teachers based in part on demonstrable improvement in student skills and learning. Of course, some observers feel that "teaching to the test" has become as damaging in itself as the accountability problems tests are supposed to address. But the Obama administration has pushed (and helped to fund) a new generation of tests—

tests tied to national standards—that aim to have the following characteristics: "The tests should be aligned to . . . new high standards; they should measure deeper learning [rather than just memorization]; they should be computerized; and they should be capable of being used to evaluate not just students but educators."

In *The Two Percent Solution*, Matthew Miller suggested a creative way of pursuing all three goals at once and, in the process, focusing on the racial test score gap. Under Miller's plan the federal government would make funds available to recruit truly remarkable talent to inner-city schools (Miller suggests salaries averaging $140,000). In exchange, school districts receiving these funds would agree to modified work rules and evaluation procedures so that the salaries were closely linked to actual performance and that unsuccessful teachers could be removed, regardless of seniority. By attracting thousands of very smart young people into teaching—rather than, say, law school or business school—such a program could provide transformative teaching experiences to hundreds of thousands of black and Hispanic school children.

For the public system more broadly, one could imagine more limited measures that would help attract, reward, and keep strong teachers. Much of the money could be freed up by emulating the efficiency of the many other nations that do much more with less. These include modestly increasing class sizes and reducing the number of teachers and administrators—by easing out the weaker ones—while linking increased pay to performance.

Almost as important as higher teacher quality is a school environment that facilitates learning. Nearly every exceptional inner-city school that has attracted attention for extraordinary success has developed careful regimens for the school environment. This includes school-wide rules that require students to dress neatly, arrive on time, pay attention, be respectful, shun fighting and foul language, and finish their homework. It includes attention in the curriculum to middle-class values, such as ethical rules, polite manners, and an emphasis on personal responsibility. Successful schools also make demands of parents, explaining expectations about homework supervision, assigning reading projects for parents and their children to share, and making clear to parents that they share responsibility for their children's adherence to school rules.

Of course, it is dramatically easier to maintain rules when one can effectively threaten to expel misbehaving students. This is an important advantage that private and, to some extent, charter schools have over public ones, but it is an advantage in part because legislatures and courts have tended to err on the side of elevating individual student rights over the general learning environment of the school. A small minority of students can be so incorrigibly disruptive—especially in schools serving low-income areas—as to interfere greatly with even elemental learning. It is important to redress this balance and, if necessary, remove disruptive students to special classrooms or special schools with the resources to meet their needs.

Creating an affirmative learning environment is obviously important to make schooling *qua* schooling as effective as possible. But it can also help address the social and environmental issues that, as we have suggested, play such an important role in weak academic performance in general and the racial test score gap in particular. The key, it seems, is to seek to make the school's ethos shape the broader environment of the students rather than—as is so often the case at ineffective schools—vice versa.

Most political leaders, Republicans and Democrats alike, have so far made themselves part of the problem by protecting or accepting the status quo. Many Republicans have long reflexively opposed federal intervention in local school systems and even the most cost-effective spending increases. Similarly, many Democrats have long reflexively bowed to the status quo favored by teachers unions and other interest groups, no matter how much it conflicted with the best interests of students.

As for the courts, they played a noble and necessary role in breaking the back of state-sponsored segregation and requiring states to spend roughly as much on majority-minority urban schools as on majority-white suburban schools. But since then courts have often required massive and wasteful spending increases that did little or nothing to enhance student learning and have so greatly expanded due process and special education rights as to make it almost impossible to dismiss ineffective teachers or control disruptive students.

Teachers unions have a legitimate role to play in protecting their members from the arbitrary treatment and grossly inadequate pay that was widespread sixty years ago. But power corrupts. And the teachers unions—perhaps the Democratic Party's most potent interest group—may have more control over what goes on in K-12 schools than do principals, school superintendents, mayors, governors, and presidents combined.

The good news is that after decades when teacher unions dominated education policy, important Democratic as well as Republican leaders around the country—started in important ways by President Bush (and Jeb Bush), but now led by President Obama, Duncan, Andrew Cuomo, Mitch Daniels, and others—have pushed teachers unions to be more receptive to reforms, including performance-based teacher evaluations and merit pay. Bush's No Child Left Behind program, though flawed in its implementation, represented a welcome break from tradition in emphasizing meaningful accountability.

Obama's Race to the Top Program has gone further, providing grants to school systems that adopt merit pay and measures to dismiss ineffective teachers. For a relatively modest federal expenditure of $4.3 billion over less than four years, the program has produced highly encouraging results.

Cuomo has asserted that "our schools are not an employment program" and that officials should not support "the teachers union at the expense of the students"—unheard of talk for a liberal Democrat with presidential ambitions. He has also worked with New York City mayor Michael Bloomberg (whose enthusiasm for school reform peaks when he is not up for election) to push for more rigorous evaluations of teachers and accountability for success or failure.

The way forward is for leaders such as these to junk rigid work rules and bring about speedy dismissal of ineffective teachers in exchange for giving higher pay to all adequate teachers and much higher merit pay to outstanding teachers. That would be a great deal for good teachers—as even the unions should see—as well as for students.

As noted above, despite the formidable racial gaps in early learning, several dozen exceptional charter and private schools around the country—many created over the past twenty-five years—are helping thousands of low-income black and Hispanic kids overcome huge obstacles in order to reach a level of learning that no large urban public school system in the country appears to match. Black and Hispanic children who started school way behind whites and Asians in early learning have become hard-working, cooperative, academically self-confident students with strong preparation for rigorous college work and great futures ahead of them.

This, despite the views of many experts that, as the seminal report by James Samuel Coleman and others on equality of educational opportunity said in 1966, schools alone cannot solve the problem of black underachievement in urban schools. To the contrary, write Will Dobbie and Roland Fryer, recent evidence suggests that "schools alone can dramatically increase the achievement of the poorest minority students—other community and broader investments may not be necessary."

Many of these are charter schools, including the more than one hundred Knowledge Is Power Program (KIPP) schools around the country, "the largest and arguably most successful network of charter schools in the country," with thirty-three thousand students; Geoffrey Canada's Harlem Children's Zone (HCZ); New York City's astonishingly successful Success Academy Charter Schools; North Star Academy, in Newark; DC Prep, in Washington, DC; and many more. Many others are private and religious schools, including Catholic schools.

Unlike almost all regular public schools as currently run, these charters and private schools are not unionized, do not hesitate to ease out ineffective teachers as well as any incorrigibly disruptive students, and can give merit pay to their best teachers. Most of the charters admit applicants by lottery, without considering test scores or academic records.

Joel Klein, who headed New York City's public school system for eight years, is persuaded that charter schools offer an excellent model for creating the necessary elements for broad-based reform. Klein has pointed out that students in the city's charter schools outperform not only other public school students in the city but also the statewide average, even though the charter schools have high proportions of students who are poor, racial minorities, or both. Demand for places in the city's charter schools now far exceeds the supply.

On our book's website (www.mismatchthebook.com) we examine briefly one group of unusually successful charter schools, the Harlem Children's Zone's Promise Academy, and we take a longer look at privately funded Eastside College Preparatory School in East Palo Alto, California, which has helped low-income Hispanic and black students achieve astonishing academic successes. Coauthor Taylor was fortunate to visit Eastside in April 2012 with his wife, Sally Ellis, who reads to middle school kids as a library volunteer at another inspiring school, DC Prep, in inner-city Washington, DC.

If we could make most or even many of America's ninety-five thousand public schools more like the best of the five thousand charter schools, and like Eastside, racial gaps would be narrowed and international competitiveness and economic growth would be enhanced at the same time. Longer school days and school years along with preschool programs with rich learning environments would help. And unlike unduly shrunken class sizes, they would be well worth the very substantial cost—much of which could be paid for by modest increases in class size and cutting the vast waste that now characterizes most school systems. A renewed emphasis on teaching a culture of hard work and middle-class values as well as academics might be even more essential.

Of course, the best schools can produce even better results if we can reduce the racial gaps among children before they enter kindergarten. But that will be a long process of cultural evolution. The immediate imperative is to continue creating excellent charter and private schools as escape routes from bad public schools and models for radical reform of the ordinary public schools.

CHAPTER EIGHTEEN

CONCLUSION

W E THINK THAT WE HAVE DEMONSTRATED
that the present system of racial admissions preferences has grave
problems and has shown a remarkable incapacity to heal itself.
Given the established inability of our elected officials to confront mismatch
and other problems with preferences as well as the sometimes perverse unintended consequences of ballot measures such as Proposition 209 in California, the US Supreme Court seems to be the only hope for serious and stable
reform.

But the Supreme Court decisions that have purported to put limits on
racial preferences in admissions, in 1978 and 2003, have, as we have seen,
been sadly ineffective. The question this raises is whether, as reasonable critics
of racial preferences argue, the only alternative to the rotten system we have
now is immediate, total abolition—that is, a Supreme Court ruling that the
Constitution and civil rights laws simply prohibit any consideration of race in
college admissions.

We think that immediate abolition might go too far, unless it turns out
that there is no other way expeditiously to escape the very bad status quo.
More important, five of the Supreme Court's current justices have said that
they are not prepared to abolish racial preferences. We suspect that these justices' main reason, like ours, is that abolition might produce an alarmingly
sudden and drastic plunge in black and Hispanic presence at our selective

schools. In addition, such a ruling would be a sharp and sudden break from a substantial line of Supreme Court constitutional precedents, a break that should be entertained only as a last resort, after more modest adjustments of legal doctrine have failed. We also think that the Supreme Court can do much better than it has in the past.

But what is the right path to reform? Traditionally, moderate critics of the racial preference system have found themselves facing the dilemma that economist Glenn Loury eloquently captured when, in 1996, he wrote about the merits of Prop 209:

> I do not think the color-blind absolutism which undergirds advocacy for Prop 209 is a logically coherent or morally correct position. . . . I think the proposition is too extreme. Race is a reality in this society; its social meaning is so powerful that sometimes the state cannot discharge its essential responsibilities, like educating the young, or maintaining order in the cities, without taking race into account. . . . [But while] I am genuinely torn about this . . . the bottom line is that I would probably vote for the initiative [if I were a Californian].

For all of its problems, Loury said, a complete ban on racial preferences might be preferable to "the maintenance of a corrupt and excessive status quo." He explained:

> Affirmative action desperately needs to be reformed, [but] the political realities are such that significant change is not likely to come from the bureaucrats who develop and administer such programs, absent dramatic, outside intervention of the sort which CCRI represents. . . . For many years now reasoned criticism of particular affirmative action programs—like an admissions policy at UC Berkeley which results in a three hundred point gap in SAT scores, or a race-based procurement policy which drives white men out of certain lines of business—have been met not with reasoned responses, but with hysterical charges that the critics are racists.

The choice Proposition 209 presented to Loury and other thinkers was all or nothing: Ban racial preferences or see them perpetuated and extended indefinitely. But the Supreme Court has more flexible tools for engineering serious reform short of an immediate ban. And we have some specific proposals for how the justices might use those tools to resolve the dilemmas racial preferences pose in a way that, though far from perfect, would be a vast improvement on the status quo. In this final chapter we shall briefly review what we have learned, outline our reform proposals, and explain why the pending Supreme Court case of *Fisher v. University of Texas* provides an opportunity for the Court to start us down this better path.

* * *

We have suggested that there are really three reasonable sides to the debate over racial preferences: the principled argument for preferences, the principled argument against them, and the so-far-less-visible empirical assessment of the preference system, which in our view is critical as we look to the future. The two arguments based on principle are often expressed in stark, one-dimensional terms. But suppose we found an honest insider on each side of the debate. Consider what they might say:

The defender of racial preferences: "It is true that affirmative action programs are flawed. But consider what they have accomplished. In the space of two generations we have gone from a society of glaring racial castes to one with a genuinely integrated leadership class. America has changed radically, and its ability to change peacefully and to operate effectively as a multiracial society without paralyzing racial conflict is an extraordinary achievement, both by historical standards and by comparison with almost any country in the world. We can never know how important affirmative action has been to this progress, but even if it was only partly responsible, that by itself justifies our efforts.

"Affirmative action today keeps open to minorities a vital path of access. Without preference programs to integrate our elite universities, many fewer minorities will end up in the management and leadership ranks of other social institutions. That is why corporate and military leaders join university and civil rights leaders in virtually unanimous support for current programs.

"Critics complain about the undesirable aura of secrecy around preference programs. But the American public has never supported the idea of large racial preferences, and the signs of its hostility have only grown over time. This is unfortunate but not by itself a reason to eliminate preferences. Does the average voter understand the severity of the racial disparities in academic preparation? Do they realize how the tenuous level of integration at top schools would plunge if we eliminated preferences? The Supreme Court's rulings have essentially told us to dissemble. So we have dissembled, and the nation has been better for it.

"Moreover, we have shown a capacity for reform. As researchers have demonstrated an absence of socioeconomic diversity at elite colleges, at least some of these schools have made themselves more accessible. Harvard, Yale,

Princeton, and Stanford are now essentially tuition-free for anyone with an income below $60,000, and Columbia has sharply increased its actual proportion of working-class and lower-income students in recent years. But given our understandable fear of being demagogued on our well-intentioned use of preferences, the path to reform is to work constructively on the inside, not to tear things down from the outside."

We see merit to this argument. But many critics of racial preferences argue with equal eloquence in support of pure and simple abolition.

The critical view of racial preferences: "Affirmative action—a misleading euphemism for racial preferences—may have been justified in the late 1960s, when it arguably helped to knock down barriers and open doors that needed to be opened, both as a matter of basic fairness and as a safety valve at a time when racial tensions in American society seemed building to some sort of explosion. But it was always no more than a highly imperfect fix to a challenging social problem; by now racial preferences have become more a fig leaf for bureaucrats than an enlightened way of opening the doors of opportunity for students. Hidden preferences enable college presidents to pose as leaders of integrated communities that, just under the surface, are actually segregated. Far from breeding tolerance, preferences breed resentment and negative stereotypes among Asians and whites, who feel that they are being discriminated against—and they are. Far from breeding a sense of access and social equality among blacks and Hispanics, preferences put these students in environments where they will struggle academically, and this generates more resentment, a perception of discrimination, and a sense of racial grievance and entitlement.

"The real revolution that occurred in the 1960s was an embrace of equality across racial lines and a society in which advancement is based on objective merit, not skin color. Scholars have provided strong reasons to doubt that racial preferences played much part in the advance of many blacks and Hispanics into our leadership classes, including the large percentage of these leaders who do not come from elite universities. There is a good reason why most Americans oppose racial preferences; they directly undercut the post-1960s social contract. They elevate the importance of skin color at a time when young Americans increasingly see that as an irrelevant distinction. They increasingly single out Asian Americans—a group that has suffered historical discrimination and includes millions of struggling individuals who do not fit the 'model minority' stereotype—for particularly invidious discrimination, to the point that "the 'Asian penalty'" in university admissions has become a term of art among experts. They systematically and enormously favor affluent blacks and Hispanics over working-class Asians and whites.

They encourage students with mixed racial backgrounds to present themselves as being part of a group that will maximize their admissions preference, and they provide incentives for every black and Hispanic student to play up, as much as possible, any past experience that can validate her status as a victim deserving compensation.

"Racial preference advocates argue that without preferences, some universities will only have a 'token' black presence, but they seem to have forgotten what 'tokenism' means. Placing students into classrooms where they will struggle to compete, all for the purpose of demonstrating a university's open-mindedness and making sure that the supposed 'point of view' of every racial group is heard in the classroom is the quintessence of tokenism as well as racial stereotyping and essentialism. Preferences stigmatize the recipients in the eyes of classmates, teachers, and themselves, and they throw into perpetual doubt the value of the degrees the recipients have earned. Far from preventing tokenism, racial preferences foster a lifetime of it.

"The racial preference regime also creates institutional pressures to discriminate in grading and make grading systems and graduation standards less rigorous. It shifts the preeminent mission of universities from the pursuit of excellence to the pursuit of diversity. It fosters cynical games of campus racial politics. And it distracts us all from the real problem that we must address: the racial gaps in K-12 academic achievement that tremendously handicap Hispanics and, especially, blacks."

What light has our empirical journey shed on this debate? On the whole, it has tended to seriously undercut many of the racial preference proponents' claims. There is no serious dispute that large preferences greatly undermine paths to success for blacks in STEM fields and in academia. They substantially increase the risk that black and Hispanic law students will fail bar exams. The University of California experience under Prop 209 strongly suggests that shrinking the largest preferences improves black and Hispanic graduation rates. To the extent we can get at the ultimate question of whether large preferences generate learning mismatch, the evidence is limited but growing and, thus far, entirely consistent with the hypothesis that it does.

The general claim that boosting blacks and Hispanics up to more elite institutions is essential for their long-term success relies on outdated assumptions and falls apart on close examination. Perhaps our best data on this issue comes from the field of law. Fifty years ago elite law firms hired overwhelmingly from elite law schools, so it made sense to think that the best way to integrate these firms racially was to place minorities in elite schools. But hiring patterns have changed radically since then and are now driven by a search for cognitive horsepower and success in law school. Large preferences have become an obstacle rather than a catalyst toward top positions in the law. Many methodologically sound studies of postcollege careers, like that of Loury and Garman, strongly suggest that the same thing is true for undergraduates: Performance trumps elite credentials.

Empirical research has also undermined the "social cohesion" arguments for racial preferences. The "warming effect" at the University of California suggests that many if not most black and Hispanic students are eager to avoid the stigma of racial preferences. Large academic gaps among classmates of different races undermine cross-racial friendships and cluster blacks in particular in non-STEM fields and near the bottom of the class. The available evidence suggests that preferences aggravate rather than ameliorate minority self-image problems like stereotype threat, and the failure of the noisy field of diversity research to tackle the obvious issue of how preferences affect stereotyping speaks volumes.

Our review of institutional behavior in Part III identifies plenty of malfeasance and powerful institutional mechanisms that block meaningful efforts to address the mismatch problem. And Chapters Sixteen and Seventeen show how far we have to go—and how much potential for progress there is—on both K-12 reform and the improvement of socioeconomic opportunity in higher education.

Nearly all of this evidence weighs in on the side of the abolitionists. Indeed, it is this growing body of evidence that has caused the present authors to slowly drift over the past twenty-five years toward greater sympathy for the abolitionists. And from a purely legal standpoint, one can imagine that if the Supreme Court were faced with a case that squarely posed the mismatch problem, its own jurisprudence on preferences ("narrow tailoring . . . requires that a race-conscious admissions program not unduly harm members of any racial group") might compel a decision prohibiting preferences in the absence of clear evidence that they are helping rather than hurting recipients.

Yet abolitionism has some serious difficulties. The three most serious are that (1) ending racial preferences (were that possible) would lead to drastic declines—probably more drastic than in the unique circumstances of the University of California after proposition 209—in black, Native American, and, to some extent, Hispanic enrollments at scores of the nation's top universities; (2) because of the peculiar workings of the cascade effect, the case against preferences is weakest at the most elite schools; and (3) because of universities' determination to circumvent any ban, outlawing preferences would *not* end them but rather would lead—and has led—to universities evading bans, thus possibly making mismatch worse, not better.

First, in a hypothetical world totally purged of racial preferences, the proportion of blacks at the most elite universities and professional schools could fall dramatically. Our "cascade" simulation in Chapter Two implies that black enrollment at the most elite schools could, if they admit students predominantly on academic criteria, fall as low as 1 percent. (This would be true, for example, at law schools.) Other simulations that take into account athletic preferences or the current mild socioeconomic preferences predict smaller but still rather dramatic declines for blacks (drops of 50 percent or more from current levels) as well as smaller but still substantial declines for Hispanics (drops of 30 percent or more from current levels).

Second, due to the peculiar workings of the cascade effect, explained in Chapter Two, the racial gaps in academic credentials—and thus race-related manifestations of mismatch—are smaller at the very top universities than at institutions even a little below them on the eliteness scale. Most or all of the black and Hispanic students admitted to these top schools are so smart and able that a substantial minority might be admitted without preferences, and the rest with preferences smaller than those that less elite schools use. In addition, the institutional resources to help any struggling students succeed are abundant. Another advantage is that preferentially admitted students at these top schools will get to know many classmates who will be future leaders. After graduation, the reputational and networking benefits of a super-elite degree are in some ways unique. So all graduates of these very top institutions have good odds of finding niches where they will thrive.

For all these reasons, a black or Hispanic student receiving a preference to Harvard or Yale is probably a good deal less likely than her counterparts at less elite schools to end up in the bottom tenth of her class—and even if she does, she will probably do just fine, or much better than fine, after graduation. In short, abolishing racial preferences would reduce the black and Hispanic presence most dramatically at the very schools where the effect is most benign.

Third, the post-209 experience at the University of California (UC), like the somewhat similar post-*Hopwood* experience at the University of Texas, illustrates vividly how hard it is to enforce an absolute ban on racial preferences and how damaging universities' evasive tactics can be. Where university leaders are ideologically convinced that the ban is a bad thing, where important political actors continue to push for higher minority headcounts, and where minority students feel aggrieved, the pressures for ill-conceived workarounds and outright (if usually covert) violation of the law become very strong and often irresistible.

One of us (Taylor) thinks that some evasion would have its attractions if the effect were to make preferences smaller without making them disappear and, thus, to avoid the drastic drop in minority presence in the top schools that we just discussed. But the lesson of experience is that some of the ostensibly race-neutral proxies for racial preferences have brought in students who encounter even greater mismatch problems than under the racial-preference regime. Such has proven to be the case at both the University of California and the University of Texas. After Prop 209, UC greatly favored students attending the weakest high schools in the state, gave large weight to other proxies linked to race, and, at professional schools, engaged in blatant evasions of the law. These measures blunted the effect of Prop 209 in reducing mismatch, and as greater evasions have returned, mismatch will foreseeably be as serious a problem at the UCs as it was before Prop 209. After the 1996 *Hopwood* decision discussed in Chapter Seven, the Texas legislature automatically admitted to its flagship university the top 10 percent of students from every high school in the state, including many who were at greater risk of academic mismatch than recipients of racial preferences had been.

If a ban on racial preferences were broad enough to punish evasion and block use of such proxies, with a new enforcement agency that aggressively monitored admissions practices, then racial preferences really would fade away. But we know of no initiative that has included such features and cannot imagine any court taking such steps.

The main tool now available to enforce a legal ban on preferences—private lawsuits by disappointed applicants—is very ineffective, as we discussed in Chapter Thirteen. Few college applicants want to start their adult lives by becoming plaintiffs against universities. If they do, there is a good chance they will graduate from some other college long before achieving any relief and see their lawsuits dismissed for mootness or lack of standing. Proving that schools are using disguised racial preferences is difficult and complex. Judges are wary of overturning the practices of highly respected universities.

Is there another way? We think there is. Below we outline three reforms, each of which would address a serious problem in the current system; together, they could set in motion a virtuous cycle of further improvements and reforms. We then discuss the pending Supreme Court case, *Fisher v. University of Texas*, that could advance these reforms. We do not think that our mix of recommendations is well tailored as a basis for the Court's decision in the current Texas case, given the importance of judicial self-restraint and the fact that the sole remaining plaintiff, Abigail Fisher, has not raised the mismatch problem at all during the case and has not asked for anything remotely like the remedies that we propose. But we believe that the Court could—and we hope that it will—point the way toward these or similar reforms.

REFORM ONE: THE POWER OF TRANSPARENCY

Nearly a decade ago the late, legendary liberal Senator Ted Kennedy proposed that universities be required to disclose the size and extent of any legacy preferences they use in admissions. He argued that legacy preferences were unfair throwbacks to an earlier time. If universities had to reveal the economic status and race of those admitted through legacy preferences, the sunlight shone on these practices would encourage schools to end them or to at least reconsider their policies.

Kennedy's bill did not pass, but we think (and one of us wrote at the time) that he was on the right track. The single-most important step toward reforming affirmative action is to adopt a comprehensive system of disclosure. The Supreme Court could mandate that any university that wishes to take students' race into account in admissions must do so in a way that makes both the use of preferences and their consequences transparent to applicants and the public. This would have three specific components:

First, each school that uses racial preferences should so state in its admissions materials, should disclose the size of the preferences it uses, and should provide each admitted student with information about the academic outcomes of past enrollees with comparable entering credentials. The data disclosed should be sufficiently aggregated to protect the privacy of past enrollees but detailed enough to allow interested observers to discern and report on the weight given in admissions to race and other relevant factors (including, per Kennedy, legacy status). Admitted students should also be given broader data disclosing the overall process of creating the student body, its characteristics, and its outcomes.

Second, schools should provide any information they have available or can reasonably obtain on learning outcomes for past students similar to the admitted student. For example, a student admitted to a college with a given SAT score and high school GPA should receive its best estimate of the past graduation rates of comparable students, their college GPAs, and their rates of attrition from intended majors. Ideally, schools should also be encouraged (perhaps required as part of the accreditation process) to gather and make available data on students' postcollege outcomes: What proportion of past students similar to the applicant ended up attending graduate school? What proportion were employed five years after graduation, and what were the median earnings of those graduates? For law schools this would include data on bar passage rates or, preferably, bar scores. For medical schools this would include data on the outcomes of national boards and eventual rates of licensing in chosen fields. For colleges this would include scores on exams taken in anticipation of graduate school (e.g., GRE scores) and any results from participation in exams like the Collegiate Learning Assessment.

Third, these data on outcomes as well as on the size of all admissions preferences should be made publicly available so that researchers, legislators, the media, and all other citizens can evaluate the accuracy and completeness of the information provided to applicants.

Universities are well equipped to gather such data through mechanisms including national networks that create samples of alumni to track outcomes. If any complain that these duties are burdensome, the answer is that, for the sake of their own students, they should have been gathering and analyzing such data for many years.

Transparency would create many positive-feedback cycles, in contrast to the perverse negative-feedback cycles racial preferences create, such as the cascade effect and the campus dynamics of unequal performance. Consider the following:

Disclosure would empower minority students to make their own assessments of the mismatch risks of enrolling in a particular school based on a preference of known size. Networks would quickly spring up to promote discussions among applicants, their parents, current students, graduates, high school guidance counselors, and others. These conversations would be far deeper and more useful than today's choice-of-school conversations, which are dominated by the simple rankings generated by *U.S. News* and its kin.

The universities themselves would be drawn into these conversations. No longer able to deny the fact or scale of preferences, administrators would suddenly find themselves accountable for the preferences that they use and also for the struggles of students whose academic problems are foreseeable based on their incoming grades and scores. More importantly, the competition for students would no longer be limited to glossy brochures and scholarship offers but rather actual outcomes. Schools would have very substantial incentives to minimize these mismatch problems or risk being shunned by many high school seniors.

With results exposed to sunlight, some colleges and universities would probably choose to reduce preferences significantly. Others would try to develop more effective academic support programs. One way or another, mismatch effects would likely be addressed and steadily eroded.

The most likely objection to a transparency requirement is that it would, by exposing the poor outcomes that often result from preferences, undercut the academic confidence of vulnerable students. But, as documented in Chapter Six, students' grades tend to reflect their preparation levels relative to their classmates, not their expectations when they enroll. Administrators' assurances that every admitted student is equipped to flourish are not true; they only mislead the students and their parents, often to the students' detriment. Cole and Barber have richly documented the tremendous loss of academic self-confidence that disproportionately plagues students receiving large preferences. In a more transparent regime students will have a better sense of the odds they are up against and be able to make more realistic and, certainly, more informed choices.

Happily, a transparency mandate is already implicit in the Supreme Court's rulings on racial preferences. *Grutter,* along with the logic of a more recent ruling on K-12 schools, require universities to prove that their consideration of race in admissions is "narrowly tailored" to promote a healthy diversity. Among other things, "narrow tailoring . . . requires that a race-conscious admissions program not unduly harm any racial group" (as noted above) and that schools must engage in "serious, good faith consideration of workable race-neutral alternatives" to minimize such harm.

As both logic and experience under *Grutter* have shown, these narrow-tailoring requirements are largely meaningless without full disclosure of the operation and effects of preferences. How can anyone know which schools have considered or incorporated race-neutral alternatives without better knowledge of what they are individually doing? How can one minimize the harms of racial preferences to the minorities that receive them without providing information that allows prospective students to understand their likely outcomes at schools that do and do not use racial preferences? How can unsuccessful applicants assess whether they might have a valid discrimination claim worth pursuing? And how can courts monitor and enforce compliance with the constitutional narrow-tailoring requirement? In short, secret admissions can't possibly be narrow tailoring.

To be sure, as we described in Chapter Thirteen, the *Gratz* decision and Justice O'Connor's opinion for the *Grutter* majority created such strong incentives for universities to keep their veils of secrecy that it seems likely that was the way she wanted it. But only majority holdings—and certainly not any justice's private purposes—are relevant to future cases. Although no decision has ever squarely addressed the question of whether narrow tailoring requires transparency, no precedent stands in the way of imposing such a requirement, and the logic of the most relevant precedents argues strongly in favor of doing so.

REFORM TWO: TARGETING ECONOMIC NEED BEFORE RACIAL IDENTITY

Despite the Supreme Court's explicit assertion that racial preferences must not unduly harm members of any racial group—and the fact that undue harm is a function of how large the preferences are—the Court has never imposed a specific size limit. And it's easy to imagine that the difficulty of determining in any principled way how large is too large may have deterred the Court from doing so.

One solution to this dilemma—which would also have the highly beneficial side effect of returning affirmative action to its original social-mobility goal—would be to require that *the racial preferences a university uses be no larger than the average size of preferences based on an individual applicant's financial need or socioeconomic status (SES).* As Chapter Sixteen demonstrates, socioeconomic diversity is every bit as compelling an interest as racial diversity, but most selective schools have grossly neglected the former.

Creating an "SES cap" on racial preferences would accomplish several goals: It would ensure that pursuit of campus diversity includes meaningful consideration of each applicant's individual circumstances rather than just her skin color. It would ensure that universities actually pay attention to race-neutral ways of pursuing diversity and, thus, would inhibit unconstitutional racial balancing.

An SES cap on racial preferences would also foster simple justice to the economic have-nots who have been so sorely neglected by our selective universities. As discussed in Chapter Sixteen, racial minorities have much better access to our universities than do Asians and whites of modest means. Indeed, blacks are about 30 percent more likely to enter college than are whites with similar socioeconomic backgrounds and academic credentials. (They are less likely than comparable whites to graduate—in part, we are confident, because of mismatch.) In contrast, students from the bottom quarter of the SES spectrum are about 80 percent less likely to enter college than are students with similar academic credentials from the top fifth of the spectrum. This is a shocking state of affairs, especially at a time of rising concern about economic inequality, and our proposed remedy would help change it.

Note that socioeconomic criteria can (and should, we think) be cognizant of and capture the manifold ways that race and disadvantage intersect in our society. For example, blacks with family incomes of $40,000 are likely to live in significantly poorer neighborhoods than are whites at the same income level. Even blacks with higher incomes tend to have much less wealth than do whites with similar incomes. A careful SES measure can take into account such nuances.

How would one actually implement this cap on racial preferences? Peter Schuck and commentator Michael Kinsley have memorably warned that SES preferences would be complicated, messy, and prone to abuse. But Sander actually devised and implemented a sophisticated system of SES preferences at UCLA after the passage of Proposition 209, and the system worked exceedingly well. Audits against financial aid statements showed little abuse; the preferences substantially changed the social makeup of the class and never, to our knowledge, prompted complaints of unfairness. Compared, for instance, to the complexity of Supreme Court rules on racial gerrymandering, our proposed SES mandate would be straightforward.

The most significant challenge in this proposal, from an enforcement point of view, is the task of actually comparing the size of socioeconomic versus racial preferences. But as detailed in the endnotes, we think this is quite doable. This sort of reliance on the specific weight assigned to race (as well as to SES status) may seem to run afoul of the Supreme Court's decision in *Gratz* to ban any admissions systems that assign a specific number of bonus points to each preferred-minority applicant. But we think—and we suspect that at least five justices think—that the *Gratz* rule has proven unworkable. As Chapter Thirteen shows, *Gratz* was based on false assumptions about how college admissions works, as all admissions decisions involve implicit assignments of relative weights to the various criteria, including race, even if only in the subconscious of the decision maker. The *Gratz* ban on making that weighting process explicit perversely makes narrow tailoring all but impossible.

REFORM THREE: OUTLAWING RACE-BASED AID AWARDS

Our third proposed reform would reinforce the effectiveness of the second and is eminently warranted in its own right: The Court should, in a proper case, prohibit state schools from using racial preferences in awarding financial aid and scholarships. Such awards produce little if any diversity benefit because they do not increase by much, if at all, the number of preferred-minority university students. Rather, the main function of race-based financial aid is to fuel zero-sum bidding wars among competing campuses for the limited supply of blacks with strong academic qualifications. Because a large proportion of those blacks are from well-off families, they need financial aid much less—but are much more likely to get it—than better-qualified, less well-off white and Asian students. Race-exclusive scholarships are already clearly unconstitutional, and if the Supreme Court takes the narrow-tailoring requirement at all seriously—as at least five of the current justices clearly do—it would strike down in a heartbeat all consideration of race in financial aid awards.

Our proposed reforms would reinforce one another. For example, one objection to creating an incentive for schools to make more use of SES preferences might be that this would just bring the mismatch effect in through another door. Certainly that is a danger, and we would not favor this step if it were not accompanied by a complete transparency that allows both students and outside experts to monitor whether the SES preferences are excessive and doing damage. But SES preferences used for their own sake (and not as an evasion of racial restrictions) are likely to be modest. As we noted in Chapter Sixteen, simply making current admissions processes more fair and better directing financial aid to those with real need would improve SES diversity significantly. Because of the large, untapped supply of academically strong, low-SES students, modest SES preferences can produce a dramatic increase in current levels of SES diversity. (Moreover, schools using very aggressive SES preferences would likely find the demands for financial aid and the demands on their own resources quite daunting, and this would also encourage moderation.)

The combined effect of our proposed reforms would thus be to give schools incentives both to increase their SES diversity and to avoid large preferences—and the mismatch they cause—while also requiring healthy transparency. Admitted applicants and their parents could assess for themselves the mismatch risks, if any, posed by this or that college. A very elite, very rich school that produces good outcomes for nearly all of its students could continue using substantial racial preferences as long as its SES preferences were just as substantial. And schools would have a new incentive to develop superb academic support programs to improve their appeal as places where preferred-minority students need not fear being left behind.

FISHER AND THE OPPORTUNITY FOR REFORM

As we finish this book, the Supreme Court is receiving briefs in *Fisher v. University of Texas*, its first case since *Grutter* and *Gratz* to deal with racial preferences in higher education. The Court has set the oral argument for October

10, 2012. It is expected to decide the case by the end of June 2013. The decision could be momentous, or it could be based on fairly narrow grounds. But for reasons we discuss below, we are hopeful that the Court's decision will mark a notable and constructive break with the patterns we criticized in Chapter Thirteen.

Abigail Noel Fisher, of Sugar Land, Texas, applied in 2008 for freshman admission to the state's flagship campus, the University of Texas at Austin (UT). Because she did not finish in the top 10 percent of her high school class, she did not qualify for automatic admission under the state's "Top Ten Percent" law, which the legislature had adopted in 1998. Instead, she competed for admission against other in-state candidates for the 19 percent of seats in the next entering class that the top 10 percent admits and out-of-state students did not fill. Though her academic credentials exceeded those of many admitted black and Hispanic applicants, UT denied her application. Fisher filed suit in 2008, challenging UT's use of race in undergraduate admissions as contrary to the Fourteenth Amendment guarantee of "equal protection of the laws," as interpreted by *Grutter* and other precedents. She lost in federal district court and appealed. A three-judge panel of the Fifth Circuit Court of Appeals ruled unanimously against her. One member, Judge Emilio Garza, harshly criticized UT's preferences and said the Supreme Court should overrule *Grutter* and strike them down. But Garza added that, as a lower court judge, he was bound to follow *Grutter*, which left him no choice but to uphold UT's preferences. The full Fifth Circuit, sitting en banc, declined by 9–7 to rehear the panel's decision, with the votes of the seven dissenters showing that they disagreed with Garza and saw UT's preferences as contrary to *Grutter.*

Fisher then filed a petition for Supreme Court review, arguing both that the UT preferences were contrary to *Grutter* and that if the Court disagreed, it should overrule *Grutter* as suggested by Judge Garza. The justices announced in February 2012 that they would hear Fisher's case. Court watchers could immediately see that—because of changes in the Court's membership since *Grutter*—this might become the biggest case ever on racial preferences in university admissions.

Four of the nine current Justices—including Samuel Alito, whom President Bush appointed to Justice O'Connor's seat when she retired—are on record saying that most or all state-sponsored racial preferences are unconstitutional. A fifth, Anthony Kennedy, strongly dissented in *Grutter* on the ground that the then-majority's purported narrow-tailoring requirement was toothless. Many saw the Court's decision to hear the Texas case as suggesting that Kennedy would provide the fifth vote to strike down UT's racial preferences. To be sure, the justices sometimes surprise. And the state's well-crafted brief, filed on August 6, 2012, was clearly written to persuade Kennedy that, even under the logic of his *Grutter* dissent, he should uphold the Texas preferences.

Critics see at least three characteristics of UT's preference program as making it vulnerable even under *Grutter*. First, UT is one of the few elite universities that already had a facially race-neutral system in place for creating racial diversity—the top 10 percent law, which has given the university a higher percentage of black and Hispanic students than most state schools—before it added its current racial preferences to that system. (There have been modifications since 2008, when Fisher applied.) Because some Texas high schools are heavily black or Hispanic, the top 10 percent system generates much more diversity than the typical college admissions system. In 2008, for example, nearly a quarter of UT's entering students were black or Hispanic even without counting the relatively small additional number who were admitted via conventional direct racial preferences. Fisher's lawyers and others argue that there can be no constitutional justification for using racial preferences to produce at most a marginal increase in diversity at a school that is already unusually diverse.

Second, UT has explicitly set a goal of moving toward enrolling a student body with roughly the same proportion of each racial group as the state's population. But this seems hard to distinguish from the "racial balancing" that *Grutter* declared to be flatly unconstitutional. And third, UT has also set a goal of using racial preferences until there are black and Hispanic students in every classroom. But that could take many, many decades because the reason so many tough classes now have no or few black or Hispanic students is that students with relatively weak preparation avoid such classes.

And the racial gaps in academic qualifications at UT are very large indeed. Among freshmen entering UT in 2009 who were admitted outside the top-ten-percent system, for example, Asians had a mean SAT score that would put them at the 93rd percentile nationwide; whites were at the 89th percentile, Hispanics at the 80th percentile, and blacks at the 52nd percentile. A staggering 467 points (on a 2,400-point scale) separated the mean SAT scores of Asians and blacks admitted with explicit preferences. (Note that the black-white gaps at Texas are similar to those estimated for Tier 3 or 4 schools in our cascade effect model from Figure 2.1, p. 24.)

We do not suggest that there is no coherent legal argument for UT's preferences, but we doubt that there is an argument that Justice Kennedy will find persuasive. He has been a pragmatic skeptic of racial preferences; he has never declared that all such preferences are unconstitutional, but he has also never voted to uphold such a program. Instead, he has suggested that any racial preference program is unconstitutional unless it can pass some fairly rigorous tests, which no racial preference yet to come before Kennedy has ever passed.

We therefore suspect—and hope—that Justice Kennedy will be engaged in his review of UT's practices in a process similar to our own more general review of racial preferences in higher education. He will not take an absolutist position either for or against preferences but instead will try to give substance and specificity to the Court's standards of "strict scrutiny" and "narrow tailoring." In the process of doing that, it would be both plausible and logical for him to articulate some type of transparency requirement and some limit on the size of racial preferences.

Indeed, Justice Kennedy could cite Justice Ruth Bader Ginsburg, perhaps the most liberal current justice, in support of transparency. Recall her assertion in her *Gratz* dissent that "if honesty is the best policy, surely [an] accurately described, fully disclosed . . . affirmative action program is preferable to achieving similar numbers through winks, nods, and disguises."

Fisher does not directly pose the problem of mismatch. The plaintiff is a white woman who was not admitted and who made no argument that racial preferences harmed anyone except rejected applicants from nonpreferred groups like her own. But the mismatch issue lurks in the background. For example, part of the reason that UT's preferences have not produced classroom diversity is, as noted above, the tendency of mismatched students to drop or avoid tough courses in which competing is particularly difficult. Simply increasing the aggressiveness of preferences is not a plausible way of solving this problem. And for the reasons we have detailed, preferences on the scale used by UT are almost certain to backfire on the students they purport to help.

The alternatives to a Supreme Court requirement of muscular reforms seem stark: either perpetuation of large and, thus, harmful racial admissions preferences into the far-distant future, or immediate abolition of any and all consideration of race. We think there is a better way. And there is reason to hope that the Court's deliberations in *Fisher*—and the broader national deliberation that will accompany it—will start us down that better path.

BIBLIOGRAPHY

Alon, Sigal, and Marta Tienda, "Assessing the 'Mismatch' Hypothesis: Differentials in College Graduation Rates by Institutional Selectivity." *Sociology of Education* 78 (2005): 294.

Antonoivcs, Kate, and Richard Sander. "Affirmative Action Bans and the 'Chilling Effect.'" *American Law and Economics Review* (forthcoming, 2013).

Arcidiacono, Peter, Esteban Aucejo, Patrick Coate, and V. Joseph Hotz. "The Effects of Proposition 209 on College Enrollment and Graduation Rates in California." Unpublished working paper.

Arcidiacono, Peter, Esteban M. Acejo, and Ken Spenner. "What Happens After Enrollment? An Analysis of the Time Path of Racial Differences in GPA and Major Choice." Duke University, 2011, http://www.seaphe.org/working-papers/.

———. "What Happens After Enrollment?" *IZA Journal of Labor Economics* (forthcoming, 2012).

Arcidiacono, Peter, Shakeeb Khan, and Jacob L. Vigdor. "Representation versus Assimilation: How Do Preferences in College Admissions Affect Social Interactions?" *Journal of Public Economics* 95, no. 1–2 (February 2011): 1–15.

Arum, Richard. "How Expanding Student Rights Undermined Public Schooling." *Atlantic*, April 6, 2012, http://www.theatlantic.com/national/archive/2012/04/how-expanding-student-rights-undermined-public-schooling/255393/

Arum, Richard, Irenee Beattie, Richard Pitt, Jennifer Thompson, and Sandra Way. *Judging School Discipline: The Crisis of Moral Authority in American Schools.* Cambridge, MA: Harvard University Press, 2003.

Arum, Richard, and Josipa Roksa. *Academically Adrift: Limited Learning on College Campuses.* Chicago: University of Chicago Press, 2011.

Ashburn, Elyse. "At Elite Colleges, Legacy Status May Count for More Than Was Previously Thought." *Chronicle of Higher Education*, January 5, 2011.

Ayres, Ian, and Richard Brooks. "Does Affirmative Action Reduce the Number of Black Lawyers?" *Stanford Law Review* 57 (2005): 1807.

Ball, Howard. *The Bakke Case: Race, Education, and Affirmative Action*, 86. Lawrence: University Press of Kansas, 2000.

———. *The Bakke Case: Race, Education, and Affirmative Action.* Lawrence, University Press of Kansas, 2000.

Barnes, Katherine. "Is Affirmative Action Responsible for the Achievement Gap Between Black and White Students?" *Northwestern Law Review* 101 (2007): 1759.
———. "Is Affirmative Action Responsible for the Achievement Gap Between Black and White Law Students? A Correction, A Lesson, and an Update." *Northwestern Law Review* 105 (2011): 791.

Biskupic, Joan. "O'Connor Could Hold Key to Her Great Friend's Legacy." *USA Today*, March 25, 2003, http://www.usatoday.com/life/2003-03-25 -affirmative_x.htm.

Bowen, William G., and Derek Bok. *The Shape of the River: Long-Term Consequences of Considering Race in College and University Admissions.* Princeton, NJ: Princeton University Press, 1998.

Bowen, William G., and Sarah Levin. *Reclaiming the Game: College Sports and Educational Values.* Princeton, NJ: Princeton University Press, 2003.

Boxall, Bettina "A Political Battle Grinds on as a War of Wording." *Los Angeles Times*, October 1, 1996.

Boxall, Bettina, and Sandy Banks. "Police, Protesters Clash at Duke-Hicks Debate." *Los Angeles Times*, September 26, 1996.

Brill, Steven. *Class Warfare: Inside the Fight to Fix American Schools.* New York: Simon and Schuster, 2011.

Brodhead, Richard H. "Brodhead: Duke and the Legacy of Race." *Duke Today*, March 22, 2012, http://today.duke.edu/2012/03/rhbfacultytalk/.

Bronner, Ethan. "Fewer Minorities Entering University of California." *New York Times*, May 21, 1998, A28.

Brooks, David. "Kerry's Good Intentions." *New York Times*, January 24, 2004.

Brown, Ryan P., Tonyamas Charnsangavej, Kelli A. Keough, Matthew L. Newman, and Peter J. Rentfrow. "Putting the 'Affirm' into Affirmative Action: Preferential Selection and Academic Performance." *Journal of Personality and Social Psychology* 79, no. 5 (2000): 736–747.

Bruni, Frank. "Blacks at Berkeley Are Offering No Welcome Mat." *New York Times*, May 2, 1998.

Buck, Stuart. *Acting White: The Ironic Legacy of Desegregation.* New Haven, CT: Yale University Press, 2010.

Bush, George W. "President Applauds Supreme Court for Recognizing Value of Diversity." The White House, June 2003, http://georgewbush-white - house.archives.gov/news/releases/2003/06/20030623.html.

"California Bar Lawsuit." Project Seaphe, http://www.seaphe.org/topic -pages/california-bar-lawsuit.php.

Card, David, and Alan B. Krueger. "Would the Elimination of Affirmative Action Affect Highly Qualified Minority Applicants? Evidence from California and Texas." *Industrial & Labor Relations Review* 58 (2005): 416.

Chavez, Lydia. *The Color Bind: California's Battle to End Affirmative Action.* Berkeley, CA: University of California Press, 1998.

Citrin, Jack. "Affirmative Action in the People's Court." Working Paper, Berkeley, CA: Institute of Governmental Studies, University of California: 43–44.

Clegg, Roger. "CEO Praises Supreme Court's Decision to Hear Fisher v. University of Texas." Center for Equal Opportunity, http://www.ceousa.org/ affirmative-action/affirmative-action-news/ education/.

———. "Latest Numbers on Unmarried Births." *National Review Online*, November 18, 2011, http://www.nationalreview.com/corner/283539/ latest-numbers-unmarried-births-roger-clegg.

Clydesdale, Timothy. "A Forked River Runs Through Law School: Toward Understanding Race, Gender, Age, and Related Gaps in Law School Performance and Bar Passage." *Law and Social Inquiry* 29 (2004): 711.

Cole, Stephen, and Elinor Barber. *Increasing Faculty Diversity: The Occupational Choices of High-Achieving Minority Students*. Cambridge, MA: Harvard University Press, 2003.

Coleman, J. S., E. Q. Campbell, C. J. Hobson, J. McPartland, A. M. Mood, F. D. Weinfeld, and R. L. York. *Equality of Educational Opportunity*. Washington, DC: U.S. Government Printing Office, 1966.

Coleman, William T., with Donald Bliss. *Counsel for the Situation: Shaping the Law to Realize America's Promise*. Washington, DC: Brookings Institution Press, 2010.

College Board. "2011 SAT Trends—SAT Mean Scores by Race/Ethnicity over 10 Years." http://professionals.collegeboard.com/data-reports-research/sat/ cb- seniors-2011/tables.

Congress and the Nation, volume IX, 1993-96. Washington DC: Congressional Quarterly, Inc., 1998, 748–749.

Connerly, Ward. *Creating Equal: My Fight Against Race Preferences*. San Francisco, CA: Encounter Books, 2000.

Cose, Ellis. *The End of Anger: A New Generation's Take on Race and Rage*. New York, NY: Ecco, 2011.

Council on Foreign Relations. "U.S. Education Reform and National Security." http://www.cfr.org/united-states/us-education-reform-national -security/p27618/.

Crosby, Faye. *Affirmative Action Is Dead, Long Live Affirmative Action*. New Haven, CT: Yale University Press, 2004.

Dale, Stacy, and Alan B. Krueger. "Estimating the Payoff to Attending a More Selective College." *Quarterly Journal of Economics* 117 (2002): 1491.

Davis, James. "The Campus as a Frog Pond: An Application of the Theory of Relative Deprivation to Career Decisions of College Men." *American Journal of Sociology* 72, no. 1 (July 1966): 17–31.

DeParle, Jason. "Two Classes, Divided by 'I Do.'" *New York Times*, July 14, 2012, http://www.nytimes.com/2012/07/15/us/two-classes-in-america -divided-by-i-do.html?_r=1&ref=todayspaper/.

Dinovitzer, Ronit, Bryant Garth, Richard Sander, Joyce Sterling, and Gitz Wilder. *After the JD: First Results of a National Study of Legal Careers*. The NALP Foundation for Law Career Research and Education and the American Bar Foundation, 2004.

Dobbie, Will, and Ronald G. Fryer Jr. "Are High Quality Schools Enough to Increase Achievement Among the Poor? Evidence from the Harlem Children's Zone" *American Economic Journal: Applied Economics* 3, no. 3 (July 2011): 158–187.

Dobbin, Frank. *Inventing Equal Opportunity*. Princeton, NJ: Princeton University Press, 2009.

Douglass, John. "A Brief on the Events Leading to SP-1." UC Academic Senate, 1997.

Drew, Christopher. "Why Science Majors Change Their Minds (It's Just So Darn Hard)." *New York Times*, November 4, 2011, http://www .nytimes.com/2011/11/06/education/edlife/why-science-majors-change -their-mind-its-just-so-darn-hard.html?pagewanted=all.

Duflo, Esther, Pascaline Dupas, and Michael Kramer. "Peer Effects, Teacher Incentives, and the Impact of Tracking: Evidence from a Randomized Evaluation in Kenya." *American Economic Review* 101 (2011): 1739.

Edmundson, Mark. "The Trouble with Online Education." *New York Times*, July 19, 2012.

Elliott, Rogers, A. Christopher Strenta, Russell Adair, Michael Matier, and Jannah Scott. "The Role of Ethnicity in Choosing and Leaving Science in Highly Selective Institutions." *Research in Higher Education* 37, no. 6 (1996): 681–709.

Espenshade, Thomas J., and Alexandria Walton Radford. *No Longer Separate, Not Yet Equal: Race and Class in Elite College Admission and Campus Life*. Princeton, NJ: Princeton University Press, 2009.

Espenshade, Thomas J., and Chang Y. Chung. "The Opportunity Cost of Admission Preferences at Elite Universities." *Social Science Quarterly* 86, no. 2 (2005): 293–305.

Espenshade, Thomas J., Chang Y. Chung, and Joan L. Walling. "Admission Preferences for Minority Students, Athletes, and Legacies at Elite Universities." *Social Science Quarterly* 85, no. 5 (2004): 1422–1446.

Fischer, M. J., and D. S. Massey. "The Effects of Affirmative Action in Higher Education." *Social Science Research* 36, no. 2 (June 2007): 531–549.

Freelon, Kiratiana, Marques J. Redd, and Toussaint Losier. *Black Guide to Life at Harvard*. Cambridge, MA: Harvard Black Student Association, 2002.

Fryer, Roland G. "Acting White: The Social Price Paid by the Best and Brightest Minority Students." *Education Next* 6, no. 1 (Winter 2006): l.

———. "Racial Inequality in the 21st Century: The Declining Significance of Discrimination." *Handbook of Labor Economics* 4, part B (March 2011): 855–971.

Fryer, Roland G., and Paul Torelli. "An Empirical Analysis of Acting White." *Journal of Public Economics* 94, no. 5 (2010): 380.

Fryer, Roland G., and Steven D. Levitt. "Understanding the Black-White Test Score Gap in the First Two Years of School." *Review of Economics and Statistics* 86, no.2 (2004): 447–464.

Gates Jr., Henry Louis. "Breaking the Silence." *New York Times*, August 1, 2004, http://www.ntimes.com/2004/08/01/opinion/breaking-the -silence.html.

Groseclose, Tim. "Report on Suspected Malfeasance in UCLA Admissions and the Accompanying Cover-up." August 28, 2008, http://www .sscnet.ucla.edu/polisci/faculty/groseclose/CUARS.Resignation .Report.pdf.

Gordon, Larry. "Brown Backs Federal Lawsuit." *Los Angeles Times*, July 9, 2011.

———. "UC San Diego Condemns Student Party Mocking Black History Month." *Los Angeles Times*, February 18, 2010.

———. "UC Moves Toward Holistic Review of Applicants." *Los Angeles Times*, January 20, 2011.

Hanushek, Eric A. "How Well Do We Understand Racial Achievement Gaps?" *Focus* 11, no. 2 (Winter 2010): 5–12.

———. "The Economic Value of Higher Teacher Quality." National Bureau of Economic Research, December, 2010.

———. "Valuing Teachers." *Education Next* 11, no. 3 (Summer 2011): 41–45.

Hanushek, Eric A., and Alfred A. Lindseth. *Schoolhouses, Courthouses, and Statehouses: Solving the Funding-Achievement Puzzle in America's Public Schools.* Princeton, NJ: Princeton University Press, 2009.

Hanushek, Eric A., Paul E. Peterson, and Ludger Woessman. "U.S. Math Performance in Global Perspective: How Well Does Each State Do at Producing High-Achieving Students." Program on Education Policy and Governance and Education Next, Harvard University, Kennedy School of Government, November 2010, 4.

Haskins, Ron, and Isabel Sawhill. *Creating an Opportunity Society.* Washington, DC: Brookings Institution Press, 2009.

Heckman, James J. "The American Family in Black and White: A Post-Racial Strategy for Improving Skills to Promote Equality." NBER Working Paper No. 16841, March 2011.

Herrnstein, Richard J., and Charles A. Murray. *The Bell Curve: Intelligence and Class Structure in American Life.* New York: Free Press, 1994.

Ho, Daniel. "Why Affirmative Action Does Not Cause Students to Fail the Bar." *Yale Law Journal* 114 (2005): 1997.

Hosendolph, Ernest. "Skills, Not Bias, Seen as Key to Jobs." *New York Times*, July 3, 1982, http://www.nytimes.com/1982/07/03/us/skills-not-bias-seen-as-key-for-jobs.html.

Howard, Philip K. "It's Time to Clean House." *Atlantic*, March 6, 2012, http://www.theatlantic.com/politics/archive/2012/03/its-time-to-clean -house/253921/#/.

———. *Life Without Lawyers: Liberating Americans from Too Much Law.* New York: W. W. Norton, 2009.

Jaschik, Scott. "How They Really Get In." *Inside Higher Ed*, April 9, 2012, http://www.insidehighered.com/news/2012/04/09/new-research-how -elite-colleges-make-admissions-decisions/.

Jeffries Jr., John C. *Justice Lewis F. Powell, Jr.: A Biography.* New York: Fordham University Press, 2001.

Jencks, Christopher. *Rethinking Social Policy: Race, Poverty, and the Underclass.* Cambridge, MA: Harvard University Press, 1992.

Johnson, KC. "Politics of Grievance at Duke." *Durham-in-Wonderland Blog,* January 22, 2012, http://durhamwonderland.blogspot.com/2012/01/politics-of-grievance-at-duke.html/.

———. "Brodhead's Extraordinary Address." *Durham-in-Wonderland Blog,* March 22, 2012, http://durhamwonderland.blogspot.com/2012/03/brodheads-extraordinary-address.html/.

Kahlenberg, Richard. *Affirmative Action for the Rich: Legacy Preferences in College Admissions.* New York: The Century Foundation, 2010.

———. "Obama's Affirmative-Action Brief." *Chronicle,* August 16, 2012, http://chronicle.com/blogs/innovations/obamas-affirmative-action-brief/34003.

———. *The Remedy: Class, Race, and Affirmative Action.* New Republic Book/Basic Books, 1996.

Kane, Thomas. "Racial and Ethnic Preferences in College Admission." *The Black-White Test Score Gap.* Edited by Christopher Jencks and Meredith Phillips. Washington, DC: Brookings Institute Press, 1998.

Kaplan, Thomas, and Kate Taylor. "Invoking King, Cuomo and Bloomberg Stoke Fight on Teacher Review Impasse." *New York Times,* January 17, 2012, http://www.nytimes.com/2012/01/17/nyregion/cuomo-and-bloomberg-on-attack-on-teacher-evaluations.html.

Karabel, Jerome. *The Chosen: The Hidden History of Admission and Exclusion at Harvard, Yale, and Princeton.* Boston: Houghton Mifflin, 2005.

Kinsley, Michael. "The Spoils of Victimhood." *New Yorker,* March 27, 1995. http://www.newyorker.com/archive/1995/03/27/1995_03_27_062_TNY_CARDS_0003696.

Klein, Joel. "New York's Charter Schools Get an A+." *Wall Street Journal,* July 26, 2012, http://online.wsj.com/article/SB10000872396390443343704577550781938901886.html.

Klein, Stephen. "Research on the California Bar Examination: A Ten Year Retrospective." 1982, http://www.seaphe.org/topic-pages/california-bar-lawsuit.php.

Klein, Stephen, and Roger Bolus, "Analysis of July 2004 Texas Bar Exam Results by Gender and Racial/Ethnic Group." 2004, http://www.ble.state.tx.us/one/analysis_0704tbe.htm.

Klitgaard, Robert. *Choosing Elites.* New York: Basic Books, 1985.

Kotkin, Joel. "Here Come the Mad Dog Democrats." *Wall Street Journal,* July 10, 1996.

Kozlowski, Kim. "Court to Debate Michigan Affirmative Action Ban." *The Detroit News,* March 7, 2012.

Kristof, Nicholas D. "Pay Teachers More." *New York Times,* March 12, 2011, http://www.nytimes.com/2011/03/13/opinion/13kristof.html.

Lemann, Nicholas. "Taking Affirmative Action Apart." *New York Times,* June 11, 1995.

Lempert, Richard. "Humility is a Virtue: On the Publicization of Policy-Relevant Research." *Law and Society Review* 23 (1989): 145.

Lewin, Tamar. "Law School Admissions Lag Among Minorities." *New York Times*, January 6, 2010, http://www.nytimes.com/2010/01/07/education/07law.html.

Leonhardt, David. "Top Colleges, Largely for the Elite." *New York Times*, May 24, 2011, http://www.nytimes.com/2011/05/25/business/economy/25leonhardt.html?pagewanted=all.

Li, David K., Jennifer Bain, and Yoav Gonen. "Can't Ex-Spell Idiots." *New York Post*, January 27, 2012, http://www.nypost.com/p/news/local/can_ex_spell_idiots_KPArPcPrwjOPbNzyYXOD6O.

Light, Audrey, and Wayne Strayer. "Determinants of College Completion: School Quality or Student Ability?" *Journal of Human Resources* 35 (2000): 2.

Loury, Glenn. "Affirmative Action: Is There a Middle Way?" *Slat*, October 8, 1996. http://www.slate.com/articles/news_and_politics/committee_of_correspondence/features/1996/affirmative_action_is_there_a_middle_way/_4.html.

Loury, Linda, and David Garman. "College Selectivity and Earnings." *Journal of Labor Economics* 13 (1995): 289.

Marquis, Julie. "Liposuction Doctor Has License Revoked." *Los Angeles Times*, August 26, 1998.

Martin, Douglas. "Patrick Chavis, 50, Affirmative Action Figure." *New York Times*, August 15, 2002.

National Center for Education Statistics. *NAEP 2008 Trends in Academic Progress.* National Center for Education Statistics, 2009, nces.ed.gov/nationsreportcard/pdf/main2008/2009479.pdf.

National Science Foundation. A Timeline of NSF History. "1971—September 10: Improving Minority Education." http://www.nsf.gov/news/special_reports/history-nsf/1971_student.jsp.

———. "Science and Engineering Degrees, by Race/Ethnicity of Recipients: 1995-2004." http://www.nsf.gov/statistics/nsf07308/content.cfm?pub_id=3633&id=2

Maguire, Timothy. "My Bout with Affirmative Action." *Commentary* 93 (April 1992): 50.

Mangin, Katherine. "New Issue of Stanford Law Review Will Rebut a Critic of Affirmative Action." *Chronicle of Higher Education* (April 22, 2005).

Marklein, Mary Beth. "Affirmative Action Fight Goes On." *USA Today*, March 6, 2012, http://www.usatoday.com/news/education/story/2012-03-02/affirmative-action/53389292/1.

Martin, Nathan D., and Kenneth I. Spenner. "A Social Portrait of Legacies at an Elite University." August 1, 2008, http://chronicle.com/article/Legacys-Advantage-May-Be/125812/.

Massey, Douglas S., Margarita Mooney, and Kimberly C. Torres, and Camille Z. Charles. "Black Immigrants and Black Natives Attending Selective Colleges and Universities in the United States." *American Journal of Education* 113, no. 2 (February 2007): 243–273.

Miller, Matthew. *The Two Percent Solution: Fixing America's Problems in Ways Liberals and Conservatives Can Love.* New York: Public Affairs, 2003.

Moore, Matt. "Ailing Method, Essential Motive: An Examination of Two Strategies to Improve Core Legal Learning Among Underrepresented Minority Law Students." Unpublished manuscript, 2005.

Moran, Rachael, et al. "Statement of Faculty Policy Governing Admission to Boalt Hall and Report of the Admissions Policy Task Force." August 31, 1993.

Moyers, Bill. "Jonathan Haidt Explains Our Contentious Culture." February 3, 2012, http:// billmoyers.com/wp-content/themes/billmoyers/transcript -print.php?post=3101.

Murphy, Sean. "GOP Lawmakers Push to Abolish Affirmative Action." *Tulsa World,* April 5, 2011, http://www.tulsaworld.com/site/printerfriendly story.aspx?articleid=20110405_336_0_OKLAHO614181.

Offen, Neil. "Black Alumni Join Duke Students in Concern over Duke Study." *Herald-Sun,* January 16, 2012, http://www.heraldsun.com/view/ full_story/17186264/article-Black-alumni-join-students-in-concern -over-Duke-study-.

———. "Black Students at Duke Upset over Study." *Herald-Sun,* n.d., http://www.heraldsun.com/view/full_story/17104957/article-Black-students-at-Duke-upset-over-study—.

———. "Duke Responds to Black Students' Concerns." *Herald-Sun,* January 19, 2012, http://www.heraldsun.com/view/full_story/17231824/ article-Duke-responds-to-black-students%E2%80%99-concerns-/.

Ogbu, John U. *Black American Students in an Affluent Suburb: A Study of Academic Disengagement.* Mahwah, NJ: Erlbaum Associates, 2003.

Oliver, Melvin L., and Thomas M. Shapiro. *Black Wealth/White Wealth: A New Perspective on Racial Inequality.* New York: Routledge, 1995.

O'Neill, June E., and Dave M. O'Neill. The Declining Importance of Race and Gender in the Labor Market: The Role of Federal Anti-Discrimination Policies and Other Factors. Washington, DC: AEI Press, 2012.

Ordo Lodus College Rankings, Academics—data, http://www.ordoludus.com/academics_details.php.

Orfield, Gary, and Edward Miller. *Chilling Admissions: The Affirmative Action Crisis and the Search for Alternatives.* Cambridge, MA: Civil Rights Project, Harvard University Press, 1998.

Orfield, Gary, and Dean Whitla. "Diversity and Legal Education: Student Experiences in Leading Law Schools." In *Diversity Challenged: Evidence on the Impact of Affirmative Action,* Chapter 6. Edited by Gary Orfield. Harvard University: Civil Rights Project, 2001.

Quinnipiac University, "U.S. Voters Disagree 3-1 With Sotomayor on Key Case, Quinnipiac University National Poll Finds; Most Say Abolish Affirmative Action." May 26–June 1, 2009, http://www.quinnipiac .edu/institutes-and-centers/polling-institute/national/release-detail ?ReleaseID=1307.

Robinson, Eugene. *Disintegration: The Splintering of Black America.* New York: Doubleday, 2010.

Rojstaczer, Stuart, and Christopher Healy. "Where A Is Ordinary: The Evolution of American College and University Grading, 1940–2009." *Teachers College Record,* 2012, http://gradeinflation.com/tcr2011grading.pdf.

———. "Grading in American Colleges and Universities." *Teachers College Record,* (March 4, 2010), http://gradeinflation.com/tcr2010grading.pdf.

Rothstein, Jesse, and Albert H. Yoon. "Affirmative Action in Law School Admissions: What Do Racial Preferences Do?" NBER Working Paper No. 14726, 2008.

Samuels, Alison. "Michelle Hits Her Stride." *Daily Beast,* May 1, 2009, http://www.thedaily beast.com/newsweek/2009/05/01/michelle-hits-her-stride.html.

Sander v. State Bar of California, 196 Cal. App. 4th 614 (2011).

Sander, Richard H. "A Systemic Analysis of Affirmative Action in American Law Schools." *Stanford Law Review* 57, no. 2 (2004): 367–384, 377.

———. "Class in American Legal Education." *Denver University Law Review* 88, no. 4 (2011): 631–682, http://www.law.du.edu/documents/denver-university -law-review/v88-4/Sander%20Final_ToPrinter_917.pdf.

———. "Experimenting with Class-Based Affirmative Action." *Journal of Legal Education* 47, no. 4 (1997): 472.

———. "Listening to the Debate on Reforming Law School Admissions Preferences." *Denver University Law Review* 88 (2011): 889.

———. "The Racial Paradox of the Corporate Law Firm," *North Carolina Law Review* 84 (2006).

———. "A Reply to Critics." *Stanford Law Review* 57 (2005): 1963, 1984–1986.

Sander, Richard H., and Jane Yakowitz, "The Secret of My Success: How Status, Prestige and School Performance Shape Legal Careers." 2011, http://www.seaphe.org/pdf/thesecret.pdf.

———. "The Secret of My Success: How Status, Eliteness and School Performance Shape Legal Careers." *Journal of Empirical Legal Studies* (forthcoming).

Sandler, Ross, and David Schoenbrod. *Democracy by Decree: What Happens When Courts Run Government.* New Haven, CT: Yale University Press, 2003.

Saulny, Susan, and Jacques Steinberg. "On College Forms, a Question of Race, or Races, Can Perplex." *New York Times,* June 13, 2011, http://www.nytimes.com/2011/06/14/us/14admissions.html?pagewanted=all.

Sawhill, Isobel. "20 Years Later, It Turns Out Dan Quayle Was Right About Murphy Brown and Unmarried Moms." *Washington Post,* May 25, 2012, http://www.washingtonpost.com/opinions/20-years-later-it-turns-out-dan -quayle-was-right-about-murphy-brown- and-unmarried-moms/2012/05/ 25/gJQAsNCJqU_story.html/.

Schuck, Peter H. *Diversity in America: Keeping Government at a Safe Distance.* Cambridge, MA: Belknap Press of Harvard University Press, 2003.

Schuman, Howard, Charlotte Steeh, Lawrence Bobo, and Maria Krysan. *Racial Attitudes in America: Trends and Interpretations.* Cambridge, MA: Harvard University Press, 1998.

Schmidt, Peter. "Sandra Day O'Connor Revisits and Revives Affirmative-Action Controversy." *Chronicle of Higher Education*, January 14, 2010, http://chronicle.com/article/Sandra-Day-OConnor- Revisits/63523/.

Shuit, Douglas. "Minority Doctors Skeptical of Health Reforms." *Los Angeles Times*, June 1, 1993.

Sidanius, Jim, Shana Levin, Colette van Laar, and David O. Sears. *The Diversity Challenge: Social Identity and Intergroup Relations on the College Campus*, 317. New York: Russell Sage, 2008.

Skrentny, John David. *The Ironies of Affirmative Action: Politics, Culture, and Justice in America*. Chicago: University of Chicago Press, 1996.

Slotnik, Daniel. "Do Asian-Americans Face Bias in Admissions at Elite Colleges?" *New York Times*, February 8, 2012.

Smyth, Frederick, and John McArdle. "Ethnic and Gender Differences in Science Graduation at Selective Colleges with Implications for Admission Policy and College Choice." *Research in Higher Education* 45, no. 4 (2004): 353–381.

Southworth, Ann. *Lawyers of the Right: Professionalizing the Conservative Coalition*. Chicago: Chicago Series in Law and Society, 2008.

Sowell, Thomas. "The Plight of Black Students in the United States." *Daedalus* 103, no. 2 (Spring 1974): 179–196.

Steele, Claude, and Joshua Aronson. "Stereotype Threat and the Test Performance of Academically Successful African Americans," In *The Black-White Test Score Gap*, Chapter 11. Edited by Christopher Jencks and Meredith Phillips. Washington DC: Brookings, 1998.

Summers, Clyde. "Preferential Admissions: An Unreal Solution to a Real Problem." *University of Toledo Law Review* 2 (1970): 377.

Sweet, Lynn. "Obama on ABC's 'This Week with George Stephanopoulos'." *Chicago Sun-Times*, May 13, 2007, http://blogs.suntimes.com/sweet/2007/05/obama_on_abcs_this_week_with_g.html.

Taylor Jr., Stuart. "Affirmative Action and Doublespeak." *Legal Times*, May 13, 1996, http://stuarttaylorjr.com/content/affirmative-action-and-doublespeak/.

———. "Do African-Americans Really Want Racial Preferences?" *National Journal*, December 20, 2002.

———. "Glimpses of the Least Pretentious of Men." *Legal Times* (February 8, 1993), http://stuarttaylorjr.com/content/glimpses-least-pretentious-men/.

———. "Gore-Lieberman: Racial Preferences Forever?" *National Journal*, September 2, 2000.

———. "How Courts and Congress Wrecked School Discipline." *National Journal*, November 15, 2003, http://nationaljournal.com/magazine/opening-argument -how-courts-and-congress-wrecked- school-discipline-20031115/.

———. "Powell on His Approach: Doing Justice Case by Case." *New York Times*, July 12, 1987, http://www.nytimes.com/1987/07/12/us/powell-on-his-approach -doing-justice-case-by-case.html?pagewanted=all&src=pm/.

———. "Racial Preferences Meet Democracy," *Legal Times*, December 20, 1996. http://stuarttaylorjr.com/content/racial-preferences-meet-democracy.

———. "Ted Kennedy's Excellent Idea: Disclosing Admissions Preferences." *National Journal*, January 31, 2004, http://nationaljournal.com/magazine/opening-argument-ted-kennedy-39-s-excellent-idea-disclosing-admissions-preferences-20040131.

———. "The Affirmative Action Decisions." *A Year at the Supreme Court*. Edited by Neal Devins and Davison M. Douglas. Durham, NC: Duke University Press, 2004.

Teachman, Jay, Kathleen Paasch, Randal Day, and Karen Carver. "Poverty During Adolescence and Subsequent Educational Achievement." In *Consequences of Growing Up Poor*. 1997.

Teles, Steven M. *The Rise of the Conservative Legal Movement: The Battle for Control of the Law*. Princeton, NJ: Princeton University Press, 2012.

The Journal of Blacks in Higher Education. "Doctoral Degree Awards to African Americans Reach Another All-Time High." http://www.jbhe.com/news_views/50_black_doctoraldegrees.html

The State Bar of California. "Statistics." http://admissions.calbar.ca.gov/Examinations/Statistics.aspx

Thernstrom, Abigail M., and Stephan Thernstrom. *No Excuses: Closing the Racial Gap in Learning*. New York: Simon and Schuster, 2003.

———. "Secrecy and Dishonesty: The Supreme Court, Racial Preferences, and Higher Education." *Constitutional Commentary* 21 (March 2004): 211.

Thernstrom, Stephan, and Abigail Thernstrom. *America in Black and White: One Nation, Indivisible*. New York: Simon and Schuster, 1997.

———. "Reflections on The Shape of the River." *UCLA Law Review* 46, no. 5 (1999): 1583–1632, 1583, 1587, 1588,1590.

Traub, James. "Mildly Ambitious." *New York Times Sunday Magazine*, June 10, 2001.

———. "The Class of Prop 209." *New York Times Magazine*, May 2, 1999.

Trounson, Rebecca. "A Startling Statistic at UCLA." *Los Angeles Times*, June 3, 2006.

University of California Office of the President. UC Statfinder, http://statfinder.ucop.edu/.

———. "The Use of Socio-Economic Status in Place of Ethnicity in Undergraduate Admissions: A Report on the Results of an Exploratory Computer Simulation." Occasional Paper 5, May 1995.

University of California Office of the President, Student Affairs. "University of California: Application, Admissions, and Enrollment of California Resident Freshmen for Fall 1989 through 2010." March 2011.

U.S. Commission on Civil Rights. "Affirmative Action in American Law Schools." April 2007, http://www.usccr.gov/pubs/AALSreport.pdf.

———. "Affirmative Action in American Law Schools: A Briefing before the United States Commission on Civil Rights, Held in Washing ton, D.C., June 16, 2006." Briefing Report. Washington, DC: US Commission on Civil Rights, 2007.

———. "Encouraging Minority Students in Science Careers." October 2010, http://www.usccr.gov/pubs/EncouragingMinorityStudentsinScienceCareers.pdf.

US Department of Education. Biennial Evaluation Report—FY 93–94. "Minority Science and Engineering Improvement Programs (MSIP)." http://www2.ed.gov/pubs/Biennial/518.html.

U.S. News and World Report, Best Colleges 2012, http://colleges.usnews.rankingsandreviews.com/bestcolleges.

Wallace, Amy, and Dave Lesher. "UC Debates Affirmative Action Policy." *Los Angeles Times*, July 21, 1996.

Washington Post/Kaiser/Harvard. "Racial Attitudes Survery." March 8–April 22, 2001, http://www.washingtonpost.com/wp-srv/nation/sidebars/polls/race071101.htm.

Welch, Susan, and John Gruhl. *Affirmative Action and Minority Enrollment in Medical and Law Schools*. Ann Arbor: University of Michigan Press, 1998.

Wightman, Linda F. *User's Guide: LSAC National Longitudinal Data File*. Newtown, PA: Law School Admission Council, 1999.

———. "The Consequences of Race-Blindness: Revisting Prediction Models with Current Law School Data." *Journal of Legal Education* 53, no. 2 (2003).

Wilbur, Susan. "Investigating the College Destinations of University of California Freshman Admits." In *Equal Opportunity in Higher Education*, Chapter 4. Edited by Eric Grodsky and Michal Kurlaender. Harvard Education Press, 2010.

Williams, Doug, Richard Sander, Marc Luppino, and Roger Bolus. "Revisiting Law School Mismatch: A Comment on Barnes." *Northwestern Law Review* 105 (2011): 813.

Willingham, Warren. *Success in College: The Role of Personal Qualities and Academic Ability*. New York: The College Board, 1985.

Wilson, Robin. "The Unintended Consequences of Affirmative Action." *Chronicle of Higher Education* 49, no. 21 (2003): 10–12.

Wood, Peter. "Mobbing for Preferences." Innovations Blog, *Chronicle of Higher Education*, September 22, 2011, http://chronicle.com/blogs/innovations/mobbing-for-preferences/30402/.

Yakowitz, Jane. "Marooned: An Empirical Investigation of Law School Graduates Who Fail the Bar Exam." *Journal of Legal Education* 60, no. 1 (2010): 3–40.

———. "Tragedy of the Data Commons." *Harvard Journal of Law and Technology* 25 (2011): 1.

Zwick, Rebecca, and Jeffrey G. Sklar. "Predicting College Grades and Degree Completion Using High School Grades and SAT Scores: The Role of Student Ethnicity and First Language." *American Education Research Journal* 42, no.3 (2005): 439–64.

ACKNOWLEDGMENTS

We have had a great deal of help from more people than we can name.

Tim Bartlett, our excellent editor at Basic Books, showed rare good will, talent, and patience under enormous time pressure. He greatly improved our writing and presentation, kept us focused on the big questions we sought to answer, made deft cuts, and did all the other things that great editors do.

Many of Tim's colleagues at Basic Books worked hard and took risks to bring this book out in time for the Supreme Court's oral arguments in *Fisher v. University of Texas*, and they have our heartfelt thanks. We are especially grateful to Lori Hobkirk of the Book Factory, who was unfailingly generous and supportive in working with us to accelerate the production process without sacrificing exactitude.

Two of Stuart's colleagues from *National Journal*, Ryan Morris and Peter Bell, worked closely with us to capture important ideas from our text with imaginative and powerful graphics. Their ability to get inside key concepts in the book, and express them in new ways, fills us with awe.

Gay Jervey enriched both the book and our understanding by finding and interviewing—and skillfully drafting the stories of—dozens of African American and Hispanic former students and current college administrators and counselors who have experienced or witnessed harms done by racial preferences to intended beneficiaries.

Special thanks also to Professor Phillip Richards, Arnold Sio Chair of Diversity and Community, Department of English, Colgate University, who spoke with us for hours, shared his insightful book manuscript about harms done by racial preferences to black students, and allowed us to quote portions of it.

Peter Schuck and Vik Amar, who kindly agreed to be peer reviewers, spent many hours reading a rougher-than-ragged early draft and gave us invaluable advice. Peter's important work on race and Ameican social policy helped shape many of our views, and his conversations with both of us over the years helped us test our evolving ideas. Vik, although a critic of the mismatch theory, has steadfastly and substantively supported efforts to bring out better data for testing the theory; his unwavering intellectual integrity made his voice and thoughts very valuable to us.

We were also very fortunate that six other distinguished thinkers—Henry Aaron, Gerard Alexander, Roger Clegg, KC Johnson, Alan Morrison, and Rick Nagel—kindly offered to read and comment on our draft manuscript. Each gave us extremely helpful insights.

Stuart's agent, Gail Ross, did a wonderful job of interesting several leading publishers in our book proposal and helping us see why Tim Bartlett and Basic Books was the best choice for our project.

Stuart conducted wide-ranging interviews as part of his research for this book. Among those who gave him (and in some cases Gay) generous helpings of time, insights and good will are: Vik Amar, Sheri Anis, Peter Arcidiacono, Ryan Atkins, Chris Bishof, Esther Cepeda, Linda Chavez, Jesse Choper, Roger Clegg, Ward Connerly, Brian Corpening, Glynn Custred, Rog Elliott, John Ellis, Charles Geshekter, Jareau Hall, Erik Hanushek, Joe Hicks, Gary Hull, Dr. William Hunter, Ibby Jeppson, Jocelyn Ladner-Mathis, Rick Nagel, Suney Park, Peter Schuck, Arnie Steinberg, Carol Swain, Abigail and Stephan Thernstrom, Tom Wood, and numerous African American veterans of the preference system and administrators who chose to remain anonymous.

The Brookings Institution, with contributions from Roger Hertog and Harlan Crow, generously assisted Stuart's work.

Above all, Stuart thanks Sally, Sarah, and Molly.

For Rick, this book arises from more than a decade of research, much of it carried on under challenging conditions. He has been blessed from the start with some remarkable help. Patrick Anderson, now a distinguished attorney at Munger, Tolles in Los Angeles, worked with Rick full-time for a year before starting law school, and was the intended coauthor of a stillborn, early version of this book. Jane Yakowitz, now a law professor at the University of Arizona and a leading scholar in the field of privacy law, worked closely with Rick for three years to develop many of the databases used in this book and helped to galvanize a community of scholars to engage in the study and evaluation of many issues we explore here. Any professor would be lucky to have one right-hand associate of the caliber of either Patrick or Jane during his career. To have had two such people dedicate themselves to this body of work was, for Rick, incredible good fortune.

Rick's work benefited from many other exceptionally able research assistants. Many of them came from social science programs at UCLA: Jennifer Flashman (sociology), Bongoh Kye (sociology), Margot Jackson (sociology), Yana Kucheva (sociology), Marc Luppino (economics), Greg Midgette (policy), Juan Pantano (economics), Flori So (political science), and Robert Sockloskie (psychology), all made invaluable contributions. Many law students at UCLA did original, creative work with Rick in seminars, or did careful, helpful work for him over various summers, including David Burke, Matthew Butterick, Carol Chao, Christian Dubois, Michael Jussaume, John Kohler, Mark Metzge, Mike Minnick, Matthew Moore, Matthew Morris, Drew Patterson, Jon Raney, Lucas Ryono, and Allison Woods. Ben Backes, Will Harper, and Sarah Lowe each provided valuable help en route to graduate work at other universities.

Doug Williams, the Wilson Professor of Economics at Sewanee, the University of the South, has been Rick's closest professional collaborator for a generation, and he played an instrumental role in helping to translate Rick's intuitions about the mismatch effect into rigorous tests, and in evaluating critics of law school mismatch. Many other colleagues around the country shared research, data, and ideas about racial preferences and student outcomes, and helped this book in a variety of ways, including Kate Antonovics, Peter Arcidiacono, Esteban Aucejo, Bernard Black, Roger Bolus, Roger Clegg, Tom Espenshade, Tim Groseclose, Stacy Hawkins, William Henderson, Gail Heriot, Joe Hotz, Richard Kahlenberg, Stephen Klein, David Leonhardt, Jim Lindgren, Adam Liptak, Terry Pell, Rick Peltz, Dan Polsby, Tom Sowell, Rob Steinbuch, Steve and Abby Thernstrom, and Bob Zelnick.

UCLA Law School has provided Rick with a wonderful environment for conducting scholarship, and is especially supportive of interdisciplinary research. June Kim of the Darling Law Library has provided invaluable help both in her own research and in training some of Rick's research assistants. Daisy Ding expertly and patiently generated over a dozen early versions of the manuscript, and Tal Greitzer brought his formidable knowledge and patient support far beyond the call of duty to all facets of document production. Many of Rick's colleagues have generously shared ideas, wisdom and criticism on his evolving work on racial preferences, including Alison Anderson, Paul Bergman, Joe Doherty, Mark Grady, Russell Korobkin, Jerry Lopez, Dan Lowenstein, Bill McGovern, Steve Munzer, Jonathan Varat, Eugene Volokh, Adam Winkler, Jonathan Zasloff, and Eric Zolt.

Rick received generous research funding from the Searle Freedom Trust, the Randolph Foundation, the UCLA Academic Senate, and the Dean's Fund at UCLA Law School. Early phases of his work on student outcomes were aided by grants from the National Science Foundation, the Law School Admissions Council, the National Association of Law Placement, the Soros Fund, and the National Conference of Bar Examiners.

Kim Dennis and Jim Reische played unique roles in fostering this book, in ways they each well understand.

As described in Chapter Fifteen, the effort to secure crucial data from the California Bar turned into one of the most important and revealing episodes in the story of the mismatch effect, and will likely be resolved by the California Supreme Court within the next few months. Regardless of how that case turns out, Rick can never adequately express his gratitude to the many people who donated their expertise, time and commitment to the causes of transparency and letting the data speak. James Chadwick has been unique and extraordinary in his dedication, but many others also provided invaluable help: Vik Amar, Sharon Browne, Guylyn Cummins, Evgenia Fkiaras, Bill Henderson, Gail Heriot, Joe Hicks, Jean-Paul Jassy, Gerald Reynolds, Peter Scheer, David Snyder, Josh Thompson, and Jane Yakowitz.

My wife, astrophysicist Fiona Harrison, has inspired and improved my work in countless ways, some of which she knows well and others she barely suspects. She has been unfailingly patient and supportive throughout this project. My son, Robert, has always helped me think about the evolution of social mores in America, and increasingly shares with me a fascination with economics and empiricism. My daughter, Joanna, has shown great forbearance during "the book project" and is counting on soon having her father back.

We alone, of course, remain responsible for any and all flaws that remain.

—*Rick Sander*   —*Stuart Taylor*
Los Angeles, CA   Washington, DC

NOTES

A note from the authors: An expanded version of these notes is available at the book's website, http://www.mismatchthebook.com, which will include further documentation, discussion of sources, and additional figures.

PREFACE

xv   a chapter in a book entitled *A Year at the Supreme Court:* Neil Devins and Davison M. Douglas, eds., *A Year at the Supreme Court* (Durham, NC: Duke University Press Books, 2004).

xvi   "Well," Marshall continued, "you owe something.": Stuart Taylor Jr., "Glimpses of the Least Pretentious of Men," *Legal Times,* February 8, 1993, http://stuarttaylorjr.com/content/glimpses-least-pretentious-men/. See also Howard Ball, *The Bakke Case: Race, Education, and Affirmative Action* (University Press of Kansas 2000), 86 ("Damn right. They owe us.").

CHAPTER ONE

5   With every class we teach: Mark Edmundson, "The Trouble with Online Education," *New York Times,* July 19, 2012.

7   Recent years have seen: U.S. Commission on Civil Rights, "Encouraging Minority Students in Science Careers," October 2010, http://www.usccr.gov/pubs/EncouragingMinorityStudentsinScienceCareers .pdf; U.S. Commission on Civil Rights, "Affirmative Action in American Law Schools," April 2007, http://www.usccr.gov/pubs/AALSreport.pdf.

8   The total number of black and: We elaborate on this claim in Chapter Ten. The number of black B.A.s granted by UCLA dipped modestly, while the number of Hispanic B.A.s grew fairly steadily—but the real point is that in both cases, drops in enrollment were coupled with similar surges in the proportion of black and Hispanic admittees who graduated, surges that were, if anything, greater for blacks. Across the entire University of California, there were large, absolute increases in the number of blacks and Hispanics earning B.A.s over time.

9   Black students are, today: See Chapter Sixteen for more on this point. See also Jay Teachman, Kathleen Paasch, Randal Day, and Karen Carver, "Poverty During Adolescence and Subsequent Educational Achievement," in *Consequences of Growing Up Poor* (1997), 382–418.

12   vestiges of slavery and [government-sanctioned] . . . racial discrimination:
      William T. Coleman, with Donald Bliss, *Counsel for the Situation: Shaping the
      Law to Realize America's Promise* (Washington, DC: Brookings Institution
      Press, 2010), 339, 438n9.

12   In late 2010 Cose wrote: Ellis Cose, *The End of Anger: A New Generation's Take
      on Race and Rage* (New York: Ecco, 2011), 8.

13   the black upper-middle class: Eugene Robinson, *Disintegration: The Splintering
      of Black America* (New York: Anchor, 2010), chapters 9 and 10.

CHAPTER TWO

15   did not simply pass through "old boy networks.": John David Skrentny, *The
      Ironies of Affirmative Action: Politics, Culture, and Justice in America* (Chicago:
      University of Chicago Press, 1996).

16   colleges would never take their students seriously: Richard Sander, "A Systemic
      Analysis of Affirmative Action in American Law Schools," *Stanford Law
      Review* 57, no. 2 (2004): 367–484, 377.

16   But starting in 1967: For an account of the origins of racial preferences at law
      schools, see Sander, "A Systemic Analysis," 384–382.

16   focus from institutional reform to racial preferences: Faye Crosby, *Affirmative
      Action Is Dead, Long Live Affirmative Action* (New Haven, CT: Yale University
      Press, 2004), 7–10; Skrentny, *The Ironies of Affirmative Action*, 56.

16   heavily rely upon in making admissions decisions: For an in-depth discussion
      of academic indices, see Sander, "A Systemic Analysis," 418–424.

17   about 130 points below those of white applicants: College Board, "2011 SAT
      Trends—SAT Mean Scores by Race/Ethnicity over 10 Years," http://
      professionals.collegeboard.com/data-reports-research/sat/cb-seniors
      -2011/tables.

17   add 130 points to each black applicant's SAT I score: Richard Sander and Jane
      Yakowitz, "The Secret of My Success: How Status, Prestige and School Perfor-
      mance Shape Legal Careers," working paper, 2011,
      http://www.seaphe.org/pdf/thesecret.pdf.

17   will not readily concede that colleges "race-norm" applications: Rachael Moran
      et al., "Statement of Faculty Policy Governing Admission to Boalt Hall and
      Report of the Admissions Policy Task Force," August 31, 1993.

17   decision in *Gratz v. Bollinger*, discussed in Chapter Thirteen: The Civil Rights
      Act of 1991, which does not apply to college admissions, makes it unlawful "to
      adjust the scores of, use different cutoff scores for, or otherwise alter the results
      of, employment related tests on the basis of race, color, religion, sex, or
      national origin." 42 U.S.C. 2000e(2)(K)(1)(A)(ii).

17   described in *Inside Higher Education*, is quite common at elite schools: See
      Scott Jaschik, "How They Really Get In," *Inside Higher Ed*, April 9, 2012,
      http://www.insidehighered.com/news/2012/04/09/new-research-how-elite
      -colleges-make-admissions-decisions/.

17 hovered in that range for the past twenty years: College Board, "2011 SAT Trends."

18 relative to whites and more relative to Asians: Thomas J. Espenshade and Alexandria Walton Radford, *No Longer Separate, Not Yet Equal: Race and Class in Elite College Admission and Campus Life* (Princeton, NJ: Princeton University Press, 2009), 93, 127.

18 a white applicant with the same academic index score: A widely used method for describing racial preferences is the "odds-ratio" technique. Such measures were used by the plaintiffs in the *Gratz v. Bollinger* and *Grutter v. Bollinger* suits (which we discuss in Chapter Thirteen). The Center for Equal Opportunity (CEO) has played a leading role in documenting the extent of racial preferences at public universities (sometimes using data obtained through litigation, such as the important case of *Osborn v. University of Wisconsin*). CEO regularly reports the size of racial preferences in odds-ratio terms. The difficulty with such measures is that odds ratios are produced by multiplying two ratios (the greater probability that Group A will enjoy a positive outcome relative to Group B, times the inverse of the probability that Group A will suffer some negative outcome relative to Group B), which can arguably produce a misleadingly high number. (With racial preferences, findings of odds ratios of one hundred or higher are common.) In this book (particularly in Chapter Fourteen) we use the square root of a conventional odds ratio to convey the relative probability that someone in Group A will be admitted with a particular academic index relative to someone in Group B. For examples of conventional odds ratios at various undergraduate colleges before 2003 (before the Supreme Court's latest rulings on racial preferences), see pp. 41–43 of http://www.eric.ed.gov/PDFS/ED454804.pdf/. For post-2003 numbers, see Roger Clegg, "CEO Praises Supreme Court's Decision to Hear Fisher v. University of Texas, Center for Equal Opportunity, http://www.ceousa.org/ affirmative-action/affirmative-action-news/education/.

18 they also use them consistently: See Robert Klitgaard, *Choosing Elites* (New York: Basic Books, 1985); Espenshade and Radford, *No Longer Separate, Not Yet Equal.*

19 might have been better matched at a lower-tier school: See, for example, *U.S. News and World Report*, Best Colleges 2012, http://colleges.usnews.rankingsandreviews.com/best-colleges; Ordo Lodus College Rankings, Academics—data, http://www.ordoludus.com/academics_details.php.

20 other students at the college if only given the chance: Espenshade and Radford, *No Longer Separate, Not Yet Equal,* 228, 245–252; Sander, "A Systemic Analysis," 425–441.

21 Figure 2.1: The key source for this table is data from the College Board on the distribution of high-school GPAs and SAT scores, by race, for a very large sample of SAT takers who expected to graduate in 2008. From this data, we computed an academic index and generated a percentile distribution of black and non-black test takers, which is shown graphically under point "2." The

assumption that roughly the top fifth or quarter of college students end up attending schools that use racial preferences comes from Kane, "Racial and Ethnic Preferences in College Admission," in *The Black-White Test Score Gap*, edited by Christopher Jencks and Meredith Phillips (Washington, DC: Brookings Institution Press, 1998), 439–464, and from our own calculations with data from the National Educational Longitudinal Survey.

25 contribution to the university community and our future society.": Richard H. Brodhead, "Brodhead: Duke and the Legacy of Race," *Duke Today*, March 22, 2012, http://today.duke.edu/2012/03/rhbfacultytalk/.

25 largely gauged by the credentials of its students): *Choosing Elites*, 92; Rebecca Zwick and Jeffrey G. Sklar "Predicting College Grades and Degree Completion Using High School Grades and SAT Scores: The Role of Student Ethnicity and First Language," *American Education Research Journal* 42, no.3 (2005): 439–464.

25 their class rank remains static or declines further: See, for example, Espenshade and Radford, *No Longer Separate, Not Yet Equal*, 228, 249, 255–256.

26 race (or other individual characteristics) irrelevant: Thomas Kane, "Racial and Ethnic Preferences in College Admission" in *The Black-White Test Score Gap*, edited by Christopher Jencks and Meredith Phillips (Washington, DC: Brookings Institute Press, 1998), 431–456.

27 the proportion is about the same at medical schools: Sander, "A Systemic Analysis," 410–417.

27 to the size and pervasiveness of these preferences: Thomas J. Espenshade and Chang Y. Chung, "The Opportunity Cost of Admission Preferences at Elite Universities," *Social Science Quarterly* 86, no. 2 (2005): 293–305; Espenshade and Radford, *No Longer Separate, Not Yet Equal*, 250–251.

27 athletic preferences are much smaller than racial preferences: See, for example, Elyse Ashburn, "At Elite Colleges, Legacy Status May Count for More Than Was Previously Thought," *Chronicle of Higher Education*, January 5, 2011 (study by Michael Hurwitz noted in passing that "legacy students, on average, had slightly higher SAT scores than nonlegacies"); Rogers Elliott, unpublished manuscript on file with authors (OCR investigation of Harvard in 1990 found that admitted legacies averaged 1380 on SAT, about 20 points below the "merit group" and 120 points above admitted blacks); Espenshade and Radford, *No Longer Separate, Not Yet Equal*, 252 and Table 6.2 (showing that black students graduate with a class rank that is more than seventeen percentile points lower than otherwise equivalent white students at the same school; the class rank "penalty" is 4.6 percent for athletes and only 1.7 percent for legacies); p. 208 within (University of Michigan as of 2003 gave 20 admissions "points" for minority race and four points for legacy status); Nathan D. Martin and Kenneth I. Spenner, "A Social Portrait of Legacies at an Elite University," August 1, 2008, 16, http://chronicle.com/article/Legacys-Advantage-May-Be/125812/. Epenshade, Chung, and Walling estimate the admissions preference shown to different student groups at elite

universities in terms of SAT points on a 1600-point scale. Net of other factors, black applicants receive a 230 point advantage, Latino applicants get 185 points, recruited athletes get 200 points, and legacy applicants receive the equivalent of a 160-point boost (Thomas J. Espenshade, Chang Y. Chung, and Joan L. Walling, "Admission Preferences for Minority Students, Athletes, and Legacies at Elite Universities," *Social Science Quarterly* 85, no. 5 [2004]: 1422–1446, 1433, 1437, 1443–1445, noting that "160 points" overstates size of legacy preferences). See also http://www.soc.duke.edu/%7Ejmoody77/ProSem/ Spenner_Legacies-ASA-2008.pdf/.

27   the same mismatch effects we document for racial minorities: See also Richard Kahlenberg, *Affirmative Action for the Rich: Legacy Preferences in College Admissions* (New York: The Century Foundation, 2010); William Bowen and Sarah Levin, *Reclaiming the Game: College Sports and Educational Values* (Princeton, NJ: Princeton University Press, 2003).

28   usually with two college-educated parents: See Kiratiana Freelon, Marques J. Redd, and Toussaint Losier, *Black Guide to Life at Harvard* (Cambridge, MA: Harvard Black Student Association, 2002); Douglas S. Massey, Margarita Mooney, and Kimberly C. Torres, and Camille Z. Charles, "Black Immigrants and Black Natives Attending Selective Colleges and Universities in the United States," *American Journal of Education* 113, no. 2 (February 2007): 243–273; William G. Bowen and Derek Bok, *The Shape of the River: Long-Term Consequences of Considering Race in College and University Admissions* (Princeton, NJ: Princeton University Press, 1998), 46–50.

28   white applicants from middle- and-upper-middle-class backgrounds.": Espenshade and Radford, *No Longer Separate, Not Yet Equal*, 98–100, 382–384. They also state that nonwhite students "on average, come from lower socioeconomic backgrounds than do white or Asian students" (381).

29   just how affluent the typical racial-preference beneficiary is: William G. Bowen and Derek Bok, *The Shape of the River: Long-Term Consequences of Considering Race in College and University Admissions* (Princeton, NJ: Princeton University Press, 1998), 48–49.

29   socioeconomic disadvantage, and the data is more mixed: Richard H. Sander, "Class in American Legal Education," *Denver University Law Review* 88, no. 4 (2011): 631–682, http://www.law.du.edu/documents/denver-university-law-review/v88-4/Sander%20Final_ToPrinter_917.pdf.

29   less likely to be admitted if they are Asian: See Jerome Karabel, *The Chosen: The Hidden History of Admission and Exclusion at Harvard, Yale, and Princeton* (Boston: Houghton Mifflin, 2005), 499–505.

29   from nearly 18 percent to more than 23 percent.": Thomas J. Espenshade and Chang Y. Chung, "The Opportunity Cost of Admission Preferences at Elite Universities," *Social Science Quarterly* 86, no. 2 (June 2005): 293–305. They based their conclusions on a study funded by the Andrew W. Mellon Foundation of more than 124,000 applicants to elite universities.

CHAPTER THREE

33   leaders and intellectuals, particularly in the sciences: One of our spouses, now a Caltech astrophysicist, was first attracted to physics as a Dartmouth undergraduate.

33   not producing very many black or American Indian scientists: The main source for the following narrative is Rogers Elliott, A. Christopher Strenta, Russell Adair, Michael Matier, and Jannah Scott, "The Role of Ethnicity in Choosing and Leaving Science in Highly Selective Institutions," *Research in Higher Education* 37, no. 6 (1996): 681–709.

35   mandatory curves that tail off with low grades: Stuart Rojstaczer and Christopher Healy, "Where A Is Ordinary: The Evolution of American College and University Grading, 1940–2009," *Teachers College Record*, 2012, http://gradeinflation.com/tcr2011grading.pdf; Stuart Rojstaczer and Christopher Healy, "Grading in American Colleges and Universities," *Teachers College Record*, March 4, 2010, http://gradeinflation.com/tcr2010grading.pdf.

36   with data from two additional elite colleges: Warren Willingham, *Success in College: The Role of Personal Qualities and Academic Ability* (New York: The College Board, 1985).

36   to achieve her goal at School C rather than at School A: This effect is tempered somewhat by the fact that more elite schools tend to give a greater percentage of their total degrees in STEM fields. Still, the difference between the STEM percentages of the third tercile at School A and top tercile at School C is so vast that the claim holds.

36   accounted for 20 percent of black college enrollment: Elliott et al., "The Role of Ethnicity in Choosing and Leaving Science in Highly Selective Institutions," 22; Cullotta 1992; Phillips 1991.

37   A number of federal programs: National Science Foundation, "A Timeline of NSF History," September 10, 1971; Improving minority education, http://www.nsf.gov/news/special_reports/history-nsf/1971_student.jsp; U.S. Department of Education.

37   promising minority scientists at various stages in the PhD pipeline: National Science Foundation, A Timeline of NSF History, "1971—September 10: Improving Minority Education," http://www.nsf.gov/news/special_reports/history-nsf/1971_student.jsp; US Department of Education, Biennial Evaluation Report—FY 93–94, "Minority Science and Engineering Improvement Programs (MSIP)," http://www2.ed.gov/pubs/Biennial/518.html.

38   appeared on the work in the five years after its publication: The only academic article we have found that even cited Elliott's work in the five years after it appeared was a piece by Stephen and Abigail Thernstrom, both critics of affirmative action, that criticized Bowen and Bok for ignoring Elliott.

38   did not even mention Elliott and Strenta's work: William G. Bowen and Derek Bok, *The Shape of the River: Long-Term Consequences of Considering Race in College and University Admissions* (Princeton, NJ: Princeton University Press, 1998).

38 big frog in a little pond or a little frog in a big pond): James Davis, "The Campus as a Frog Pond: An Application of the Theory of Relative Deprivation to Career Decisions of College Men," *American Journal of Sociology* 72, no. 1 (July 1966): 17–31.

39 establishment leaders dismissed his warnings: Clyde Summers, "Preferential Admissions: An Unreal Solution to a Real Problem," *University of Toledo Law Review* 2 (1970), 377; Thomas Sowell, "The Plight of Black Students in the United States," *Daedalus* 103, no. 2 (Spring 1974): 179–196.

39 tens of thousands of elite college students: The following section is largely based on Frederick Smyth and John McArdle, "Ethnic and Gender Differences in Science Graduation at Selective Colleges with Implications for Admission Policy and College Choice," *Research in Higher Education* 45, no. 4 (2004): 353–381.

41 but that was survivable: Interview of anonymous young Dartmouth graduate by Gay Jervey, June 4, 2012, and brief follow-up calls.

41 they are just worn out when they leave.": Interviews of anonymous black college administrator by Gay Jervey, June 1, 2012; e-mail from interviewee to Jervey, July 13, 2012.

42 a path to success, it was a doorway to failure.": Interview of Dr. William Hunter by Gay Jervey, May 10 and 13, 2012; e-mail exchange on July 17, 2012.

45 In 1995 black doctorates: See, for example, "Science and Engineering Degrees, by Race/Ethnicity of Recipients," 1995–2004, National Science Foundation http://www.nsf.gov/statistics/nsf07308/content.cfm?pub_id=3633&id=2; see also http://www.jbhe.com/news_views/50_black_doctoraldegrees.html.

45 a seed grant from the Council of Ivy League Presidents: Stephen Cole and Elinor Barber, *Increasing Faculty Diversity: The Occupational Choices of High-Achieving Minority Students* (Cambridge, MA: Harvard University Press, 2003).

47 book sold few copies and generated no discussion: Robin Wilson, "The Unintended Consequences of Affirmative Action," *Chronicle of Higher Education* 49, no. 21 (2003): 10–12.

47 they adhere to them regardless of the evidence.": Interview of Stephen Cole by Stuart Taylor, November 7, 2011.

CHAPTER FOUR

52 According to the bar's published reports: The State Bar of California compiles a "General Statistics Report" for each semiannual exam; recent reports are posted here: http://admissions.calbar.ca.gov/Examinations/Statistics.aspx; earlier reports are available from the authors.

53 a conjecture that was proven several years later: See Stephen Klein and Roger Bolus, "Analysis of July 2004 Texas Bar Exam Results by Gender and Racial/Ethnic Group," (2004), available at http://www.ble.state.tx.us/one/analysis_0704tbe.htm.

54   The California Bar Exam had introduced: Some of the research behind the
     development of the Performance Exam in California is summarized in Stephen
     Klein, "Research on the California Bar Examination: A Ten Year Retrospec-
     tive" (1982), available at http://www.seaphe.org/topic-pages/california
     -bar-lawsuit.php.

55   the single-most important piece of information: Exceptions to this policy
     were made for students at the very top of the grade distribution for pur-
     poses of applying for highly coveted and prestigious judicial clerkships.
     Judges were much too likely simply to pass UCLA by if it refused to reveal
     who its very best students were, so the school made at least this concession
     to reality.

56   The proposed study was funded: The development and initial findings of the
     study are detailed in Ronit Dinovitzer, Bryant Garth, Richard Sander, Joyce
     Sterling, and Gitz Wilder, *After the JD: First Results of a National Study of Legal
     Careers* (2004).

56   In the late 1980s LSAC: An overview of the LSAC's study of bar passage, and
     its detailed methods, can be found in Linda F. Wightman, *User's Guide: LSAC
     National Longitudinal Data File* (Newtown, PA: Law School Admissions
     Council, 1999).

57   Dr. Wightman was soon to publish: Linda Wightman, *The Consequences of
     Race-Blindness: Revisting Prediction Models with Current Law School Data*, 53
     J. Legal Educ. 229 (2003).

58   Taking the twenty-odd thousand: The analysis in the following pages is sum-
     marized from Richard Sander, "A Systemic Analysis of Affirmative Action in
     American Law Schools," *Stanford Law Review* 57, no. 357 (2004).

61   An analysis by LSAC's Dr. Wightman: See Wightman, "The Consequences of
     Race-Blindness."

62   harmful for law graduates who never passed the bar: My friend and colleague
     Jane Yakowitz undertook a study several years ago to try to assess *how* harmful
     it is to law graduates not to have a license. Her picture is qualified and
     nuanced, but does indeed find that bar failers experience harm in both their
     personal and professional lives. See Yakowitz, "Marooned: An Empirical Inves-
     tigation of Law School Graduates Who Fail the Bar Exam," *Journal of Legal
     Education* 60, no. 1 (2010): 3–40.

63   I would later explore this question: This discussion is elaborated upon in
     Richard Sander, "The Racial Paradox of the Corporate Law Firm," *North
     Carolina Law Review* 84, no. 1755 (2006); and Richard Sander and Jane
     Yakowitz, "The Secret of My Success: How Status, Eliteness and School
     Performance Shape Legal Careers," forthcoming, *Journal of Empirical Legal
     Studies* (2013).

64   paid particularly close attention to black candidates' grades: Note the finding
     that black students themselves perceive their grades to be particularly impor-
     tant in determining their job outcomes.

CHAPTER FIVE

68   A recurring subtheme: See andré douglas ponds cummings, "Open Water: Affirmative Action, Mismatch Theory, and Swarming Predators—A Response to Richard Sander," *Brandeis Law Journal* 44, no. 795 (2006) ("Sander's Systemic Analysis engages in a paternalistic exercise. . . . Paternalism has been defined as attempting to exercise control over another individual that purports to be implemented in the best interests of that individual. . . . Sander figuratively casts himself as the 'Great White Father.'") Journalist Emily Bazelon, in a Slate.com column published on April 29, 2005, inaccurately claimed that Sander's published response in the *Stanford Law Review* "compares his work to Galileo's. That's not really the comparison that comes to mind." Michelle Dauber, a Stanford professor, complained to the *Chronicle of Higher Education* that "Stanford's name is being tied up with a piece of crap that never should have been published and has no merit of any sort. . . . " Katherine Mangin, "New Issue of *Stanford Law Review* Will Rebut a Critic of Affirmative Action," *Chronicle of Higher Education*, April 22, 2005.

69   All of its tables, models: The identity of various independent scholars who replicated the analyses in *Systemic Analysis* are described in Richard Sander, "A Reply to Critics," *Stanford Law Review* 57, no. 1963 (2005), at 1984–1986.

71   Their letter to the Review: E-mail from David Chambers to Richard Sander, July 2, 2004, available from the authors.

72   LSAC's president wrote: Letter to Paula Patton from Phil Shelton, July 8, 2004, available from the authors. See also e-mail from Terry Adams to other members of the AJD, July 12, 2004, discussing the LSAC letter, also available from the authors.

74   On October 17, Edley: E-mail from Chris Edley to Eric Feigin, October 17, 2004, available from the authors.

75   Almost simultaneously with Edley's note: Letter from James Vaseleck to Richard Sander, October 21, 2004, on file with the authors.

75   The irony was biting: Richard Lempert, "Humility Is a Virtue: On the Publicization of Policy-Relevant Research," *Law and Society Review* 23, no. 145 (1989).

76   Clydesdale. Two months before: The original Clydesdale paper is Timothy Clydesdale, "A Forked River Runs Through Law School: Toward Understanding Race, Gender, Age, and Related Gaps in Law School Performance and Bar Passage," *Law and Social Inquiry* 29, no. 711 (2004).

77   Ayres and Brooks. The single: This section examines Ian Ayres and Richard Brooks, "Does Affirmative Action Reduce the Number of Black Lawyers?" *Stanford Law Review* 57, no. 1807 (2005).

83   Barnes. Whether I: The Barnes article is Katherine Barnes, "Is Affirmative Action Responsible for the Achievement Gap Between Black and White Students?" *Northwestern Law Review* 107, no. 1759 (2007).

84 a restatement of Barnes's results: The revised Barnes results appeared in Katherine Barnes, "Is Affirmative Action Responsible for the Achievement Gap Between Black and White Law Students? A Correction, A Lesson, and an Update," *Northwestern Law Review* 105, no. 791 (2011).

84 a comment by Williams: See Doug Williams, Richard Sander, Marc Luppino, and Roger Bolus, "Revisiting Law School Mismatch: A Comment on Barnes," *Northwestern Law Review* 105, no. 813 (2011).

85 Stanford professor Dan Ho: See Daniel Ho, "Why Affirmative Action Does Not Cause Students to Fail the Bar," *Yale Law Journal* 114, no. 1997 (2005).

86 A similar problem affects: Jesse Rothstein and Albert H. Yoon, "Affirmative Action in Law School Admissions: What Do Racial Preferences Do?" NBER Working Paper, no. 14726 (2008).

86 In the summer of 2006: See U.S. Commission on Civil Rights, "Affirmative Action in American Law Schools," April 2007, http://www.usccr.gov/pubs/AALSreport.pdf.

88 But Kim could not say that, either: Interview of unnamed law teacher number one by Stuart Taylor, June 11, 2011, and follow-up discussions.

89 which ones they want working on the most important cases: Interview of unnamed law teacher number two by Stuart Taylor, May 31, 2011, and follow-up discussions.

CHAPTER SIX

94 Several years ago: The Kenyan study is described in Esther Duflo, Pascaline Dupas, and Michael Kramer, "Peer Effects, Teacher Incentives, and the Impact of Tracking: Evidence from a Randomized Evaluation in Kenya," *American Economic Review* 101, no. 1739 (2011).

95 the general effectiveness of college education in America: Richard Arum and Josipa Roksa, *Academically Adrift: Limited Learning on College Campuses* (Chicago: University of Chicago Press, 2011).

96 times as likely as whites to end up in the bottom tenth: Ibid., 246.

96 An unusually careful study at Duke: Peter Arcidiacono, Esteban Aucejo, and Ken Spenner, "What Happens After Enrollment?" forthcoming, *IZA Journal of Labor Economics* (2012).

97 consider a well-known study by Gary Orfield: The study is Gary Orfield and Dean Whitla, "Diversity and Legal Education: Student Experiences in Leading Law Schools," Chapter 6 of Gary Orfield, ed., *Diversity Challenged: Evidence on the Impact of Affirmative Action* (Boston: Harvard University, Civil Rights Project, 2001).

97 But when, without any racial prompts: Personal communication with Thomas Espenshade, April 2006.

98 And so they very well may end up leaving.": Interview of unnamed administrator by Gay Jervey, June 1, 2012, and brief follow-up calls; e-mail from same to Jervey, July 13, 2012.

99   which then triggers a host of psychological maladies.": Interview of Gary Hull
      by Stuart Taylor, June 23, 2012, and follow-up e-mails.
99   academic competence, which in turn harms performance: See Ryan P. Brown,
      Tonyamas Charnsangavej, Kelli A. Keough, Matthew L. Newman, and Peter J.
      Rentfrow, "Putting the 'Affirm' into Affirmative Action: Preferential Selection
      and Academic Performance," *Journal of Personality and Social Psychology* 79,
      no. 5 (2000): 736–747; Stephen Cole and Elinor Barber, *Increasing Faculty
      Diversity: The Occupational Choices of High-Achieving Minority Students* (Cam-
      bridge, MA: Harvard University Press, 2003), 116–121 (see also the discussion
      of their work in Chapter Three of this volume); M. J. Fischer and D. S.
      Massey, "The Effects of Affirmative Action in Higher Education," *Social Sci-
      ence Research* 36, no. 2 (June 2007): 531–549.
99   and conclude that they are failures: Interview of Hull by Taylor, June 23,
      2012, and follow-up e-mails.
99   essential part of my reasserting and rediscovering myself.": Interviews of Dr.
      William Hunter by Gay Jervey, May 10 and 13, 2012, with brief follow-up
      conversations and July 17, 2012, e-mail exchange.
100   creating structures that maintain a sense of separation.": Interviews of Brian
      Corpening by Gay Jervey, May 25 and July 20, 2012, with shorter follow-up
      calls and July 19, 2012, e-mail exchange.
100   fostering a healthy racial diversity on campus: In one widely discussed 2003
      study, scholars surveyed a random sample of more than sixteen hundred stu-
      dents and twenty-four hundred faculty members and administrators at 140
      American colleges and universities on various aspects of preferential admis-
      sions. They found that 85 percent of students (including 71 percent of non-
      white students) and a majority of faculty specifically rejected the use of racial
      or ethnic "preferences." The authors also found that, controlling for other col-
      lege characteristics, a rising proportion of blacks was associated (in both stu-
      dent and faculty evaluations) with lower student satisfaction, higher reported
      levels of discrimination, and lower assessments of the quality of their educa-
      tion. We are skeptical of this second finding, because we think there may have
      been inadequate controls for objective aspects of college quality. But the results
      are very suggestive, and this type of cross-sectional research that tries to com-
      pare the effects of varying diversity conditions on college outcomes and experi-
      ences—with careful controls—is plainly needed. Stanley Rothman,
      "Affirmative Action—and Reaction; Is Diversity Overrated?" *New York Times*,
      March 29, 2003; http://www.nytimes.com/2003/03/29/opinion/affirmative-
      action-and-reaction-is-diversity-overrated.html?pagewated=2&src=pm (sum-
      marizing Rothman, Seyour Martin Lipset, and Neil Nevitte, "Does
      Enrollment Diversity Improve University Education?" *International Journal of
      Public Opinion Research* 15, no. 1 (2003).
101   returned to Colgate and obtained his bachelor's degree: Interview of Jareau
      Hall by Gay Jervey, June 2, 2012, with several shorter follow-up calls and e-
      mail exchanges on July 10, 2012.

101 So you just knew.": Interview of anonymous Dartmouth graduate by Gay Jervey, June 4, 2012.

102 this type of condescending mentality.": Carol M. Swain, *The New White Nationalism in America: Its Challenge to Integration* (New York: Cambridge University Press, 2002), xiv–xx.

102 You can lose your mind basically.": Interview of Jocelyn Ladner-Mathis by Gay Jervey, May 31 and July 10, 2012, with short follow-up calls and e-mail exchanges on July 16, 17, 18, and 20, 2012.

102 grow up in a dump.": Esther Cepeda, "The Year I Became a 'Minority,'" *Chicago Tribune*, March 2, 2012; interview of Cepeda by Stuart Taylor, March 13, 2012.

103 "an exceptionally self-destructive form of alienation.": Unpublished manuscript 23, 27, 20.

103 community of scholars, teachers, and students at Colgate: Ibid., 8–9.

103 underlies the institution's central social knowledge: Ibid., 17.

103 inadequate and consequently miserable as they: Ibid., 18–19.

104 And then there is a study: Peter Arcidiacono, Shakeeb Khan, and Jacob Vigdor,"Representation versus Assimilation: How Do Preferences in College Admissions Affect Social Interaction?" *Journal of Public Economics* 95, no. 1 (2011).

104 for same-race friendships and cross-racial friendships: Peter Arcidiacono, Shakeeb Khan, and Jacob L. Vigdor, "Representation versus Assimilation: How Do Preferences in College Admissions Affect Social Interactions?" *Journal of Public Economics* 95, no. 1–2 (February 2011): 1–15.

104 Another suggestive example: See Matt Moore, "Ailing Method, Essential Motive: An Examination of Two Strategies to Improve Core Legal Learning Among Underrepresented Minority Law Students," (2005) (unpublished manuscript on file with the authors).

105 In a famous series of experiments: See Claude Steele and Joshua Aronson, "Stereotype Threat and the Test Performance of Academically Successful African Americans," Chapter 11 of Jencks and Phillips, *The Black-White Test Score Gap*.

105 One of the best studies: See Jim Sidanius, Shana Levin, Colette van Laar, and David O. Sears, *The Diversity Challenge: Social Identity and Intergroup Relations on the College Campus* (New York: Russell Sage, 2008), 317.

106 respectively the former presidents of Princeton and Harvard: William G. Bowen and Derek Bok, *The Shape of the River: Long-Term Consequences of Considering Race in College and University Admissions* (Princeton, NJ: Princeton University Press, 1998).

107 Economists Linda Loury and David Garman: See Linda Loury and David Garman, "College Selectivity and Earnings," *Journal of Labor Economics* 13, no. 289 (1995).

107 Economists Audrey Light and Wayne Strayer: See Audrey Light and Wayne Strayer, "Determinants of College Completion: School Quality or Student Ability?" *Journal of Human Resources* 35, no. 2 (2000).

107   Sociologist Marta Tienda: See, for example, Sigal Alon and Marta Tienda,
       "Assessing the 'Mismatch' Hypothesis: Differentials in College Graduation
       Rates by Institutional Selectivity," *Sociology of Education* 78, no. 294 (2005).

108   Stacy Dale and Alan Krueger: See Stacy Berg Dale and Alan B. Krueger, "Esti-
       mating the Payoff to Attending a More Selective College," *Quarterly Journal of
       Economics* 117, no. 1491 (2002).

109   Starting in the mid-1980s: The Michigan surveys, and our analysis of this
       data, are described in more detail in Richard Sander and Jane Yakowitz,
       "The Secret of My Success: How Status, Eliteness and School Performance
       Shape Legal Careers," forthcoming, *Journal of Empirical Legal Studies*
       (2013).

CHAPTER SEVEN

116   "a reality of reverse discrimination that actually engenders racism.": David
       Brooks, "Kerry's Good Intentions," *New York Times*, January 24, 2004.

117   in favor of somebody based on the group they represent.": Stuart Taylor Jr.,
       "Gore-Lieberman: Racial Preferences Forever?," *National Journal*, September 2,
       2000.

117   In April 1995 Congress eliminated: See Congress and the Nation, volume IX,
       1993–1996 (Washington, DC: Congressional Quarterly, Inc., 1998), 748–
       749.

118   thus, was not eager to get into racial issues at UC: Ward Connerly, *Creating
       Equal: My Fight Against Race Preferences* (San Francisco, CA: Encounter Books,
       2000), 113.

118   had grades and test scores well below his son's: Ibid., 117–124.

118   the existence of such practices"—even to a regent: Ibid., 118.

118   "affirmative action" in admission, let alone racial preferences: "Dear Col-
       leagues" letter from UC President J. W. Peltason to Chancellors et al., March
       3, 1994, and attachments (on file with authors). One could argue that the
       meaning of the word "discriminate" had been changed for all purposes by
       Supreme Court rulings that the 1964 Civil Rights Act, which mandated that
       people not "discriminate" based on race, did not outlaw racial preferences
       advantaging minorities over whites. But how many readers of UC's boilerplate
       would have assumed that two Supreme Court decisions had overthrown hun-
       dreds of years of English usage?

118   fell over the room after I finished talking," Connerly recalled: Connerly, *Creat-
       ing Equal*, 126.

119   such a statement is blatantly false: John Douglass, "A Brief on the Events Lead-
       ing to SP-1," UC Academic Senate, 1997.

119   too much a life of their own and were being abused: Connerly, *Creating Equal*,
       127–128, 133.

120   anyone thought of this as an electoral plus.": E-mail from John Ellis to Stuart
       Taylor, June 7, 2012; interview of John Ellis by Stuart Taylor, June 2, 2011; see

Lydia Chavez, *The Color Bind: California's Battle to End Affirmative Action* (Berkeley, CA: University of California Press, 1998), 48–50.

120   the UC President's Office gave: See "The Use of Socio-Economic Status in place of Ethnicity in Undergraduate Admissinos: A Report on the Results of an Exploratory Computer Simulation," Occasional Paper 5, University of California Office of the President, 1995.

121   and a 50 percent drop in Hispanics: University of California Office of the President, "The Use of Socio-Economic Status in Place of Ethnicity in Undergraduate Admissions: A Report on the Results of an Exploratory Computer Simulation," Occasional Paper 5, May 1995. Much of the report consisted of simulations showing that large socioeconomic preferences could offset much but not all of the racial drop.

121   apparently larger than at any other major college in the nation: Richard J. Herrnstein and Charles A. Murray, *The Bell Curve: Intelligence and Class Structure in American Life* (New York: Free Press, 1994), 452.

122   Jackson led a chorus of "We Shall Overcome.": Chavez, *The Color Bind*, 64; Amy Wallace and Dave Lesher, "UC Debates Affirmative Action Policy," *Los Angeles Times*, July 21, 1996; see also Chavez, *The Color Bind*, 62–67.

122   Regents' vote to the Japanese bombing of Pearl Harbor: Wallace and Lesher, "UC Debates Affirmative Action Policy."

122   protesters in public appearances around the state: Connerly, *Creating Equal*, 188.

122   educate the public about racial and gender preferences.": American Civil Rights Institute, http://www.acri.org.

123   he was then a nominal Republican but "quite apolitical.": Interview of Glynn Custred by Stuart Taylor, July 17, 2011; interview of Tom Wood by Stuart Taylor, July 5, 2011, along with numerous follow-up e-mail exchanges with each.

123   in state university admissions and private employment: *Regents of University of California v. Bakke*, 438 U.S. 265 (1978); *United Steelworkers v. Weber*, 443 U.S. 193 (1979).

124   two hundred thousand signatures and seemed a lost cause: Chavez, *The Color Bind*, 72–73; interview of John Ellis by Stuart Taylor, June 2, 2011.

124   Connerly became CCRI chairman in December 1995: Connerly, *Creating Equal*, 160, 164–165.

125   many more than enough to qualify for the ballot: Chavez, *The Color Bind*, 75–76; Connerly, *Creating Equal*, 168.

125   preferential programs as examples of its meaning: "Affirmative action has never had much public support, 'with little evidence of change over time.' . . . A leading study of public attitudes toward affirmative action finds, consistent with other studies, that 'the most fundamental factor behind opposition to affirmative action is one of principle.' . . . Researchers on public attitudes toward affirmative action understand that the phraseology of the question asked, as well as other contextual factors, can affect survey results and that

multiple interpretations of these data are possible. For this reason, it is hard to know the precise division of opinion. No researcher in this field doubts, however, that the public's opinion remains decidedly and intensely negative, pretty much regardless of how the questions are formulated." Peter H. Schuck, *Diversity in America: Keeping Government at a Safe Distance* (Cambridge, MA: Belknap Press of Harvard University Press, 2003), 170–171 (citing, among other works, Howard Schuman, Charlotte Steeh, Lawrence Bobo, and Maria Krysan, *Racial Attitudes in America: Trends and Interpretations* (Cambridge, MA: Harvard University Press, 1998), 58–98, 182; Jack Citrin, "Affirmative Action in the People's Court," Working Paper, Berkeley, CA: Institute of Governmental Studies, University of California, 43–44; and Stuart Taylor Jr., "Do African-Americans Really Want Racial Preferences?" *National Journal*, December 20, 2002. The latter article collects polls, including a *Washington Post*/Kaiser Family Foundation/Harvard University racial attitudes survey in spring 2001: "In order to give minorities more opportunity, do you believe race or ethnicity should be a factor when deciding who is hired, promoted, or admitted to college, or that hiring, promotions, and college admissions should be based strictly on merit and qualifications other than race or ethnicity?" *Of the 1,709 adults surveyed, 5 percent said, "race or ethnicity should be a factor," 3 percent said, "don't know," and 92 percent said, "should be based strictly on merit and qualifications other than race/ethnicity"* (emphasis added). More surprising, of the 323 African American respondents, 12 percent said, "race or ethnicity should be a factor," 2 percent said, "don't know," and 86 percent said, "should be based strictly on merit and qualifications other than race/ethnicity." See also Bettina Boxall, "A Political Battle Grinds on as a War of Wording," *Los Angeles Times*, October 1, 1996. Lydia Chavez, a 209 opponent, cites (at 19–20 of *Color Bind*) a single Harris Poll that showed majority support for "affirmative action"—*in 1988*. But that poll was an outlier, done eight years and hundreds of other polls before the 209 campaign.

125 won in lower court, but lost, on appeal, in August 1996: See Boxall, "A Political Battle Grinds on as a War of Wording."

126 supported it by a 77 percent to 17 percent margin: Chavez, *The Color Bind*, 104.

126 "You know what to do. Go and disrupt his class.": Interview of Custred by Taylor, July 17, 2011; email exchange July 13, 2012; see Joel Kotkin, "Here Come the Mad Dog Democrats," *Wall Street Journal*, July 10, 1996; e-mail from Tom Wood to Stuart Taylor, June 9, 2010.

127 sex discrimination by the government will be expressly allowed.": Stuart Taylor Jr., "Affirmative Action and Doublespeak," *Legal Times*, May 13, 1996; Erwin Chemerinsky and Laurie Levinson, "Sex Discrimination Made Legal," *Los Angeles Times*, January 10, 1996; see Chavez, *The Color Bind*, 84, 98, 136–38, 152–57, 230–34.

127 discriminate against men in casting women's roles: See Chavez, *The Color Bind*, 152, 230–34; Taylor, "Affirmative Action and Doublespeak."

128 But many leading opponents of 209 were quick to praise it: Chavez, *The Color Bind*, 199–203, 226–230, 250–251. See also Connerly, *Creating Equal*, 190–91, 200.

128 But his heart was no longer in it: Interview of Joe Hicks by Stuart Taylor, July 14, 2011, along with follow-up calls and e-mails; see Bettina Boxall and Sandy Banks, "Police, Protesters Clash at Duke-Hicks Debate," *Los Angeles Times*, September 26, 1996.

128 my allies, about how unscrupulous they could be.": Interview of Hicks by Taylor, July 14, 2011; see Chavez, *The Color Bind*, 227–229.

128 had that nice line at the end, 'bring us together.'": Chavez, *The Color Bind*, 251.

128 played a decidedly subordinate role in the public debate: Vikram Amar, e-mail to Richard Sander and Stuart Taylor, July 1, 2012; Stuart Taylor Jr., "Affirmative Action and Doublespeak," *Legal Times*, May 13, 1996, http://stuarttaylorjr.com/content/affirmative-action-and-doublespeak/.

129 and narrowed 209's margin of victory: Interview of Arnie Steinberg by Stuart Taylor, July 12, 2011; Connerly, *Creating Equal*, 195–198; see interview of Tom Wood by Stuart Taylor, July 5, 2011; interview of Custred by Taylor, July 17, 2011.

130 keeping the entire apparatus of affirmative action intact.": James Traub, "Mildly Ambitious," New York Times *Sunday Magazine*, June 10, 2001.

CHAPTER EIGHT

131 As University of California administrators: Much of the material in this chapter comes from Kate Antonoivcs and Richard Sander, "Affirmative Action Bans and the 'Chilling Effect,'" forthcoming, *American Law and Economics Review* (2013).

132 UC Berkeley Chancellor Chang-Lin Tien: See *Los Angeles Times*, October 21, 1996, A3.

132 A senior administrator at Mills College: See *San Francisco Chronicle*, November 7, 1996, A21.

132 the most privileged racial and ethnic communities.": Gary Orfield and Edward Miller, *Chilling Admissions: The Affirmative Action Crisis and the Search for Alternatives* (Cambridge, MA: Civil Rights Project, Harvard University Press, 1998).

132 The change in total unique applications: University of California: Application, Admissions, and Enrollment of California Resident Freshmen for Fall 1989 through 2010, UC Office of the President, Student Affairs (March 2011).

135 In May 1998 the *New York Times*: See Ethan Bronner, "Fewer Minorities Entering U. of California," *New York Times*, May 21, 1998, A28.

135 Another May 1998 *Times* story: See Frank Bruni, "Blacks at Berkeley Are Offering No Welcome Mat," *New York Times*, May 2, 1998.

136 David Card and Alan Krueger: See David Card and Alan B. Krueger, "Would the Elimination of Affirmative Action Affect Highly Qualified Minority

Applicants? Evidence from California and Texas," *Industrial & Labor Relations Review* 58, no. 416 (2005).

CHAPTER NINE

143   The warming effect we documented: Most of the material in this chapter comes the authors' analysis of the UCOP dataset, which is described in Antonovics and Sander. We supplemented this with official data from the University of California Office of the President, from the online resource UC Statfinder (http://statfinder.ucop.edu), and from other administrative records of the university. Much of this data will be available on this book's website (www.mismatchthebook.com).

147   A team of economists: See Peter Arcidiacono, Esteban Aucejo, Patrick Coate, and V. Joseph Hotz, "The Effects of Proposition 209 on College Enrollment and Graduation Rates in California," unpublished working paper available from the authors.

CHAPTER TEN

155   In the Spring of 1999: See James Traub, "The Class of Prop 209," *New York Times Magazine*, May 2, 1999.

156   Consider, for example, a report: See Susan Wilbur, "Investigating the College Destinations of University of California Freshman Admits," Chapter 4 in Eric Grodsky and Michal Kurlaender, *Equal Opportunity in Higher Education* (Boston: Harvard Education Press, 2010).

159   By 2002 Boalt was admitting: We secured data on the 2002 and 2003 admission cycles from Boalt from its admissions office; the data and analysis are available from the authors.

159   Subtlety, however, went out the window: We secured data on the 2002 and 2003 "special" admissions data from the UCLA School of Law's Office of the Dean. Analysis of data available from the authors.

160   studied conscientiously and received strong grades: ELC was closely modeled on the much better-known "Top Ten percent" plan adopted by the Texas state legislature to create a diverse path of admission to the University of Texas after the Fifth Circuit struck down racial preferences there.

161   compared with everyone else, increased only slightly: In response to the concerns that the holistic system was a subterfuge around Prop 209, the university commissioned an analysis by Professor Michael Hout, a Berkeley sociologist. Hout concluded that holistic admissions had not been applied in a racially discriminatory way, and though there was some evidence in his report that contradicted this conclusion, the effect was no more than small.

161   In the spring of 2006: See Rebecca Trounson, "A Startling Statistic at UCLA," *Los Angeles Times*, June 3, 2006.

162   sinister and harmful to minorities was afoot at UCLA: Groseclose, 64–65.

163 We have an unusual window: Much of the this section is based on Tim Grose-close's report, which is posted here: http://www.sscnet.ucla.edu/polisci/faculty/groseclose/CUARS.Resignation.Report.pdf.

166 but even from those applied to Hispanics: Though this is speculative, we assume that UCLA's admissions office used explicit preferences for blacks but none (or much smaller ones) for Hispanics, because the political pressure focused almost entirely on low black enrollment.

167 The fuse was thus set: An account of the "Compton Cookout" can be found at Larry Gordon, "UC San Diego condemns student party mocking Black History Month," *Los Angeles Times*, February 18, 2010.

168 This broadened into the idea: An account of the progress of holistic admissions can be found at Larry Gordon, "UC Moves Toward Holistic Review of Applicants," *Los Angeles Times*, January 20, 2011.

CHAPTER ELEVEN

176 a paper titled, "What Happens After Enrollment?": Peter Arcidiacono, Esteban M. Acejo, and Ken Spenner, *What Happens After Enrollment? An Analysis of the Time Path of Racial Differences in GPA and Major Choice*, Duke University, working paper, 2011, http://www.seaphe.org/working-papers/.

177 black students?" and "Does GPA have a color?": For these and subsequent paragraphs, see Neil Offen, "Black Students at Duke Upset over Study," *Herald-Sun*, n.d., http://www.heraldsun.com/view/full_story/17104957/article-Black-students-at-Duke-upset-over-study—; Neil Offen, "Black Alumni Join Duke Students in Concern over Duke Study," *Herald-Sun*, January 16, 2012, Black+alumni+join+students+in+concern+over+Duke+study+%20&id=17186 264/; Neil Offen, "Duke Responds to Black Students' Concerns," *Herald Sun*, January 19, 2012, http://www.heraldsun.com/view/full_story/17231824/article-Duke-responds-to-black-students%E2%80%99-concerns-/.

178 urging the Supreme Court to hear [the *Fishe*r case]: See KC Johnson, *Durham-in-Wonderland* blog, January 22, 1012 and March 22, 2012, http://durham-wonderland.blogspot.com/2012/01/politics-of-grievance-at-duke.html/, http://durhamwonderland.blogspot.com/2012/03/brodheads-extraordinary-address.html/.

181 both were hired away to still loftier academic posts: Karen W. Aronson, "University of Michigan President Is Nominated to Lead Columbia," *New York Times*, October 4, 2001; Elizabeth Kassab and Louie Meizlish, "Provost to Leave U. Michigan for Top Illinois Post," *Michigan Daily*, April 18, 2001; Cantor's "quest to ban what she believed was its racist mascot, Chief Illiniwek, soured [her] chancellorship in 2004 when the board refused to back her." She moved on to a controversial tenure as chancellor of Syracuse University, which on her watch has slid down the U.S. News rankings while she has spent tens of millions of dollars attempting to revitalize the rust-belt city; Robin Wilson, "Syracuse's Slide; As Chancellor Focuses on the 'Public Good,' Syracuse's Reputation Slides," *Chronicle of Higher Education*, Oct. 2, 2011.

182 would, in principle, be sympathetic to reform: See, for example, Rothman, "Affirmative Action—and Reaction."

182 some persons equally, we must treat them differently.": From Blackmun's concurring and dissenting opinion in *Bakke* (joined by no other justice), 438 U.S. 265, 407 (1978).

182 their diversity-value.": Peter H. Schuck, *Diversity in America: Keeping Government at a Safe Distance* (Cambridge, MA: Belknap Press of Harvard University Press, 2003), 165.

182 of Afro-Americans: 'race.'": Orlando Patterson, *The Ordeal of Integration: Progress and Resentment in America's "Racial" Crisis* (New York: Basic Books, 1997), 2–4.

183 our group says is going to help them, you go with: Bill Moyers, "Jonathan Haidt Explains Our Contentious Culture," February 3, 2012, http://billmoyers.com/wp-content/themes/billmoyers/transcript-print.php?post=3101.

183 not much I can do about that.'": Interview of Carol Swain by Stuart Taylor, September 30, 2001.

184 his official university account: "Students were awesome.": Peter Wood, "Mobbing for Preferences," Innovations Blog, *Chronicle of Higher Education*, September 22, 2011, http://chronicle.com/blogs/innovations/mobbing-for-preferences/30402/.

CHAPTER TWELVE

185 admissions offices: the problem of multiracial candidates: Susan Saulny and Jacques Steinberg, "On College Forms, a Questions of Race, or Races, Can Perplex," *New York Times*, June 13, 2011, http://www.nytimes.com/2011/06/14/us/14admissions.html?pagewanted=all.

188 A Washington Post/Kaiser poll from 2001: Washington Post/Kaiser/Harvard, "Racial Attitudes Survey," March 8–April 22, 2001, http://www.washingtonpost.com/wp-srv/nation/sidebars/polls/race071101.htm.

188 A Quinnipiac poll in 2009: Quinnipiac University, "U.S. Voters Disagree 3-1 With Sotomayor On Key Case, Quinnipiac University National Poll Finds; Most Say Abolish Affirmative Action," May 26–June 1, 2009, http://www.quinnipiac.edu/institutes-and-centers/polling-institute/national/release-detail?ReleaseID=1307.

189 One fascinating analysis: See Frank Dobbin, *Inventing Equal Opportunity* (Princeton University Press, 2009).

189 corporate America from the 1960s to the turn of the century: Frank Dobbin, *Inventing Equal Opportunity*, Princeton, NJ: Princeton University Press, 2009.

191 Michigan's 5-year-old affirmative action ban: Kim Kozlowski, "Court to debate Mich. affirmative action ban," *The Detroit News*, March 7, 2012.

191 The U.S. Supreme Court has agreed: Bloomberg, "The Race Case: Supreme Court Picks Up Affirmative Action Debate," *Chicago Tribune*, February 22, 2012.

191 Gov. Jerry Brown added his voice: Larry Gordon, "Brown backs federal lawsuit," *Los Angeles Times*, July 9, 2011.

191   she plans to transfer to Eastern Michigan University.": Mary Beth Marklein,
       "Affirmative Action Fight Goes On," *USA Today*, March 6, 2012,
       http://www.usatoday.com/news/education/story/2012-03-02/affirmative
       -action/53389292/1.

192   considered whether Asians are penalized: Daniel Slotnik, "Do Asian-
       Americans Face Bias in Admissions at Elite Colleges?," *New York Times*, Febru-
       ary 8, 2012.

192   a handful of state scholarships that target minority student: Sean Murphy,
       "GOP Lawmakers Push to Abolish Affirmative Action," *Tulsa World*, April 5,
       2011, http://www.tulsaworld.com/site/printerfriendlystory
       .aspx?articleid=20110405_336_0_OKLAHO614181.

193   their student bodies remained shockingly affluent.": David Leonhardt, "Top
       Colleges, Largely for the Elite," *New York Times*, May 24, 2011, http://www
       .nytimes.com/2011/05/25/business/economy/25leonhardt.html?page
       wanted=all.

193   switching to other subjects or failing to get any degree.": Christopher Drew,
       "Why Science Majors Change Their Minds (It's Just So Darn Hard)," *New
       York Times*, November 4, 2011, http://www.nytimes.com/2011/11/06/
       education/edlife/why-science-majors-change-their-mind-its-just-so-darn-hard
       .html?pagewanted=all.

193   headlined "Law School Admissions Lag Among Minorities.": Tamar Lewin,
       "Law School Admissions Lag Among Minorities," *New York Times*, January 6,
       2010, http://www.nytimes.com/2010/01/07/education/07law.html.

195   ran a cover story about Patrick Chavis: Nicholas Lamann, "Taking Affirmative
       Action Apart," *New York Times*, June 11, 1995

195   about Chavis's run-ins: Douglas Shuit, "Minority Doctors Skeptical of Health
       Reforms," *Los Angeles Times*, June 1, 1993.

195   California's medical board: "Liposuction Doctor Has License Revoked," *Los
       Angeles Times*, August 26, 1998.

195   2002 obituary: Douglas Martin, "Patrick Chavis, 50, Affirmative Action Fig-
       ure," *New York Times*, August 15, 2002.

196   have treated the preferences debate as toxic and dangerous: As Peter Schuck
       observed, most politicians, including Republicans, "with their eyes on His-
       panic and Asian voters (and money), are unwilling to rock the affirmative
       action boat and risk being pilloried as racist or insensitive to minority inter-
       ests. It is hardly surprising, then, that the battles against affirmative action
       (and bilingual education) in California and elsewhere have been spearheaded
       primarily by private political entrepreneurs in ballot referenda, not by elected
       politicians." Schuck, *Diversity in America*, 173.

196   makes it easy to decide to stay away from the issue.": Interview of anonymous
       congressman by Stuart Taylor, August 18, 2012.

196   recognizing the value of diversity on our nation's campuses.": George W. Bush,
       "President Applauds Supreme Court for Recognizing Value of Diversity,"
       TheWhite House, June 2003, http://georgewbush-whitehouse.archives.gov/
       news/releases/2003/06/20030623.html.

196 diminishing tool for us to achieve racial equality in this society.": Lynn Sweet, "Obama on ABC's 'This Week with George Stephanopoulos'," *Chicago Sun-Times*, May 13, 2007, http://blogs.suntimes.com/sweet/2007/05/ obama_on_abcs_this_week_with_g.html.

197 better—and instead fell back on stale thinking.": Richard Kahlenberg, "Obama's Affirmative-Action Brief," *Chronicle*, August 16, 2012, http:// chronicle.com/blogs/innovations/obamas-affirmative-action-brief/34003.

CHAPTER THIRTEEN

200 and led the Court to dismiss the action in 1974: *Defunis v. Odegaard*, 416 U.S. 312 (1974).

200 hospital as a candy striper—a rare thing for a man: John C. Jeffries Jr., *Justice Lewis F. Powell, Jr.: A Biography* (New York: Fordham University Press, 2001), 455–456; Howard Ball, *The Bakke Case: Race, Education, and Affirmative Action* (Lawrence, University Press of Kansas, 2000), 46–48.

200 return to virtually all-white professional schools.": Ball, *The Bakke Case*, 82, 69.

201 without preferences, have become much whiter: See p. 279 in this volume.

201 schools from using race as a factor in admissions: *Bakke v. Regents of University of California*, 18 Cal. 3d 34, 38 (1976).

201 victimized by anti-Jewish quotas, supported Bakke: Jeffries, *Justice Lewis F. Powell, Jr.*, 462; Ball, *The Bakke Case*, 84.

201 totaling 156 pages, none speaking for a majority: *Regents of University of California v. Bakke*, 438 U.S. 265 (1978).

201 the Fourteenth Amendment equal protection clause: Ibid., 408 (Stevens, J., concurring in part and dissenting in part).

201 Stevens insisted on avoiding the constitutional issue: Jeffries, *Justice Lewis F. Powell, Jr.*, 483–484.

201 who also wrote separate individual dissents: 438 U.S. at 324, 328, 362, 400 (Brennan, J. concurring in part and dissenting in part). In subsequent cases Stevens and White would switch sides, with the former coming to support and the latter to oppose most racial preferences.

202 as a normal way of life in this country.": Stuart Taylor Jr., "Powell on His Approach: Doing Justice Case by Case," *New York Times*, July 12, 1987, http://www.nytimes.com/1987/07/12/us/powell-on-his-approach-doing -justice-case-by-case.html?pagewanted=all&src=pm/.

202 "so that race-consciousness would not become the norm.": Jeffries, *Justice Lewis F. Powell, Jr.*, 469–473.

202 no reason other than race or ethnic origin.": 438 U.S. at 269, 289, 290–291, 307–308 (internal quotations omitted).

203 or other qualifications deemed important.": 338 U.S. at 293, 299, 307, 313–318.

203 Indeed, all eight shunned the diversity rationale: 438 U.S. at 307–308 (Powell, J.). Of course, the four who would have struck down all racial admissions preferences necessarily rejected the diversity rationale for allowing preferences. As

for the other four, none joined Powell's opinion, which they would presumably have done had they agreed with the diversity rationale. In addition, Brennan's opinion for White, Marshall, Blackmun, and himself conspicuously shunned the diversity rationale at two junctures. First, Brennan specified that "the central meaning of today's opinions" is that "government may take race into account when it acts not to demean or insult any racial group, *but to remedy disadvantages cast on minorities by past racial prejudice*" (emphasis added). Second, Brennan agreed the Harvard plan approved by Justice Powell would be "constitutional under our approach, *at least so long as the use of race to achieve an integrated student body is necessitated by the lingering effects of past discrimination.*" Ibid., at 326n1 (emphasis added). *Bakke*, 438 U.S. at 325, 326n1 (emphasis added). Not a trace of "diversity" in either statement—only Brennan's own, compensatory rationale for racial preferences.

203   merely a convenient way to broach a compromise.": Jeffries, *Justice Lewis F. Powell, Jr.*, 500.

203   farm may tip the balance in other candidates' cases.": 338 U.S. at 316–317, 323.

203   preferring racial minorities so long as you do not say so.'": Ibid., at 318; Jeffries, *Justice Lewis F. Powell, Jr.*, 484.

203   prospect of generation upon generation of racial quotas.": Jeffries, *Justice Lewis F. Powell, Jr.*, 487.

204   variations in the applicant pool from year to year: See *Transparency*.

204   Enrollments also remained constant.": Richard Sander, "A Systemic Analysis of Affirmative Action in American Law Schools," *Stanford Law Review* 57, no. 2 (2004): 367–484, 383.

204   they used after *Bakke* were at least as large as before: Susan Welch and John Gruhl, *Affirmative Action and Minority Enrollment in Medical and Law Schools* (Ann Arbor: University of Michigan Press, 1998), 61, 70–71, 131–132.

204   involving government employment and contracting: For example, *Adarand Constructors v. Peña*, 515 U.S. 200 (1995); *Richmond v. J. A. Croson, Co.*, 488 U.S. 469 (1989); *Wygant v. Jackson Board of Education*, 476 U.S. 267 (1986).

204   in *America in Black and White: One Nation, Indivisible*: Stephan Thernstrom and Abigail Thernstrom, *America in Black and White: One Nation, Indivisible* (New York: Simon and Schuster, 1997).

204   the other diversity factors listed by Powell combined: Abigail Thernstrom and Stephan Thernstrom, "Secrecy and Dishonesty: The Supreme Court, Racial Preferences, and Higher Education," *Constitutional Commentary* 21 (March 2004), 211; see Timothy Maguire, "My Bout with Affirmative Action," *Commentary* 93 (April 1992), 50.

204   struggling with low grades and high dropout rates: *Shape*; *Transparency*. (Also cite Klitgaard, *Choosing Elites*).

205   the continued use of explicit racial preferences: Christopher Jencks, *Rethinking Social Policy: Race, Poverty, and the Underclass* (Cambridge, MA: Harvard University Press, 1992), 68–69.

205 important players in bringing activist litigation: Steven M. Teles, *The Rise of the Conservative Legal Movement: The Battle for Control of the Law* (Princeton, NJ: Princeton University Press, 2012); Ann Southworth, *Lawyers of the Right: Professionalizing the Conservative Coalition* (Chicago: Chicago Series in Law and Society, 2008).

205 contained before signing and sending it to Meek: Stephan Thernstrom and Abigail Thernstrom, "Reflections on *The Shape of the River,*" *UCLA Law Review* 46, no. 5 (1999), 1585–1586 and note 7.

205 without ever qualifying to practice law: Ibid.

206 three Fifth Circuit states, Texas, Louisiana, and Mississippi: *Hopwood v. Texas*, 78 F. 3d 932 (5th Cir. 1996).

206 ever more deeply entrenched in the universities: See Maranto et al 2009.

206 where preferences had not been much used in the 1970s: US Commission on Civil Rights, "Affirmative Action in American Law Schools: A Briefing before the United States Commission on Civil Rights, Held in Washington, D.C., June 16, 2006," Briefing Report (Washington, DC: US Commission on Civil Rights, 2007).

207 19 opposed, and 5 in between: Joan Biskupic, "O'Connor Could Hold Key to Her Great Friend's Legacy," *USA Today*, March 25, 2003, http://www.usatoday.com/life/2003-03-25-affirmative_x.htm.

207 we will have virtually no black students: *Grutter v. Bollinger*, Brief of the Law School Admission Council as *Amicus Curiae* in Support of Respondents 8–9, http://www.law.duke.edu/publiclaw/supremecourtonline/additional/gruvbol.html/.

208 Alumni children received a 4-point boost: See Stuart Taylor Jr., "Ted Kennedy's Excellent Idea: Disclosing Admissions Preferences," *National Journal*, January 31, 2004, http://nationaljournal.com/magazine/opening-argument-ted-kennedy-39-s-excellent-idea-disclosing-admissions-preferences -20040131.

209 strong distaste for race-based election districting: *Richmond v. J. A. Croson Co.*, 488 U.S. 469 (1989); see, for example, *Shaw v. Reno*, 509 U.S. 630 (1993) (O'Connor, J.).

209 which she said could not be quantified: 539 U.S. at 318–319, 329–330, 333, 335–336, 340.

209 racial preferences will no longer be necessary.": Ibid., at 329–330 (quoting Powell in *Bakke*), 342, 343 (quoting Nathanson and Bartnik, "The Constitutionality of Preferential Treatment for Minority Applicants to Professional Schools," 58 Chicago Bar Rec. 282, 293 (May–June 1977)) (internal quotation marks omitted).

210 of paramount importance in the fulfillment of its mission.": Ibid., at 380 (citations omitted).

210 conscious admissions program as soon as practicable.": Ibid., at 343.

211 achieve numerical goals indistinguishable from quotas.": Ibid., at 378, 385 (Rehnquist, C. J., dissenting) and at 387, 388 (Kennedy, J. dissenting).

211   group of educational have-nots is morally unacceptable.": Thernstrom and
      Thernstrom, "Secrecy and Dishonesty," 232. Indeed, as if to help pave the way
      for perpetual preferences, O'Connor wrote in an essay years after her retire-
      ment in 2005 that her reference to twenty-five years was not really a deadline.
      Peter Schmidt, "Sandra Day O'Connor Revisits and Revives Affirmative-
      Action Controversy," *Chronicle of Higher Education*, January 14, 2010,
      http://chronicle.com/article/Sandra-Day-OConnor-Revisits/63523/.
211   high grades and test scores has indeed increased.": 539 U.S. at 343.
211   had been level or growing for fifteen years—not shrinking: The most authori-
      tative assessment of national trends in academic preparation is the congres-
      sionally authorized National Assessment of Educational Progress (NAEP). The
      most recent NAEP report, on levels of academic preparation for a variety of
      demographic groups, analyzes data through 2008. The report shows that
      although black-white performance gaps narrowed substantially from 1971
      until the late 1980s, the gaps widened in the years around 1990 and have been
      essentially unchanged since then. The same is true of the Hispanic-white gaps.
      National Center for Education Statistics, *NAEP 2008 Trends in Academic
      Progress*, National Center for Education Statistics (2009), *nces.ed.gov/nationsre-
      portcard/pdf/main2008/2009479.pdf*.
212   Freedom of Information Act request and subsequent lawsuits: 539 U.S. at
      297–298 (Souter, J., dissenting), 305 (Ginsburg, J., dissenting).
212   race might make to UM's educational environment: *Transparency*.
214   which no justice had ever mentioned before: 539 U.S. at 349, 371–374
      (Thomas, J., concurring in part and dissenting in part, joined by Scalia, J.).
      None of the briefs filed on Barbara Grutter's side mentioned mismatch with
      the exception of the Reason's Foundation's amicus brief, which contained an
      excellent three-page discussion of the then-available literature.
214   and it was wrong to give that kind of false hope.": See Ernest Hosendolph,
      "Skills, Not Bias, Seen as Key to Jobs," *New York Times*, July 3, 1982,
      http://www.nytimes.com/1982/07/03/us/skills-not-bias-seen-as-key
      -for-jobs.html.
215   and appropriately so, as one of us wrote in 2004: Stuart Taylor Jr., "The Affir-
      mative Action Decisions," in *A Year at the Supreme Court*, edited by Neal
      Devins and Davison M. Douglas (Durham, NC: Duke University Press,
      2004), 87, 107 ("The best argument by far for upholding racial preferences in
      university admissions is that the unelected justices should not lightly disregard
      the unique near-unanimity of establishment leaders on this issue, and should
      not seek to stop selective universities from using the admissions criteria that
      virtually all of them want to use.").

CHAPTER FOURTEEN

218   As we saw: The material in Chapter 14 comes predominantly from unpub-
      lished documents and datafiles obtained from George Mason University Law
      School through public record requests. These materials are available from the

authors, and much of the material is posted on the book's website (www.mis-matchthebook.com).

CHAPTER FIFTEEN

234 The simplest way to protect privacy: An excellent overview of this subject, and the issues, is Jane Yakowitz, "Tragedy of the Data Commons," *Harvard Journal of Law and Technology* 25, no. 1 (2011).

236 All this prompted: The restrictions on the College and Beyond data are detailed in Stephan Thernstrom and Abigail Thernstrom, "Reflections on The Shape of the River," *UCLA Law Review* 46, no. 1583 (1999).

236 observe in a scathing review of *The Shape of the River*: Stephan Thernstrom and Abigail Thernstrom, "Reflections on *The Shape of the River*," *UCLA Law Review* 46, no. 5 (1999): 1583–1632, 1583, 1587, 1588, 1590 (footnotes omitted).

239 Some support was forthcoming: Extensive archival materials on the effort to secure data from the California Bar, including supporting materials, correspondence, letters sent in support of or opposition to the request, peer reviews of the proposal, and key documents in the subsequent litigation, are posted at http://www.seaphe.org/topic-pages/california-bar-lawsuit.php.

240 Perhaps most striking of all: Memorandum from Richard Lempert to the Board of Governors, November 6, 2007, available from the authors.

244 In June 2011 the First Amendment Coalition: *Sander v. State Bar of California,* 196 Cal. App. 4th 614 (2011).

CHAPTER SIXTEEN

247 The 1968 Kerner Commission: These quotes, and a larger discussion of the class-based origins of affirmative action, can be found in Richard Kahlenberg, *The Remedy: Class, Race, and Affirmative Action* (New York: New Republic Book/Basic Books, 1996), 10–15 and *passim.*

249 When we talk about class: Much of the analysis in this chapter comes from two pieces that opened and closed a symposium held in 2011 by the Denver University Law Review: Richard Sander, "Class in American Legal Education," *Denver University Law Review* 88, no. 631 (2011), and Richard Sander, "Listening to the Debate on Reforming Law School Admissions Preferences," *Denver University Law Review* 88, no. 889 (2011). A detailed discussion of how SES indices are constructed can be found in the appendix to the first of these two articles.

252 grow another 21 percent by 2015, to over 6.4 million: SAUS 2012 Table 10.

253 who need help but are often utterly overlooked: Eugene Robinson, *Disintegration: The Splintering of Black America* (New York: Doubleday, 2010).

255 In the wake of Prop 209: The UCLA Law School experiment with socioeconomic preferences is described in detail in Richard Sander, "Experimenting with Class-Based Affirmative Action," *Journal of Legal Education* 47, no. 472 (1997).

257   It is well documented that: See Rojstaczer, Stuart, and Christopher Healy.
      "Where A Is Ordinary: The Evolution of American College and University
      Grading, 1940–2009." *Teachers College Record*, (2012),
      http://gradeinflation.com/tcr2011grading.pdf.

CHAPTER SEVENTEEN

261   important civil rights battle of the twenty-first century.": June E. O'Neill
      and Dave M. O'Neill, *The Declining Importance of Race and Gender in the
      Labor Market: The Role of Federal Anti-Discrimination Policies and Other Fac-
      tors* (Washington, DC: AEI Press, 2012); Roland G. Fryer, "Racial Inequality
      in the 21st Century: The Declining Significance of Discrimination," *Hand-
      book of Labor Economics* 4, part B (March 2011): 855–971, 855, 858–860,
      925, 926.

262   The data provides no basis for complacency: Roland G. Fryer and Steven D.
      Levitt, "Understanding the Black-White Test Score Gap in the First Two Years
      of School," *Review of Economics and Statistics* 86, no.2 (2004): 447–464, 447,
      449.

263   through age five, could fully explain group differences: Ibid., 447–448.

263   changes in parents' educational attainment or income.": Fryer, "Racial Inequal-
      ity in the 21st Century," 890; Fryer and Levitt, "Understanding the Black-
      White Test Score Gap," 452.

263   and 17 percent of Asian American children: "Births: Preliminary Data for
      2010," National Vital Statistics Reports, vol. 60, no. 2, November 17, 2011,
      table 1; see link at Roger Clegg, "Latest Numbers on Unmarried Births,"
      National Review Online, November 18, 2011,
      http://www.nationalreview.com/corner/283539/latest-numbers-unmarried-
      births-roger-clegg.

264   finish college, find good jobs and form stable marriages.": Jason DeParle, "Two
      Classes, Divided by 'I Do,'" *New York Times*, July 14, 2012, http://www
      .nytimes.com/2012/07/15/us/two-classes-in-america-divided-by-i-do
      .html?_r=1&ref=todayspaper/; see Ron Haskins and Isabel Sawhill, *Creating
      an Opportunity Society* (Washington, DC: Brookings Institution Press, 2009);
      Isobel Sawhill, "20 Years Later, It Turns Out Dan Quayle Was Right About
      Murphy Brown and Unmarried Moms," *Washington Post*, May 25, 2012,
      http://www.washingtonpost.com/opinions/20-years-later-it-turns
      -out-dan-quayle-was-right-about-murphy-brown-and-unmarried-moms/2012/
      05/25/gJQAsNCJqU_story.html/.

264   says a black youth with a book is acting white.": See Henry Louis Gates Jr.,
      "Breaking the Silence," *New York Times*, August 1, 2004,
      http://www.ntimes.com/2004/08/01/opinion/breaking-the-silence.html.

264   for 'acting white' when she got good grades.": Alison Samuels, "Michelle Hits
      Her Stride," *Daily Beast*, May 1, 2009, http://www.thedailybeast.com/
      newsweek/2009/05/01/michelle-hits-her-stride.html.

264   blaming poor academic performance on teachers: John U. Ogbu, *Black American Students in an Affluent Suburb: A Study of Academic Disengagement* (Mahwah, NJ: Erlbaum Associates, 2003).

264   true of blacks, especially boys, in integrated schools: Roland G. Fryer and Paul Torelli, "An Empirical Analysis of Acting White," *Journal of Public Economics* 94, no. 5 (2010): 380; Roland G. Fryer, "Acting White: The Social Price Paid by the Best and Brightest Minority Students," *Education Next* 6, no. 1 (Winter 2006), l; Stuart Buck, *Acting White: The Ironic Legacy of Desegregation* (New Haven, CT: Yale University Press, 2010), 9–40; Abigail M. Thernstrom and Stephan Thernstrom, *No Excuses: Closing the Racial Gap in Learning* (New York: Simon and Schuster, 2003), 144–147, 296n54.

265   what black parents want for their children, too.": E-mail from Rick Nagel to Stuart Taylor, July 21, 2012.

266   disproportionately few low-income and minority students: Joel Klein, "New York's Charter Schools Get an A+," *Wall Street Journal*, July 26, 2012, http://online.wsj.com/article/SB10000872396390044334370457755507819389 01886.html; see also Steven Brill, *Class Warfare: Inside the Fight to Fix America's Schools* (New York: Simon and Schuster, 2011).

266   no evidence that higher spending is related to better achievement.": Eric A. Hanushek and Alfred A. Lindseth, *Schoolhouses, Courthouses, and Statehouses: Solving the Funding-Achievement Puzzle in America's Public Schools* (Princeton, NJ: Princeton University Press, 2009), 31, 52, 56.

266   school district that has ever closed the racial achievement gap.": See Fryer references and others.

266   public schools—without raising their students' test scores: Thernstrom and Thernstrom, *No Excuses*, 164–166; Hanushek and Lindseth, *Schoolhouses, Courthouses, and Statehouses*, 5–6, 54–55, *passim*; Brill, *Class Warfare* 47, 347, 434.

266   students per class in kindergarten through grade three: Hanushek and Lindseth, *Schoolhouses, Courthouses, and Statehouses*, 52, 56.

267   "No one is even asking the question.": Philip K. Howard, "It's Time to Clean House," *Atlantic*, March 6, 2012, http://www.theatlantic.com/ politics/archive/2012/03/its-time-to-clean-house/253921/#/; Hanushek and Lindseth, *Schoolhouses, Courthouses, and Statehouses*, 50–51, 255–257.

267   nearly as important in determining student achievement.": Eric A. Hanushek, "Valuing Teachers," *Education Next* 11, no. 3 (Summer 2011): 41–45,; Brill, *Class Warfare*, 77–79, 150–154.

267   teachers were compensated according to their effectiveness.": Hanushek, "Valuing Teachers," 45.

267   counterpart is true as well: A bad teacher can do great harm: Ibid., 1. See also Hanushek and Lindseth, *Schoolhouses, Courthouses, and Statehouses*, 6–9, 147, 236–237, 246, 280; Brill, *Class Warfare, passim*; Philip K. Howard, *Life Without Lawyers: Liberating Americans from Too Much Law* (New York: W. W. Norton, 2009), 98–101.

268 the 'basic' level in reading, math, and science skills.": Hanushek and Lindseth, *Schoolhouses, Courthouses, and Statehouses*, 30, 37. For example, in standardized tests administrated by the OECD to assess math, science, and reading for fifteen-year-olds, in 2009 the United States ranked twenty-fifth in math and seventeenth in science out of the fifty-six participating countries. Brill, *Class Warfare*, 27. The US ranking for students who scored at the international equivalent of the "advanced" level on our National Assessment of Educational Progress (NAEP) tests was an even more abysmal thirtieth out of fifty-six. Brill, *Class Warfare*, 27; Eric A. Hanushek, Paul E. Peterson, and Ludger Woessman, "U.S. Math Performance in Global Perspective: How Well Does Each State Do at Producing High-Achieving Students," Program on Education Policy and Governance and Education Next, Harvard University, Kennedy School of Government, November 2010, 4. Indeed, in a March 20, 2012 report a council on foreign relations task force headed by Condoleezza Rice and Joel Klein asserted that "the education crisis is a national security crisis," producing adults without the math, science, and language skills necessary to ensure American leadership or equip students for the workforce, and that many have stopped teaching the sort of basic civics that prepares students for leadership. All this, the report said, puts the nation's future economic prosperity, global position, and physical safety at risk. Council on Foreign Relations, "U.S. Education Reform and National Security," http://www.cfr.org/united-states/us-education-reform-national-security/p27618/.

268 teachers on average earn more than lawyers and engineers.": Nicholas D. Kristof, "Pay Teachers More," *New York Times*, March 12, 2011, http://www.nytimes.com/2011/03/13/opinion/13kristof.html (summarizing Eric A. Hanushek, "The Economic Value of Higher Teacher Quality," National Bureau of Economic Research, Working Paper #16606, December 2010); Hanushek and Lindseth, *Schoolhouses, Courthouses, and Statehouses*, 279–280; see also Brill, *Class Warfare*, 348.

268 relieving them of mind-numbing paperwork and bureaucratic rules: Hanushek and Lindseth, *Schoolhouses, Courthouses, and Statehouses*, 6–9, 147, 236–237, 246, 280; Brill, *Class Warfare*, 2–5, *passim*; Howard, *Life Without Lawyers*, 98–101.

268 life tenure no matter how execrable their performance: Brill, *Class Warfare*, 89–90, 283, 363–370; Hanushek and Lindseth, *Schoolhouses, Courthouses, and Statehouses*, 7, 276, 283; Howard, *Life Without Lawyers*, 98–101, 107–121, 122–149.

268 for example, it was blocked in half the cases: David K. Li, Jennifer Bain, and Yoav Gonen, "Can't Ex-Spell Idiots," *New York Post*, January 27, 2012, http://www.nypost.com/p/news/local/can_ex_spell_idiots_KPArPcPrwj OPbNzyYXOD6O.

269 in the process, focusing on the racial test score gap: Matthew Miller, *The Two Percent Solution: Fixing America's Problems in Ways Liberals and Conservatives Can Love* (New York: PublicAffairs, 2003).

269   weaker ones—while linking increased pay to performance: See, for example,
      Hanushek and Lindseth, *Schoolhouses, Courthouses, and Statehouses*, 272–273;
      Brill, *Class Warfare*, 16, 37, 347, 434.

269   responsibility for their children's adherence to school rules: See, for example,
      Richard Arum, "How Expanding Student Rights Undermined Public School-
      ing," *Atlantic*, April 6, 2012,
      http://www.theatlantic.com/national/archive/2012/04/how-expanding-stu-
      dent-rights-undermined-public-schooling/255393/; Howard, *Life Without
      Lawyers*, 101–107, 118–119; Stuart Taylor Jr., "How Courts and Congress
      Wrecked School Discipline," *National Journal*, November 15, 2003,
      http://nationaljournal.com/magazine/opening-argument-how-courts-and-con-
      gress-wrecked-school-discipline-20031115/. See also Richard Arum, Irenee
      Beattie, Richard Pitt, Jennifer Thompson, and Sandra Way, *Judging School Dis-
      cipline: The Crisis of Moral Authority in American Schools* (Cambridge, MA:
      Harvard University Press, 2003); Howard, *Life Without Lawyers*, 142–149.

270   dismiss ineffective teachers or control disruptive students: See, for example,
      Hanushek and Lindseth, *Schoolhouses, Courthouses, and Statehouses* 4–6, 83–
      171; Ross Sandler and David Schoenbrod, *Democracy by Decree: What Happens
      When Courts Run Government* (New Haven, CT: Yale University Press, 2003).
      Also see Howard, *Life Without Lawyers*, 122–149.

270   grossly inadequate pay that was widespread sixty years ago: Brill, *Class Warfare*,
      31–34.

270   superintendents, mayors, governors, and presidents combined: Ibid., 34, 41,
      passim.

271   the program has produced highly encouraging results: Ibid., 4–9, *passim*.

271   evaluations of teachers and accountability for success or failure: For example,
      Thomas Kaplan and Kate Taylor, "Invoking King, Cuomo and Bloomberg
      Stoke Fight on Teacher Review Impasse," *New York Times*, January 17, 2012,
      http://www.nytimes.com/2012/01/17/nyregion/cuomo-and-bloomberg-on-
      attack-on-teacher-evaluations.html.

271   solve the problem of black underachievement in urban schools: J. S. Coleman,
      E. Q. Campbell, C. J. Hobson, J. McPartland, A. M. Mood, F. D. Weinfeld,
      and R. L. York, *Equality of Educational Opportunity* (Washington, DC: U.S.
      Government Printing Office, 1966).

271   community and broader investments may not be necessary.": Fryer, "Racial
      Inequality in the 21st Century," 924; see Will Dobbie and Ronald G. Fryer Jr.,
      "Are High Quality Schools Enough to Increase Achievement Among the Poor?
      Evidence from the Harlem Children's Zone," *American Economic Journal:
      Applied Economics* 3, no. 3 (July 2011): 158–187.

271   in the country," with thirty-three thousand students: Brill, *Class Warfare*, 23,
      72–75.

271   private and religious schools, including Catholic schools: See, for example,
      Schuck, *Democracy in America*, 298–299.

272   economic growth would be enhanced at the same time: Brill, *Class Warfare*, 9, 422.

272   preschool programs with rich learning environments would help: Studies of
      the federal Head Start program and numerous other preschool programs for
      three- to five-year-old poor children have shown uneven results, with most
      programs showing temporary gains in academic preparedness that dissipated
      within a few years and others showing lasting gains. The bottom line appears
      to be that "if we truly want to eliminate the racial achievement gap, early
      interventions may or may not be necessary but the evidence forces one to con-
      clude that they are not sufficient." Fryer, "Racial Inequality in the 21st Cen-
      tury," 880; Hanushek and Lindseth, *Schoolhouses, Courthouses, and Statehouses*,
      206–211; Thernstrom and Thernstrom, *No Excuses*. See Eric A. Hanushek,
      "How Well Do We Understand Racial Achievement Gaps?" *Focus* 11, no. 2
      (Winter 2010): 5–12, 9–10; James J. Heckman, "The American Family in
      Black and White: A Post-Racial Strategy for Improving Skills to Promote
      Equality," NBER Working Paper No. 16841, March 2011.

CHAPTER EIGHTEEN

274   would probably vote for the initiative [if I were a Californian]: Glenn Loury,
      "Affirmative Action: Is There a Middle Way?" *Slate*, October 8, 1996,
      http://www.slate.com/articles/news_and_politics/committee_of_correspon-
      dence/features/1996/affirmative_action_is_there_a_middle_way/_4.html.
274   "the maintenance of a corrupt and excessive status quo.": Stuart Taylor, Jr.,
      "Racial Preferences Meet Democracy," *Legal Times*, December 20, 1996,
      http://stuarttaylorjr.com/content/racial-preferences-meet-democracy.
276   tuition-free for anyone with an income below $60,000: On Harvard's $60,000
      threshold, which it soon plans to raise to $65,000, see Financial Aid Office,
      Harvard College, http://www.fao.fas.harvard.edu/icb/icb.do.
276   these leaders who do not come from elite universities: See, for example,
      Schuck, *Diversity in America*, 158–159.
276   admissions has become a term of art among experts: See Thomas J. Espen-
      shade and Alexandria Walton Radford, *No Longer Separate, Not Yet Equal: Race
      and Class in Elite College Admission and Campus Life* (Princeton, NJ: Princeton
      University Press, 2009), 345.
278   admissions program not unduly harm members of any racial group.": *Grutter
      v. Bollinger*, 539 U.S. 306, 341 (2003).
278   circumstances of the University of California after proposition 209: On how
      the "UC eligibility" component of UC admissions led to a cascading of stu-
      dents from more elite to less elite UC campuses rather than to a sudden
      plunge in black and Hispanic admissions at the UC campuses collectively, see
      Chapter Eight in this volume.
279   smaller but still substantial declines for Hispanics: See, for example, Espen-
      shade Radford, *No Longer Separate, Not Yet Equal*, 343–348 (based on statisti-
      cal analysis of eight highly selective colleges, eliminating consideration of race
      in admissions would cut the number of blacks admitted by more than half and
      the number of Hispanics by about one-fourth); William G. Bowen and Derek

Bok, *The Shape of the River: Long-Term Consequences of Considering Race in College and University Admissions* (Princeton, NJ: Princeton University Press, 1998), 35–36 and Figure 2.10, using 1989 data from five unidentified, "roughly representative" elite private colleges: "If all institutions of higher education were required to adopt race-neutral admissions policies, . . . the hypothetical black share in the freshman classes of these [five] institutions would [be about] 3.6 percent— . . . far below the 7.1 percent actual share." See pp. 19–20 in this volume on data showing that the most elite schools use smaller racial preferences than do many others.

281 wrote at the time) that he was on the right track: Stuart Taylor Jr., "Ted Kennedy's Excellent Idea: Disclosing Admissions Preferences," *National Journal*, January 1, 2004, http://nationaljournal.com/magazine/opening-argument-ted-kennedy-39-s-excellent-idea-disclosing-admissions-preferences-20040131/.

281 action is to adopt a comprehensive system of disclosure: Schuck, *Diversity in America*, 193–197. Schuck suggested ending racial preferences at state universities while allowing them at private institutions, conditioned on full disclosure.

281 their consequences transparent to applicants and the public: A note on why we generalize about "universities" rather than speaking of "state universities": Only state universities and other government actors are limited by the Constitution; private universities such as Princeton, Stanford, and Yale are not. However, the 1964 Civil Rights Act's Title VI has long been construed as applying the same rules that the Constitution imposes on state institutions to private institutions receiving federal financial assistance—as virtually all private colleges and universities do. Of course, if the Court were to ban or tightly restrict racial preferences in a state-university case, there might be a massive effort to change Title VI.

283 workable race-neutral alternatives" to minimize such harm: *Parents Involved in Cmty Sch. v. Seattle Sch. Dist. No. 1*, 551 U.S. 701, 735 (2007); *Grutter v. Bollinger*, 539 U.S. at 339, 341.

285 have much less wealth than do whites with similar incomes: The classic work on this issue is Melvin L. Oliver and Thomas M. Shapiro, *Black Wealth/White Wealth: A New Perspective on Racial Inequality* (New York: Routledge, 1995).

285 would be complicated, messy, and prone to abuse: Schuck, *Diversity in America*, 188–89, quoting Michael Kinsley, "The Spoils of Victimhood," *New Yorker*, March 27, 1995, http://www.newyorker.com/archive/1995/03/27/1995_03_27_062_TNY_CARDS_000369619: "Is it worse to be a cleaning lady's son or a coal miner's daughter? Two points if your father didn't go to college, minus one if he finished high school, plus three if you have no father? (Or will that reward illegitimacy, which we're all trying hard these days not to do?) Communist societies tried this kind of institutionalized reverse discrimination—penalizing children of the middle class—without any enviable success. Officially sanctioned affirmative action by 'disadvantage' would turn today's festival of competitive victimization into an orgy."

285 to our knowledge, prompted complaints of unfairness: See Richard Sander, "Experimenting with Class-Based Affirmative Action," *Journal of Legal Education* 47, no. 4 (1997): 472.

285 detailed in the endnotes, we think this is quite doable: Admissions offices routinely create databases that comprise all of the students who apply for admission to an entering class. These databases may include information on both the academic and the demographic characteristics of applicants. If one conducts a regression analysis of such data, one can find the weight given to each admissions factor—that is, one can measure how much an applicant's chance of admission goes up if, say, her GPA is 3.4 rather than 3.3. One can similarly measure the weight given to a demographic characteristic such as race, legacy status, or in-state residency. A few more calculations can effectively determine the weight a school gives to race in terms of, for example, how many additional SAT points an applicant from a nonpreferred group would need in order to match a preferred applicant's race-based "plus" factor. Similar calculations can determine the weight a college gives to low-SES status and compare that with the weight given to race. It's a little more complicated, but not much. In evaluating an applicant's socioeconomic status a college might use only a simple, single factor such as whether he is the first person in his family to attend college. More often colleges take into account several SES factors, including parental income and educational attainment as well as the poverty rate of the applicant's neighborhood, for example. A school might or might not combine these various factors into an explicit index. But even if the school does not, a regression analysis of admissions decisions can determine what the implicit index would look like if it were explicit, and then derive the aggregate weight attached to SES factors.

289 similar numbers through winks, nods, and disguises.": *Grutter v. Bollinger*, 539 U.S. at 305 (Ginsburg, J., dissenting).

INDEX